Boston Printers, Publishers and Booksellers: 1640-1800

Isaiah Thomas

Boston Printers, Publishers, and Booksellers: 1640-1800

**Edited by
Benjamin Franklin V**

G. K. Hall & Co.   Boston, Massachusetts

Library of Congress Cataloging in Publication Data
Main entry under title:

Boston printers, publishers, and booksellers, 1640-1800.

Includes indexes.
1. Printers—Massachusetts—Boston—Biography.
2. Book industries and trade—Massachusetts—
Boston—Biography. 3. Boston-Biography.
4. Printing—Massachusetts—Boston—History—
17th century. 5. Printing—Massachusetts—
Boston—History—18th century. 6. Book industries
and trade—Massachusetts—Boston—History—
17th century. 7. Book industries and trade—
Massachusetts—Boston—History—18th century.
I. Franklin, Benjamin, 1939-
Z209.B7B67   070.5092'2   80-17693
ISBN 0-8161-8472-0

to Paul Engsberg,
John Oliver,
and Richard Martin
        mentors

Contents

Contributors

Elizabeth Nelson Adams, University of South Carolina
Robert E. Burkholder, The Penn. State University, Wilkes-Barre
Jacob L. Chernofsky, AB Bookman's Weekly
Charles E. Clark, University of New Hampshire
Michael Clark, University of Michigan
Sue Cunha-Cheesman, University of South Carolina
Jessica Kross Ehrlich, University of South Carolina
Thomas Goldstein, University of South Carolina
Alice S. Haynes, University of South Carolina
John B. Hench, American Antiquarian Society
Marta Paul Johnson, University of South Carolina
David Kaser, Indiana University
C. R. Kropf, Georgia State University
Donna Nance, Cooper Library, University of South
    Carolina
James P. O'Donnell, University of South Carolina
Tony J. Owens, University of South Carolina
David W. Pitre, University of South Carolina
Leslie Todd Pitre, University of South Carolina
David Paul Ragan, University of South Carolina
Jean Rhyne, Cooper Library, University of South
    Carolina
Richard W. Ryan, Clements Library, University of
    Michigan
Mark S. Shearer, University of South Carolina
MaryAnn Yodelis Smith, University of Wisconsin
Phyllis A. Smith, University of Texas
Madeleine B. Stern, New York City
John Tebbel, Southbury, Connecticut
Jane Isley Thesing, Cooper Library, University of South
    Carolina
Gary R. Treadway, Cooper Library, University of South
    Carolina
Charles Wetherell, University of New Hampshire
Richard Ziegfeld, University of South Carolina
All unsigned entries are by the editor.

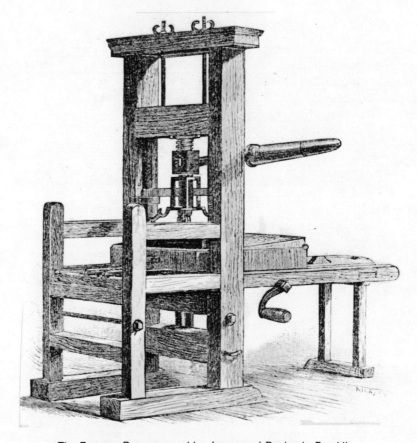

The Ramage Press as used by James and Benjamin Franklin

Preface

American printing and publishing began in Cambridge, in the Massachusetts Bay Colony, within two decades of the Pilgrims' arrival on the <u>Mayflower</u>. After the early years of only the Cambridge press, small amounts of type, and few publications, the book trade became established in Boston, where it soon began to flourish. This volume documents the first 160 years of printing and publishing in that most important colonial town by providing succinct professional histories of every person known to have appeared in a Boston (including Cambridge) imprint through the year 1800.

Each entry for a significant figure includes an essay preceded by an introductory paragraph, a list of major authors he published, and, when applicable, names of publishers he served. Less important individuals (generally those appearing in fewer than twenty-five imprints) warrant as little as a sentence or at most a brief paragraph or two. Some who might be considered major figures are not designated as such because their careers were dominated by their partners. For example, while hundreds of imprints bear the name of Ebenezer T. Andrews, he receives only cursory treatment, for his accomplishments were considerably less important than, and are difficult to isolate from, those of his partner Isaiah Thomas, surely the major American bookman of his time. Similarly, John Nourse receives passing notice because his name appears only in imprints alongside that of the more significant Thomas Adams. Other partners, such as Benjamin Edes and John Gill, were so inextricably linked and equally important that they receive a joint entry. Silent partners have been omitted unless the name is hinted at in an imprint, as in the case of Sarah Hood Russell. There are no entries for individuals who have been identified incorrectly as appearing

in an early Boston imprint. William Dodge and Richard
Fry are two such men. Yet because some legitimate
scholar has asserted that John Ewing, for example,
appeared in an imprint that is not now known to exist,
Ewing receives an entry.

Care has been taken with factual material. Ar-
chival research has established the accuracy of dates
of birth and death given in this volume that are at
variance with previously published dates. Titles of
individual works have been verified. Bibliographical
terminology has been used as precisely as possible.
The sharp distinction between printer and publisher,
or bookseller, is recognized throughout, but the last
two terms are often used interchangeably. A person
described as a bookseller in an early imprint would
usually be called a publisher today.

The contributors to this volume have examined a
variety of secondary materials, and every source con-
sulted has been cited as a reference, with the following exceptions. Because the monumental work of Charles
Evans and that of his successors Roger P. Bristol,
Clifford K. Shipton, and James E. Mooney has been con-
sulted for every entry, there are no references to
Evans's American Bibliography (Shipton compiled the
last volume), Bristol's Supplement to Charles Evans'
American Bibliography, or to Shipton and Mooney's
National Index of American Imprints through 1800: The
Short-Title Evans. For the same reason, references are
omitted to such standard biographical sources as the
Dictionary of American Biography and the National Cyclo-
paedia of American Biography.

The editor welcomes addenda and corrigenda. He
wishes to thank his contributors for their efforts and
accomplishments; the Interlibrary Loan Department,
Thomas Cooper Library, University of South Carolina,
for its support and patience; and the William L. Clements
Library, University of Michigan, and the American Antiquarian Society for access to their superlative
collections.

B. F.

Abijah Adams

Abijah Adams (c. 1754-1816), a tailor by trade, was the brother of Thomas Adams, for whom he worked as clerk in the office of the Independent Chronicle. When the newspaper criticized the Alien and Sedition Acts, Abijah was prosecuted and served thirty days in jail for libel. After Thomas Adams's death in 1799, Abijah and Ebenezer Rhoades assumed control of the paper and published their first number in May 1800. They continued with the Chronicle until June 1817, when they sold it to Edmund Wright, Jr. and Davis C. Ballard, a former partner.

References:

Brigham, Clarence S. History and Bibliography of American Newspapers: 1690-1820. Vol. 1. Worcester, Mass.: American Antiquarian Society, 1947.

Buckingham, Joseph T. Specimens of Newspaper Literature. Vol. 1. Boston: Little and Brown, 1850.

Samuel Adams

Samuel Adams (c. 1771-1802) was active as a printer, newspaper publisher, and bookseller in Delaware and Baltimore from 1786 until 1800. He possibly printed A Mournful Lament in Boston in 1781 when he was only ten years old and in his first month of apprenticeship.

Seth Adams

Seth Adams (1740-1782), printer and bookseller, was
active in Boston from 1762 to 1772, first at the shop
of Samuel Kneeland in Queen Street (1762-1764), then in
partnership with John Kneeland in Milk Street (1765-
1772). He printed some sixty-three works, nearly all
religious in nature, before quitting the trade to become a post rider.

   Major Authors: Amos Adams, Charles Chauncy,
Andrew Croswell, Nathaniel Low, Thaddeus MacCarty,
Samuel Mather, Samuel Phillips.

   Publishers Served: Nicholas Bowes, Joseph
Edwards, Phillip Freeman, John Perkins, Thomas
Leverett, Samuel Webb, John Wharton.

   Adams was born on 3 December 1740 in Milton,
Massachusetts, to John and Sarah Swift Adams. Little
is known of his early life, but around 1755 he was
apprenticed to Samuel Kneeland, the father of his fu-
ture partner John Kneeland. The first book bearing
Adams's imprint appeared in 1762 and was printed at
Kneeland's shop in Queen Street where, in all likeli-
hood, Adams worked until 1764. In 1763 he married Ann
Lowder, whose father was the first post rider between
Boston and Hartford, Connecticut.

   In 1765 Adams entered into partnership with John
Kneeland and together they opened a shop in Milk Street,
but the firm of Kneeland and Adams was in some respects
an adjunct to the business of Daniel Kneeland, John's
brother. The auxiliary nature of Kneeland and Adams's
business is most clearly seen in the publication of
Nathaniel Low's almanacs, a series which would come to
rival the New England almanacs of Nathaniel Ames. The

2

Low almanacs first appeared in 1762, printed by Daniel
and John Kneeland. From 1762 to 1765, they were printed
exclusively by the Kneeland brothers (probably with the
help of Adams as an employee). There was no almanac
for 1766 because of the Stamp Act, but from 1767 to
1770, Low's calendar was printed jointly by Daniel
Kneeland in Queen Street and by Kneeland and Adams in
Milk Street. Only in 1771 and 1772 did Kneeland and
Adams alone print the almanac.

Kneeland and Adams printed mainly religious
works: sermons, Psalters, and hymnals. Low's almanacs
and one Latin grammar were the only patently secular
books they printed. Their clientele was the New England ministry. While they served the major Boston publishers of the day, their record suggests that they
were publishers in their own right as well. Of the
forty-seven religious works they printed, twenty-three
were done explicitly for publishers. Twenty-four carry
no publisher credit, but Kneeland and Adams both printed
and sold all of those works.

Kneeland and Adams mutually dissolved their partnership in February 1772. Kneeland continued to print
alone until 1775, when he retired from the trade. Adams
became a post rider from Boston to Hartford, but he did
not leave the trade entirely. In the summer of 1772 he
published--and John Kneeland printed--Benjamin Wadsworth's Dialogue between a Minister and His Neighbour.
In that same year, moreover, Ebenezer Watson began to
print Low's almanac in Hartford, Connecticut, the same
almanac that Kneeland and Adams had printed--and that
John Kneeland printed annually until 1775--suggesting
Adams's continued activity in the business.

Adams died on 12 October 1782 in Milton, Massachusetts. He had spent close to ten years as a post rider,
after an equal number of years in printing. He was not

3

a major figure in the Boston trade. His significance stems largely from his association with the Kneelands-- first as apprentice, then as employee, and finally as partner--an often repeated pattern among printers and publishers of Boston in the eighteenth century.

Charles Wetherell

Reference:

Thomas, Isaiah. The History of Printing in America. Worcester, Mass.: Isaiah Thomas, Jr., 1810; 2nd ed., revised, Albany, N.Y.: J. Munsell for the American Antiquarian Society, 1874; ed. Marcus A. McCorison, Barre, Mass.: Imprint Society, 1970.

4

Thomas Adams

Thomas Adams (c. 1757-1799), printer to the Massachusetts General Court (the state legislature), was also
the printer, publisher, and editor from 1784 to 1799
of the Independent Chronicle in Boston, which was the
most articulate, ideologically committed, and influential voice of Jeffersonian Republicanism in New England
in the 1790s. As such, Adams and his newspaper were
principal targets for Federalist repression during the
era of the Alien and Sedition Acts. Adams was in fact
indicted in 1798 under both the federal Sedition Act
and, in state court, under the common law of seditious
libel, but his terminal illness and death prevented him
from ever coming to trial under either charge.

Adams's printing and publishing enterprises were
carried out mainly in a series of partnerships. From
1778 to 1780, he and James White, a Boston bookseller,
printed and published books and newspapers (the Evening
Post from 17 October 1778 to 26 February 1780, and the
Morning Chronicle from 9 March to 11 May 1780). In
mid 1783 Adams formed a partnership with a younger man,
John Nourse, a native of Salem, Massachusetts, and six
months later purchased the Independent Chronicle from
Nathaniel Willis. After Nourse died six years later to
the day, on 1 January 1790, Adams worked alone for three
years until 4 July 1793, when Isaac Larkin, one of
Adams's journeymen and former apprentices, joined Adams
as a partner, owning one-third of the business. Following Larkin's death on 4 December 1797, Adams managed
his printing and publishing enterprise alone until,
beset by illness and legal problems arising out of the
Sedition Act proceedings, he sold the business to his
friend and former partner, James White, in May 1799.

During Adams's proprietorship and for some years after, the Chronicle printing office was located "opposite the new Court-House," in Boston's Court Street at the corner of Dorsett's Alley. The premises housed, in addition to the Chronicle establishment, the offices of the auctioneers Russell and Clap and the book and stationery store of James White ("at the sign of Franklin's Head"). The business of the firm was sufficient to require the shop to have three printing presses. About 250 books, pamphlets, and broadsides, besides the hundreds of numbers of the Chronicle, are known to have been printed, published, or sold by Thomas Adams alone or in association with several partners. About three-quarters of these imprints were jobs that came to Adams in his capacity as state printer. Beyond that, however, Adams's chief significance lies in his proprietorship of the Chronicle.

Major Authors: Benjamin Austin, Jr., Ebenezer Bradford, James Sullivan.

Publishers Served: The Massachusetts General Court (legislature).

Only the sketchiest of biographical details about Adams exist. He was born about 1757, probably in Boston and probably the son of Abijah and Mary (Lamson) Adams. It is not known whether he was trained as a printer, for no record of his apprenticeship has been found. His first recorded involvement in the printing trades was the partnership he formed with White in 1778. There is no evidence of how he occupied his time between the dissolution of that partnership in 1780 and the formation of the Adams and Nourse firm in 1783. Adams kept largely to his own business and was not as prominent or active in the affairs of his trade or community as a number of his colleagues were.

Politics and government interested Adams greatly, however, and he eagerly sought the preferment of the Massachusetts legislature. After its founding in 1783, the firm of Adams and Nourse quickly took away much of the commonwealth's printing business from such better established printers as Nathaniel Willis and Benjamin Edes. Their first job was to print the acts and re-solves of the legislature in June 1783 at the price of 1 1/2d per sheet. Half a year later they purchased the Chronicle from Willis. For the next twelve years Adams and his partners retained most of the commonwealth's printing business--bills, debates, election sermons, acts and resolves, and other documents ranging from broadsides to large volumes.

This patronage was clearly an important factor in Adams's success as a printer and publisher of a news-paper as well as of separate imprints, perhaps as much because of the prestige he gained thereby as because of the actual payments he received from government. The government was not, in Rollo Silver's words, "an ideal customer." The legislature knew well the virtue of playing competing printers against one another. The volume of work ordered varied according to the legisla-ture's needs, and there were no guarantees for more work than was contracted. The state, moreover, did not always pay its printing bills promptly. Worst of all, the legislature kept forcing the printers to hold down their prices. Besides the printing of the laws and other official business as separates, the Chronicle, by virtue of a 1781 resolve of the General Court, also had the duty and privilege of publishing, at the rate of six shillings per square, advertisements for the sale of confiscated estates.

By the mid 1790s the political climate in Massa-chusetts had changed sufficiently to loosen Adams's grip on state printing. After several unsuccessful challenges, the firm of Young and Minns, printers with Federalist connections, in 1796 won the right to the legislative printing. As a result, Adams's nonnewspaper printing business declined to practically nothing.

The Chronicle, which Adams and Nourse purchased on 1 January 1784, was for many years a highly success-ful newspaper in terms of its financial support and its

7

influence. A weekly at first, measuring about 11 x 19
inches, the Chronicle had a generous amount of advertising support and a respectable circulation. The paper
became a semiweekly (published Mondays and Thursdays)
with the number of 19 August 1793, about a month after
Larkin was admitted to partnership.

Politically, the Chronicle was, like most Boston
papers, relatively nondescript in the 1780s. It supported the drafting and ratification of the federal
Constitution, and later favored the addition to the
Constitution of a bill of rights. On this latter issue,
later on the domestic policies of the Washington administration, and, most of all, on the issue of the French
Revolution, the Chronicle's Jeffersonian Republican
position became manifest. With these issues and others
as a basis, Adams's Chronicle engaged in bitter political and journalistic rivalry with Benjamin Russell's
Columbian Centinel, the leading Federalist journal in
Boston.

As a newspaper editor, Adams was not as conspicuous as some of his colleagues in the craft, especially
his chief adversary, Russell. The pronounced ideolog-
ical slant of the Chronicle was largely the result of
Adams's selection of other people's writings rather
than of his own. In fact, the Chronicle office became
the meeting place for many of Boston's leading Repub-
licans, who discussed the events of the day and in
response to them penned brief paragraphs and longer
essays for the newspaper.

Beyond his principal contributions as public
printer and newspaper editor and publisher, the output
of Adams's press had little lasting significance. Alone
or with partners, he published several almanacs, including editions for 1780, 1784, and 1786, and a few sermons, including some by Shippie Townsend and Ebenezer
Bradford, and some other religious publications. In
addition, he published several works of timely political or social significance. Chief among these was
Observations on the Pernicious Practice of the Law by

Benjamin Austin, Jr., writing under the pseudonym
Honestus. These essays by a Boston merchant and
frequent contributor to the Chronicle (in which they
first appeared) stirred up considerable controversy
when they were published by Adams and Nourse in 1786.
Other publications of this sort include two works
attributed to James Sullivan, a leading lawyer and
political figure, Biographical Sketch of the Life and
Character of His Late Excellency Governor Hancock
(Adams and Larkin, 1793) and The Altar of Baal Thrown
Down (Adams and Larkin, 1795).

The printing house of Thomas Adams made no contribution to American belles-lettres. Rather, its
significance lies in its service to the legislature of
one of the largest of the new united states and in its
publication of the Independent Chronicle, the leading
Republican paper in Boston and New England in the 1790s.
Although he never actually came to trial for sedition,
Thomas Adams was nevertheless a martyr to that phase of
political intolerance in being a leading champion of
the cause of a free press.

John B. Hench

References:

Buckingham, Joseph T. Specimens of Newspaper Literature. Vol. 1. Boston: Little and Brown, 1850.

Hench, John B. "The Newspaper in a Republic: Boston's
Centinel and Chronicle, 1784-1801." Ph.D. dissertation, Clark University, 1979.

Silver, Rollo G. "Government Printing in Massachusetts,
1751-1800." Studies in Bibliography, 16 (1963).

Smith, James Morton. Freedom's Fetters: The Alien and
    Sedition Laws in American Civil Liberties. Ithaca
    and London: Cornell University Press, 1966.

Bezoune Allen

Bezoune Allen (dates unknown) printed approximately sixteen titles bearing his name on the title page. All but
two appeared in 1743. Allen worked alone from 1734 to
1736; he was a partner with his brother-in-law Bartholomew Green, Jr. and John Bushell from 1736 to 1743 and
with Bushell and John Green (not Bartholomew's son of
that name) from 1745 until 1747. Allen and partners
printed for Daniel Henchman, Samuel Eliot, Thomas Fleet,
Timothy Green, Nathaniel Proctor, and for the booksellers. They printed mainly religious titles, including
works by Nathaniel Appleton, Thomas Barnard, Charles
Chauncy, Jonathan Edwards, Thomas Hooker, and Samuel
Willard, all eminent divines. Allen was the son of
John Allen.

Reference:

Thomas, Isaiah. The History of Printing in America.
    Worcester, Mass.: Isaiah Thomas, Jr., 1810;
    2nd ed., revised, Albany, N.Y.: J. Munsell for
    the American Antiquarian Society, 1874; ed.
    Marcus A. McCorison, Barre, Mass.: Imprint
    Society, 1970.

John Allen

John Allen (c. 1660-c. 1727), printer and bookseller, arrived in Boston on 10 February 1686 with considerable experience in the book trade. He had begun printing and selling books in London as early as 1669, when he was located at the White Horse in Wentworth Street near Bell Lane. In 1687 Allen's name appeared in only one imprint as a publisher. In 1691, however, numerous imprints bore his name as co-printer, some in conjunction with Benjamin Harris, others with Bartholomew Green. The partnership with Harris lasted only about two years, that with Green for a decade after 1694. From 1704 until 1707 Allen was probably in England, but late in 1707 he opened his own Boston printing shop in Pudding Lane near the post office, and thereafter he was the sole printer of the imprints bearing his name. His shop was destroyed by the great fire of 2 October 1711, but within months he reopened for business in Newbury Street, where he remained until his death.

Major Authors: John Hale, Cotton Mather, Increase Mather, Samuel Mather, Samuel Sewall.

Publishers Served: Nicholas Boone, Daniel Henchman, Robert Starke.

Why Allen left his business in London in 1685 to come to Boston is not clear. John Dunton, with whom he sailed to the new world, reports in his Letters that Allen came at the request of his uncle, the Reverend James Allen, then pastor of the First Church in Boston. But Isaiah Thomas records that Allen came at the encouragement of the Mathers. Whatever the case, Allen was certainly instrumental in the dissemination of the Mathers' works. In London he had printed Increase

Mather's <u>Mystery of Israel's Salvation</u> (1669), and he
had published John Eliot's <u>Brief Narrative of the Gospel
in New England</u> (1671), the first publication of the Society for the Propagation of the Gospel amongst the
Indians in New England after Charles II had renewed its
charter. These activities doubtless called him to the
Mathers' attention. In Boston Allen was responsible,
or partly responsible, for printing a large number of
the Mathers' works. For example, in 1691, the first
year in which Allen's name appears in a substantial
number of imprints, he helped print seven titles by
Cotton Mather, four in partnership with Green and three
in partnership with Harris. During the years that
Allen and Green were in partnership, they were the most
frequent printers of the Mathers' works; their titles,
in turn, formed a major part of Allen and Green's business. In 1697 they printed twenty-seven titles, of
which eight are by Cotton Mather, two are by Increase
Mather, and one is by Samuel Mather.

Allen's association with Benjamin Harris early in
his career in America was brief but interesting. In
1691 they printed three works by Cotton Mather, five
by Samuel Willard, and an edition of the <u>Shorter Cate-
chism</u>. The works they printed were sold through a
sales outlet at the London Coffee House. Judging by
the imprints, Allen was in partnership with Harris in
the sale as well as in the printing of their titles,
the only time Allen was involved with the bookselling
business in America.

Allen's partnership with Green was considerably
more significant. Isaiah Thomas maintains that although
in fact Allen and Green never entered into a formal
partnership, their collaboration is of considerable
historical interest, however formal or informal it may
have been. In addition to being the main printers of
the Mathers' works, in 1695 they became the "Printers
to the Governour and Council," and after that date such
official documents as proclamations, acts, and legal
codes formed the bulk of their business. They also
printed a number of works of particular interest to

12

historians of the period. In 1696, for example, they printed one of the most valuable documents in early New England history, Joshua Scottow's collection of letters entitled Massachusetts or the First Planters of New-England, printed for the publisher Richard Wilkins. Historians are further indebted to Green and Allen for printing Cotton Mather's The Bostonian Ebenezer (1698), the first history of the city of Boston, and for printing the same author's Decennium Luctuosum (1699). Published by Samuel Phillips, this work is a history of the ten years' war with the Indians.

Other titles printed by Allen and Green and of interest to the historian include an edition of the Bay Psalm Book in 1698 for Michael Perry; it was probably the first book printed in America to include musical notation. During the same year they became the first in Boston (not including Cambridge) to print a book in an Indian language; this was an edition of Increase Mather's Greatest Sinners Called, which Samuel Danforth had translated into Massachuset, an Algonquian language. In 1700 they printed one of the earliest antislavery tracts in America, Samuel Sewall's The Selling of Joseph, and in 1702 they printed John Hale's Modest Enquiry into the Nature of Witchcraft for Nicholas Boone.

The Allen and Green partnership came to an end in 1704, and from then until 1707 Allen's name disappears entirely from the book trade records. Presumably he spent those years in England. Then with the number for 10 November 1707 Allen took over printing the Boston News-Letter for the publisher John Campbell, a printing job that Green had done until that date. Except for a few months during 1709 when its publication was apparently suspended, this weekly newspaper was Allen's main source of business until the fire that destroyed his shop in October 1711. Other than the newspaper, Allen printed little during these years except an occasional title by Cotton Mather and an edition of John Bunyan's Sighs from Hell (1708). After he moved to his new quarters in Newbury Street, however, his business

13

increased sharply. In 1717, his best year in this
phase of his career, he printed twenty-one titles.
None of these is of particular historical interest,
but they testify to the extensive connections Allen
enjoyed among the publishers in Boston. Of those
titles, the imprint of only one does not indicate a
publisher. Of the others, Allen printed nine for
Nicholas Boone, four each for Daniel Henchman and
Robert Starke, and one each for Nicholas Buttolph,
Benjamin Eliot, and Thomas Fleet. During the course
of his career, Allen also printed titles for Joseph
Browning (or Brunning), Duncan Campbell, Samuel
Gerrish, Michael Perry, Samuel Phillips, Samuel
Sewall, Jr., and Richard Wilkins. After 1717 Allen's
business gradually declined until in 1725 he printed
only one work, an edition of John Bunyan's The Heavenly
Foot-Man. That is the last known imprint in which his
name appears.

Allen's name appears in the imprints of some 375
works, of which slightly more than one-third are volumes by the Mathers. Allen's major historical importance probably lies in that fact, for the Mathers,
especially the prolific Cotton, wielded an influence
over the life and thought of Massachusetts in general
and Boston in particular that cannot be overestimated.
Any assessment of Allen's historical significance must
also take into account his association with Green in
printing Scottow's Massachusetts and the invaluable
documents they produced as printers for the colonial
government.

C. R. Kropf

References:

Dunton, John. Letters Written from New-England.
     Boston: Prince Society, 1867; reprint edition,
     New York: Burt Franklin, 1966.

John Allen

Littlefield, George E. Early Boston Booksellers:
    1642-1711. Boston: Club of Odd Volumes, 1900;
    reprint edition, New York: Burt Franklin, 1969.

Plomer, Henry R. A Dictionary of the Printers and
    Booksellers Who Were at Work in England, Scotland,
    and Ireland from 1668 to 1725. Oxford: Biblio-
    graphical Society, 1968.

Thomas, Isaiah. The History of Printing in America.
    Worcester, Mass.: Isaiah Thomas, Jr., 1810;
    2nd ed., revised, Albany, N.Y.: J. Munsell for
    the American Antiquarian Society, 1874; ed.
    Marcus A. McCorison, Barre, Mass.: Imprint
    Society, 1970.

John Wincoll Allen

John Wincoll Allen (dates unknown) was active as a
Boston printer and publisher in 1787 and 1788. He
listed his place of business variously as "No. 49,
Marlborough-Street," "in Ann-Street, near the Conduit,"
and "the north side of the State-House, in State-
Street." He printed and sold two volumes of Minutes
of the Warren Association, a Peter Thacher sermon, and
probably A Table, Calculated to Shew in an Instant the
Contents (in Feet and Twelfth Parts of a Foot) of Any
Sled Load or Cart Load of Wood. In June 1787 Samuel
Hall admitted Allen as a partner in publishing the
Massachusetts Gazette. Hall left in September 1787
and Allen continued alone until the paper's last number
on 11 November 1788. Before his years in Boston, Allen
had been active in Charlestown, Massachusetts, and
after a stay in Harrisburg, Pennsylvania, in 1792 and
1793, he worked in Baltimore until 1796. He spent
most of his career in Philadelphia, where he worked as
a printer from 1800 until 1833.

Reference:

Brigham, Clarence S. History and Bibliography of
    American Newspapers: 1690-1820. Vol. 1.
    Worcester, Mass.: American Antiquarian Society,
    1947.

John Amory

John Amory (dates unknown) was a Boston bookseller and binder who became an eminent merchant. His name is reportedly in the imprint of Isaac Watts's Orthodoxy and Charity United (1749), but no copy of that book is known to exist.

Reference:

Thomas, Isaiah. The History of Printing in America. Worcester, Mass.: Isaiah Thomas, Jr., 1810; 2nd ed., revised, Albany, N.Y.: J. Munsell for the American Antiquarian Society, 1874; ed. Marcus A. McCorison, Barre, Mass.: Imprint Society, 1970.

Ebenezer Turell Andrews

Ebenezer Turell Andrews (1766-1851) was apprenticed to
Isaiah Thomas from 1781 to 1788. In 1788 Thomas took
Andrews and John Sprague as partners, but when Sprague
left, the firm became Thomas and Andrews in 1789. It
was located at the sign of Faust's head (or statue) in
Newbury Street. Business increased so rapidly that
Thomas and Andrews established a house in Baltimore in
1793, one in Albany, New York, in 1796 and another in
1797, one in Troy, New York, in 1799, and one in
Walpole, New Hampshire, in 1807 and another the next
year. By the time the firm of Thomas and Andrews dissolved in 1822, it had become the largest printing
establishment in America.

References:

Shipton, Clifford K. Isaiah Thomas: Printer, Patriot
    and Philanthropist, 1749-1831. Rochester, N.Y.:
    Leo Hart, 1948.

Thomas, Isaiah. The History of Printing in America.
    Worcester, Mass.: Isaiah Thomas, Jr., 1810;
    2nd ed., revised, Albany, N.Y.: J. Munsell for
    the American Antiquarian Society, 1874; ed.
    Marcus A. McCorison, Barre, Mass.: Imprint
    Society, 1970.

Loring Andrews

Loring Andrews (1768-1805) printed, with Edmund Freeman, the Herald of Freedom, and the Federal Advertiser from its inception in September 1788 to the end of the second volume a year later. Andrews and Freeman, "opposite the north door of the State-House," printed only one other known item, Candid Considerations on Libels (1789). Andrews published newspapers in other towns after leaving the Herald of Freedom.

Reference:

Brigham, Clarence S. History and Bibliography of American Newspapers: 1690-1820. Vol. 1. Worcester, Mass.: American Antiquarian Society, 1947.

John Asplund

John Asplund (d. 1807) first published in Albany, New York, in 1792. In Boston he published John Leland's A Circular Letter of Valediction in 1794 and Richard Burnham's Hymns in 1796. Asplund also published in Dover, New Hampshire, in 1798.

19

Mary Woodmansey Tappin Avery

Mary Woodmansey Tappin Avery (c. 1629-1707) was the
first American woman publisher. She sold books in
Boston from 1678 to 1707, first as Mary Tappin and
then, beginning in 1679, as Mary Avery, the wife of
William Avery. In 1682, "near the Blue Angel," she
published at least two titles bearing her imprint:
The Rule of the New-Creature and William Perkins's
The Foundation of Christian Religion Gathered into Six
Principles, the latter printed by Samuel Green.

      Reference:

Tebbel, John. A History of Book Publishing in the
      United States. Vol. 1. New York and London:
      Bowker, 1972.

20

William Avery

William Avery (c. 1621-1687), Mary Avery's husband, published only one known book, William Adams' The Necessity of the Pouring out of the Spirit from on High upon a Sinning Apostatizing People, printed by John Foster in 1679. Avery might have had Elkanah Pembrooke as a clerk.

Reference:

Littlefield, George E. Early Boston Booksellers: 1642-1711. Boston: Club of Odd Volumes, 1900; reprint edition, New York: Burt Franklin, 1969.

Thomas Baker

Thomas Baker (dates unknown) published one known book, Benjamin Keach's Sion in Distress (1683). It was printed by Samuel Green.

Andrew Barclay

Andrew Barclay (1738-1823), a Scot, was a binder and bookseller who began business in 1764 at the "2d door north of
Three Kings, Cornhill." In 1769 he identified his shop as
"at the Sign of the Gilt Bible." He and Samuel Taylor were
the only eighteenth-century American binders to have signed
their work. As a Boston bookseller he published approximately fourteen works, almost all of which are either
almanacs or Psalters. Perhaps his most significant title
was one of his first, Tom Thumb's Play-Book (1764), a work
that Isaiah Thomas printed toward the end of his apprenticeship with Zechariah Fowle. Barclay was active as a
binder and bookseller in New York from 1777 until 1783.

References:

French, Hannah D. "The Amazing Career of Andrew Barclay,
    Scottish Bookbinder, of Boston." Studies in Bib-
    liography, 14 (1961).

Thomas, Isaiah. The History of Printing in America.
    Worcester, Mass.: Isaiah Thomas, Jr., 1810; 2nd
    ed., revised, Albany, N.Y.: J. Munsell for the
    American Antiquarian Society, 1874; ed. Marcus A.
    McCorison, Barre, Mass.: Imprint Society, 1970.

William Barrett (see Job Weeden and William Barrett)

Gillam Bass

Gillam Bass (1746-1814) sold one known book bearing his name in the imprint, William Billings's New-England Psalm-Singer (1770).

Ebenezer Battelle

Ebenezer Battelle (1754-1818) published approximately fifteen titles from 1781 or 1783 to 1787. Although Charles Evans lists Battelle's 1783 edition of a Thomas almanac as his first publication, John Tebbel cites Battelle editions of The Fair and Nurse Truelove's New Year's Gift, both published in 1781. Battelle's publications are undistinguished. Proprietor of the Boston Book Store until 1785, he conducted business in Marlborough Street, "near the State House."

Reference:

Tebbel, John. A History of Book Publishing in the United States. Vol. 1. New York and London: Bowker, 1972.

23

Joseph Belknap and
Thomas Hall

Joseph Belknap (1769-1800) and Thomas Hall (d. 1798) were printers, booksellers, and binders. Over two dozen works published from 1792 to 1794 bear their joint imprint, including the Collections of the Massachusetts Historical Society; the American Apollo, a weekly newspaper; the first edition of the Farmer's Almanack; and various sermons, devotional works, and plays. In 1792 their shop, the Apollo Press, was located at "State Street"; in August 1793 they relocated at "no. 8, Dock Square, North Side of the Market," where they remained throughout their partnership.

Major Authors: Jeremy Belknap, Daniel Gookin.

Belknap was born in Dover, New Hampshire, on 2 December 1769, the son of Jeremy Belknap and Ruth Eliot, daughter of Samuel Eliot, the Boston bookseller. His father became a prominent Congregational clergyman in Boston and served in the Federal Street Church from 1787 until 1798. From November 1783 until the summer of 1787, the younger Belknap was apprenticed to Robert Aitken in Philadelphia, followed by an apprenticeship under John Mycall of Newburyport, Massachusetts, from September 1787 until December 1790. He worked briefly in the Boston shop of Ebenezer Andrews before beginning business for himself.

Belknap began his career as a printer in August 1791, in partnership with Alexander Young. Initially their shop was located at "No. 34, Newbury Street," but they soon moved to the "north side of the State-House, State-Street." In 1792 they named their establishment the Apollo Press, a name that Belknap retained for his shop throughout his printing career in Boston. They printed only a small number of titles together,

24

including several works about the French Revolution, as
well as the third and final volume of Jeremy Belknap's
History of New-Hampshire (1792), a diligently researched
and well-written study of the state through the 1780s.

On 6 January 1792 they began publishing the American Apollo, a weekly octavo paper that initially included in each number a separately paged section of the
publications of the Massachusetts Historical Society.
Belknap's father, Jeremy, had been one of the founders
of the Society in 1791, and it apparently gave some support to the newspaper as a vehicle for publishing its
Collections. Printed on the first printing press made
completely in Boston, the paper attracted nearly 1,200
subscribers at first, but the subscriptions soon began
to decrease at a disappointingly rapid rate. Young became discouraged, and Belknap bought out his interest
in early May 1792, ending their association. Before
the end of the month Belknap was joined by a new partner, Thomas Hall.

Little is known of Hall, but his partnership with
Belknap apparently served as his introduction to the
world of printing. Both men continued to publish the
Apollo, even though the number of 28 September 1792
was the last to contain the Historical Society's publications. Thereafter the newspaper assumed a regular
folio format. Belknap and Hall continued to work for
the Historical Society, however, printing its annual
Collections in 1792 and 1793. Other historical works
that they printed include Jeremy Belknap's Discourses,
Intended to Commemorate the Discovery of America by
Christopher Columbus and Daniel Gookin's Historical
Collections of the Indians in New England, both in
1792.

The partners' duties as newspaper publishers and
printers for the Historical Society did not preclude
their printing other works, which included more than a
dozen sermons and devotional works, but these items are
of an undistinguished nature. One of their most

important publications was Robert B. Thomas's Farmer's
Almanack. They published the first edition of this
best known New England almanac in 1792, and it sold
3,000 copies. The second edition, which they printed
a year later, was so great a success--9,000 copies were
sold--that it provoked Isaiah Thomas to rail against
its intrusion into territory previously dominated by
his Massachusetts, Connecticut, Rhode-Island, New-
hampshire & Vermont Almanack. It was such valuable
property that Hall retained his share in it even after
he and Belknap ended their partnership. One of the
last books that Belknap printed was the 1796 edition
of this work.

Belknap and Hall profited from Boston's first
theater season in 1794, printing a number of plays "As
performed at the Theatre, in Boston." Since 1750 plays
had been forbidden in Massachusetts, but after the repeal of the acting ban in 1793, the Boston Theatre was
speedily built and opened for the first time in February
1794. Belknap and Hall printed two collections of the
plays that appeared on stage at the new theater during
its first season. The first collection, American Selection of Farces, Operas, Etc., was printed for William
Blake and William Clap, and includes a dozen works.
The second, American Selection of Plays, printed in two
volumes for David and John West, contains thirteen titles. Both collections consist of plays written by
such popular contemporary playwrights as David Garrick
and John O'Keefe, in addition to ones by such established
masters as Oliver Goldsmith and William Shakespeare.

The American Apollo, initially plagued by declining subscriptions, apparently continued to give its publishers problems, for with the number of 10 July 1794,
their partnership ended and the paper was continued by
Belknap alone until it ceased on 25 December 1794. The
Collections of the Massachusetts Historical Society
never proved very profitable for Belknap, either. After
the dissolution of Belknap's partnership with Hall, the
society decided to publish the Collections at its own
risk, and although Belknap requested that he be allowed

26

to continue printing them, the society heeded complaints about the quality of his work and contracted with another printer. Belknap's printing did not surpass that of his competitors in quality; the composition was neat, but the press work was often mediocre or poor.

After Hall left the business, Belknap continued alone for a year, during which time he printed several works by his father, including Sacred Poetry; Dissertations on the Character, Death and Resurrection of Jesus Christ; and a broadside entitled Queries Respecting the Introduction, Progress and Abolition of Slavery in Massachusetts. All of these appeared in 1795. He also printed the Farmer's Almanack for 1796. No later title bears his imprint. He died 2 August 1800 in Petersburg, Virginia.

Thomas Hall continued to print for two years after his partnership with Belknap ended, until 1796. In 1794 he printed one of the first American editions of Thomas Paine's Age of Reason. In the same year he began a short-lived newspaper publishing venture in partnership with a man surnamed Macclintock. The Times: or the Evening Entertainer was intended as a triweekly and was begun on 4 October. But Macclintock withdrew from the enterprise with the 5 November number, and the paper ceased altogether with the number of 8 November. For the next year Hall was the partner of Joseph Nancrede, and together they printed several political titles, including a translation of the new French Republic's constitution and a discussion of the Jay Treaty entitled Treaties with France, Great Britain, and the United States Pro and Con. No titles bear Hall's imprint after 1796.

During the three years of their partnership, from 1792 until 1794, Joseph Belknap and Thomas Hall printed over two dozen works, including a newspaper and the Collections of the Massachusetts Historical Society.

Joseph Belknap and Thomas Hall

They also printed various sermons, devotional works, plays, and the earliest editions of the Farmer's Almanack.

Gary R. Treadway

References:

Deane, Charles and Charles C. Smith. "Introduction." Proceedings of the Massachusetts Historical Society, 1 (1876).

Hitchings, Sinclair H. "Joseph Belknap's Printing in Boston." Printing and Graphic Arts, 6 (1958).

Nathaniel Belknap

Nathaniel Belknap (dates unknown) was principally a
binder who published fewer than two dozen known volumes
from 1722 to 1729. He was a cousin to John Phillips's
wife. Cotton Mather assisted Belknap in the business
by permitting him to publish Love Triumphant in 1722.
In fact, most of Belknap's titles are by Mather. Belknap
conducted business "at his shop the corner of Clarke's
Wharffe, and next door to the Mitre Coffee-House." He
used Thomas Fleet, Samuel Gerrish, Bartholomew Green,
and Samuel Kneeland as printers, and he published two
books in conjunction with Kneeland and Bennet Love.

References:

Tebbel, John. A History of Book Publishing in the
     United States. Vol. 1. New York and London:
     Bowker, 1972.

Thomas, Isaiah. The History of Printing in America.
     Worcester, Mass.: Isaiah Thomas, Jr., 1810;
     2nd ed., revised, Albany, N.Y.: J. Munsell
     for the American Antiquarian Society, 1874;
     ed. Marcus A. McCorison, Barre, Mass.: Imprint
     Society, 1970.

Edward Berry and
Edward Cox

Edward Berry (dates unknown) and Edward Cox (dates unknown) published approximately one dozen titles from
1767 to, probably, 1776. About half of their publications are reprints; they published their own catalogue
in 1772. They conducted business first "two doors
above the British Coffee-House" and later in "Cornhill,"
where they specialized in English goods and jewelry.
In 1778 Cox and Berry moved to New York City.

        Reference:

Thomas, Isaiah. The History of Printing in America.
        Worcester, Mass.: Isaiah Thomas, Jr., 1810;
        2nd ed., revised, Albany, N.Y.: J. Munsell
        for the American Antiquarian Society, 1874;
        ed. Marcus A. McCorison, Barre, Mass.: Imprint
        Society, 1970.

William Billings

William Billings (1746-1800) was America's first native composer. Best known for his New-England Psalm-Singer, he sold several of his own works from 1770 to 1786.

References:

Damon, S. Foster. "Varnum's 'Ministerial Oppression,' A Revolutionary Drama." Proceedings of the American Antiquarian Society, 55 (1945).

Foote, Henry W. "Musical Life in Boston in the Eighteenth Century." Proceedings of the American Antiquarian Society, 49 (1939).

Caleb Bingham

Caleb Bingham (1757-1817) was a bookseller and minor Boston publisher whose career extended into the nineteenth century. He was an educator who entered the book business primarily to publish his own work. From 1795 to 1800 he published approximately thirty titles at his shop at "No. 44, Cornhill."

Major Authors: Caleb Bingham, Hannah Foster, Abraham Weatherwise, Benjamin West.

After taking a degree at Dartmouth in 1782, Bingham became master of Moor's Indian Charity School

(1782-1784), a teacher in a private Boston school for young ladies (1784-1789), and then a teacher in the Boston public schools (1789-1795). He also served as director of the state prison. In 1795 he became a bookseller.

Bingham published only one volume during 1795, the second edition of his American Preceptor, a book that, in its sixty-four editions and 640,000 copies sold, replaced Noah Webster's as the most popular American reader. In 1796 Bingham published eight titles, half of which bear his name as author. He published the third edition of the American Preceptor; the second edition of his Astronomical and Geographical Catechism, a title that eventually sold 100,000 copies; the ninth edition of his popular Young Lady's Accidence, the second American grammar; and the fifth edition of his Child's Companion, a speller that eventually sold 120,000 copies. That year he also published--in collaboration with seven other publishers--editions of Benjamin West's Astronomical Diary and The Federal Advocate, the 1797 Weatherwise Almanack, and Thomas Hayes's address on the danger of neglecting common colds.

Between 1797 and 1800 about half of Bingham's publications were his own compilations, including the Columbian Orator (1797), a book on eloquence that ultimately went through twenty-three editions and sold approximately 200,000 copies. The non-Bingham titles he published are mainly religious volumes or practical works, such as almanacs. In his only venture into literature, in 1798 he published, with others, Hannah Foster's The Boarding School. Bingham was the sole publisher of only about half of the volumes bearing his imprint.

Caleb Bingham's importance is not as a publisher but as a compiler of books that helped shape the minds of American children for almost a century.

References:

Littlefield, George E. Early Schools and School-Books of New England. Boston: Club of Odd Volumes, 1904.

Tebbel, John. A History of Book Publishing in the United States. Vol. 1. New York and London: Bowker, 1972.

Lemuel Blake

Lemuel Blake (1775-1861) spent the first half of his
life as a Boston bookseller and publisher, his name
appearing in the imprints of some seventy-five titles
published in that city. Until 1806 he was allied with
his brother as W. P. and L. Blake at No. 1 Cornhill,
where he subsequently operated in his own name for
three years. From 1809 to 1814 he was a partner in the
bookselling firm of West and Blake, located at No. 56
Cornhill, after which time he left the book trade.

Major Authors: James Boswell, Lord Byron,
Sir Walter Scott, William Shakespeare.

Blake was born in Dorchester, Massachusetts, on
9 August 1775. The son of William and Rachel (Glover)
Blake, he was apprenticed early to the Boston firm of
Guild and Blake, proprietors of the Boston Book Store,
in which his older brother William was a partner. By
the time Lemuel attained his majority, Benjamin Guild
had died, and William had taken over sole direction of
the store. On 27 September 1796 Lemuel entered into
partnership with his brother, and thereafter for a
decade they operated under the style of W. P. and
L. Blake.

The Blakes published catalogues of their stock in
1798 and 1800 that reveal exceptionally strong holdings
in fiction. More than half of the titles listed are
novels, which was an unusually high percentage at that
time, especially in Boston where many considered novel-
reading to be pernicious frivolity at best and the work
of the devil at worst. History and biography constituted ten percent of their stock at the turn of the
century; plays, poems, and essays another ten percent;
and geography and travel an additional five percent.

The remaining quarter of their holdings was spread among such fields as philosophy and religion, science and technology, commerce and political economy. Clearly they strove to purvey the more popular literature of their time.

A like concern for popular literature that would retail well pervaded W. P. and L. Blake's publishing activities during this period. Lemuel had published two plays on his own account even before becoming a partner in the firm. In subsequent years the Blakes published, in concert with others in the Boston book trade, such marketable titles as Walley Oulton's Wonderful Story-Teller (1797), August von Kotzebue's Constant Lover (1799), George Colman's Poor Gentleman (1802), and Susanna Keir's Interesting Memoirs (1802). They also shared responsibility for the appearance of much general literature, including Roger L'Estrange's Seneca's Morals (1800), Eulogies . . . on the . . . Death of Washington (1800), and Lord Chesterfield's Man of Education (1801). Some works of scholarship also carry their imprint, including Stewart Kyd's Treatise on the Law of Bills of Exchange (1798), Alexander Adam's Rudiments of Latin and English Grammar (1799), and Joseph Townsend's Elements of Therapeutics (1802).

Business declined, however, and early in 1805 all property belonging to the firm was assigned to Thomas and Andrews for disposal. William left the store and opened the Boston Circulating Library on his own account on School Street, but Lemuel remained at the old stand, operating now in his own name. From 1807 to 1809 Lemuel published several of his most important books, including an edition of Shakespeare, Boswell's Johnson, Watts's Hymns, and Jane Porter's Thaddeus of Warsaw.

In 1809 Blake became a partner in the firm of West and Blake, booksellers, at 56 Cornhill. Although David West died the following year, the style of the firm remained the same until 1814, but with Blake directing its operations. West and Blake brought out

Scott's Marmion (1801), Byron's Corsair (1814), and his English Bards and Scotch Reviewers (1814). When the firm was dissolved in 1814, Blake left the book trade.

Lemuel Blake was an auctioneer and commission merchant with Blake and (Joseph L.) Cunningham from 1815 to 1823, and he operated a paper warehouse in Boston from 1824 to 1832. He was later a rubber goods merchant, an agent for a chemical company, and president, from 1839 to 1844, of the Mutual Insurance Company of Boston. He never married. Blake died in Boston on 4 March 1861.

David Kaser

Reference:

Bolton, Charles K. "Circulating Libraries in Boston 1765-1865." Publications of the Colonial Society of Massachusetts, 11 (1907).

William Pynson Blake

William Pynson Blake (1769-1820) served the popular
reading needs of two cities through his publishing,
bookselling, and circulating library activities. He
had some fifty books printed for his firm alone, and
his imprint was joined with others in an additional
fifty-nine titles. Of singular significance was his
publishing of plays and general literature. His operation was located in Boston at No. 59 Cornhill (1792-
1796), No. 1 Cornhill (1796-1805), and No. 3 School
Street (1805-1808); he later moved to New York City.

Major Authors: Oliver Goldsmith, Samuel Johnson,
Junius, Susanna Rowson, Isaac Watts.

Blake, the eldest son of William and Rachel
(Glover) Blake, was born into a family of Congregation-
alists in Dorchester, Massachusetts, just south of
Boston, on 9 January 1769. He was baptized two weeks
later at the New South Church. Little is known of
William's early life and education, but when he attained
his majority he was the junior partner in the firm of
Guild and Blake, proprietors of the Boston Book Store.

Blake's senior partner was Benjamin Guild, a well-
connected Harvard man, sometime college tutor, and minister who had taken over the Boston Book Store from
Ebenezer Battelle in 1785. Locating at No. 59 Cornhill,
Guild soon added a circulating library to his operation
and developed an extensive trade in books "to be Let or
Sold." The catalogues he published in 1788, 1789, and
1791 exhibit a balanced stock of carefully selected
titles, of which about a third were novels and the remainder were spread among science, law, religion,
belles-lettres, and other fields. The situation

provided the young Blake with a good opportunity to learn thoroughly the trade that was to be his livelihood.

Benjamin Guild, however, died on 15 October 1792, and Blake helped administer the estate. A few days later he took over direction of the Boston Book Store and its circulating library and began shaping them to his own predilections. Within a few months he was also publishing under his own name. In 1796 he removed his operation from 59 Cornhill (a few doors north of School Street on the west side of the present Washington Street) to No. 1 Cornhill, at the north corner of Spring Lane. In the following year he took his brother Lemuel, six years his junior, into partnership with him, and thereafter for a decade they worked together under the style of W. P. and L. Blake. Lemuel had previously been apprenticed to Guild and Blake and had done some limited publishing under his own imprint.

Blake set out from the beginning to develop a more popular and less scholarly stock of books in his store and library than had Guild. His published catalogues of books for sale or circulation in 1793, 1796, 1798, and 1800, show considerable and steady shifts in emphasis. Whereas one in seven of his 1,350 titles in 1793 concerned science or technology, he offered nothing in those fields seven years later. The representation of religion and philosophy was cut by two-thirds over the same period. Fiction, on the other hand, was increased substantially. Whereas novels constituted thirty-seven percent of his stock in 1793, they rose to fifty percent of the total in 1796, to fifty-four percent in 1798, and to sixty-three percent in 1800.

Blake entered modestly into publishing in 1793, with little to distinguish his early work. In that year he produced a perennial favorite in Goldsmith's Deserted Village, as well as a couple of children's books. Early in 1794, however, Boston's first real theater opened its doors, and Blake was quick to capitalize on its great popularity. He published eleven plays, farces, comic operas, and other stage

38

presentations in that year and a considerably larger
number in 1795. These works, most of which were then
being performed at the new Federal Street Theatre, included plays by David Garrick, John O'Keefe, George
Colman, Jr., Thomas Shadwell, Thomas Hurlstone, and
many others. As the novelty of the theater in Boston
diminished, however, so did Blake's publication of
plays, and following 1798 he published none except for
Pizarro and Self-Immolation by the popular sentimental-
ist August von Kotzebue.

Most of Blake's other titles during this decade
were published in concert with other Boston booksellers.
Ann Radcliffe's Romance of the Forest (1795), Ducray-
Dumenil's Alexis (1796), Fanny Burney's Camilla
(1797), and T. S. Surr's George Barnwell (1800) were
among novels published jointly by him and others. He
also allied himself with his fellow booksellers to produce religious books such as the New Testament (1794)
and the Psalms of David, Imitated (1799), as well as
William Paley's View of the Evidences of Christianity
(1795), James Fordyce's Sermons to Young Women (1796),
and Stephen Sewall's Scripture History (1796). There
were also the ubiquitous almanacs and several editions of
Caleb Bingham's popular American Preceptor. Pilgrim's
Progress was brought out in 1800, and John Locke's Essay
Concerning Human Understanding appeared in 1803.

Several of W. P. and L. Blake's most significant
titles were published by them alone in 1804. In that
year they published a pocket edition of Samuel Johnson's
Dictionary, the first in the United States. They also
produced a popular edition of Isaac Watts's Psalms,
Hymns, and Spiritual Songs, as well as Susanna Rowson's
Miscellaneous Poems. Also in 1804 they published
Junius's Letters in two volumes. After that year, however, William P. Blake published no more books.

In addition to his publishing and bookselling,
Blake was important as the proprietor of a circulating
library. His appears to have been the only commercial
library in Boston at the time he took over its direction

39

in 1792; if not the only one, it was certainly the strongest one in town. The conditions governing use of his library, as published in the Independent Chronicle on 31 July 1800, called for a quarterly subscription of two dollars for use of two volumes at a time for up to a month; nonsubscribers could rent duodecimos and smaller books for seven cents per week and octavos for twelve cents.

Especially in the early years Blake's Boston Book Store, with its publishing, retail selling, and circulating library, appears to have prospered. When the great conflagration occurred in Portsmouth, New Hampshire, the day after Christmas 1802, burning out many of the merchants, including booksellers, the Association of Boston Booksellers contributed more than $400 for their relief, of which Blake put in $30. That was a tidy sum in those days, indicative of Blake's thriving business.

The success of Blake's library, however, soon inspired imitators. Joshua Thomas opened a small library "opposite the Treasurer's Office" in 1793, and when Blake removed from No. 59 Cornhill in 1796, William Pelham established another competing library at the vacated old stand. Much of the patronage of the circulating libraries came from women, who for reasons of propriety were often reluctant to frequent commercial establishments. To capitalize upon this modesty, an enterprising milliner named Mary Sprague opened a library in her store on Milk Street in 1802, and two years later another milliner, Keziah Butler, did likewise "at the south part of town."

By 1805 there were at least eight circulating libraries in Boston, a city of scarcely 30,000 inhabitants. The competition proved too much for Blake, and in the face of declining public support, he was forced in March 1805 to dispose at auction of his library along with his Boston Book Store. Later that same year, however, he opened a new Boston circulating library, this time apparently without a book store

40

conjoined, at No. 3 School Street. He remained at this
stand until 1808, at which time his new library was
also offered for sale, probably on account of assign-
ment, and was taken over by Elias Penniman, Jr., who
soon sold it to Charles Metcalf. William's brother
Lemuel meanwhile left the partnership in 1806, continuing for a decade thereafter to sell books on his own
account.

William P. Blake's life and activities after 1808
are difficult to trace. In 1813 he was selling books
and stationery in New York City, as well as advertising
himself as a dry goods merchant. In 1818 he was located
there at 249 Broadway, where he was again operating a
small circulating library after the style of William P.
Blake and Co. A catalogue of his stock published in
that year, however, lists only between 500 and 600 titles on hand. In contrast to his earlier emphases,
moreover, his inventory in 1818 comprised only seventeen
percent novels and twenty-five percent religious and
philosophic works. Clearly much had changed.

William P. Blake, who never married, died in New
York on 5 June 1820 at age 51.

David Kaser

References:

Bolton, Charles K. "Circulating Libraries in Boston
    1765-1865." Publications of the Colonial Society
    of Massachusetts, 11 (1907).

Kaser, David. A Book for a Sixpence. Pittsburgh:
    Beta Phi Mu, 1980.

Joshua Blanchard

Joshua Blanchard (1718-1786) was a stationer and bookseller who dealt largely in British editions. He published only twenty-five titles, over half of which are
reprints. He is perhaps best remembered as one of the
original proprietors of the American Magazine and Historical Chronicle. His shop was located at the "Sign
of the Bible and Crown in Dock-Square."

   Major Authors: Charles Chauncy, Jonathan
Dickinson, Ebenezer and Ralph Erskine, Elizabeth
Singer Rowe, Isaac Watts.

   Blanchard was born in 1718 and died 28 April 1786
in Boston. Although little is known for certain of
Blanchard's personal history, the best evidence indicates that he was the eldest son of Joshua Blanchard,
a mason, builder of the Old South Meeting House, and
husband to Elizabeth Hunt, whom he married in Boston on
26 November 1745. The younger Blanchard sustained himself as a stationer and a dealer in English goods prior
to, during, and following his relatively brief stint as
a publisher.

   Isaiah Thomas relates that Blanchard was "an
enterprising but not a successful bookseller." Certainly his publishing output was modest. In the thirteen years that he was active, he produced only
twenty-five titles; many are reprints of earlier
British works and many were jointly published. He
began his career in 1742, intending, no doubt, to
capitalize upon a heightened demand for religious publications inspired by the Great Awakening. His beginning was auspicious. Of the eight titles he published
in that year, two, at least, are significant today.
Charles Chauncy's Enthusiasm Described and Cautioned

42

Against survives as a classic statement of antirevivalist sentiment. As pastor of the First Church in Boston,
Chauncy was both the Awakening's most prestigious and
most outspoken critic. Contemptuous of the spiritual
presumption and self-righteousness displayed by George
Whitefield and his imitators, he railed against enthusiasm in all of its manifestations, describing it as "a
kind of religious frenzy" and as "a disease, a sort of
madness." He cautioned sane men against trusting in
those afflicted. In a more ecumenical vein, Blanchard
also published the first American edition of Elizabeth
Singer Rowe's Devout Exercises of the Heart. A collection of her prayers published posthumously in England
by Isaac Watts, the book proved popular and went through
a number of editions. Other works published by
Blanchard during his initial year include one each by
three British nonconformist divines, Giles Firmin,
Thomas Gouge, and James Janeway; an edition of Ralph
Erskine's popular Gospel Sonnets; and a sermon by an
American Congregational minister, Benjamin Lord.

Beginning in 1743, Blanchard was associated with
the publication of the American Magazine and Historical
Chronicle, a monthly miscellany derivative of contemporary British journals and styled after the London Magazine. Blanchard began as one of the magazine's original
publishers and proprietors, sharing the honor with
Samuel Eliot; in the second and subsequent years, when
the printers Rogers and Fowle took over its publication,
he remained as a selling agent. The magazine was edited by Jeremiah Gridley, a devotee of British literary
and political authority, and reflected, therefore,
largely British tastes and interests. Its run of
three years, four months was the longest of any general
magazine established prior to 1786.

Blanchard published several other important titles from 1743 until 1746, among them A Collection of
Sermons on Several Subjects (1744) by Ebenezer and
Ralph Erskine, the famous Scottish revivalists (the
first published work of Ebenezer Erskine in America);
and Jonathan Dickinson's Familiar Letters to a

43

Gentleman upon a Variety of Seasonable and Important
Subjects in Religion (1745), a treatise aimed in part
at combatting revivalist enthusiasm. Colonial Governor
William Shirley's letter to the Duke of Newcastle (1745)
describing the successful siege of Louisburg is the
only nonreligious title of note. After 1746 Blanchard's
publishing career was virtually at an end. He reprinted
four more titles by the ever-appealing Isaac Watts, the
last appearing in 1755, but he produced no original
titles.

Blanchard maintained many connections in the publishing business. Samuel Eliot was his most frequent
co-publisher, appearing in the imprint of the American
Magazine, Chauncy's Enthusiasm Described, and a work by
Jonathan Dickinson. Other names sharing imprints with
Blanchard are John Amory, Joseph Edwards, Charles
Harrison, and Daniel Henchman. In addition, Blanchard
seems to have engaged in reciprocal selling agreements
with Benjamin Franklin. For example, Blanchard sold
copies of Franklin's printing of Isaac Watts's A Pre-
servative from the Sins and Follies of Childhood and
Youth (1744), while Franklin sold Blanchard's collection of Erskine sermons. The printers most often employed by Blanchard were Gamaliel Rogers and Daniel
Fowle; John Draper also served.

Joshua Blanchard was a minor but not an insignificant publisher. Several of his works, particularly
those by Charles Chauncy and Jonathan Dickinson, are
valuable documents of the religious controversy surrounding the Great Awakening. In addition, the American
Magazine and Historical Chronicle is of interest from
the standpoint of social history, expressing as it does
a strong social and cultural alliance between the colonies and England.

Donna Nance

|Joshua Blanchard

References:

Richardson, Lyon N. A History of Early American
    Magazines, 1741-1789. New York: Nelson, 1931;
    reprint edition, New York: Octagon, 1966.

Thomas, Isaiah. The History of Printing in America.
    Worcester, Mass.: Isaiah Thomas, Jr., 1810;
    2nd ed., revised, Albany, N.Y.: J. Munsell
    for the American Antiquarian Society, 1874;
    ed. Marcus A. McCorison, Barre, Mass.: Imprint
    Society, 1970.

John Bonner

John Bonner (1662-1726) made a map of Boston that he
and William Price sold "against ye Town House" in 1722.
Francis Dewing engraved and printed it. The map "is
the first detailed contemporary map of the town."

Reference:

Whitehill, Walter M. Boston: A Topographical History.
    Cambridge: Belknap Press of Harvard University
    Press, 1959.

45

Nicholas Boone

Nicholas Boone (1679-1738) was a Boston publisher, bookseller, and author with approximately 100 imprints to his credit. In 1701 he wrote and published <u>Military Discipline</u>, the first book on military science written by an American, and in 1704 he entered into an agreement with postmaster John Campbell to sell copies of Campbell's <u>Boston News-Letter</u>, the first long-term newspaper in the colonies. He also published what is considered to be the first historical print in America, Samuel Blodget's <u>A Prospective Plan of the Battle of Lake George</u> (1755), engraved by Thomas Johnston. He opened his first store in 1700 "over against the Old Meeting House," and in 1706, his business prospering, he moved to larger quarters "near the Corner of School-House Lane." In 1708 he adopted the logo of Benjamin Harris, and, until he retired in 1729, his imprints directed the reader to "the sign of the Bible in Cornhill near the Corner of School Street."

<u>Major Authors</u>: Joseph Alleine, Samuel Clough, Benjamin Colman, William Dyer, James Janeway, Massachusetts House of Representatives, Cotton Mather, Increase Mather, Rhode Island Colony, Solomon Stoddard, Samuel Willard, John Wise.

Boone was born in Boston and was most probably apprenticed to bookseller and postmaster Duncan Campbell around 1693. When Campbell changed locations in 1697, Boone retained Campbell's old shop and released his first imprint, James Janeway's <u>A Token for Children</u>, in 1700. He moved a few doors away in 1704, to the coffee shop and tavern operated by the Widow Campbell, but his imprints remained the same. There he sold coffee, tea, ale, and chocolate as well as

46

books. Needing more space in 1706, he purchased another
store in School-House Lane, although he continued to
own the tavern, and there he remained, selling books
and chocolate until he retired in 1729. Boone's combination coffee shop and bookstore burned to the ground
in the Boston fire of 1711, but it was quickly rebuilt,
and he bought the new brick building and lot in 1715
for £855. He was a civic-minded man and held a number
of posts, including clerk of Boston market, collector
of tithes, and constable. Boone was married twice,
having one child by his first wife and five children
by Hannah, his second.

Boone published all three of his own books. Military Discipline, a collection of precepts garnered from
a number of sources and rewritten by Boone, appeared in
1701. His second, An Account of the Behaviour and Last
Dying Speeches of the Six Pirates (1704), is a caution-
ary tract narrating the terrible punishment of Captain
John Quelch and five of his men who were hanged in the
summer of 1704 for the piracy of nine Portuguese ships.
Boone's third book grew out of his experiences as town
constable, and The Constable's Pocket-Book (1710), in
the form of a dialogue between an old constable and a
young one, offers sensible advice on how to discharge
the duties of the job.

The most striking features of Boone's work as a
publisher were his piety and his practicality. He was
evidently a sincerely devout man, and religious tracts
form a substantial part of his total output. In 1703,
for example, he published Joseph Alleine's An Alarm to
Unconverted Sinners and James Janeway's Invisibles,
Realities, Demonstrated in the Holy Life and Triumphant
Death of Mr. John Janeway. Also his are William Dyer's
Christ's Famous Titles (1704, 1722); Thomas Shepard's
The Saint's Jewel (1708); Solomon Stoddard's A Guide to
Christ (1714); the sixth edition of Michael Wiggles-
worth's The Day of Doom (1715); the fifth edition of
his Meat out of the Eater (1717); and John Flavel's
Sacramental Meditations (1729). Boone's religion was
conservative in nature, and this may be why he chose

47

to reprint a number of John Bunyan's works hitherto un-
published in America. Apart from Pilgrim's Progress,
which had appeared in 1681, and Sighs from Hell in
1708, no Bunyan title was published in this country
until Boone started to do so, although copies were no
doubt imported from England. In 1716 and again in
1725 Boone published The Heavenly Foot-Man, in 1717
and 1729 Grace Abounding, and in 1728 he published
Come and Welcome. These editions apparently sparked
a minor revival of Bunyan in America, for a number of
other publishers began to follow Boone's lead. An
American edition of Jerusalem-Sinner was released in
1733, The Holy War in 1736, and Rest for a Wearied
Soul in 1735.

The more secular side of Boone's business can be
seen in his publication of yearly almanacs and his own
three books, and in 1704 in his role as vendor of the
first long-lived American newspaper, the Boston News-
Letter, which survived, with frequent name changes,
until 1776. In 1708, responding to the need of the
populace to doctor themselves, he published Nicholas
Culpeper's The English Physician, a useful book in a
country of few doctors and long distances for them
to travel. Boone also published Culpeper's companion
piece, the Pharmacopoeia Londinensis; Or the London
Dispensatory (1720). Similarly practical books published by Boone were the fifth edition of John Hill's
The Young Secretary's Guide (1718), a reprinting of
John Smith's The Husbandman's Magazine (1718), and the
anonymous A Useful and Necessary Companion in Two Parts
(1708), the two parts consisting of advice for clerks
and, secondly, for jurymen, surveyors, and constables.
On occasion Boone was able to publish a work combining
both religious and practical subject matter, as he did
with John Flavel's Navigation Spiritualized: Or, A
New Companion for Sea-Men (1726), although the book is
short on nautical advice and long on moralizing.

The most significant authors published by Boone
were Increase and Cotton Mather. The prolific father
and son team was an important source of copy for every

other Boston publisher as well, but for Boone they
accounted for twenty percent of his total productions.
Boone's second imprint was Cotton Mather's The Resolved
Christian (1700), which is a collection of four sermons
that had first seen print in 1689 as Small Offers.
Other Cotton Mather books published by Boone were
Corderius Americanus (1708), an eloquent funeral sermon
on Mather's old schoolmaster, Ezekiel Cheever; Elizabeth
in Her Holy Retirement (1710); Pastoral Desires (1712);
his attack on Deism, Reason Satisfied and Faith Established (1712); Advice from the Watchtower (1713), which
lists some twenty common vices and the remedies for
each; Parentalia (1715); Instructions to the Living,
From the Condition of the Dead (1717); and Zelotes
(1717). For Increase Mather he published, among others,
The Blessed Hope (1701), The Excellency of a Publick
Spirit (1702), Solemn Advice to Young Men (1709), the
second edition of Some Important Truths about Conversion
(1721), and Ichabod (1729), a jeremiad on the gradual
decline of Massachusetts piety.

Boone's religious conservatism also led him to
play a minor role in the heated debates over the Proposals of 1705. The controversy began when Benjamin
Colman was appointed the first pastor of the Brattle
Street Church in 1699. The Mathers considered the
practices of the church heterodox since they revised
the Congregationalist principles set down in the
Cambridge Platform of 1649. At issue were such matters
as whether the minister should simply read the scriptural text, as Colman wished, or whether it should be
expounded, as the Mathers believed; whether a minister
should be chosen by all the adult church communicants
or whether the vote should be limited to just the adult
males; and whether or not a prospective member should
be allowed into the church without a public recital of
his conversion experience. In 1705, after an exchange
of pamphlets on both sides, Cotton Mather had published
his Proposals for the Preservation of Religion in the
Churches, which attempts to suppress heterodoxy by the
formation of a council of ministers to examine and
judge the fitness of ministerial candidates. The

49

Mathers were, in short, trying to return to the spirit of the Cambridge Platform by grafting a presbytery onto Congregationalism, thus taking away much of the cherished autonomy of the New England churches. The Proposals met with stiff resistance from religious conservatives and were defeated largely because of John Wise's two witty and graceful attacks on them in The Churches Quarrel Espoused and A Vindication of the Government of New-England Churches, the second edition of the former being published by Boone in 1715 and the first edition of the latter in 1717.

Boone must have known that by publishing Wise's books and offending the Mathers he stood to lose a substantial part of his business; yet he did so and went even further. In the Vindication, Wise had complained that the principles of the Cambridge Platform were growing dim in men's minds because so few copies were available to read. To remedy the situation, Boone immediately caused another edition to be printed (1717). The publisher's assistance to Wise must have been too much for Cotton Mather, who stopped employing Boone after 1717, although his father, perhaps of a more generous spirit, did not abandon Boone.

Boone's conservatism led him to oppose the Mathers again in 1721, but this time it led him astray. In the summer of 1721 smallpox ravaged Boston and the city was divided into two camps, with the Mathers favoring the new and still experimental practice of inoculation and the opposition, led by the physician William Douglass, condemning it. Into this bitterly fought dispute came Boone, who published an anonymous attack on inoculation, A Letter from One in the Country, To His Friend in the City (1721). It is not certain whether Boone published this pamphlet as another jab at the Mathers or whether it was merely an item published in the normal course of business. The answer is probably both, for the controversy was heated and Boone could have expected a good sale for the title.

Boone's business acumen in taking a stand on an issue had been tested earlier in 1719 when he defied an order of Governor Shute and published a title without license. On 4 November 1719 Shute had criticized the province for not conserving the forests, which were necessary to the royal shipyards. The Massachusetts House of Representatives replied to the charge with a remonstrance, accusing the surveyor who had brought the information to Shute with malfeasance. The governor defended the surveyor and ordered the colony's printers not to print the remonstrance in the House Journal. The official printer to the House, Bartholomew Green, refused to disobey Shute, but when the House asked Boone, he agreed, and the Journal, with the remonstrance in it, was duly published on 14 December 1719. Shute did not attempt to punish Boone, and the House rewarded him by appointing him as their publisher, a post he held until 1722.

Nicholas Boone is a paradigm of the New England Puritan: devout, practical, shrewd, and willing to act in accord with his principles despite the consequences. He was, moreover, a successful publisher. His tavern and his combined bookstore and coffee shop made him a comparatively wealthy man; when he died his estate was inventoried at £1,918. The record of his publications shows he was often embroiled in the theological and political disputes of his time, and that he published his most memorable imprints as a controversialist.

James P. O'Donnell

References:

Drake, Samuel G. The History and Antiquities of Boston. Boston: Stevens, 1856.

Duniway, Clyde A. The Development of Freedom of the Press in Massachusetts. New York: Longmans, Green, 1906.

Littlefield, George E. Early Boston Booksellers: 1642-1711. Boston: Club of Odd Volumes, 1900; reprint edition, New York: Burt Franklin, 1969.

Silver, Rollo G. "Government Printing in Massachusetts-Bay, 1700-1750." Proceedings of the American Antiquarian Society, 68 (1958).

S. S. "Early American Book on Military Science." Historical Magazine, 4 (1860).

Bowen

Bowen (given name and dates unknown) was a printer and engraver whose name appears in two 1785 imprints. He and John Norman printed and sold, "in Marshall's Lane, near the Boston-Stone," Isaac Watts's The Psalms of David, Imitated, and they printed the second edition of The Constitutions of the Several Independent States of America. This man was not Abel Bowen (1790-1850), a printer and engraver in Boston after 1812.

52

Daniel Bowen

Daniel Bowen (1760-1856) was a printer who, with Edward
Savage, opened the Columbian Museum in Boston in 1795.
Bowen printed fewer than ten known works bearing his
name, most of which are broadsides advertising his
printing business. A 1797 broadside announces the
appearance of an elephant at the museum.

Reference:

Nichols, Charles L. "The Portraits of Isaiah Thomas:
     With Some Notes Upon His Descendants." Proceed-
     ings of the American Antiquarian Society, 30
     (1920).

Nicholas Bowes

Nicholas Bowes (d. 1790) published in Boston from 1761
to 1777. He began in partnership with John Wharton "in
Corn-hill" at the former shop of Daniel Henchman, whose
stock they retained. Together they published ten known
titles through 1767, all of which are almanacs or religious works. They had Henry Knox and John Langdon as
apprentices. Bowes began publishing alone in 1768 "opposite the Brick Meeting-House." There he published
approximately twenty-five volumes, almost all of which
are religious. Daniel Kneeland was the printer Bowes
used most frequently. Bowes continued as a bookseller
until his death.

Reference:

Thomas, Isaiah. The History of Printing in America.
    Worcester, Mass.: Isaiah Thomas, Jr., 1810;
    2nd ed., revised, Albany, N. Y.: J. Munsell
    for the American Antiquarian Society, 1874;
    ed. Marcus A. McCorison, Barre, Mass.: Imprint
    Society, 1970.

John Boydell

John Boydell (c. 1690-1739) came to Boston from England with Governor Shute, to whom he was secretary. He was appointed postmaster, and he became publisher of the Boston Gazette in 1732. Until his death in 1739 he "conducted the paper with excellent judgment and ability," according to Justin Winsor. When he left the post office he changed the cut on the Gazette from a postman on horseback to a pine tree.

References:

Thomas, Isaiah. The History of Printing in America. Worcester, Mass.: Isaiah Thomas, Jr., 1810; 2nd ed., revised, Albany, N. Y.: J. Munsell for the American Antiquarian Society, 1874; ed. Marcus A. McCorison, Barre, Mass.: Imprint Society, 1970.

Winsor, Justin. The Memorial History of Boston. Vol. 2. Boston: Osgood, 1881.

John Boyle (or Boyles)

John Boyle (or Boyles) (1746-1819), printer and bookseller, served an apprenticeship with Green and Russell
before beginning business on his own in 1769 "opposite
to the New Court House in Queen-Street." In 1770 he
relocated "in Marlborough-Street," and in 1771 he
stocked his shop with types purchased in Halifax, Nova
Scotia. He announced his business as "next door to the
Three Doves in Marlborough-Street" in 1773, at which
address he remained until he went into partnership
with Richard Draper in May 1774. A year later he moved
to Hingham, Massachusetts, but he returned to Boston in
March 1776. He conducted business for a month with his
father-in-law in Union Street before returning again
and finally to Marlborough Street in June. He remained
a bookseller until his death.

Major Authors: Isaac Backus, Ebenezer Chaplin,
Lord Chesterfield, Mary Rowlandson, Benjamin Rush,
Phillis Wheatley, John Wise.

Boyle published approximately 125 volumes from
1769 to 1800, although his productivity waned considerably after the outbreak of the War of Independence.
Despite the length of his career and the number of
titles for which he was responsible, Boyle published
few important books. He specialized in the practical
and the religious. His first two publications suggest
the nature of most of his subsequent works: The Base-
ness and Perniciousness of the Sin of Slandering and
Backbiting and An Abstract of Geminiani's Art of Playing on the Violin (both 1769). He published ten
Psalters and seven primers; after 1795 he published
only ten known titles, nine of which are almanacs.
The most notable of Boyle's publications are Phillis
Wheatley's elegy on George Whitefield (two editions,

56

1770) and John Wise's <u>Vindication of the Government of New England Churches</u> (two editions, 1772), a democratic statement in keeping with America's mood just before the Revolution.

Boyle is most significant as a newspaper publisher and as a diarist. In May 1774 he formed a partnership with Richard Draper, who died one month later. Boyle continued in partnership with Margaret Draper, Richard's widow, and helped her publish the <u>Massachusetts Gazette</u> through August of that year. Boyle felt uneasy being associated with a Tory newspaper, so he divorced himself from it by dissolving the partnership. Also, beginning in 1759 and continuing through 1778, Boyle kept a diary of events occurring in Boston. Although not published until the twentieth century, it has value as an historical document.

Boyle published many titles of little significance. He was a minor figure in Boston publishing during the last third of the eighteenth century.

References:

Boyle, John. "Boyle's Journal of Occurrences in Boston, 1759-1778." <u>The New England Historical and Genealogical Register</u>, 84 (1930); 85 (1931).

Buckingham, Joseph T. <u>Specimens of Newspaper Literature</u>. Vol. 1. Boston: Little and Brown, 1850.

John Boyles (see John Boyle)

Thomas Bromfield

Thomas Bromfield (dates unknown) was a Boston bookseller from 1755 to 1769. He joined Samuel Kneeland
in printing and selling Richard Pearsall's The Power
and Pleasure of the Divine Life (1755), and in 1760
he sold David Jones's Discourse on the 1666 London
fire.

Elisha Brown

Elisha Brown (dates unknown) printed and sold one known
title, A Sermon in Praise of Swearing (1767).

George Brownell

George Brownell (dates unknown), who taught dancing,
writing, music, and navigation, among other subjects,
was a mentor of the young Benjamin Franklin. In 1715
Brownell published Increase Gatchell's The Young American Ephemeris.

John Browning

John Browning (dates unknown) sold only one volume
bearing his name in the imprint, Increase Mather's
Heavens Alarm to the World (1682). This second edition was printed for Samuel Sewall.

Joseph Browning (or Brunning)

Joseph Browning (or Brunning) (d. 1691) emigrated from
Amsterdam to Boston in 1682 to sell books. He established his shop "at the corner of the Prison-Lane next
the Town-House [or Exchange]," an establishment that
was destroyed when Prison Lane was widened. Browning
published twenty-five volumes from 1682 through 1691.
Of his publications, all but four are by the Mathers:
eleven are by Increase, nine are by Cotton, and one
is by Samuel. Among his most significant Mather titles are Increase's Discourse Concerning Comets (1683)
and Cotton's Memorable Providences (1689). Browning
was, according to John Tebbel, the Mathers' favorite
publisher. The only other authors whose works he published were John Corbet, Joshua Moody, and Samuel
Willard.

Joseph Browning (or Brunning)

References:

Littlefield, George E. Early Boston Booksellers:
    1642-1711. Boston: Club of Odd Volumes,
    1900; reprint edition, New York: Burt Franklin,
    1969.

Tebbel, John. A History of Book Publishing in the
    United States, Vol. 1. New York and London:
    Bowker, 1972.

Joseph Brunning (see Joseph Browning)

James Buck

James Buck (dates unknown), who conducted business "at
ye Spectacles" or "opposite the Crown and Comb in
Queen-Street," published Thomas Johnston's engraving
of Yale College in 1749 and Nathaniel Hurd's engraving
of the Boston Court House in 1751.

Joseph Bumstead

Joseph Bumstead (c. 1768-1838), printer, bookseller, and minor publisher, conducted business at "No. 20, Union-Street." He began as a printer in 1790, and his name appears in approximately seventy imprints through the year 1800. Bumstead printed insignificant religious works and useful, popular almanacs. Of the books he printed or published, only The Poetical Works of John Milton (1796) and Pilgrim's Progress (1800) are noteworthy. In the latter volume he used the woodcuts that first appeared in Isaiah Thomas's edition of Bunyan's work in 1791. Bumstead printed the Courier Politique, with English and French in corresponding columns, in December 1792 and January 1793, but there are no extant copies.

References:

Brigham, Clarence S. History and Bibliography of American Newspapers: 1690-1820. Vol. 1. Worcester, Mass.: American Antiquarian Society, 1947.

Silver, Rollo G. The American Printer: 1787-1825. Charlottesville: University Press of Virginia, 1967.

Tebbel, John. A History of Book Publishing in the United States. Vol. 1. New York and London: Bowker, 1972.

William Burdick

William Burdick (1774-1817), a printer and publisher, was active in eighteenth-century Boston only in 1795. In business with Benjamin Sweetser "at their Printing-Office, opposite the Court-House, Court-Street," they published a broadside and possibly Thomas Taylor's Vindication of the Rights of Brutes, a burlesque on Thomas Paine and Mary Wollstonecraft. Beginning on 1 July 1795, Burdick and Sweetser published the Courier, a semi-weekly newspaper, until Burdick withdrew from it in December. After leaving Boston, he was active publishing in Portland, Maine, before returning to Boston as a printer in 1804.

Reference:

Brigham, Clarence S. History and Bibliography of American Newspapers: 1690-1820. Vol. 1. Worcester, Mass.: American Antiquarian Society, 1947.

John Bushell

John Bushell (c. 1715-1761) printed approximately
twenty-five titles bearing his name in an imprint.
Fifteen of them appeared in 1743. Bushell did not
work alone. He was a partner with Bezoune Allen and
Bartholomew Green, Jr. from 1736 to 1743. In 1743
and 1744 he was with John Green (not Bartholomew's
son of that name), and Allen joined them in 1745.
Bushell, Green, and Allen dissolved their partnership
in 1747. Bushell and his various partners printed for
Daniel Gookin, Daniel Henchman, Samuel Eliot, Thomas
Fleet, Timothy Green, Nathaniel Proctor, and for the
booksellers. They printed mostly religious titles,
including works by Nathaniel Appleton, Thomas Barnard,
Charles Chauncy, Jonathan Edwards, Thomas Hooker, and
Samuel Willard, all eminent divines.

Alford Butler

Alford Butler (c. 1696-1742) served an apprenticeship
with Daniel Henchman. He published eight known titles
from 1726 to 1734. His first volume, Cotton Mather's
Fasciculus Viventium, printed by Thomas Fleet, is the
only one of significance. Butler conducted business
"at the lower end of King-Street, near the Crown
Coffee-House."

Alford Butler, Jr.

Alford Butler, Jr. (c. 1739-1828) was an apprentice
with William M'Alpine. Primarily a binder, in 1762
he published James Forester's The Polite Philosopher,
and in 1766, "in Corn-hill," Butler had Zechariah
Fowle print Samuel Pike's Plain and Full Account of
the Christian Practices. His name appears in no
other known volume.

Reference:

Thomas, Isaiah. The History of Printing in America.
    Worcester, Mass.: Isaiah Thomas, Jr., 1810;
    2nd ed., revised, Albany, N.Y.: J. Munsell
    for the American Antiquarian Society, 1874;
    ed. Marcus A. McCorison, Barre, Mass.: Imprint
    Society, 1970.

Nicholas Buttolph

Nicholas Buttolph (1668-1737), bookseller and publisher,
published mainly religious items. Of the thirty books
bearing his imprint, over twenty are either sermons,
theological discourses, or Psalms and hymns. Buttolph
began his business in 1690 at the corner of Washington
and Court Streets, next to Gutteridge's Coffee House.

Major Authors: Cotton Mather, Increase Mather,
Benjamin Wadsworth.

64

Buttolph was born on 3 March 1668, the fifth and youngest child of Thomas and Mary Buttolph. His grandfather, Thomas Buttolph, had emigrated from London in 1635, establishing himself in Boston in leather goods. His rapid success allowed him to invest in considerable real estate. Eventually he owned eight parcels of land in Boston, including an area known as Buttolph Pasture. In 1701 the pasture was divided into lots of two and two-thirds acres by Nicholas and his two sisters, Abigail Belknap and Mary Gutteridge. Thus Nicholas operated his business in its various locations on Buttolph family property. He died on 29 January 1737, having served his town as constable, assessor, and businessman.

The first book Buttolph published was a volume by Cotton Mather entitled <u>Addresses to Old Men, and Young Men, and Little Children</u> (1690). According to George Littlefield, as "Cotton Mather was always ready to lend a helping hand, it is possible that he recognized the ability of Buttolph while serving his apprenticeship in one of the neighboring bookshops, and advised him to open a shop on his own account, showing his faith in the enterprise by giving him this book to publish, and thus bringing him before the public under the most favorable auspices." Whether or not Mather actually served as Buttolph's patron, his works comprise one-fourth of Buttolph's total publications. Other works by Cotton Mather carrying Buttolph's imprint include <u>Fair Weather</u> (1691), <u>A Scriptural Catechism</u> (1691), <u>Things to be Look'd For</u> (1691), <u>The Everlasting Gospel</u> (1700), and <u>A Faithful Man</u> (1705). The first three titles would support Littlefield's suggestion of Mather's patronage, since Buttolph was given these volumes to publish in a single year, his second year in business. In addition to Mather's works, Buttolph published works by fifteen other authors, including Increase Mather, Benjamin Wadsworth, and Thomas Foxcroft.

One of Buttolph's early publications, a sermon on witchcraft by Deodat Lawson, is particularly significant because of its awesome impact. Entitled <u>Christ's</u>

Fidelity the Only Shield against Satan's Malignity
(1693), it was delivered in 1692 to an easily influenced congregation. In noting Lawson's remark that
witches were "contracted" by Satan to be his "instru-
ments," Littlefield states that the "ideas advanced in
the sermon were so in accord with the feelings of the
people that its publication was asked for." Nineteen
persons were executed in Salem during the emotional
fervor generated in part by this sermon.

Buttolph was also involved in publishing several
editions of the Bay Psalm Book. The tenth edition,
printed for him by Bartholomew Green and John Allen in
1702, contains the ten pages of music that had first
appeared in the ninth edition. Buttolph was thus involved in promoting the first American book to which
music was appended. In addition, Buttolph published
the thirteenth edition; a year later he joined Benjamin
Eliot in producing still another.

Other types of publications by Nicholas Buttolph
include an almanac by Daniel Travis (1707); a poem about
Great Britain by Francis Knapp (1723); and a collection
of the sayings of John Dod (1731). In addition to pub-
lishing these, Buttolph joined Samuel Phillips and
Benjamin Eliot in selling a pseudonymous volume by
Cotton Mather, A Memorial of the Present Deplorable
State of New-England, by Philopolites (1707).

Although Nicholas Buttolph was not a prolific
publisher, records indicate that he was highly depend-
able and was respected as a businessman. Certainly his
relationship with Cotton Mather justifies a close look
at this bookseller-publisher. Isaiah Thomas, in praising Buttolph's character, makes a puzzling comment:
"I have discovered many books which were printed for
him." Since standard bibliographies list only thirty
volumes, either Thomas's "many books" is not greater

than thirty, or else Buttolph published additional volumes that are now lost.

Alice S. Haynes

References:

Littlefield, George E. Early Boston Booksellers: 1642-1711. Boston: Club of Odd Volumes, 1900; reprint edition, New York: Burt Franklin, 1969.

Thomas, Isaiah. The History of Printing in America. Worcester, Mass.: Isaiah Thomas, Jr., 1810; 2nd ed., revised, Albany, N.Y.: J. Munsell for the American Antiquarian Society, 1874; ed. Marcus A. McCorison, Barre, Mass.: Imprint Society, 1970.

Samuel Cabot

Samuel Cabot (1758-1819), a bookseller in Boston from 1784 to 1796, joined with others to publish John Moore's journal in 1794. After living in Milton, Massachusetts, and London, he returned to Boston in 1804. He became president and then director of the Boston Marine Insurance Company.

Charles Cambridge

Charles Cambridge (c. 1761-1831), printer, publisher, and bookseller, was in business by himself from 1786 until he formed a partnership with Joseph White "near the Charles-River Bridge" in 1788. From 1788 to 1792 they published twenty-two known titles. They began slowly with a Bickerstaff almanac in 1786 and a Weatherwise almanac in 1788, but they increased their business with five volumes in 1789, seven in 1790, and five in 1791. They published only three volumes in 1792. Most of their publications are practical or religious in nature, although they published three volumes by Daniel Defoe (1790-1791). Cambridge was a bookseller in Boston from 1807 until his death.

Duncan Campbell

Duncan Campbell (d. 1702), a Scot, emigrated to Boston for religious reasons. He was made postmaster in 1693, and in that capacity he established postal service between Portsmouth, New Hampshire, and James City, Virginia. Since he had franking privileges, he was able to distribute his publications free of charge between those two locations. Only six known titles bear Campbell's imprint. Two of them are sermons by Cotton Mather, one is a sermon by Gurdon Saltonstall, and the most significant is a list of books for sale by Samuel Lee (1693). The last is the earliest work of its kind published in America. Campbell conducted business out of the lower floor of the George Tavern at the south corner of Elm and Union streets. When he moved to the south corner of State and Washington streets in 1697, his apprentice Nicholas Boone kept the old shop. Campbell was the father of John Campbell, the publisher of the Boston News-Letter.

References:

Littlefield, George E. Early Boston Booksellers: 1642-1711. Boston: Club of Odd Volumes, 1900; reprint edition, New York: Burt Franklin, 1969.

Littlefield, George E. The Early Massachusetts Press: 1638-1711. Boston: Club of Odd Volumes, 1907; reprint edition, New York: Burt Franklin, 1969.

Tebbel, John. A History of Book Publishing in the United States. Vol. 1. New York and London: Bowker, 1972.

69

Thomas, Isaiah. The History of Printing in America.
   Worcester, Mass.: Isaiah Thomas, Jr., 1810;
   2nd ed., revised, Albany, N.Y.: J. Munsell
   for the American Antiquarian Society, 1874;
   ed. Marcus A. McCorison, Barre, Mass.: Imprint
   Society, 1970.

John Campbell

John Campbell (1653-1728), son of Duncan Campbell, was
a bookseller and postmaster who became the founder, editor, and publisher of the Boston News-Letter, the first
regularly published American newspaper. The first number was 24 April 1704, and Campbell published it through
1722, at which time he sold it to Bartholomew Green,
his long-time printer.

References:

Brigham, Clarence S. History and Bibliography of American Newspapers: 1690-1820. Vol. 1. Worcester,
   Mass.: American Antiquarian Society, 1947.

Buckingham, Joseph T. Specimens of Newspaper Literature. Vol. 1. Boston: Little and Brown, 1850.

Thomas, Isaiah. The History of Printing in America.
   Worcester, Mass.: Isaiah Thomas, Jr., 1810;
   2nd ed., revised, Albany, N.Y.: J. Munsell for
   the American Antiquarian Society, 1874; ed.
   Marcus A. McCorison, Barre, Mass.: Imprint
   Society, 1970.

Winterich, John T. Early American Books & Printing.
   Boston and New York: Houghton Mifflin, 1935;
   reprint edition, Detroit: Gale Research, 1974.

Hopestill Capen

Hopestill Capen (dates unknown) possibly sold The Life, and Strange, Unparallel'd and Unheard of Voyages of Ambrose Gwinett (1782). No copy of this book is known to exist.

Osgood Carleton

Osgood Carleton (1742-1816) is most noted for his almanacs that appeared from 1790 to 1797. He also instructed Robert B. Thomas, another almanac maker. Carleton, a mathematician and astronomer as well as an almanac calculator, published two known titles. In 1789 he and Matthew Clark published Clark's map of the American coast. Carleton conducted business that year "in his School near Oliver's Dock." In 1795 Thomas and Andrews published and John Norman and Carleton sold Carleton's own Accurate Map of the District of Maine.

References:

Anon. "The Colonial Scene--1620-1800." Proceedings of the American Antiquarian Society, 60 (1950).

Nichols, Charles L. "Notes on the Almanacs of Massachusetts." Proceedings of the American Antiquarian Society, 22 (1912).

Isaac Cazneau

Isaac Cazneau (dates unknown) published three known books during his first stay in Boston (1793-1795). In 1793, while located "near the Mill-Bridge," Cazneau had Joseph Bumstead print a discourse by Henry Grove. In 1795 Thomas Hall printed volumes by Emanuel Swedenborg and James Winthrop for Cazneau, who identified his shop as "in Marshall's Lane." He was a bookseller in Andover, Massachusetts, from 1796 to 1831, at which time he returned to Boston, where he remained until 1849.

John Checkley

John Checkley (1680-1754) was a Boston bookseller from 1717 to 1724. He sold Charles Leslie's The Religion of Jesus Christ the Only True Religion in 1719 and his Short and Easie Method with the Deists in 1723, a volume that includes "Discourse Concerning Episcopacy." For publishing material praising Anglicanism and criticizing Congregationalism, Checkley was prosecuted and fined for "a false and seditious libel."

Reference:

Thomas, Isaiah. The History of Printing in America. Worcester, Mass.: Isaiah Thomas, Jr., 1810; 2nd ed., revised, Albany, N.Y.: J. Munsell for the American Antiquarian Society, 1874; ed. Marcus A. McCorison, Barre, Mass.: Imprint Society, 1970.

William T. Clap

William T. Clap (1770-1818) published twenty-two known
volumes from 1792 to 1798, first at "No. 90, Newbury
Street" and beginning in 1795 in "Fish-street, corner
of Proctor's Lane." His first title was a Benjamin
West almanac in 1792; he published nothing more until
1794 when he published twelve titles, eleven of them
with William P. Blake, most of which were plays being
performed at the new Federal Street Theatre. From 1795
to 1798 Clap published only nine titles, none of any
consequence. He continued as a bookseller in Boston
until he moved to Cincinnati in 1814.

Matthew Clark

Matthew Clark (dates unknown) made a map, A Complete
Chart of the Coast of America, that he published jointly
with Osgood Carleton in 1789.

John Coles

John Coles (dates unknown) published John Norman's engravings of George and Martha Washington in 1782. He
is probably the Coles, with no given name, who, with
Norman, made and published a map of New England in 1785.

James Foster Condy

James Foster Condy (c. 1746-1809) was a bookseller in Boston from 1768 to 1785. In 1772 he published the seventh edition of Robert Blair's The Grave.

Obadiah Cookson

Obadiah Cookson (1709-c. 1770) was a Boston grocer and bookseller. In 1749 he reportedly published the third edition of Joseph Morgan's Love to Our Neighbour Recommended, although no copy is known to exist.

Jonathan S. Copp

Jonathan S. Copp (dates unknown), a native of New London, Connecticut, printed and edited the Constitutional Telegraphe from July to September 1800 "at his printing-office, south side State-street." The paper, which began in October 1799, was staunchly Republican. Joseph T. Buckingham notes that its "typography and mechanical execution were miserable specimens of mechanic art."

Reference:

Buckingham, Joseph T. Specimens of Newspaper Literature. Vol. 2. Boston: Little and Brown, 1850.

Solomon Cotton

Solomon Cotton (1775-1806), bookseller and stationer, conducted business at "No. 51, Marlborough-Street" in 1796. His only known Boston publication is a Collection of the Speeches of the President of the United States to Both Houses of Congress, printed by Manning and Loring in 1796. He was later a bookseller in Baltimore.

Nathaniel Coverly

Nathaniel Coverly (c. 1744-1816) was an enterprising, often itinerant printer, publisher, and bookseller whose imprints illustrate the increasing secularization of New England in the last quarter of the eighteenth century. His publications reflect an interest in education, juvenilia, and politics, and he helped to encourage early American attempts at belles-lettres. He may have published as many as ninety titles in Boston, and many more in various New England towns. His earliest known Boston location was at "Black-Horse Lane, North-End," in 1770, although he may have published at least one title as early as 1767. Coverly announced his business variously as "near Liberty-Tree" (1771), "near Christ's-Church, at the North-End" (1774), in "Newbury Street" (1779), "between Seven-Star Lane and the Sign of the Lamb" (1780), again in "Newbury Street" (1781), at the "sign of the Lamb and the White Horse" (1783), at the "corner of Back-Street, leading to Charles River Bridge" (1788), and finally "near Sign of the Indian Chief, North-End" (1793). Coverly, as well as his son, published at various Boston locations after 1800.

Major Authors: Joseph Addison, Daniel Defoe, James Murray, Alexander Pope, Mary Rowlandson, Isaac Watts.

Little is known of Coverly's early life except that he married Susanna Cowell on 2 November 1769 in a ceremony performed in Boston by Charles Chauncy. Possibly his earliest imprint is 1767, which is an unconfirmed date; the first imprint that can be verified is a 1768 publication by Coverly and Zechariah Fowle. Coverly published intermittently in Boston until 1775, in Chelmsford, Massachusetts, in 1775 and 1776, and in

76

Concord in 1776. Coverly returned to Boston in 1777
and remained until 1784, when he moved to Plymouth and
from there to Middleborough. He returned to Boston a
third time in 1788 and apparently left again in 1794.
(Charles Evans, however, lists two Boston imprints
with unconfirmed dates of 1796 and 1799.) He then
traveled to New Hampshire where he founded, in 1795,
the first newspaper of that area, the Amherst Journal
and New Hampshire Advertiser, and the same year formed
a partnership with his son, Nathaniel Coverly, Jr. He
then appeared in Haverhill, New Hampshire, and Salem,
Massachusetts, returning to Boston in 1800. He conducted business in Salem in 1801 and 1802, and he returned to Boston for the last time in 1803. Coverly's
Boston activity was often sporadic. Only four times
did he publish more than five titles in one year, publishing seven in 1782, eight in 1790, ten in 1792, and
eleven in 1793. His greatest activity occurred during
the second (1777-1784) and third (1788-1794) Boston
residencies, during which he published twenty-seven and
forty-seven titles, respectively.

Coverly published a diverse assortment of works
by a variety of authors, but one of his most important
activities was the publication of educational volumes
and juvenilia. He published at least nineteen titles
that can be classified under one of these headings.
Some works are specifically educational, such as the
New-England Primer Improved published in 1779, 1791,
and 1793, the American Primer Improved (1792), and two
different grammar books. Other works combining instruction with amusement, such as in Tom Thumb's Little Book
(1794), were designed to teach language to children.
Much of Coverly's juvenilia is religious, such as his
1782 children's Bible. Yet another type of juvenilia
combines religious teaching with fiction in moral tales
whose titles sufficiently describe their contents.
Among these are the History of Little Goody Two-Shoes
(1783) and the History of Two Good Boys and Girls, To
Which is Added the Story of Three Naughty Girls and
Boys (1793). Several of Coverly's titles reveal an
interest in fantasy. Also significant is Coverly's

77

publication of musical literature, an example of which
is John Wright's Spiritual Songs for Children (1784).
These titles reveal Coverly's role in the important
early development of juvenile literature.

Several of Coverly's titles depict the growing
importance of belles-lettres in late eighteenth-century
Boston. His reprints of such significant English works
as Defoe's Robinson Crusoe (1779), Pope's Essay on Man
(1780), and Addison's Cato (1782) indicate the popularity of these works. Coverly also reprinted an important American work, Mary Rowlandson's Narrative of the
Captivity (1770). However, Coverly's most important
role in the development of an indigenous literature was
his journalistic venture, the editing and publishing of
the Gentlemen and Ladies Town and Country Magazine.
Begun in February 1789, the ill-printed magazine tried
unsuccessfully to compete with Isaiah Thomas's Massachusetts Magazine (1789-1796). As Lyon N. Richardson
observes, Coverly "was no match for Thomas," and his
magazine ceased publication in August 1790. Richardson
further states that Coverly's magazine lacked diversi-
fication in its thorough devotion to "sentimentality
and sensibility in fiction," but it did arouse the support and contributions of local women. In his fifty-
page numbers Coverly published original essays, stories,
poems, and romances, often crudely illustrated with
copperplates. In spite of its brevity and localized
following, the magazine reflected the literary tastes
of the day and encouraged original attempts at literary
composition.

Coverly's publications also reflect important
political controversies of the American Revolution.
For instance, in 1774 he published the broadside An
Address to New England, a poetical exhortation by "a
daughter of Liberty." Then during the war he published
a satiric anti-Tory attack entitled The Motley Assembly
(1779), probably by Mercy Otis Warren, and Ethan Allen's
Narrative of . . . Captivity (1780). Of historical as
well as political importance is Coverly's three-volume
publication of James Murray's popular Impartial History

of the War in America (1781, 1782, 1784). These works
reveal Coverly's patriotic sentiments and the public's
interest in war-related literature.

   Like most New England publishers, Coverly published a considerable amount of religious literature,
including sermons and other theological tracts such as
Moses Hemmenway's discourse on baptism (1781). In 1775
Coverly formed, according to Worthington C. Ford, a
"public connection" in Chelmsford, Massachusetts, with
Elisha Rich, a Baptist teacher and blacksmith who wrote
religious poetry. This association resulted in at
least one Boston publication, Rich's Poetical Dialogues
(1775). Coverly's three publications of Isaac Watts's
Divine Songs (1775, 1778, 1794) indicate the importance
and popularity in New England of religious music.

   Especially toward the end of his career Coverly
was a prolific publisher of almanacs. He published
twenty-two of them, eighteen of which appeared from
1790 to 1794, including the Weatherwise and Bickerstaff
almanacs.

   Coverly printed, published, and sold almost
all of his titles, but occasionally he printed
educational material for other men: John Norman
in 1784 and William P. Blake in 1793. In addition to the 1795 New Hampshire partnership with
his son, Coverly formed at least two brief partnerships in Boston. The first was a two-year association
(1781-1782) with Robert Hodge in Newbury Street. Under
the second, in 1789 with William Hoyt, he published the
August and September numbers of the Gentlemen and Ladies
Town and Country Magazine.

   Nathaniel Coverly's long and varied career provides an important example of the growing diversifica-
tion and secularization of early American printing and
publishing. Although often sporadic and occasionally
crudely prepared, Coverly's titles played an important
role in the early development of children's literature
and in the promulgation of indigenous belles-lettres.

His Gentlemen and Ladies Town and Country Magazine,
although short-lived, was an ambitious attempt to produce a literary magazine based primarily on the contributions of local writers.

Tony J. Owens

References:

Brigham, Clarence S. History and Bibliography of
    American Newspapers: 1690-1820. Vol. 1.
    Worcester, Mass.: American Antiquarian Society,
    1947.

Ford, Worthington C. "Ballads in the Isaiah Thomas
    Collection." Proceedings of the American Anti-
    quarian Society, 33 (1923).

Richardson, Lyon N. A History of Early American
    Magazines, 1741-1789. New York: Nelson, 1931;
    reprint edition, New York: Octagon, 1966.

Tebbel, John. A History of Book Publishing in the
    United States. Vol. 1. New York and London:
    Bowker, 1972.

Nathaniel Coverly, Jr.

Nathaniel Coverly, Jr. (c. 1775-1824) was primarily a
newspaper printer and publisher. With his father he
published papers in New Hampshire in 1795 and 1796
before publishing, alone, the Orange Nightingale in
Newburyport, Vermont, in 1796 and 1797. He published
many broadsides in Boston after 1800; possibly he published some there as early as 1796. He printed the
Boston Idiot in 1818 and 1819.

References:

Allen, Gardner W. "Naval Songs and Ballads." Pro-
    ceedings of the American Antiquarian Society,
    35 (1925).

Brigham, Clarence S. History and Bibliography of
    American Newspapers: 1690-1820, 2 vols.
    Worcester, Mass.: American Antiquarian Society,
    1947.

Ford, Worthington C. Broadsides, Ballads &c. Printed
    in Massachusetts, 1639-1800, Vol. 75 of the
    Collections of the Massachusetts Historical
    Society. Boston: Massachusetts Historical
    Society, 1922.

Ford, Worthington C. "Ballads in the Isaiah Thomas
    Collection." Proceedings of the American Anti-
    quarian Society, 33 (1923).

James Cowse

James Cowse (dates unknown) came to America from England for religious reasons in 1684. In Boston he became established as a bookseller and stationer next to the Rose and Crown Tavern, a shop that Samuel Phillips probably occupied in 1694. Two known books bear Cowse's name in imprints. Richard Pierce printed Richard Steere's Monumental Memorial of Marine Mercy for Cowse in 1684, and the next year Samuel Green printed Pierre Berault's The Church of Rome Evidently Proved Heretick. With the death of Charles II in 1685, Cowse returned to England.

References:

Littlefield, George E. Early Boston Booksellers: 1642-1711. Boston: Club of Odd Volumes, 1900; reprint edition, New York: Burt Franklin, 1969.

Littlefield, George E. The Early Massachusetts Press: 1638-1711. Boston: Club of Odd Volumes, 1907; reprint edition, New York: Burt Franklin, 1969.

Edward Cox (see Edward Berry and Edward Cox).

Thomas Cox

Thomas Cox (dates unknown) was an Englishman who specialized in English editions. Even during the time of his Boston bookshop, "at the Lamb on the south-side of the Town-House," he lived in London while an agent conducted the Boston business. In 1733 Cox published two titles. One is a sermon by William Beveridge, and the other is John Rawlet's The Christian Monitor. The next year Cox published his own Biblioteca Curiosa, a list of books available at his shop. Cox discontinued his Boston business in 1744 and auctioned off his stock.

Reference:

Thomas, Isaiah. The History of Printing in America. Worcester, Mass.: Isaiah Thomas, Jr., 1810; 2nd ed., revised, Albany, N.Y.: J. Munsell for the American Antiquarian Society, 1874; ed. Marcus A. McCorison, Barre, Mass.: Imprint Society, 1970.

Thomas Crump

Thomas Crump (dates unknown) was a Boston printer who
began his career in an informal partnership with Thomas
Fleet that lasted from 1714 until 1717. Together,
Fleet and Crump printed approximately thirty titles for
a number of booksellers, primarily Samuel Gerrish and
Daniel Henchman. There are ten known texts bearing
Crump's imprint alone, all printed in 1717 and 1718
for several booksellers, including Gerrish, Gillam
Phillips, Robert Starke, and Benjamin Gray.

Major Authors: Benjamin Colman, James Janeway,
Cotton Mather, Isaac Watts.

Publishers Served: Samuel Gerrish, Benjamin
Gray, Daniel Henchman, Gillam Phillips, Robert Starke.

The relationship between Crump and Fleet is un-
clear. Isaiah Thomas suggests that their partnership
was one of many such connections undertaken by printers
who lacked either the type or the labor necessary to
complete a job. In such cases the partnership simply
ceased until it was formed again for another job. This
accounts for the fact that some books printed in the
same year bear the imprint of Fleet and Crump, others
that of Fleet or Crump separately.

Although Fleet was primarily known in his years
with Crump for small pamphlets, children's books, and
ballads, together they printed more substantial texts,
beginning in 1714 with a proclamation by George I and
in 1715 with several sermons by Cotton Mather. The
next year, ten of their sixteen titles were sermons by
Mather and Benjamin Colman. In addition to works by
those two eminent divines, Fleet and Crump also printed
several editions of James Janeway's Three Practical

Discourses (1716), the selected hymns of Isaac Watts, and the seventh edition of Matthew Henry's The Communicant's Companion (1716).

When Crump began printing on his own in 1717, his work was confined to minor religious tracts, with the exception of Thomas Paine's almanac (also published by Fleet and Crump). Crump was thus a minor Boston printer who is most notable for his association with Thomas Fleet.

Michael Clark

Reference:

Thomas, Isaiah. The History of Printing in America. Worcester, Mass.: Isaiah Thomas, Jr., 1810; 2nd ed., revised, Albany, N.Y.: J. Munsell for the American Antiquarian Society, 1874; ed. Marcus A. McCorison, Barre, Mass.: Imprint Society, 1970.

James Cutler

James Cutler (1774-1818), son-in-law to Benjamin
Russell, published fewer than ten known titles from
1795 to 1800. Two of them are by Thomas Fiske. Cutler
is best known as the last publisher of the Massachusetts Magazine (November-December 1796) and as co-
publisher of the Boston Gazette, beginning in 1800,
with John Russell, with whom Cutler had served his
apprenticeship. He died on 18 April 1818.

References:

Buckingham, Joseph T. Specimens of Newspaper Literature. Vol. 2. Boston: Little and Brown, 1850.

Mott, Frank Luther. A History of American Magazines:
1741-1850. New York and London: Appleton, 1930;
Cambridge: Harvard University Press, 1938;
Cambridge: Belknap Press of Harvard University
Press, 1957.

Nathaniel Davis

Nathaniel Davis (dates unknown), a printer, was in business with Daniel Kneeland "in Queen-Street." Active
from 1772 to 1774, they printed for Nicholas Bowes,
Thomas Leverett, Samuel Webb, and for themselves. They
printed approximately a dozen books, three of which are

by Isaac Skillman. Davis conducted a printing business without Kneeland from 1774 until 1777, although his name appears in no imprints from those years. He was jailed in 1777 for printing counterfeit Massachusetts bills.

Matthew Day (or Daye)

Matthew Day (or Daye) (c. 1620-1649), the son of Stephen Day, may have been apprenticed to a printer in England at age fourteen. He came to America in 1638, where he possibly became the first printer in America. Perhaps he was the real head of the Cambridge Press before succeeding his father as manager in 1641. Matthew's name appears in only one known imprint, the 1647 Danforth almanac. For a discussion of the Days, see the essay in this volume on Stephen Day.

References:

Littlefield, George E. The Early Massachusetts Press: 1638-1711. Boston: Club of Odd Volumes, 1907; reprint edition, New York: Burt Franklin, 1969.

Oswald, John C. "Matthew, not Stephen, Day was America's First Printer." American Printer, 91 (1930).

Winship, George P. The Cambridge Press: 1638-1692. Philadelphia: University of Pennsylvania Press, 1945.

Stephen Day (or Daye)

Stephen Day (or Daye) (c. 1594-1668) helped to establish, in 1638 at Cambridge, Massachusetts, the first press in America, and he is considered by many to be the first printer in the colonies. Some believe that his son, Matthew, who may have served a four-year apprenticeship to a printer in England, was the first printer of the Cambridge Press. Uncertainty exists because Stephen is not known to have had any experience as a printer before coming to America and, until 1647, at which time Matthew's name appears on the imprint of Samuel Danforth's almanac, no work of the press bears its printer's name. Whether Stephen Day was an actual printer or served only as supervisor is a matter of conjecture. Nevertheless, either alone or in conjunction with his son, he may have printed at his house on Holyoke Street and later at the house of Henry Dunster as many as twenty works, of which only four are extant. Most notable of his works are The Oath of a Free-Man, the first publication of the Cambridge Press, of which there is no known copy; the Bay Psalm Book (1640), the first American book; and Danforth's 1646 almanac, the earliest extant American almanac and perhaps the last work that Day produced.

Major Authors: Samuel Danforth, Richard Mather, John Winthrop.

Publishers Served: Hezekiah Usher (?).

Day was born in Cambridge, England, about 1594. Little is known of his life before he came to America in 1638. In 1618 he bound himself to William Bordman, then four years old, for £ 50, promising to feed, clothe, and educate him until he reached his majority. Shortly after signing the bond, Day married William's mother,

Rebecca Bordman, who bore him two sons, Stephen, Jr. (1619-1639) and Matthew (c. 1620-1649). Day, a skilled mechanic expert in the working of iron, worked as a locksmith, employing three assistants in his shop. His importance in the history of American printing began on 7 June 1638, when he signed a contract with Jose Glover, rector of a church in Sutton, County Surrey, England. In this contract Day obligated himself to work for Glover in America for two years. Glover agreed to pay transportation costs for Day's family and assistants and purchased for him kettles and iron tools, equipment Day would need in setting up an iron works.

In late July 1638, Glover and Day boarded the John of London. Glover carried with him a printing press that had cost £20, a font of type, and paper costing £60. Glover's move to America was prompted by religious and financial considerations. As part of the great migration of Puritans between 1630 and 1643, he sought to escape the religious and political repressions in England, particularly those instituted by Charles I and Archbishop Laud, and his bringing of a press was connected with the general desire for greater religious freedom. During the 1630s the Puritans found it increasingly difficult to publish their polemical writings and sermons. Glover and seven other men, who subscribed £50 for the purchase of a press and paper, desired a press in the colonies, where it would be beyond the control of Charles' censors. Glover himself paid for the font of type. Although he had had no prior training in printing, he apparently expected to assume duties as manager of the press, perhaps employing Matthew Day to do the actual printing.

Glover also expected to profit from a mining venture. He and his father, a London merchant, were among the original subscribers to the stock of the Massachusetts Bay Company, whose stockholders believed that great mineral wealth would be discovered in the new country. Although no mention is made of prospecting or of valuable metals in the contract between Glover and Day, Glover apparently intended to employ Day in erecting and supervising an ironworks. Day himself expected to profit from the discovery of iron.

After his arrival, Day spent a good deal of his time prospecting for iron ore in the bogs and marshes around a few rivers in Massachusetts. From 1642 until 1654 he was involved, at considerable expense to himself, in an effort to establish a town and an iron works at Nashaway Plantation (later Lancaster) on the Nashaway River. In 1643, as a result of his initial efforts, Day was in some financial and legal trouble. That year he was jailed temporarily for allegedly defrauding several men, and he either mortgaged or sold all his property, which amounted to about 182 acres. In 1667 he petitioned the General Court of Massachusetts for approximately forty acres of land as recompense for trying to settle Nashaway Plantation, noting that he had had to entertain, at his expense, "English and Indians at my own house, from day to day, for some yeares together."

Day's duties as possibly the first printer in America came to him unexpectedly. En route to Boston, Glover died of a fever, leaving the press to his wife. Mrs. Glover and her party arrived in Boston sometime between 7 September and 10 October 1638. Finding no suitable housing, she almost immediately proceeded to Cambridge, where several houses lay vacant, their well-to-do owners having moved to more suitable farmland in the Connecticut River valley. Mrs. Glover moved into the Haynes mansion, and Day and the press occupied a house on Holyoke Street. She entrusted Day with the task of setting up the press and supervising its operation, and within six months the first item appeared. Whether Day was involved in the actual printing of the first works of the press is unknown. While the General Court of Massachusetts granted him 300 acres of land on 10 December 1641 for being "the first that set upon printing," his name does not appear on any existing imprint. Some scholars theorize that his son Matthew produced the first and subsequent publications under the supervision of his father since Matthew,

90

not Stephen, was likely experienced as a printer. In
the bond between Glover and Day no mention is made of
printing, and no evidence has been found to indicate
that either Day or his assistants knew anything about
printing or had ever been employed at a printing press.
One of Day's letters indicates that he was an atrocious
speller and had difficulty composing a sentence. Nevertheless, the press remained at Holyoke Street until
shortly after 21 June 1641. On this date Mrs. Glover
married Henry Dunster, President of Harvard College,
and the press was then moved to Dunster's house on
the present site of Massachusetts Hall.

In his Journal, John Winthrop states that the
first publications of the Cambridge Press were the
"freemen's oath," next an "almanac made for New England by Mr. William Peirce, mariner," and "the Psalms
newly turned into metre." Printed on a half-sheet of
paper in 1638 or early the next year, The Oath of a
Free-Man, an oath every man over twenty years of age
and six months a householder was required to sign in
order to become a legal citizen, was Day's first work.
No copy of the original edition has survived. Day
printed William Peirce's (or Pierce's) almanac sometime before 25 March 1639. Although no copy of the
almanac has survived, this work marks the beginning of
printed literature in America, for an almanac was published every year afterwards up to the present time.
Day is supposed to have produced almanacs for each
year from 1640 to 1645. However, none of them has been
found, and no writer of that period has mentioned their
appearance.

The third publication of Day's press is the most
important. In 1640, The Whole Booke of Psalmes Faithfully Translated into English Metre appeared in an edition of 1,700 copies. Known as the Bay Psalm Book, it
is the earliest extant work and the first book printed
in America. Few copies have survived. In spite of its
crude workmanship, evidenced among other things by typographical errors, curiosities of spelling, and irregular spacing, the Bay Psalm Book is important for its

literary merit. The earliest example of the famous
Puritan style, its translators strove for faithful-
ness to the Hebrew original in a style free of literary embellishments and ornamental imagery. Richard
Mather (or John Cotton) wrote in the preface, "If
therefore the verses are not alwayes so smooth and
elegant as some may desire or expect; let them consider that God's Altar needs not our pollishings . . .
for wee have respected rather a plaine translation,
then to smooth our verses with the sweetnes of any
paraphrase, and soe have attended Conscience rather
than Elegance, fidelity rather than poetry. . . ."
The Bay Psalm Book may have been sold in the shop of
Hezekiah Usher, the earliest bookseller in America.

    The exact number of titles Day printed from 1641
to 1645 is not known. Five works are certain, and he
may have printed as many as eight others. In the autumn
of 1642 he printed a list of theses for the first commencement of Harvard College. Although no copy of the
broadside has been discovered, authority for its printing is given in New England's First Fruits, published
in London in 1643. The first of the Eliot Indian
tracts, its first part accounts for the colonists'
earliest attempts to civilize and convert the Massachusetts Indians; the second part treats "the progress of
learning in the colledge at Cambridge." The names of
the nine men who first graduated from Harvard and the
titles of their theses are preserved in this pamphlet.
Represented by a single copy printed in 1643, the second extant publication of the Day press is the Theses
Philologicas, which lists four graduates at the college's second commencement, the most notable of which
was Samuel Danforth, compiler of the earliest extant
almanac in America. This same year Day printed for
the General Court of Massachusetts the Capitol Lawes
for 1641 and 1642. Although no copy of this work has
been found, these laws are printed in full in John
Child's New Englands Jonas Cast up at London (1647)
from a copy Child had in his possession. In 1643 Day
also printed A Spelling Book, no copy of which is
extant. The third extant work of Day's press is John

92

Winthrop's <u>Declaration of Former Passages and Proceedings Betwixt the English and the Narrowgansetts</u> (1645).
In this declaration of war Winthrop, on behalf of all
the commissioners of the Massachusetts Bay Company,
justifies the colonists' decision to subdue the hostile
Indians.

In addition to the six almanacs published from
1640 to 1645, Day may have printed three other titles.
In 1641 he possibly printed <u>The Liberties of the Massachusetts Colonie in New England</u>, a code of laws that
served as the foundation of legislation in Massachusetts.
In his <u>Journal</u> John Winthrop mentions a catechism "which
might be put forth in print," also in 1641, referring
to James Noyes's <u>A Short Catechism, Agreed Upon by the
Elders at the Desire of the General Court</u>. According to
Robert F. Roden, this work, as well as a 1644 election
sermon by Richard Mather, does not appear to have been
printed.

In 1646 Day brought out Samuel Danforth's almanac,
probably the last work printed under Day's direction of
the press. Day's association with the press may have
ended not long afterward because of trouble with President Dunster and a change in circumstances that caused
Day either to resign or to be deposed from management
of the press. Until her death in 1643, Mrs. Glover,
who had married Dunster in 1641, owned Day's house on
Holyoke Street. Whether she willed her house to him or
to one or all of her five children by Jose Glover is
not known. Sometime in 1646, however, Day's house was
sold to John Fownell, at which time Day, his wife, and
stepson moved into a house his son Matthew had bought
on the corner of Massachusetts Avenue and Dunster
Street. It is thought that Dunster retained the younger
Day's services at the press until the latter's death in
1649, not long after which Samuel Green became printer.
In 1647 Matthew Day's name appeared on the title page
of the second almanac by Samuel Danforth; it was the
first appearance of a printer's name in an American
imprint. From 1646 to 1654 Stephen Day appears to have
devoted his time to settling a town and erecting an

iron works at Nashaway. In April 1656, he brought suit
against President Dunster in an effort to recover £100
for former services, but he gained only court costs.
After the death of his wife Rebecca in 1658, Day married Mary Fitch in 1664. He died on 22 December 1668,
apparently having devoted the last fifteen years of his
life to his trade as a locksmith.

Stephen Day helped to establish the first press
in America and is considered by many to be the first
printer in the colonies. Compared with later Cambridge
printers, his workmanship, whether as actual printer or
as supervisor of the press, was amateurish and crude.
Dividing his time between the press and prospecting for
iron ore and settling a town in the wilderness, Day's
output was meager. He was responsible for some twenty
titles from 1638 to 1646. Day's chief importance lies
in his being designated the first printer of the colonies and in his having helped to print the Bay Psalm
Book, one of the most important literary monuments of
early American literature.

Mark S. Shearer

References:

Haraszti, Zoltán. The Enigma of the Bay Psalm Book.
    Chicago: University of Chicago Press, 1956.

Littlefield, George E. The Early Massachusetts Press:
    1638-1711. Boston: Club of Odd Volumes, 1907;
    reprint edition, New York: Burt Franklin, 1969.

Roden, Robert F. The Cambridge Press: 1638-1692.
    New York: Dodd, Mead, 1905; reprint edition,
    New York: Burt Franklin, 1970.

Winship, George P. "The First Press in English Amer-
    ica." Gutenberg Jahrbuch, 14 (1939).

Winthrop, John. <u>A History of New England from 1630 to</u>
<u>1649</u>. Boston: Phelps and Farnham, 1825-1826;
edited by James Savage, Boston: Little, Brown,
1853; republished as <u>Winthrop's Journal, "History</u>
<u>of New England": 1630-1649</u>, edited by James K.
Hosmer, New York: Scribners, 1908; reprint edition, New York: Barnes & Noble, 1946.

[signature: Stephen Daye]

Matthew Daye (see Matthew Day)

Stephen Daye (see Stephen Day)

L. Deming

L. Deming (given name and dates unknown) sold, through
1800, one known title bearing his name in the imprint.
At his shop, "No. 1 Market Square corner, of Merchant's
Row," he sold <u>A Lamentation for Gen. Washington</u> (1800).

Michael Dennis

Michael Dennis (1715-1763), a bookseller and binder, conducted business "near Scarlet's Wharf." He published approximately ten titles from 1741 to 1761. His most significant publication is Samuel Mather's The Walk of the Upright (1753).

Francis Dewing

Francis Dewing (dates unknown), who emigrated from England in 1716, was probably America's first professional engraver. In 1717 he engraved the first map on metal in America, thus establishing copperplate engraving in this country. His name appears in the imprint of only one known publication, however: John Bonner's important 1722 map of Boston. Dewing engraved and printed the map that Bonner and William Price sold.

References:

Lehmann-Haupt, Hellmut. The Book in America. New York: Bowker, 1939; revised and enlarged, New York: Bowker, 1951.

Tebbel, John. A History of Book Publishing in the United States. Vol. 1. New York and London: Bowker, 1972.

Whitehill, Walter M. Boston: A Topographical History.
    Cambridge: Belknap Press of Harvard University
    Press, 1959.

Doyle

Doyle (given name and dates unknown) joined with
Nathaniel Mills in printing, for Joseph Hovey, the
1791 Weatherwise Massachusetts Almanack. No other
volume is known to bear his imprint.

Edward Draper

Edward Draper (1749-1831), printer, publisher, and
bookseller, placed his imprint on approximately forty
titles from 1776 through 1799. His first titles designate "Draper and Phillips at the New Printing-Office,
next door but one to the Sign of the Lamb Tavern, in
Newbury-Street." Phillips's given name is not known.
In 1777 Draper remained in Newbury Street, but without
a partner; the next year he went into partnership with
John West Folsom. Draper and Folsom located first at
Draper's old shop in Newbury Street near the Lamb
Tavern, and in 1779 they moved to the corner of Water
Street. In 1783 they were named among the printers to
the Commonwealth of Massachusetts. In November of that
year they dissolved their partnership. Draper continued in business by himself until his death, but after
1783 he printed only eleven eighteenth-century titles
bearing his name in an imprint.

Major Authors: Ethan Allen, Isaac Backus, William Billings, Daniel George, John Lathrop.

Publishers Served: John Boyle, Philip Freeman, James White.

There is almost no biographical information about Draper. As the brother of Samuel Draper, the nephew of John Draper, and the cousin of Richard Draper, however, his was a family of printers. His relatives probably trained him in the craft.

Edward Draper's first printed work was Daniel George's 1777 almanac (1776). Printed and sold at the Draper and Phillips Printing Office, it represents the kind of useful works that Draper would continue to print. He also printed George's almanac for the years 1779 and 1780. In 1777 Draper printed the New-England Primer Improved, and in 1778 he and John West Folsom printed William Billings's The Singing Master's Assistant, or Key to Practical Music, a work they would reprint in 1779 and 1781.

Draper printed primarily secular volumes. Among them are Gerard van Swieten's The Diseases Incident to Armies (1777) and A Narrative of Colonel Ethan Allen's Captivity (1779). In June 1778 Draper and Folsom founded the Independent Ledger, and American Advertiser, a newspaper for which they selected contents reflecting their Whig political bias. After Draper left Folsom in November 1783, Folsom continued publishing the paper for only a few weeks.

Not all of Draper's work was secular, however. He printed such religious items as the first volume of Isaac Backus's History of New-England, with Particular Reference to the Denomination of Christians Called Baptists (1777) and Policy, as Well as Honesty, Forbids the Use of Secular Force in Religious Affairs (1779). In 1785 he printed a sermon by David Osgood.

98

Edward Draper

Less is known about Edward than any of the other printing Drapers. He was a printer, a publisher, and for a short time a bookseller. Works bearing his name spanned the American Revolution, although only the Independent Ledger was overtly political. Most of his titles were secular and practical.

Jessica Kross Ehrlich

Reference:

Thomas, Isaiah. The History of Printing in America. Worcester, Mass.: Isaiah Thomas, Jr., 1810; 2nd ed., revised, Albany, N.Y.: J. Munsell for the American Antiquarian Society, 1874; ed. Marcus A. McCorison, Barre, Mass.: Imprint Society, 1970.

99

John Draper

John Draper (1702-1762), printer and publisher, placed his imprint on more than 450 publications. In 1732 he inherited the printing shop and apparently the connections of Bartholomew Green, Sr., his father-in-law. His building in Newbury Street burned in 1734, but Draper rebuilt it. From 1743 until 1745 he was possibly a member of the firm of Bartholomew Green and Company, this Green being Draper's brother-in-law. All of Draper's printing was done in Newbury Street, although from 1757 until his death he also had a shop in Cornhill.

Major Authors: Nathaniel Ames, Nathaniel Appleton, Mather Byles, Charles Chauncy, Benjamin Colman, Samuel Cooper, William Cooper, Samuel Mather, Joseph Sewall, Gilbert Tennent.

Publishers Served: The Boston booksellers.

Draper was born in Roxbury, Massachusetts, the seventh child of Richard Draper, merchant, and Sarah Kilby Draper. He was apprenticed to the Boston printer Bartholomew Green, and in 1726 he married Green's daughter, Deborah. Their son Richard was born the next year. Deborah died in 1736, and John next married Elizabeth Avery. They apparently had two children. He died on 29 November 1762.

John Draper was one of the busiest and most prolific printers in Boston. His name first appeared in John Webb's Practical Discourses on Death, Judgment, Heaven, & Hell (1726), a volume he printed for Daniel Henchman. Within five years he was printing the Boston Weekly Rehearsal, a newspaper. He printed it from its first number in September 1731 until August 1732, when

100

Thomas Fleet succeeded him as printer. The paper was
financed by a private club headed by the lawyer Jeremiah
Gridley, who also served as editor.

Upon Bartholomew Green's death in 1732, Draper
acquired Green's printing office and many of his accounts. These included the governor and council of
Massachusetts Bay and the Boston Weekly News-Letter
(originally the Boston News-Letter), the newspaper
that Green had printed from 1704 until his death, with
the exception of four years. Under Draper the News-
Letter added new features such as letters to the publisher, clippings, and verse, and devoted more space
to advertising. He also increased its size. His son
Richard succeeded him with the News-Letter upon John's
death in 1762.

Under the governorships of Shirley, Pownall, and
Bernard--and Lieutenant Governor Phips as well--Draper
printed the acts and proclamations of the governor and
the council. These various official documents account
for a little more than one-half of his titles. He also
printed, under official auspices, such reports as
William Shirley's Letter . . . to His Grace the Duke
of Newcastle (1746) and A Journal of the Proceedings at
Two Conferences Begun to be Held at Falmouth in Casco-
Bay (1754).

The most famous of Draper's items is the Ames
almanac, which came out every year from 1735 to 1762
and thereafter was continued by Draper's son. The
elder Draper had printed Ames for the booksellers, but
with the 1759 volume he, Green and Russell, and Thomas
Fleet published Ames themselves and forced the other
booksellers to buy it from them at an inflated price.
Other useful works Draper printed include 2,000 copies
of The English Instructor or, the Art of Spelling Improved (1736) by Henry Dixon, The Dealers Pocket Companion. Containing Tables for the Ready Knowing the
Amount, or Value, of Any Commodity (1745), the fourth
edition of The Child's New Play-Thing (1750), and Sir
Richard Cox's Letter . . . to Thomas Prior Esq; Shewing

from Experience, a Sure Method to Establish the Linnen-Manufacture (1750).

Most of Draper's other works are religious in nature. Many of them are sermons preached for specific occasions. Some, such as Daniel Lewis's (or Lewes's) Good Rulers the Fathers of Their People (1748), were preached before the governor and the council. Other sermons celebrate the ordination of a minister (Samuel Whittelsey's A Sermon Preach'd at the Ordination of Mr. Samuel Whittelsey, Jun., 1739) or mark a funeral (Mather Byles's God the Strength and Portion of His People, 1752). Draper often printed sermons that were delivered to such organizations as the Ancient and Honourable Artillery Company (by Samuel Cooper, 1751; printed for Joseph Edwards) or the Society for Encouraging Industry and Employing the Poor (by Samuel Cooper, 1753; printed for Daniel Henchman). Draper also printed and sold the annual Dudleian Lectures at Harvard beginning in 1756 with John Barnard's A Proof of Jesus Christ His Being the Ancient Promised Messiah. Draper printed such other religious works as Thomas Shepard's The Sound Believer, or a Treatise of Evangelical Conversion (1736), A New Version of the Psalms of David (1754), and A Specimen of the Unrelenting Cruelty of Papists in France (1756). He printed John Bunyan's Pilgrim's Progress (1744).

The years of the Great Awakening saw John Draper print works by some of the best known of the New Light ministers and their critics. In 1740 Draper printed the first part of George Whitefield's Life, and in 1741 he printed Gilbert Tennent's The Righteousness of the Scribes and Pharisees Considered. Draper also printed tracts by those who had doubts about the revival. Foremost was Charles Chauncy, whose Enthusiasm Described and Caution'd Against Draper printed in 1742.

Most of Draper's printing was sold through booksellers, but a few things he sold himself. These include his newspaper and some religious works, the first of which was Samuel Niles's Tristitiae Ecclesiarum or,

102

John Draper

A Brief and Sorrowful Account of the Present State of the Churches in New-England (1745). Thereafter, at irregular intervals, Draper would both print and sell a religious tract. The next one, Nathaniel Appleton's *The Cry of Oppression Where Judgment is Looked for and the Sore Calamities Such a People May Expect from a Righteous God*, appeared in 1748, and in 1749 he published John Beach's *A Calm and Dispassionate Vindication of the Professors of the Church of England* and Henry Caner's *The Piety of Founding Churches for the Worship of God*.

John Draper was one of eighteenth-century Boston's longest lived and most prolific printers. He edited the *Boston Weekly News-Letter*, which he inherited from his father-in-law Bartholomew Green, and then passed it on to his own son thirty years later. He was one of the official printers for the Massachusetts Bay Colony, and this account he also gave to his son. In the course of his three decades in Newbury Street he trained other printers, including his nephew, Samuel, and probably his own son, Richard. His titles include the popular Ames almanac and many sermons and religious tracts written by the foremost ministers of his day.

Jessica Kross Ehrlich

References:

Bates, Albert C. "Check List of Connecticut Almanacs, 1709-1850." *Proceedings of the American Antiquarian Society*, 24 (1914).

Brigham, Clarence S. *History and Bibliography of American Newspapers: 1690-1820*. Vol. 1. Worcester, Mass.: American Antiquarian Society, 1947.

103

Thomas, Isaiah. <u>The History of Printing in America</u>.
    Worcester, Mass.: Isaiah Thomas, Jr., 1810;
    2nd ed., revised, Albany, N.Y.: J. Munsell
    for the American Antiquarian Society, 1874;
    ed. Marcus A. McCorison, Barre, Mass.: Imprint
    Society, 1970.

John Draper

Margaret Draper

Margaret Draper (1727-c. 1807), a member of the famous
Green family of printers, became even more intimately
connected with the Boston printing establishment by
marrying her cousin, Richard Draper, in 1750. When
her husband died in June 1774, Margaret assumed control of the business. During 1774 and 1775 she
printed approximately one dozen titles bearing her
name, about half of which are broadsides. She printed
and sold primarily English or governmental documents
as "Printer to his excellency the Governor, and the
honourable his Majesty's Council," but her most important publication was the <u>Massachusetts Gazette</u>.
The date of her first number was 9 June 1774, only
four days after Richard's death. Her partner was
John Boyle, but after they dissolved their partnership
she published the <u>Gazette</u> alone until she formed a
partnership with John Howe. Hers was the only news-
paper--pro-British as it was--published during the
siege. Her Tory sympathies caused her to flee Boston
with the British troops to Halifax, Nova Scotia, in
March 1776. From there she moved to England, where
she died.

104

| Margaret Draper

References:

Brigham, Clarence S. History and Bibliography of Amer-
     ican Newspapers: 1690-1820. Vol. 1. Worcester,
     Mass.: American Antiquarian Society, 1947.

Buckingham, Joseph T. Specimens of Newspaper Litera-
     ture. Vol. 1. Boston: Little and Brown, 1850.

Demeter, Richard L. Primer, Presses, and Composing
     Sticks: Women Printers of the Colonial Period.
     Hicksville, N.Y.: Exposition Press, 1979.

Hudak, Leona M. Early American Women Printers and
     Publishers: 1639-1820. Metuchen, N.J., and
     London: Scarecrow Press, 1978.

Thomas, Isaiah. The History of Printing in America.
     Worcester, Mass.: Isaiah Thomas, Jr., 1810;
     2nd ed., revised, Albany, N.Y.: J. Munsell
     for the American Antiquarian Society, 1874;
     ed. Marcus A. McCorison, Barre, Mass.: Imprint
     Society, 1970.

Richard Draper

Richard Draper (1727-1774) was a loyalist printer, publisher, and bookseller active in the quarter century before the American Revolution. He began his career as an independent printer in 1751 when his first imprint appeared, and he spent his entire working life in his shop "in Newbury Street." He assumed control of the Boston Weekly News-Letter from his father John in 1762 and continued to publish it until his own death. From 1763 to 1767 he was in partnership with his cousin Samuel, and in May 1774, a month before he died, he took John Boyle as his partner. In 1762 he began printing for Harvard College, and in the following year he was appointed "Printer to his excellency the Governor, and the honorable his Majesty's Council," a position he held until he died. His last imprint was in 1774. Excluding the weekly numbers of the newspaper, Draper printed or published more than 200 titles, approximately half of which were for either the Massachusetts government or Harvard.

Major Authors: Nathaniel Ames, Mather Byles, Charles Chauncy, Samuel Davies, Thomas Dilworth, Charles Ferne, Ebenezer Gay, Harvard College, William Hooper, Massachusetts Bay Province, Jonathan Mayhew, Rhode Island Colony, George Whitefield.

Draper was born in Boston on 24 February 1727, the only child of John and Deborah Draper. He was apprenticed to his father, the publisher of the Boston Weekly News-Letter and printer to the governor and the council of Massachusetts, and evidently remained in his father's shop after taking up his freedom, acting as a silent partner and not appearing in the imprints he helped produce. His father having gone into semi-retirement in 1751, Draper took charge of the shop in

106

Newbury Street and released his first known imprint in
that year. Draper was a frail, sickly man, often confined to his bed, and it is likely that his father continued to assist him in the day-to-day operations of
the press. After his father died in 1762, Draper hired
his cousin Samuel Draper, who had been associated with
Zechariah Fowle from 1757 to 1762, as overseer of the
press. Samuel died in 1767 and Draper continued the
business alone, although he may have been assisted by
his wife Margaret, whom he had married in 1750 and who
was his cousin and the granddaughter of Bartholomew
Green, the most distinguished Boston printer and publisher of the time. After forming a partnership with
John Boyle in May 1774, Draper died on the fifth day
of the following month.

     Although he inherited a long-established business,
Draper's publishing career started slowly, perhaps because of his chronic sickliness. In his first six
years he produced only nine titles, and none at all
in 1752, 1754, and 1756. Not until 1763, when he was
appointed to succeed his father as printer to the governor and the council, and with the assistance of
Samuel, did the number of his imprints increase. His
request that he be allowed to follow his father in
printing for the governor and the council is the earliest example of a printed petition in Massachusetts
history.

     Beginning with Isaiah Thomas in 1810, the histo-
rians of American publishing have, with some justifica-
tion, treated Draper as primarily a newspaper publisher.
The demands of putting out a weekly paper, even the
four-page News-Letter, placed a heavy burden on Draper's
supplies and press time, and if the frequent printing
orders of government proclamations, acts of parliament,
and supplements to the laws are added, it becomes obvious that Draper had little capacity to spare for other
business. Yet he did print or publish a fairly substantial number of books and pamphlets. To compensate
for his other obligations, Draper apparently split his
book business into two lines: titles that could be

expected to have a limited appeal and hence a short
press run he printed in his own shop, but for more
popular titles, with much longer press runs, he preferred to ally himself with other publishers, sharing
the costs but not burdening his overtaxed shop with
the actual printing. Among the books produced solely
by Draper are a reprinting of Roger Clap's Memoirs
(1766), Peter Clark's Man's Dignity and Duty as a
Reasonable Creature (1763), George Whitefield's Observations on Some Fatal Mistakes (1764), and Stephen
Sewall's An Hebrew Grammar (1763), which was intended
as a textbook for Harvard students.

     Comparatively few books were published by Draper
alone. More usual was his practice of teaming with
other Boston publishers in the production of titles
that could be expected to have a large sale. The popular almanacs of Nathaniel Ames, father and son, for
example, were published by Draper, Green and Russell,
Edes and Gill, and the Fleet brothers; William Hooper's
A Sermon Preached in Trinity Church at the Funeral of
Thomas Green (1763) was published with Thomas and John
Fleet; John Shearman's The Last Words and Dying Speech
of John Shearman, Executed at Newport . . . for Burglary
(1764) was printed by Draper and Green and Russell;
Thomas Dilworth's A New Guide to the English Tongue
(1768) was reprinted by Kneeland and Adams for Draper;
and the North American Almanack for 1772 (1771), by
Samuel Stearns, was printed by Draper, the Fleets, and
Edes and Gill.

     An instructive example of the flexible working
arrangements among the Boston publishers is offered by
the publications of Jonathan Mayhew, the fiery rector
of the West Church. From the very start of his ministry in 1740, Mayhew had been in the center of virtually
every controversy in Boston. His sermons against the
Sugar and Stamp Acts helped fuel the rising anti-
British feeling, and one of them may have helped spark
the riot on 14 August 1765 that led to the destruction
of Governor Hutchinson's mansion. Despite his strong
and oft expressed Tory sentiments, Draper was not slow

to realize that Mayhew was highly salable and, in conjunction with several other houses, soon began publishing his writings. In 1755 Draper and Edes and Gill published Mayhew's Expected Dissolution of All Things and A Discourse on Rev. XV, and in 1760 the same printers, with Green and Russell, published The Late Smiles of Providence Represented. Green and Russell left the consortium in 1760 and Thomas and John Fleet were added for the publication of four more Mayhew titles. In 1763 the same three firms released Christian Sobriety and Mayhew's two attacks on the New England Company, the leading advocate of episcopacy for the American churches: Observations on the Charter and Conduct of the Society for the Propagation of the Gospel in Foreign Parts and A Defence of the Observations. In 1766, a few months before Mayhew died, Draper and his colleagues published The Snare Broken, a thanksgiving address on the repeal of the Stamp Act.

It is as a newspaper publisher, however, that Draper is chiefly regarded. The paper he took over from his father was the first regularly published paper in the colonies and had been started by John Campbell in 1704 as the Boston News-Letter. In 1730 Campbell died and Bartholomew Green assumed control, rechristening it the Boston Weekly News-Letter. He in turn relinquished it three years later to his son-in-law, John Draper, who published it for approximately thirty years. In December of 1762 Draper inherited the paper and, in an attempt to widen the circulation, renamed it the Boston Weekly News-Letter and New England Chronicle. On 7 April 1763 Draper again changed the name, this time to the Massachusetts Gazette and Boston News-Letter, as a result of being appointed printer to the governor and council.

Draper continued the policies of his father, retaining the paper's progovernment slant and its policy of providing news of interest to the local merchants, but he did make a few concessions to the temper of the times by publishing some Whig pieces in it. On 7 November 1765 Draper shortened the title of

the paper to the Massachusetts Gazette and defied the
Stamp Act, which he had printed in his role as government printer, by withdrawing his name from the paper's
masthead. He even refused to follow Governor Hutchinson's strong wish that he print a scathing attack on
the Whig agitators penned by Israel Williams. When he
learned of the repeal of the Stamp Act, Draper reverted
to the previous title and the paper again became the
Massachusetts Gazette and Boston News-Letter.

However, Draper was still a staunch and outspoken
loyalist. He allowed the government to place a series
of anti-Whig pieces in his paper under a variety of
pseudonyms, and he, on occasion, also wrote some articles defending the government. In May 1768, in one of
the most unusual moves in American newspaper publishing,
Draper's paper and Green and Russell's Boston Post-
Boy and Advertiser combined to print the Massachusetts
Gazette as a supplement to each paper. The two firms
had been intimately although informally connected for
a number of years; John Green was Draper's brother-in-
law, both firms were strongly Tory, and both were
printers to the government. Each paper now appeared
in two parts. In the first half, under their original
titles, both firms printed their usual news independently of each other; in the second half, under the
banner of the Massachusetts Gazette, which proudly
proclaimed itself "published by Authority," each firm
printed the acts, proceedings, announcements, and
official government versions of the issues that were
dividing Massachusetts. With the Post-Boy coming out
on Mondays and the News-Letter on Thursdays, the government received twice as much coverage as before.

This arrangement did not last long. It was discontinued after sixteen months, the Gazette being
dropped from the News-Letter in September 1769 and
from the Post-Boy in October. The Gazette did not,
as the government had hoped, serve to quiet the dis-
sension, and it may have been even counterproductive.
The citizens derided it as the "Adam and Eve" paper
or the "Court Gazette," and apparently paid it little

110

heed. Draper did pay a price for his loyalty to the
crown. In 1771, because of his monarchism, the seniors
of Harvard voted to deny him the printing of their commencement theses, a job he had done since 1764, and
they awarded it instead to Isaiah Thomas. Draper was
unchastened, however, and he continued to use his paper
to advocate the government position until he died.

Draper's importance as a publisher lies less in
what he printed than in what he was. Although he
printed numerous documents for the government and
Harvard, and although his books and pamphlets include
some important texts, he is remembered chiefly for
being a Tory newspaper publisher in Whig Boston. A
shrewd businessman, he knew when to placate his enemies
and when to stand by his principles. He antagonized
the more fervent Whigs by his unwavering and frequently
printed support of the British government, but men of
less passionate tempers recognized his honesty and
sincerity of conviction. In his obituary in the News-
Letter, which was also reprinted in the more moderate
and judicious Boston Evening-Post, he is praised as a
man of "endearing manners and inflexible integrity."

James P. O'Donnell

References:

Brigham, Clarence S. History and Bibliography of Amer-
     ican Newspapers: 1690-1820. Vol. 1. Worcester,
     Mass.: American Antiquarian Society, 1947.

Kobre, Sidney. The Development of the Colonial News-
     paper. Pittsburgh: Colonial Press, 1944.

Mott, Frank Luther. American Journalism, A History:
    1690-1960. Third edition. New York: Macmillan,
    1962.

Schlesinger, Arthur M. Prelude to Independence: The
    Newspaper War on Britain, 1764-1776. New York:
    Knopf, 1958.

Stark, James H. The Loyalists of Massachusetts and the
    Other Side of the American Revolution. Salem:
    Salem Press, 1910.

Thomas, Isaiah. The History of Printing in America.
    Worcester, Mass.: Isaiah Thomas, Jr., 1810;
    2nd ed., revised, Albany, N.Y.: J. Munsell
    for the American Antiquarian Society, 1874;
    ed. Marcus A. McCorison, Barre, Mass.: Imprint
    Society, 1970.

Samuel Draper

Samuel Draper (1737-1767) was, with his two partners, responsible for more than 120 titles in his brief career. Apparently a skilled and industrious printer, his first partnership was with Zechariah Fowle. The firm of Fowle and Draper was located in Marlborough Street, "opposite the Lion and Bell," from 1757 to 1762. While Draper was with Fowle he helped train Isaiah Thomas, Fowle's apprentice. After the death of his uncle John Draper in 1762, Samuel went into partnership with his cousin Richard Draper who had inherited John's establishment in Newbury Street. Samuel died still a partner in the firm of Richard and Samuel Draper.

Major Authors: Nathaniel Ames, Nathaniel Appleton, Charles Chauncy, Samuel Davies, Jonathan Mayhew, Isaac Watts, Edward Wigglesworth.

Publishers Served: Richard Draper, Zechariah Fowle.

After an apprenticeship with his uncle John Draper, Samuel succeeded Benjamin Mecom as Zechariah Fowle's partner in 1757. Draper and the apprentice Isaiah Thomas did most of the work; Fowle supplied the money. Most of their titles are either sermons or discourses of a religious nature, such as the anonymous Elegy on the Death of That Worthy Friend Priscilla Coleman (1762). They also printed a few secular titles, one of which is A Journal of the Expedition up the River St. Lawrence, from the Embarkation at Louisbourg 'til After the Surrender of Quebeck (1759) and Brief Review of the Campaigns in America (1760).

113

After Draper terminated the partnership in 1762, he joined his cousin Richard Draper in the ongoing and flourishing business that had been John Draper's. They continued to print some of John's stand-bys, including the annual Ames almanac. Samuel's name was also affixed to sermons and lectures by Jonathan Mayhew, Edward Wigglesworth, and Charles Chauncy. Mayhew's works are particularly striking because many of them exhort against the Society for the Propagation of the Gospel in New England, the missionary branch of the Church of England.

Most of the imprints bearing Richard and Samuel Draper's names are religious, but a few are not. Richard was one of the official Massachusetts printers after the death of his father, but only a few governmental publications bear Samuel's name. In 1763 the Drapers published the Boston Weekly News-Letter that had been established as the Boston News-Letter by John Campbell in 1704. As a result of the governmental decision to authorize "the publication of all official notices in this paper," in April 1763 they changed its name to the Massachusetts Gazette and Boston News-Letter. They also published various acts of parliament, including the notorious Stamp Act in 1765. In 1763 Samuel was the first printer to have his name appear at the foot of a Harvard diploma.

Samuel Draper never went into business for himself, but during his nine active years as a printer and as the junior partner he lent his name and skills to the well-known printing and publishing houses of Fowle and Draper and Richard and Samuel Draper. Both Zechariah Fowle and Richard Draper went on without him--he was the printer, not the publisher or bookseller. An early teacher of Isaiah Thomas, who thought well of him as a craftsman, Draper worked actively at his trade until his death at the age of thirty.

Jessica Kross Ehrlich

References:

Brigham, Clarence S. History and Bibliography of Amer-
    ican Newspapers: 1690-1820. Vol. 1. Worcester,
    Mass.: American Antiquarian Society, 1947.

Lane, William C. "Early Harvard Broadsides." Proceed-
    ings of the American Antiquarian Society, 24
    (1914).

Thomas, Isaiah. The History of Printing in America.
    Worcester, Mass.: Isaiah Thomas, Jr., 1810;
    2nd ed., revised, Albany, N.Y.: J. Munsell for
    the American Antiquarian Society, 1874; ed.
    Marcus A. McCorison, Barre, Mass.: Imprint
    Society, 1970.

John Dunton

John Dunton (1659-1733) was an English bookseller who
spent approximately eight months in Boston during 1686.
The penurious Dunton went to Boston because of debts
owed him there. He brought a stock of books with him,
and he established business in Richard Wilkins's warehouse. Upon selling those books, he returned to London
where his wife had managed his business during his
absence. His name appears in the imprint of one known
work published in Boston, Increase Mather's Sermon
Occasioned by the Execution of a Man Found Guilty of
Murder (1686). Dunton wrote and later published biographical sketches of some of the people he met in
Boston, including booksellers, as a result of which
Worthington C. Ford has termed him an "amiable pla-
giarist and incipient madman."

References:

Dunton, John. The Life and Errors of John Dunton.
    London: Malthus, 1705; reprint edition, New
    York and London: Garland, 1974; edited by
    John B. Nichols, London: Nichols, 1818;
    reprint edition, New York: Burt Franklin,
    1969.

Dunton, John. Letters Written from New-England.
    Boston: Prince Society, 1867; reprint edition,
    New York: Burt Franklin, 1966.

Ford, Worthington C. The Boston Book Market: 1679-
    1700. Boston: Club of Odd Volumes, 1917;
    reprint edition, New York: Burt Franklin, 1972.

Littlefield, George E. Early Boston Booksellers:
    1642-1711. Boston: Club of Odd Volumes,
    1900; reprint edition, New York: Burt Franklin,
    1969.

Tebbel, John. A History of Book Publishing in the
    United States. Vol. 1. New York and London:
    Bowker, 1972.

John Dunton

Benjamin Edes and John Gill

Benjamin Edes (1732-1803) and John Gill (1732-1785),
booksellers, printers, publishers, and journalists,
were among the most prolific and radical of all
Boston publishers during the American Revolution
and the decades immediately preceding it. The Edes
and Gill imprint appears on approximately 250 publications, and Edes alone, or with his sons, accounted
for nearly 200 more publications, while John Gill's
imprint appears on approximately fifty separate publications. Of course, these figures do not include
the weekly edition of the Boston Gazette, which was
published continuously from 1755 until 1798, or the
weekly Continental Journal, which Gill founded in
1776 and published until 1785. Edes and Gill began
their business near the end of 1754 "At their Printing-
Office near the east end of the Town-House, in King-
Street." From 1755 until 1775 they were almost a
fixture "Next to the Prison in Queen-Street." After
the battles of Concord and Lexington in April 1775,
Edes was forced to flee to Watertown, where he set
up shop "near the Bridge," and remained until October
1776, when he returned to Boston and Queen Street, but
moved to Court Street by October 1777. In April 1779
the firm became Benjamin Edes and Sons, with the admission of Peter and Benjamin Edes, Jr., to the business,
and it was moved to a new "Office in State-Street"
until 1782, when it was removed to "No. 42, Cornhill."
In 1784 Peter Edes left to form his own business, and
the imprint was changed to Benjamin Edes and Son. In
September 1787 the office was moved to "No. 49,
Marlborough-Street," and in June 1788, it was moved
again, this time to "No. 7 State-Street, next to
Mr. Abiel Smith's, and directly opposite the south-
east corner of the State-House." In April 1792 Edes
moved his shop to "the house next to Col. Colman's, in

117

Kilby-Street." The departure of Benjamin Edes, Jr.,
from his father's business in June 1794 must have
created a tremendous hardship on the old printer, but
he changed his imprint to Benjamin Edes and continued
to work until 1799. In 1800 he moved his equipment
into his Temple Street home and engaged in job printing
until his death. When Edes left Boston in 1775, Gill
remained behind in the Queen Street establishment. In
September 1777, Gill moved his office to Court Street,
where he remained until he sold his business to James D.
Griffith in April 1785. Gill's final publications, except for the weekly edition of the Continental Journal,
appeared in 1784.

Major Authors: Samuel Adams, Nathaniel Ames,
Mather Byles, Charles Chauncy, Jared Eliot, John
Hancock, Nathaniel Low, Samuel Mather, Thomas Prince,
Josiah Quincy, Jr., Samuel Stearns, Ezra Stiles,
Joseph Warren, Mercy Otis Warren.

Publishers Served: The Drapers, the Fleets,
Samuel Kneeland.

Both Benjamin Edes and John Gill were born in
1732. Edes was the son of a successful Charlestown
hatter, and although little is known about the early
life or education of either man, it is generally acknowledged that before 1754 both Edes and Gill served
their apprenticeships to a printer. In fact, Rollo G.
Silver speculates that both Edes and Gill were apprentices in the shop of Samuel Kneeland, a speculation
made more plausible for the reasons that Edes and Gill
certainly spent some time in planning their enterprise
before they launched their partnership, and Kneeland
was the firm's first benefactor. It was Kneeland who
provided Edes and Gill with what would be the basis of
their printing business when he sold them the Boston
Gazette in April 1755. It was Kneeland, again, who
provided a wife for Gill in 1756 in the person of his
daughter, Ann. The marriage produced several children.
Prior to Gill's marriage, Edes had married Martha Starr

in May 1755, and they also had several children, including the printers Peter and Benjamin Edes, Jr.

Although Robert Abercrombie's Account of the Proceedings of the Presbytery was published by Edes and Gill in 1754, it is clear from the advertisements in the Boston Gazette in early 1755 that Edes and Gill began their endeavor with the intention of building a newspaper from scratch. In early February they advertised subscriptions for a new weekly they planned to call the Country-Journal; however, by late March they announced in the Gazette that they would defer the first number of the Country-Journal "for a Week or two," because they lacked "a sufficient Number of Subscribers." Perhaps it was a request from Ann Kneeland to her father combined with the new Provincial Stamp Act that caused Samuel Kneeland to discontinue publication of the Boston Gazette with the number of 1 April 1755. The first number of the Boston-Gazette, Or, Country Journal printed and published by Edes and Gill appeared on 7 April. There is little of the auspicious in that first number of the new Gazette, but within twenty years it would become what Joseph T. Buckingham states was the most "powerful influence over the feelings, opinions, and conduct of the people" in the country.

The Boston Gazette was beyond doubt the major enterprise of the firm of Edes and Gill from 1755 until 1775, but it was by no means their only one. Besides the usual job printing for local shopkeepers and others, Edes and Gill did primarily religious printing during their early years. In fact, MaryAnn Yodelis has shown that Edes and Gill depended heavily upon religious printing until 1769, when their political activities won them appointment as printers to the General Assembly. In 1763, ninety-eight percent of the work Edes and Gill printed and published was religious, whereas in 1769 more than half of their work was governmental.

119

Surely the two most important divines to have work printed and published by Edes and Gill were Jonathan Mayhew and Charles Chauncy. Mayhew was the highly respected pastor of Boston's West Church from 1744 until his death in 1766. His <u>Discourse on Rev. XV</u> was one of the first publications of the new firm of Edes and Gill in 1755. In all they published fifteen works by Mayhew, most under a combined imprint with Richard and Samuel Draper and Thomas and John Fleet, the last being Mayhew's 1765 Dudleian Lecture entitled <u>Popish Idolatry</u>. They also published Charles Chauncy's <u>Discourse Occasioned by the Death of the Revernd Jonathan Mayhew</u> in 1766.

Before Gill and, more notably, Edes became em-broiled in political controversy, they found them-selves caught up in religious debate as the printers and publishers of pamphlets authored by Mayhew. Per-haps in the hope of intensifying the controversy and interest in it and, therefore, increasing sales, the firm also published the work of Mayhew's detractors. In 1763 East Apthorp published <u>Considerations on the Institution and Conduct of the Society for Propagating the Gospel</u>, which applauded the society's work. Mayhew, through Edes and Gill, published <u>Observations on the Charter and Conduct of the Society for Propagation of the Gospel</u> (1763), which expressed Mayhew's disfavor with the society for proposing an American episcopacy and for sending missionaries to settled areas. Mayhew was answered in two more Edes and Gill publications, Henry Caner's <u>Candid Examination of Dr. Mayhew's Obser-vations</u> (1763) and a pamphlet by the Archbishop of Canterbury, Thomas Secker, entitled <u>An Answer to Dr. Mayhew's Observations</u> (1764). Not to be outdone, Mayhew responded in 1763 with <u>A Defence of the Obser-vations</u>, also published by Edes and Gill. After the publication of an anonymous response to his defense, Mayhew, once again through Edes and Gill, published <u>Remarks on an Anonymous Tract, Entitled An Answer to Dr. Mayhew's Observations</u> in 1764. Another contro-versy began in 1763, when the Reverend John Cleaveland of Ipswich took exception in print to comments Mayhew had made in two sermons delivered on a day of public thanksgiving in December 1762 concerning discrepancies between Calvinist doctrine and the Bible. Mayhew responded with A Letter of Reproof to Mr. John Cleaveland, which was published by Edes and Gill in 1764 and is noted for the caustic attack upon Cleaveland for what Mayhew termed his "wilful misrepresentation."

Chauncy's relationship with Edes and Gill also began in 1755, when they published his Earthquakes a Token of the Righteous Anger of God, and his important Letter to a Friend, Giving a Concise, but Just, Account According to Advices Hitherto Received, of the Ohio-Defeat and A Second Letter to a Friend, Giving a More Practical Narrative of the Defeat of the French Army at Lake-George. Although Edes and Gill ultimately published fewer than ten sermons and tracts by Chauncy, through their acquaintance with him they became involved in an important chapter in the history of American printing. According to Lawrence C. Wroth, in 1768, after Abel Buell of Killingworth, Connecticut, had cast the first type produced in America and set a small advertisement, the stick of type was sent to Ezra Stiles who then sent it to Chauncy in Boston. Chauncy later wrote that in order to gratify his curiosity he asked Edes and Gill to take some proofs of Buell's newly cast letters. In this way the firm of Edes and Gill had a small hand in the first type founding of America.

Other religious clients of Edes and Gill through 1769 included Samuel Mather, whose Dissertation Concerning the Most Venerable Name of Jehovah they published in 1760, and Mather Byles, whose Sermon on the Nature and Necessity of Conversion was published by Edes and Gill in 1769. They also published Ezra Stiles's Discourse on the Christian Union in 1761, which is notable because Stiles wrote little for publication and also because of its appendix, which lists the names of all New England churches and their ministers in 1760. As well as printing and publishing a significant number of election and funeral sermons,

121

Edes and Gill published the annual sermons of the Ancient and Honourable Artillery Company in 1758, 1761, 1763, 1766, and 1770, but this, too, they ceased doing as they became more involved in political and governmental printing.

In some cases, the religious clients of Edes and Gill did not furnish them with strictly religious materials. For example, in 1755 they printed two parts of Thomas Prince's important Annals of New-England "for S. Kneeland and J. and T. Leverett, Cornhill." They were also the printers and publishers of Jared Eliot's Essays Upon Field Husbandry in New England (1760), a work that remained for years the most widely recognized treatise on American agriculture.

Certainly the most important scientific work done in New England in the mid-eighteenth century was that of the Reverend John Winthrop. In 1746 Winthrop had established at Harvard the first laboratory for experimental physics in America. His experiments in physics and astronomy were transformed into lectures and these, in turn, were published. Because most of Winthrop's work was published in Philosophical Transactions of the Royal Society, it is that much more impressive that Edes and Gill printed and published two of his more important works in America, Relation of a Voyage from Boston to New Foundland for the Observation of the Transit of Venus, June 6, 1761 (1761) and Two Lectures on the Parallax and Distance of Sun (1769). In all, Edes and Gill printed and published four works by Winthrop, but none is more interesting than his Lecture on Earthquakes, which was read at Harvard on 26 November 1755 for the purpose of explaining "the great earthquake which shook New-England the week before."

Edes and Gill also printed and published some purely literary endeavors during their early years, including Benjamin Church's The Choice: A Poem, After the Manner of Pomfret, in 1757, and George Cockings's War: An Heroic Poem, in 1762.

The firm of Edes and Gill entered the comparatively lucrative almanac trade soon after their business was founded with the publication of George Wheaten's Astronomical Diary; or an Almanack for . . . 1757 in 1756. However, in 1757 they first published the almanac of Nathaniel Ames, the most successful, most popular almanac maker in New England. In conjunction with the Drapers, the Fleets, and Green and Russell, Edes and Gill published and sold Ames's almanac until 1765. Despite the number of printers involved in producing and selling Ames's almanac, in its best years more than 60,000 copies were sold and, according to MaryAnn Yodelis, a firm's involvement with Ames could yield as much as £50 annually. It must have occurred to Edes and Gill that if such profits were possible through a joint effort, it would be considerably more lucrative to produce one's own almanac. Whether that was the reasoning or not, in 1768 the first Edes & Gill's North-American Almanack appeared. It was the product of Samuel Stearns. In format Edes and Gill's almanac followed Ames's closely, except that where Ames had placed articles discussing practical instruction, Edes and Gill published political statements and public documents bearing on the colonies' relationship with Great Britain. For example, their first almanac contains a political allegory entitled "The History of Publius Clodius Britano Americano," and a copy of "The Charter of the Province of the Massachusetts-Bay." Apparently their expectations for the success of their almanac were not met, for in 1771 its name was changed to the North American Almanack, and it was published with Richard Draper and the Fleets. Nevertheless, both Edes and Gill were obviously committed to publishing almanacs and they continued to do so, most often producing the work of Ames or Stearns, for the rest of their respective careers.

Among the most important of all the publications bearing the imprint of Edes and Gill are those authored by James Otis. At the time of Otis's association with Edes and Gill he was not only a respected lawyer, but an important Massachusetts political leader; therefore, his pamphlets added some prestige to the printing firm that published them. The importance of Otis's work is borne out by the fact that Edes and Gill charged slightly more for a political pamphlet by Otis than for tracts by less significant writers. In 1762 they published Otis's Vindication of the Conduct of the House of Representatives, which deals with what some might view as a rather meaningless local issue, but which has also been acknowledged by William Tudor as the source of all arguments supporting representative taxation as the basis of constitutionally limited government. With Edes and Gill's publication of Otis's Rights of the British Colonies Asserted and Proved (1764), the taxation issue was raised from the provinciality of Otis's 1762 pamphlet into an international arena, with Otis, who based his argument upon his understanding of natural law, claiming the right to oppose the British Parliament on the grounds that the people delegate power to governments, which hold this power in trust. Otis claimed that therefore the aims of the government and the people should be shared. In two pamphlets published in 1765, A Vindication of the British Colonies and Brief Remarks on the Defence of the Halifax Libel, Otis attacks both the author of Letter from a Gentleman at Halifax, Martin Howard--who claimed that colonial representatives would destroy the purity of the House of Commons--and other critics of his arguments calling for fair treatment. It was almost certainly the aid and friendship of Otis that enabled Edes and Gill to become the sole Boston printers and publishers of John Dickinson's popular Letters from a Farmer in Pennsylvania in 1768.

Otis's pamphlets published by Edes and Gill really signify the great shift that occurred in their business in the latter 1760s. As MaryAnn Yodelis has calculated, Edes and Gill were by far the most active political printers in Boston during the decade immediately preceding the Revolution. Although political printing was not profitable, the political activities of Edes and Gill did win them an appointment as printers to the House of Representatives in 1762 and again from

1770 to 1775. This gave the firm added prestige and no
doubt contributed to their volume of work, which in
1770 reached twenty-five percent of all Boston printing.

Edes and Gill bothered local officials from the
outset, publishing such controversial religious material in the Gazette that in March 1757 the Selectmen
of Boston warned the two printers that further offenses
against the religious principles of the people of Boston would result in the withdrawal of all town business
from the firm. Apparently Edes and Gill acquiesced and
the matter was forgotten. However, by the mid 1760s
Edes, most certainly through his friendship with Otis,
had become a principal espouser of the patriot cause,
and a member of the Loyall Nine, the group that directed
operations for the Sons of Liberty. Edes's closest cir-
cle of friends now included Samuel and John Adams, Otis,
Josiah Quincy, Jr., and Joseph Warren. Gill, on the
other hand, seems to have been strangely aloof from the
fevered political activity around him. It was not until after the Boston Massacre in 1770 that Gill performed his only recorded public activity by serving on
a committee that demanded the withdrawal of British
troops from Boston. Although a quiet partner, Gill
was not silent; he worked diligently to publish the
pro-patriot pamphlets and broadsides and the controversial Boston Gazette, which made his partner famous.

Of course, the reaction of Edes and the other
patriot leaders to the Stamp Act of 1765 had been
strong enough to force its repeal, but the force of
resistance in the Boston Gazette to the Townshend
Acts was so great that in November 1767 a demand was
made in Parliament that Edes and Gill be brought to
London and tried for libel. No action was taken,
however. A few months later, an inflammatory attack
on Governor Bernard in the Gazette of 29 February 1768
by Joseph Warren (signed "A True Patriot") forced
Bernard to seek grand jury action against Edes and
Gill. But he was thwarted in his attempt and the
Gazette continued publishing the work of Samuel Adams,
Quincy, and Warren under pen names.

125

On 5 March 1770 the so-called Boston Massacre took place. The event represents, in many ways, the central moment in the history of the firm of Edes and Gill. The massacre provided Edes and Gill with the most famous story that would be printed in the Boston Gazette, complete with engravings by Paul Revere of five coffins bearing the initials of the dead. This version of the massacre from the Gazette was evidently so popular that Edes and Gill soon reprinted it as a broadside, adding to it Revere's engraving of the event, which pictures the British soldiers, standing rather conspicuously in front of Butcher's Hall, firing into the crowd of innocents. They also published such propagandistic accounts of the event as A Short Narrative of the Horrid Massacre in Boston (1770), by James Bowdoin, Joseph Warren, and Samuel Pemberton, and published John Lathrop's Innocent Blood Crying to God in the Streets of Boston (1771), which had been published originally in London. All of this was quite effective propaganda that took advantage of the anti-British sentiment in Boston, increased sales of the Gazette, and contributed significantly to making 1770 the most productive year in the history of the firm of Edes and Gill.

In fact, Edes and Gill became so closely associated with the massacre in the minds of the people of Boston that in 1771, when James Lovell spoke his Oration Delivered April 2d, 1771. At the Request of the Inhabitants of the Town of Boston; to Commemorate the Bloody Tragedy of the Fifth of March, 1770, it was Edes and Gill who printed and published it. Subsequently they printed the commemorative oration every year until their partnership ended in 1775, and even then, either Edes or Gill printed the oration until it was ended in 1783. From 1771 to 1775 they printed two commemorative orations by Warren, one by Hancock, and one by Church, along with that of Lovell.

With John Adams and Josiah Quincy defending the soldiers accused of the massacre, all of the fury of the Boston Gazette resulted in very little action, and

when the most objectionable parts of the Townshend Acts
were repealed, the tension soon lessened. However,
Edes and Gill, with the help of Samuel Adams, would
not let people forget. Adams, writing under pen names
in the Gazette, continued his scathing attacks on the
British. Edes, too, apparently intensified his polit-
ical activity, and the publications of Edes and Gill
during the early 1770s reflect this intensification.
For example, in 1773 they reprinted Locke's second
treatise on civil government, and printed and published
Governor Hutchinson's Copy of Letters Sent to Great
Britain, the contents of which inflamed the people of
Boston. In 1774 they printed and published Josiah
Quincy, Jr.'s Observations on the Act of Parliament
Commonly Called the Boston Port-Bill. Even the sermons
became political as Samuel Webster's Misery and Duty of
an Oppress'd and Enslav'd People, published by Edes
and Gill in 1774, attests. Ironically, during the same
years, as printers to the House of Representatives,
Edes and Gill were also responsible for printing the
sermons delivered before governors Hutchinson and Gage.
Edes and Gill made a dual contribution to the patriot
cause and fledgling American drama when they published
parts of Mercy Otis Warren's "The Defeat" in two numbers of the Boston Gazette in 1773. This theatrical
attack on Governor Hutchinson must have been greeted
with favor since Edes and Gill printed and published
Warren's next effort, The Group, in 1775. This topical
farce focuses upon the group of cronies Hutchinson left
behind when he was recalled, and includes references
to the Boston Tea Party.

On 29 November 1773, when the tea arrived, Edes
and Gill were in the center of the activities that led
to the Boston Tea Party. Edes helped recruit the men
who would take part in the "Indian raid," and on the
afternoon before the event, the volunteers met at
Edes's house in Brattle Street, where Edes's son,
Peter, reported they drank a great deal of punch. In
the evening, this group met other men at the printing
office of Edes and Gill in Queen Street. According to
Jonathan Daniels, the men there changed into their

127

Mohawk costumes and proceeded to Griffin's Wharf where
they unceremoniously dumped £18,000 worth of tea.

Edes's part in all this was never acknowledged
publicly, and Edes and Gill continued their political
attacks in the Gazette. Even after the appointment
of Thomas Gage to the governorship in May 1774 and the
arrival of more British troops that this appointment
brought, Edes and Gill remained untouched. However,
the Tories of Boston were apparently applying pressure
to have Edes and Gill silenced. For example, a letter
distributed to British soldiers in the fall of 1774
listing the "authors" of the "rebellion breaking out
in this province," included many of the Gazette's
most consistent contributors, and added: "N. B. Don't
forget those trumpeters of sedition, the printers Edes
and Gill, and Thomas."

The Boston Gazette suspended publication with the
number of 17 April 1775. It is clear that from the
political involvement of the firm, and especially that
of Edes, choices had to be made to avoid imprisonment
by the British. Edes's only possible choice was to
flee. He managed to load a press and some type into
a boat and he escaped on the night of 16 April 1775
up the Charles River to Watertown, where the other
patriot leaders had established themselves. There Edes
set up his shop "near the Bridge," and after only a
brief hiatus, the Boston Gazette was back into production by 5 June 1775.

Gill, on the other hand, remained in Boston but
did no business through 1775. This concession on Gill's
part might well have been a defensive measure to con-
vince the British that he and Edes had officially split
and to assure them that the propaganda war would not be
continued on twin fronts in Watertown and Boston. If
this was Gill's reasoning, it did not work. In late
August 1775 he was arrested by the British and imprisoned for printing treasonous and seditious statements,
but he served only twenty-nine days.

Despite the apparent split of the partners, the firm of Edes and Gill continued to publish works until 1779. Since all of the works published by Edes and Gill after 1775 are of a patriotic nature, they were published under that imprint clearly because of the high regard that the people of Boston had for the imprint of Edes and Gill. For example, in 1776 Thomas Paines's Common Sense and Large Additons to Common Sense were reprinted by Edes and Gill, and the 1777 and 1779 orations to commemorate the Boston Massacre, by Benjamin Hichborn and William Tudor, respectively, were published by Edes and Gill.

When Gill reestablished himself as a printer in Boston in the spring of 1776, the political philosophy behind his firm seemed less radical than it had been during the partnership of Edes and Gill. Although Isaiah Thomas claimed that Gill was "a sound whig," who "did not possess the political energy of his part- ner," Gill did continue to work for the patriot cause. In fact, both Edes and Gill saved Massachusetts valu- able capital by printing paper currency at their re- spective shops in Watertown and Boston. Finding that Edes could print money from type for approximately half the price Paul Revere asked for currency from engraved plates, the state commissioned him for the project. Edes's bills, which were released on 18 June 1776, were the first in Massachusetts to display the monetary value in both shillings and dollars. Gill was also commis- sioned to produce a run of currency, and on 18 October 1776 his notes appeared, bearing the imprint "BOSTON: Printed by John Gill October 1776."

Gill also continued printing and reprinting the work of patriots, but his reprinting of John Adams's Thoughts on Government in 1776 indicates that he had become decidedly less radical than Edes. Perhaps Gill's most important publication of 1776 was The Militia Act; Together with Rules and Regulations for the Militia, 1,000 copies of which were ordered to be printed by the General Assembly on 23 April 1776. According to Charles Evans, this work is "full of the

129

spirit of the times." In fact, it was claimed that its
sixty-nine articles of war contained enough motivation
to make every patriot a soldier. Also in 1776 Gill
printed and published The Blockheads, a pro-patriot
farce probably written by Mercy Otis Warren that is
distinguished largely by its attacks on another writer
of farces, General Burgoyne.

A steady employment for Gill from 1776 to 1783
was the printing and publication of Nathaniel Low's
annual Astronomical Diary or, Almanack. It was published by Gill and T. & J. Fleet from 1776 until 1780,
when Nathaniel Willis also joined in the publication.
As printer to the General Assembly in 1777, 1778, and
1780, and printer to the House of Representatives in
1779, Gill produced more than thirty imprints for the
state, not including five sermons preached before either
the Council or Governor Hancock that he published from
1776 to 1782. Gill also printed the annual oration to
commemorate the Boston Massacre in 1780 and had the distinction of printing the last of these in 1783 and the
first of a new series, meant to replace the massacre
oration, in 1784: Benjamin Hichborn's Oration, Delivered July 5th, 1784, at the Request of the Inhabitants
of the Town of Boston; in Celebration of the Anniversary of American Independence.

As he had done with the firm of Edes and Gill,
Gill operating on his own devoted a major part of his
time to the production of a weekly newspaper. On 30
May 1776 he began publishing the Continental Journal
and Weekly Advertiser. His promises to his readers in
the first issue of a "News-Paper of Intelligence" that
would omit "pompous representations" intimate the conservative nature of Gill's journalistic approach, and
perhaps his reaction to the sensationalism of Edes.
Nevertheless, when Gill retired and sold his entire
printing concern on Court Street to James D. Griffith,
his final public statement was a political one. The
last number of the Journal edited and published by Gill
appeared on 21 April 1785, and in it he informed his
readers that he was leaving the printing business in

130

the face of a new stamp tax levied by the Commonwealth
of Massachusetts. He implied that he had spent much
energy fighting two such taxes imposed by the British,
and was unable to continue the fight.

John Gill died in Boston on 26 August 1785. An
obituary in the Massachusetts Spy of 1 September 1785
eulogizes him for exactly those qualities his incon-
spicuous career suggests: "honesty, frugality and
industry."

After his escape to Watertown in April 1775,
Edes also had difficulty reestablishing his business.
The press and type he managed to get out of Boston
were apparently inferior, the ink he was forced to use
was second-rate, and most serious, paper was in short
supply. The most frequent advertisement in the Gazette
during the twenty months that it was printed in Watertown was Edes's own plea for "clean Cotton and Linnen
RAGS." The problem became so critical that in the
13 May 1776 number of the Gazette, Edes announced a
price increase "owing to the neglect of saving rags"
and the general scarcity of paper. Nevertheless, even
before Edes began producing the Gazette in Watertown,
he was hard at work for the provincial government. As
early as 8 May 1775 he was printing broadsides containing important information from the council for the people, as well as other official documents for the council
and House of Representatives. In 1775 Edes also
printed more than twenty official publications for
the provincial congress, including Rules and Regulations for the Massachusetts Army. In fact, through
1780 Edes's primary concern beside the Gazette was
his official duties as "Printer to the Council of
State, of Massachusetts-Bay." During those years
from 1775 to 1780, which saw his return to Boston in
early November 1776 and the entry of his sons into
the business on 12 April 1779, Edes printed more
than 150 official documents. In 1781 the firm of
Benjamin Edes and Sons was named "Printers to his
excellency the Governor, the Council and the Senate
of the Commonwealth of Massachusetts," and a short

time later "Printers to the Commonwealth." In this
capacity Edes and Sons printed approximately forty of
the state's official documents from 1881 to 1883. With
the demands made on Edes by the Gazette and his work
for the state, it is easy to understand why very little
else was done in Edes's shop during the late 1770s and
early 1780s. In 1776 alone, Edes produced more than
forty publications for the state. However, nearly all
government patronage disappeared in 1783, when Adams
and Nourse were named printers to the commonwealth.

Despite the demands made on Edes by government
work and despite the onset of old age, after 1783 he
still managed to print a variety of publications.
Of course, with the passage of the Constitution, certain parts of which Edes bitterly opposed, he had lost
the cause that had sustained the Gazette for nearly
twenty years. Without that cause, interest in the
Gazette declined, and in the early 1780s there was a
noticeable decline in subscriptions. Edes's publications in the 1780s represent another change in the
direction of his business. There are noticeably
more sermons. Some, like Samuel Mather's All Men Will
Not be Saved Forever (1782), are reminiscent of works
published at the beginning of Edes's career, but more
often the sermons commemorate the patriot cause, as
do Henry Cummings' Sermon Preached at Lexington, on
the 19th of April, 1781 (1781), Phillips Payson's
Memorial of Lexington Battle (1782), or the orations
to commemorate the Boston Massacre, which Edes published in 1778 (with the Fleets) and 1782.

Edes's publications became more eclectic as the
century moved toward its close. Between 1775 and 1783
the house's work was almost exclusively governmental
or political, but between 1783 and 1799 its publications included a religious dictionary (Hannah Adams's
Alphabetical Compendium of the Various Sects which Have
Appeared in the World from the Beginning of the Christian Era to the Present Day, 1784), a New Testament
(1788), a medical treatise (John Newman's Treatise, on
Schirrus Tumours, 1791), and a scientific work, which

132

was the most popular of Edes's publications during these later years, Bartholomew Burges's Short Account of the Solar System. This treatise went through two editions in 1789. Edes also continued his association with Samuel Stearns, publishing his almanac in 1782, 1787, 1790, and 1791.

The eclectic nature of the firm's clientele also indicated that the business was in decline. The participation of Peter and Benjamin Edes, Jr., in their father's business certainly must have contributed to the acquisition of clients and the prolongation of Edes's career. When Peter left Edes and Sons in 1784 to open his own shop on State Street, the firm was still productive, but Benjamin Jr.'s departure in 1794 signaled the final decline, during which Edes made many moves.

The final number of the Boston Gazette was published on 17 September 1798. Despite the appearance of Jeremiah Condy's Mercy Exemplified, in the Conduct of a Samaritan under Edes's imprint in 1799, the end of the Gazette marked the end of Edes's career. His editor's farewell in that final number of the Gazette speaks of Edes's condition: "the cause of Liberty is not always the channel of preferment or pecuniary reward. The little property which he acquired has long since fell a sacrifice;--the paper-evidences of his services were soon consumed by their rapid depreciation, and the cares of a numerous family were too powerful to be resisted, though he fed them with property at four shillings and sixpence in the pound, which he faithfully and industriously earned at twenty shillings." However, the disappointment of losing the Gazette after forty-five years of nearly continuous operation did not deter Edes from practicing his craft until his death on 10 December 1803.

Edes and Gill must be counted among the most important of Boston printers and publishers in the latter half of the eighteenth century, if for no other reason than their venerability; however, other more important reasons exist. As printers and publishers of the works of Chauncy and Mayhew, they produced work by the two most influential religious spokesmen of their time. Their publication of work by Winthrop and Eliot contributed substantially to the study of physics, astronomy, and agriculture in New England. From 1760, Edes and Gill printed and published political works important to the American Revolution and the founding of this country by such significant figures as Samuel Adams, Hancock, Otis, Quincy, and Warren; and through the continued publication of the Boston Gazette, Edes and Gill not only aided in inciting the Revolution but labored to keep people informed during desperate times.

Robert E. Burkholder

References:

Buckingham, Joseph T. Specimens of Newspaper Literature, Vol. 1. Boston: Little and Brown, 1850.

Daniels, Jonathan. They Will Be Heard: America's Crusading Newspaper Editors. New York: McGraw-Hill, 1965.

Silver, Rollo G. "Benjamin Edes, Trumpeter of Sedition." Papers of the Bibliographical Society of America, 47 (1953).

Thomas, Isaiah. The History of Printing in America. Worcester, Mass.: Isaiah Thomas, Jr., 1810; 2nd ed., revised, Albany, N.Y.: J. Munsell for the American Antiquarian Society, 1874; ed. Marcus A. McCorison, Barre, Mass.: Imprint Society, 1970.

Tudor, William. The Life of James Otis. Boston: Wells and Lilly, 1823.

Wroth, Lawrence C. *The Colonial Printer*. New York:
    Grolier Club, 1931; revised and enlarged,
    Portland, Me.: Southworth-Anthoensen Press,
    1938; reprint edition, Charlottesville, Va.:
    University Press of Virginia/Dominion Books,
    1964.

Yodelis, MaryAnn. *Who Paid the Piper? Publishing
    Economics in Boston, 1763-1775*, Journalism
    Monographs, 38. Lexington, Ky.: Association
    for Education in Journalism, 1975.

Benjamin Edes, Jr.

Benjamin Edes, Jr. (1755-1801) was the son of Benjamin
Edes and brother to Peter Edes. The younger Benjamin
was active in Boston from 1779 until 1794, always as a
partner in his father's business. In 1794 Edes moved
to Haverhill, Massachusetts, where he published the
Guardian of Freedom until 1795, when it ceased publication. He returned to Boston in 1798, where he remained
active as a printer until his death.

References:

Brigham, Clarence S. History and Bibliography of
    American Newspapers: 1690-1820. Vol. 1.
    Worcester, Mass.: American Antiquarian Society,
    1947.

Buckingham, Joseph T. Specimens of Newspaper Litera-
    ture. Vol. 1. Boston: Little and Brown, 1850.

Silver, Rollo G. "Benjamin Edes, Trumpeter of Sedi-
    tion." Papers of the Bibliographical Society of
    America, 47 (1953).

Thomas, Isaiah. The History of Printing in America.
    Worcester, Mass.: Isaiah Thomas, Jr., 1810;
    2nd ed., revised, Albany, N.Y.: J. Munsell
    for the American Antiquarian Society, 1874;
    ed. Marcus A. McCorison, Barre, Mass.: Imprint
    Society, 1970.

Peter Edes

Peter Edes (1756-1840), an active Boston printer and publisher from 1779 until 1787 and from 1792 until 1794, pursued his trade in several New England towns. Through 1794 he produced, or helped produce, about seventy-five titles in Boston, as well as 105 numbers of a weekly newspaper, the Exchange Advertiser. After being in partnership with his father and brother, Peter opened his office in State Street in December 1784; in the spring of 1786 he moved to 45 Marlborough Street. The next year he moved to Newport, but returned to Boston in 1792. In 1794 he moved to Haverhill, Massachusetts, and in 1795 he moved to Maine, where he spent the rest of his life.

Major Authors: James Allen, Henry Alline, John Gardiner, John Sylvester John Gardiner, Hannah More, John Trumbull, Noah Webster.

Publishers Served: Blake and Clap, Thomas and Andrews.

Edes was born in Boston on 17 December 1756, and learned his trade in his father's shop. He was a son of Benjamin Edes, who, with John Gill, published the Boston Gazette. Benjamin Edes moved his press to Watertown, Massachusetts, in the spring of 1775, not returning until the next year. In the interim Peter was imprisoned by the British on a charge of concealing firearms in his house, and was held from 19 June until 3 October 1775, when he was finally released. In 1779, after dissolution of the Edes-Gill partnership, Benjamin took his sons Peter and Benjamin, Jr. into the firm. It was known as Benjamin Edes and Sons until Peter Edes opened his own shop five years later.

137

The first number of Edes's newspaper, the Exchange Advertiser, was dated 30 December 1784, about two months after an advertisement in his father's Gazette announced that Peter was opening his own shop. The Exchange Advertiser was a small folio of four pages that appeared weekly, usually on Thursday, for the next two years, ceasing with number 105 on 4 January 1787. The paper contained local news and correspondence, foreign intelligence, shipping news, a poetry column, and articles on education, medicine, and other subjects. It served as well to advertise Edes's new publications and other phases of his business. An advertisement in the 13 January 1785 number lists about seventy-five titles of books that Edes had for sale; other advertisements show his willingness to furnish stationery and "blanks of all kinds."

More than a dozen other items appeared with his imprint during these first three years alone in Boston. The first, perhaps, was John Lathrop's Discourse on the Peace, a Thanksgiving sermon preached on 25 November 1784. The Exchange Advertiser of 17 March 1785 advertised as "Just published" a collection of thirteen of the annual orations delivered to commemorate the Boston Massacre. This ambitious project was followed a few months later by the first Boston edition of John Trumbull's M'Fingal, advertised in the 7 July number. Shortly thereafter Edes announced publication of the first part of Pierre Landais' Memorial. Landais had been relieved of command for failure to support John Paul Jones during Jones's engagement with the Serapis in 1779; this was one of a series of attempts by Landais to justify his conduct. Later in the same year Edes produced an Independence Day oration by John Gardiner, reprinted a Latin grammar, and published the new liturgy of King's Chapel. Early the next year he published a children's catechism, taken probably from the King's Chapel liturgy he had published.

In 1786 Edes published the first Boston edition of Noah Webster's Grammatical Institute of the English

<u>Language</u>, apparently receiving the opportunity through the author's dissatisfaction with the Hartford publishers of the first four editions. Also published this same year were the first works of the revivalist Henry Alline, <u>Hymns and Spiritual Songs</u>, and of John Sylvester John Gardiner, <u>An Epistle to Zenas</u>, a satire against future governor James Sullivan.

After his return from Newport in 1792, Edes apparently acted more as a printer for others than as a publisher. Of approximately fifteen items produced during this three-year period, seven were done for Thomas and Andrews. These included editions of Mary Wollstonecraft's <u>Vindication of the Rights of Woman</u> (1792), Goldsmith's <u>Miscellaneous Works</u> (1793), and Addison's <u>Cato</u> (1793). With Samuel Etheridge, Edes printed editions of a few of Garrick's farces for William P. Blake and William T. Clap. Edes and Etheridge had contracted, on 31 January 1794, to do work for the Boston Association of Booksellers, represented by a committee of James White, Thomas and Andrews, and Ebenezer Larkin, Jr.; and one book, an edition of <u>Pilgrim's Progress</u>, came out in 1794 with the imprint "Printed by Peter Edes, for the Booksellers." By late 1794, however, Edes was on the move again. Two of his 1794 imprints are from Haverhill, Massachusetts, and the next year he was in Maine.

Peter Edes's six years in Boston as printer and publisher were a small part of a long career. He lived to be eighty-four years old and operated shops in at least five cities besides Boston. He is of Boston interest not only as a son who carried on the work of a notable father, but as the first Boston publisher of important works by Hannah More, John Trumbull, and Noah Webster.

Richard W. Ryan

Reference:

Boardman, Samuel L. Peter Edes, Pioneer Printer in
     Maine: A Biography. Bangor, Me.: The
     De Burians, 1901.

John Edwards

John Edwards (d. 1725), the father of Joseph Edwards,
conducted business "on the south side of the Town-
House in King Street" (or "next door to the Light-
House Tavern in King-Street" or "at the head of
King-Street") between 1718 and 1725. Four of his
first six and fourteen of his total of twenty-four
known publications are by Increase or Cotton Mather,
including two of the former's tracts in support of
smallpox inoculation and the latter's Psalterium
Americanum (with Benjamin Eliot, Samuel Gerrish,
and Daniel Henchman). Samuel Kneeland printed all
but four of the seventeen Edwards publications
bearing the name of a printer. Edwards had Benjamin
Gray as a partner from 1719 to 1721.

Joseph Edwards

Joseph Edwards (1707-1777), son of John Edwards, was a bookseller and publisher who published primarily religious books, including sermons, eulogies, and various versions of the Bible. Among the practical material he published are the first American life insurance plan, readers for children, a book on weights and denominations, and an almanac. Active for fifty-two years, he established his business in 1725 at the corner shop on the north side of the Town House, where he remained until mid century. In 1751 he moved to the Cornhill district where he stayed until his retirement in 1772. He published fewer than 100 titles.

Major Authors: John Bunyan, Mather Byles, Benjamin Colman, William Cooper, Daniel Defoe, Jonathan Edwards, Cotton Mather, Ebenezer Turell, George Whitefield.

Edwards began his publishing career modestly, publishing one or two titles per year for the first ten years. In 1735 his activity increased and his output remained more substantial until 1744; during this period he published or sold about six books each year. In 1745 he reverted to the earlier pattern of publishing only a few titles annually, and he continued in this fashion for his final twenty-five years as a publisher. Despite his modest number of titles, he was considered, at least by Isaiah Thomas, "a very respectable, and a considerable publisher, bookseller and binder."

One of Edwards's first publications was Cotton Mather's Nails Fastened (1726), and from then until his career ended religious volumes constituted the major part of Edwards's business. He also published

141

Mather's The Comfortable Chambers, Opened and Visited
(1728), Matthew Mead's The Almost Christian Discovered
(1730), sermons by William Cooper (1730, 1732, 1740),
and John Bunyan's The Jerusalem-Sinner Saved (1733).

Edwards's most productive decade began in 1735.
That year he published the first of his many titles by
Benjamin Colman, an Ebenezer Turell eulogy, and Francis
Gregory's Nomenclatura Brevis Anglo-Latino. From 1735
to 1740 he published sermons by Mather Byles and William
Cooper, more items by Colman, and several of George
Whitefield's titles. Edwards published or sold thirteen volumes in 1741, his most productive year. (In
1740 and 1741 he was in partnership with Samuel Eliot.)
He published sermons by Charles Chauncy and Samuel
Shaw, Isaac Watts's adaptation of the Psalms, more
volumes by Whitefield, and a piece by Jonathan Edwards.
Joseph Edwards was publishing the works of the most
prominent clergymen of the day. In his last flurry of
publishing activity, he published another Shaw sermon
in 1744, as well as several nonreligious works, including the fourth edition of Daniel Defoe's Abstract of
the Remarkable Passages in the Life of a Private
Gentleman.

At that point Edwards's career as a publisher
all but ended. He was semi-active for more than three
decades after 1744, but in several years he published
nothing and in no year did he publish more than two
titles. The single most important book he published
appeared during those quiet years, however: Ebenezer
Turell's biography of Benjamin Colman in 1749.

During his long career of more than fifty years
Edwards published primarily religious titles by a small
number of venerable clergymen; however, he generally
published their minor works, so that his reputation
rests on the names of the authors he published.

Richard Ziegfeld

142

|Joseph Edwards

Reference:

Thomas, Isaiah.   The History of Printing in America.
    Worcester, Mass.:   Isaiah Thomas, Jr., 1810;
    2nd ed., revised, Albany, N.Y.:   J. Munsell
    for the American Antiquarian Society, 1874;
    ed. Marcus A. McCorison, Barre, Mass.:   Imprint
    Society, 1970.

Benjamin Eliot's Shop and the "Liberty Tree"

Benjamin Eliot

Benjamin Eliot (1665-1741), bookseller and publisher, was an official government publisher who produced eleven works specifically requested by the Massachusetts Bay Province. More than 110 other publications bear his imprint, including eighty religious works. Eliot was among the thirty or more booksellers who did business around the Town House during this period. His imprint from 1699 to 1702 located him "under the West-End of the Town House." In 1703 he enlarged his shop to include the former quarters of John Howard, scrivener. After the fire of 1711, he was located briefly in King Street; from there he moved to the south corner of Essex and Washington streets. The shop at this location was surrounded by several large elms, one of which later became famous as the Liberty Tree.

Major Authors: Benjamin Colman, Cotton Mather, Increase Mather, Solomon Stoddard, Benjamin Wadsworth, Samuel Willard.

Eliot was born in 1665, the son of Jacob and Mary Powell Eliot. He was a great-nephew of the Reverend John Eliot, the "Apostle to the Indians," whose translation of the Bible into the Algonquian language was the first Bible printed in America. Benjamin Eliot was a cousin of Michael Perry, another bookseller. They probably began their careers as apprentices to Samuel Phillips, and while they published jointly for a few years, imprints as early as 1700 show their names individually. By 1709 Eliot was running a profitable business, having enlarged his shop under the staircases at the west end of the Town House He became a leading bookseller, publishing steadi y at an average of five titles yearly between 1707 and 1727. Eliot died on 9 November 1741.

145

Benjamin Eliot

Eliot possibly began his career by publishing, with Perry, <u>Acts and Laws of His Majesties Province of Massachusetts-Bay, in New England</u> (1699); his next two publications were also contracted by Massachusetts Bay in the same year. Printed by Bartholomew Green, "Printer to His Excellency the Governour and Council," and John Allen, these volumes indicate a thriving relationship between Eliot as bookseller-publisher and the province. Although the imprints emphasize the printer, the government did not deal directly with the printer. Rather, transactions were handled with the bookseller, who bore the financial risk. Since the council and the House of Representatives functioned separately, disputes arose occasionally over which publishing firm to contract. The House of Representatives was particularly businesslike, concerning itself with printing costs and unmindful of the honor attached to government publishing. Thus Benjamin Eliot entered the publishing business by making the most satisfactory bid to the general court. In 1699 Eliot and Perry agreed to furnish the court with fifty free copies of the compilation of laws being prepared, as well as to furnish 150 additional copies at production cost. In 1714 Eliot published another compilation, and by 1722 he had gained considerable bargaining power within the House. In negotiations that year, Eliot proposed "that if he may have a Privilege of Printing the Laws of This Province for Twenty Years exclusive of all others, he will supply the several Towns of the Province and Members of the General Court with Two Hundred and Thirty Bound. . . ." Eliot was proposing a copyright; the Council failed to accept his proposal, however. Finally, after three years of arguments over his offer and that of Nicholas Boone, another bookseller, and an intervening edition of laws by John Baskett of London, Eliot was awarded the right to publish a 1726 compilation.

By the time of the next negotiation, Eliot wielded even greater influence. In 1734, when proposals for a new compilation of laws began, Eliot effectively argued for a delay because of the large

146

number of copies of the 1726 compilation yet unsold.
The decision to authorize a new edition was countered
as well during the next session, when Eliot again stated
that because of his large stock he would suffer financially. However, arguments ensued until 1741; finally
the court tired of the relationship with Benjamin Eliot
and became wary of the power of booksellers. This time
the court dealt directly with the printers Kneeland and
Green, engaging them to do the vending of the volumes
so as to avoid booksellers altogether.

Amid these discussions with the council and
House of Representatives, which resulted in eleven
major publications between 1699 and 1728, Eliot published significantly in other areas. Cotton Mather
accounted for eighteen titles. In addition, Eliot
sold the volume entitled A Memorial of the Present
Deplorable State of New-England (1707), published
under Mather's pseudonym Philopolites. This work,
probably printed in London, was also sold by Samuel
Phillips and Nicholas Buttolph. Eliot published fourteen works by Increase Mather as well; together the
Mathers represented forty percent of his religious
publications. Eliot also participated in the publishing history of the Bay Psalm Book. He joined with
Nicholas Buttolph in the edition of 1707; then, in
1716, Eliot published the seventeenth edition. In
1718 he joined Daniel Henchman, Samuel Gerrish, and
John Edwards in publishing Cotton Mather's Psalterium
Americanum.

In terms of historical significance, Eliot's
most important religious publication was perhaps Samuel
Willard's Compleat Body of Divinity (1726). Recognized
in the history of American publishing as the largest
single volume published up to that time, it measures
8 1/4 x 13 3/8 inches and is nearly 1,000 pages long.
This folio volume is significant for other reasons as
well. First, it was one of the earliest subscription
books in America, with a list of 500 subscribers.
Second, its title page is an early example of rubrication. Although it appeared eight years after the

147

earliest instance of two-color printing in the colonies, that done in Philadelphia by Andrew Bradford, the title page undertaken for Willard's volume represents laborious work. As Lawrence C. Wroth notes, the procedure was costly and painstaking, and thus unpopular with American printers, "but when the largest publication project of the first-half of the century was brought to a close in Boston in 1726, the printers signalized their pride in the volume produced, or, perhaps, their relief at its completion, by a fine display of red on its tall, well-ordered title page." The volume, printed in parts by both Bartholomew Green and Samuel Kneeland, under the joint publication of Benjamin Eliot and Daniel Henchman, contains noticeable errors in pagination. Nevertheless, it marked a considerable achievement in American publishing.

While his total output was primarily religious and political, Eliot did not exclude other areas. For example, he published almanacs by Samuel Clough in 1706, 1707, and 1708. In the field of scholarly learning, Ezekiel Cheever's Short Introduction to the Latin Tongue was published in 1709 and again in 1713 and 1724. In addition, Eliot possibly published editions of Bunyan's Pilgrim's Progress and Michael Wigglesworth's The Day of Doom.

Benjamin Eliot's publishing activities are important for several reasons. His experiences with the Massachusetts Bay government give insight into the developing role of the publisher in contract situations. Further, his frustrations in this area show the circumstances that contributed to copyright protection. Finally, his versatility and daring in several of his ventures provide a well-rounded sketch of the eighteenth-century bookseller-publisher.

Alice S. Haynes

Benjamin Eliot

References:

Littlefield, George E. Early Boston Booksellers:
     1642-1711. Boston: Club of Odd Volumes, 1900;
     reprint edition, New York: Burt Franklin, 1969.

Oswald, John C. Printing in the Americas. Chicago
     and New York: Gregg, 1937; reprint edition,
     New York: Hacker Art Books, 1968.

Silver, Rollo G. "Government Printing in Massachusetts-
     Bay, 1700-1750." Proceedings of the American
     Antiquarian Society, 68 (1958).

Wroth, Lawrence C. The Colonial Printer. New York:
     Grolier Club, 1931; revised and enlarged,
     Portland, Me.: Southworth-Anthoensen Press,
     1938; reprint edition, Charlottesville, Va.:
     University Press of Virginia/Dominion Books,
     1964.

John Eliot

John Eliot (1692-1771), nephew to Benjamin Eliot, was
a bookseller, stationer, and binder who published
approximately twenty-five titles from 1716 until 1770,
all of which are undistinguished. He published only
three titles after 1741 and before his last volume in
1770, an edition of William Billings's New-England
Psalm-Singer. He conducted business "at the South-End
of the Town" and "at the Tree of Liberty."

References:

Littlefield, George E. Early Boston Booksellers:
    1642-1711. Boston: Club of Odd Volumes, 1900;
    reprint edition, New York: Burt Franklin, 1969.

Thomas, Isaiah. The History of Printing in America.
    Worcester, Mass.: Isaiah Thomas, Jr., 1810;
    2nd ed., revised, Albany, N.Y.: J. Munsell
    for the American Antiquarian Society, 1874;
    ed. Marcus A. McCorison, Barre, Mass.: Imprint
    Society, 1970.

Samuel Eliot

Samuel Eliot (1713-1745) was a minor but competent publisher whose work was characterized by a judicious business sense. He was an unbiased participant in the
religious controversies surrounding the Great Awakening
of the 1740s and published important works by both
George Whitefield and Charles Chauncy. He also published the reputable American Magazine and Historical
Chronicle. In his brief career he published a total
of seventy titles. His business was established at
Cornhill and remained there until his widow moved it
to "South-End near the Great-Trees" in 1746.

   Major Authors: Nathaniel Appleton, Charles
Chauncy, Benjamin Colman, John Cotton, Jonathan
Dickinson, Thomas Hooker, George Whitefield.

   Almost nothing is known of Eliot's early life
from his birth, in 1713, until 1737. As a publisher,
however, he was recognized as an astute and successful
businessman and is described by Isaiah Thomas as a
"considerable bookseller." He was also a binder and
stationer. He is listed in the "Subscribers to Prince's
Chronology" as one of the "principal Literati of New
England," possessing a "specially desired" pedigree.

   Eliot's publications increased slowly from 1737
to 1740 (a total of thirteen titles), then expanded
substantially in the next three years. As almost exclusively a publisher of religious works (except for
one magazine), Eliot benefited from the level of religious feeling at this time, publishing fourteen titles
in 1741, fifteen in 1742, and seventeen in 1743. He
published only nine works in the two years before his
death; his widow possibly continued the business for two
years after 1745.

151

As evidence of his religious emphasis, Eliot published thirty-nine sermons or sermon collections. He
seems to have selected his titles with care, and published usually two types. The first consists of sermons preached on auspicious occasions, such as the
funeral of a well-known personage, ordinations, and,
in 1742, a sermon preached by Nathaniel Appleton to
Governor Shirley. In addition, Eliot published several
sermons occasioned by the religious fervor aroused by
Whitefield's visits to New England. These include
sermons by Appleton (1741) and Thomas Foxcroft (1740).
He also published sermons by such notable earlier
divines as John Cotton and Thomas Hooker. His other
religious works include theological treatises, polemical letters, reports of pastoral conventions, and a
1737 edition of the Psalms.

Eliot's most important and most frequently
appearing authors were two clergymen in theological
opposition, George Whitefield and Charles Chauncy.
In 1740 Eliot published Whitefield's account of his
life and two letters, one to John Wesley refuting
free grace and one to Presbyterian church members.
In 1741 he republished a letter to Wesley, published
several volumes of Whitefield's journal, and published
Whitefield's account of money received for his Georgia
orphanage. In 1741 Eliot also began to publish the
anti-evangelical works of Charles Chauncy. Over the
next five years, possibly as a reflection of a waning
Whitefield influence, Eliot published eight of Chauncy's
works, including six sermons (generally cautions against
religious enthusiasm), a 1745 polemical letter to
Whitefield, and, perhaps the best known of all Eliot's
publications, the first edition of Chauncy's influential Seasonable Thoughts on the State of Religion in
New England (1743).

Eliot's only secular publication, the American
Magazine and Historical Chronicle, also testifies to

his judiciousness. Described by Charles Evans as a
"well-printed" imitation of the London Magazine, the
first Boston number was published in October 1743, by
Eliot and Joshua Blanchard. The magazine was edited
by Jeremiah Gridley and consisted of fifty pages.
According to Lyon N. Richardson, it was accompanied
by "careful business supervision" and was published
monthly for three years and four months, a longevity
unequaled in America until 1786.

Although Eliot occasionally printed his own titles, he usually relied on other printers, most frequently John Draper, Gamaliel Rogers, and Daniel Fowle
(later a Rogers-Fowle partnership). He assumed a brief
partnership in 1740 and 1741, publishing several titles
under the imprint of "J. Edwards and S. Eliot." His
partner was Joseph Edwards.

Although his output was relatively small, Samuel
Eliot was an accomplished publisher whose titles depict
the significant religious controversies of the 1740s.
He helped to spread the enthusiasm of George Whitefield
to Boston and then helped to counteract that influence
with the publication of Chauncy's Seasonable Thoughts.
Although his publications illustrate a dominance of
religious concerns, he also helped to establish and
printed one of the best early American magazines.

Tony J. Owens

References:

D., S. G. "List of Subscribers to Prince's Chronology."
New England Genealogical and Historical Register,
6 (1852).

Richardson, Lyon N. A History of Early American Magazines, 1741-1789. New York: Thomas Nelson,
1931; reprint edition, New York: Octagon, 1966.

Thomas, Isaiah. <u>The History of Printing in America</u>.
Worcester, Mass.: Isaiah Thomas, Jr., 1810;
2nd ed., revised, Albany, N.Y.: J. Munsell
for the American Antiquarian Society, 1874; ed.
Marcus A. McCorison, Barre, Mass.: Imprint
Society, 1970.

Abraham Ellison

Abraham Ellison (dates unknown), a binder, published
four religious works in Boston in 1773 at his shop
"in Seven-Star Lane." He later lived in Newport,
Rhode Island, and was a bookseller in Albany, New
York, from 1793 to 1812.

Reference:

Thomas, Isaiah. <u>The History of Printing in America</u>.
Worcester, Mass.: Isaiah Thomas, Jr., 1810;
2nd ed., revised, Albany, N.Y.: J. Munsell
for the American Antiquarian Society, 1874; ed.
Marcus A. McCorison, Barre, Mass.: Imprint
Society, 1970.

Benjamin Endicott (see Benjamin Indicott)

154

Samuel Etheridge

Samuel Etheridge (1771-1817) was a printer, publisher, and bookseller who printed half of his approximately fifty titles for various Boston publishers. In 1792 he began in the business with Alexander Young. During 1794 he collaborated with Peter Edes, but by 1795 he was by himself at No. 9, Newbury Street. In 1798 he was in partnership with William Spotswood, but later that year he established his own business. He continued in Boston through 1808, although he also printed in Charlestown, Massachusetts, from 1799 to 1805.

Major Authors: Hugh Blair, Hannah Foster, David Garrick, Ann Radcliffe, Benjamin West.

Publishers Served: William P. Blake, John Boyle, Thomas and Andrews, David and John West.

The earliest record of Etheridge's work in Boston is his publication, with Alexander Young, of two titles in 1792: The Progress of Refinement by Thomas Odiorne, and William Haliburton's Effects of the Stage on the Manners of a People. During the next year Etheridge and Young printed three books--one for David West, one for the Massachusetts General Court, and one for the booksellers--but that same year they embarked upon their most ambitious project, a newspaper. On 1 January 1793 they published the first number of a quarto tri-weekly, the Massachusetts Mercury; in July they changed its size to folio, its frequency of publication to semi-weekly, and its name to the Mercury. After dissolving their partnership one month later, Young continued publishing the paper.

155

| Samuel Etheridge

Etheridge shared several projects with Peter Edes in 1794, and their most notable achievement was the printing of four titles for William P. Blake and William T. Clap's series of plays. Etheridge and Edes printed two by David Garrick (The Lying Valet and The Bon Ton), one by John O'Keefe, and one by Arthur Murphy.

On his own again in 1795, Etheridge printed, among other titles, Benjamin West's 1796 almanac. He published three other volumes in 1795, the most notable being Ann Radcliffe's The Romance of the Forest, a popular novel of the time. In 1796 Etheridge's printing and publishing were typically diverse and included Thomas Day's The History of Sandford and Merton and Lord Kames's Elements of Criticism.

Etheridge was also active in 1797. That year he printed Hugh Blair's influential Essays on Rhetoric for Thomas and Andrews, and he published what would be his most important volume, the first edition of Hannah Foster's The Coquette, a novel that received great public acclaim. In 1798 he had his last burst of productivity with, among others, a builder's guide, a cookbook, a letter-writing guide, a travel book, a children's nature book, and four histories. In 1799 Etheridge printed only five titles in Boston.

Although Samuel Etheridge was essentially a printer who handled few important literary figures and left only one book of consequence, The Coquette, the diversity of his productions is representative of the variety of books published in the last decade of eighteenth-century Boston.

Elizabeth Nelson Adams

156

|Samuel Etheridge

References:

Brigham, Clarence S. History and Bibliography of
    American Newspapers: 1690-1820. Vol. 1.
    Worcester, Mass.: American Antiquarian
    Society, 1947.

Silver, Rollo G. The American Printer, 1787-1825.
    Charlottesville, Va.: University Press of
    Virginia, 1967.

John Ewing

John Ewing (dates unknown) was a grocer at "No. 42,
Marlborough-Street" who possibly sold Gardiner on
Theatre in 1792. No copy of that book is known to
exist.

Joseph Farnham

Joseph Farnham (dates unknown) published only one
known book bearing his name in the imprint. In 1672
Marmaduke Johnson printed William Dyer's Christs
Famous Titles for Farnham and Edmund Ranger.

157

Josiah Flagg

Josiah Flagg (1737-1794), an engraver, was a "musical
enthusiast" who organized the first militia band in
Boston and managed various concerts there. His name
appears in the imprints of four known titles published
between 1764 and 1790. The first, his own Collection
of the Best Psalm Tunes, was sold by Flagg and Paul
Revere, who engraved the plates. It was the largest
collection of Psalms published in America up to that
time. In 1766 Flagg engraved and sold his Sixteen
Anthems, as he did his last title, A Curious Almanack,
in 1790. He joined with others in publishing an edition of William Billings' New-England Psalm-Singer in
1770.

References:

Foote, Henry W. "Musical Life in Boston in the Eight-
    eenth Century." Proceedings of the American Anti-
    quarian Society, 49 (1939).

Tebbel, John. A History of Book Publishing in the
    United States. Vol. 1. New York and London:
    Bowker, 1972.

Thomas, Isaiah. The History of Printing in America.
    Worcester, Mass.: Isaiah Thomas, Jr., 1810;
    2nd ed., revised, Albany, N.Y.: J. Munsell
    for the American Antiquarian Society, 1874;
    ed. Marcus A. McCorison, Barre, Mass.: Imprint
    Society, 1970.

John Fleeming

John Fleeming (dates unknown), printer, publisher, and bookseller, who had learned the printing trade in his native Scotland, arrived in Boston from Glasgow on 20 August 1764. Shortly after his arrival he entered into partnership with the already established printer and bookseller William M'Alpine, another Scot, in Marlborough Street. Fleeming left this partnership in 1765, and after a trip to Scotland to purchase materials and hire journeymen, he returned to Boston and entered partnership with John Mein, another fellow countryman. For a brief period they had a small shop in Wing's Lane, but in 1767 they moved to new quarters in Newbury Street opposite the White Horse Tavern. For a time the firm prospered, but late in 1769 Mein left the country to escape his enemies and to settle serious financial problems with his creditors in London. In 1770 an attachment was served on the shop, but a compromise allowed Fleeming to continue printing from the location under his own name. In 1771 he opened his own printing shop and bookstore in King Street opposite the south door of the Town House, but the business failed and the last imprint bearing his name appeared in 1772.

Major Authors: Oliver Goldsmith, Robert Sandeman, Laurence Sterne, Benjamin West.

William M'Alpine had been in business for about four years when Fleeming joined his firm in late 1764. The single work bearing their names in partnership for that year is Robert Sandeman's Some Thoughts on Christianity, one of the earliest works printed in America espousing the doctrines of John Glas. In 1765 nine titles appeared bearing their imprint, none of which is of any special historical interest.

Fleeming's association with John Mein is of much
greater significance. Their business started slowly
with only one title in 1765 and two in 1766, one of
which was Mein and Fleeming's Massachusetts Register.
In 1767, however, the shop became busier for they
printed the first edition of Benjamin West's (i.e.,
Bickerstaff's) Boston almanac, and on 21 December they
printed the first number of a weekly newspaper, the
Boston Chronicle, which set a new standard for typographical appearance. Perhaps most significant, that
year they printed the first American edition of Oliver
Goldsmith's popular novel, The Vicar of Wakefield.

The business continued to prosper in 1768, during
which they printed fifteen titles. The Chronicle continued to appear, and they again printed both their own
and West's almanacs. They also printed West's New-
England Almanack to be sold through Mein's London Book
Store on the north side of King Street and through
West's store in Providence. The firm made another
literary contribution by printing the first American
edition of Laurence Sterne's Sentimental Journey.

The year 1769 started well but ended disastrously.
With the number for 2 January, the Boston Chronicle began to appear twice a week, the first newspaper in New
England to do so. Throughout the partnership it is
clear that Mein was the more important partner. He
took the financial responsibility; he edited and published the Chronicle; and the titles that the firm
printed were sold almost exclusively through his shop.
Mein took a staunchly pro-British editorial position in
the Chronicle that led to his and Fleeming's being
mobbed in October 1769. In the scuffle Mein shot and
wounded a man and had to flee the country. He used the
occasion to sail to London to try to satisfy his creditors but was unsucessful.

For a time Fleeming attempted to carry on the
business alone, printing and publishing titles under his
own imprint. However, with the number for 25 June 1770,
the Chronicle ceased publication, and he moved his

business to new quarters in King Street where he sold
the titles he printed. His most ambitious project
appears in a proposal he published, probably in 1770,
to print by subscription the first complete Bible in
English in America. Nothing came of this scheme, and
after printing four titles in 1772, Fleeming closed
his business for good.

Although Fleeming's career was brief, he deserves
to be remembered as Mein's partner. They were the
first printers to use the distinct type face which was
probably cast in America by David Mitchelson, and they
printed the first American editions of Goldsmith's
Vicar of Wakefield and Sterne's Sentimental Journey.

C. R. Kropf

References:

Alden, John E. "John Mein, Publisher: An Essay in
    Bibliographic Detection." Papers of the Biblio-
    graphical Society of America, 36 (1942).

Bolton, Charles. "Circulating Libraries in Boston,
    1765-1865." Publications of the Colonial Society
    of Massachusetts, 11 (1906-1907).

Schlesinger, Arthur M. "Propaganda and the Boston
    Newspaper Press." Publications of the Colonial
    Society of Massachusetts, 32 (1933-1937).

John Fleet (see Thomas and John Fleet)

Thomas and John Fleet

Thomas (1685-1758) and John (1734-1806) Fleet, father and son, were among the most influential and successful printers in eighteenth-century America. Either singly or together, they printed the best newspaper in New England, the most popular children's books of the century, perhaps including Mother Goose, religious pamphlets and treatises by important divines, and a great number of diverse, nonreligious pamphlets and books. They are important not only because of the legendary quality of their work, but also because of the great variety of subjects their publications dealt with. They were among the first truly professional printers. Thomas Fleet established his shop in King Street in 1712. From 1713 to 1729 he announced his location as "Pudding-Lane, in King Street," and from 1729 to 1731 it was "Pudding-Lane, near the Town-House." Finally, the shop was "at the sign of the Heart and Crown, in Cornhill" from 1731 to 1764.

Major Authors: John Checkley, Benjamin Colman, Thomas Hutchinson, Cotton Mather, Increase Mather, Samuel Mather, Samuel Penhallow, Edward Wigglesworth, Michael Wigglesworth.

Publishers Served: John Draper, Samuel Gerrish, Daniel Henchman, Samuel Kneeland, Samuel Phillips.

Thomas Fleet arrived in Boston around 1712. He had left London, where he had been a printer, because his contemptuous opposition to the High Church faction brought him into conflict with the authorities. Almost immediately, he opened his own printing shop in King Street. Demonstrating the remarkable industry and business acumen that were to mark his entire life, Fleet seems quickly to have made his business successful.

162

Even before moving to the Pudding Lane address, from
where many successful publications would emanate, he
printed the fourth edition of John Hill's popular The
Young Secretary's Guide (1713). Hill's Guide includes
information on writing protocol, from deeds to proper
forms of business letters to punctuation and mechanics.
It even includes a short dictionary of difficult words.
The Guide had been popular in England, and Fleet wisely
printed an edition for the colonies with the expanded
title, Made suitable to the People of New-England.

The record of Fleet's publications before 1720
indicates his firm's quick growth and pronounced success. Between projects of large scale or with prominent
authors, Fleet apparently recognized the value of diver-
sification and high turnover. If, for example, he
printed a number of religious pamphlets, such as a hand-
ful of Benjamin Colman's sermons of 1716, he also broadened his readership--and therefore his market--with
nonreligious publications, such as Paul Dudley's Objections to the Bank of Credit Lately Projected at Boston
(1714). Further, Fleet became involved in publishing
the profitable almanacs. He printed Nathaniel Whitte-
more's long-running almanac from 1715 to 1721, and
Thomas Robie's almanac from 1714 to 1718 and again in
1721. In 1719, Fleet printed and published his own
Almanack for the Year 1720. Also during this time,
1714 to 1717, he entered into an informal partnership
with the printer Thomas Crump. Fleet's shrewd diver-
sification and prodigious output continued throughout
his life, and John, his son, junior partner, and heir,
was to rely on these same strategies.

Among Thomas Fleet's printing and/or publishing
ventures before 1720 may have been the first American
edition of Mother Goose's Melodies for Children (1719).
While Fleet's firm did publish more children's books
than any other firm of the century, recent historians of
publishing argue that Mother Goose was probably not
printed in America until later in the century. John Tebbel

163

contends that the 1719 American edition was a "persua-
sively charming legend" begun by Fleet's great-grandson,
John Fleet Eliot, in an 1860 newspaper article that
identifies Mother Goose as Thomas Fleet's mother-in-law,
Elizabeth Goose (or Vergoose or Vertigoose). Tebbel
reports that the first English edition did not appear
until 1729, and that American editions did not come
until later. Fleet's sons, John and Thomas, Jr., did,
however, print the first American edition of another
famous child's book, Tom Thumb's Folio, for Little
Giants (1780?).

At different times, under both Thomas and John
Fleet, the firm was successful in another way. Beginning in 1714 with the publication of Maternal Consolations, a sermon "On the Death of Mrs. Maria Mather the
Consort of the Eminent Dr. Increase Mather," the Fleets
printed a number of the Mathers' pamphlets and books.
Although the Mathers (Increase, Cotton, and Samuel)
used a variety of printers and publishers, they returned time and again to the Fleets. For example, in
1716 Thomas Fleet printed (for Daniel Henchman) Cotton
Mather's The Christian Cynick (popularly known then as
The Favours of the Saviour Asked For). Eleven years
later, in 1727, Mather turned once more to Thomas Fleet
to print (again for Henchman) his Agricola. Almost
fifty years later, in 1762, Samuel Mather's Of the Pastoral Care was printed by John and Thomas, Jr. The
record of the sons' printing is as impressive as their
father's; that the firm was handed down to equally
capable sons guaranteed its long influence.

One of the more controversial--and profitable--
events early in the firm's history involved a heated
exchange between the prominent Anglican clergyman John
Checkley and those opposing his belief in the Apostolic
origin of episcopacy. This protracted controversy-in-
print ultimately involved prominent theologians and
intellectuals such as Edward Wigglesworth. Throughout
the debate Thomas Fleet printed Checkley's pamphlets.
The squabble began with the publication of the seventh
edition of Charles Leslie's The Religion of Jesus

164

Christ the Only True Religion (1719), Checkley acting
as publisher. This "Apostolic Episcopacy" treatise
and another published in 1720 (also printed by Fleet),
Choice Dialogues between a Godly Minister and an Honest
Countryman Concerning Election and Predestination, written by Checkley but published without his name, brought
Checkley into legal conflict as well. As James Truslow
Adams notes in the Dictionary of American Biography, he
"alone of all Boston" was charged with "disaffection to
the king or government." Piqued by the charges,
Checkley refused to take the oath of allegiance ten-
dered him. After refusing a second time to take the
oaths, he was fined. The controversy did not end,
however.

After a trip to England in 1722 and an unsuccessful attempt to receive Holy Orders, Checkley commissioned Fleet to print his famous (or infamous) A Modest
Proof of the Order and Government Settled by Christ and
His Apostles (1723). Widely circulated, Modest Proof
was answered by Edward Wigglesworth, and a new round of
this pamphlet war began. After Checkley was sentenced
to jail for seditious libel and released, he returned
to Fleet to print A Defence of a Book Lately Re-Printed
at Boston (1724), a reply to Wigglesworth's Sober Remarks to a Modest Proof (1724), which attacked
Checkley's treatise. Continuing to benefit from
Checkley's controversial but undeniable popularity,
Fleet in 1725 printed a Checkley letter to Jonathan
Dickinson, one of the more vocal detractors of A Modest
Proof. Of greatest importance in this incident, as far
as Thomas Fleet is concerned, is that this canny printer
with a reputation for avoiding factional religious and
political controversy quickly and accurately perceived
the professional benefits of becoming involved in
Checkley's pamphlet war.

Another impressive accomplishment, perhaps the
Fleets' greatest, was the long and distinguished print-
ing and publishing of a newspaper. Indeed, Isaiah
Thomas devotes most of his lengthy entry on Thomas
Fleet to it. Thomas unequivocally calls Fleet's

165

newspaper "the best paper at that time published in New England," and John C. Oswald argues that it was the first "real" newspaper in New England. In 1733 Fleet purchased the Weekly Rehearsal from Jeremiah Gridley, and the paper flourished instantly under Fleet's guidance. In 1735 Fleet, for two years now at his famous Cornhill "Heart and Crown" location, changed his paper's name to the Boston Evening-Post.

This newspaper bore the professional mark of all the Fleets' undertakings. First Thomas, and later John (and to some extent, Thomas, Jr.), tried to broaden the scope and purpose of the colonial newspaper. While Thomas included the usual commentary that filled many early newspapers, he also set standards for the calm, rational, and objective reporting of what modern editors call hard news. In February 1744, for example, Fleet rebelled against superstition by treating the appearance of a comet as an event of interest rather than as a portent of apocalyptic significance. When his assessment of the comet did take on a speculative tone, it remained unlike the fearful musings of others, who regarded the comet as a sign of divine displeasure. Fleet once described the comet as "the most profitable Itinerant Preacher and friendly New Light that has yet appeared among us."

Another example of Fleet's journalistic polish was an attack in the Evening-Post on the charismatic English preacher George Whitefield. Few dared to attack Whitefield, whose preaching tours elicited a tremendous emotional response from hordes of colonists. Fleet complained about Whitefield and the fervor he provoked (as did the fiery John Checkley), and thus established a professional if not controversial standard for his newspaper. Indeed, Fleet's plain-spoken manner and independence got him into trouble with civil authorities in March 1741, when a somewhat political paragraph in the Evening-Post was construed by the governor and council as casting, to quote Thomas, "a scandalous and libellous Reflection upon his Majesty's Administration."

166

Fleet also strove during the Evening-Post's early years to make it professional by apparently attempting to free it--and by implication, other newspapers--from the limitations of the newspaper-bookseller system. That is, up to this time, newspapers had been printed and published for one bookseller. By expanding circulation and sales, all concerned would profit, readers by greater accessibility, printers and publishers by greater sales. After Fleet's death, the Evening-Post continued, successfully, under his capable son, until the outbreak of the War of Independence. Publication of this preeminent newspaper was not resumed after the Revolution.

The influence of the Fleets, however, surpasses even the accomplishments of the Evening-Post. In the 1750s, the decade of Thomas Fleet's death and the sons' inheriting the firm, the Fleets continued printing pamphlets and books of renown. At the beginning of the decade, Thomas was the printer of the American edition of Joseph Addison's popular play Cato (1750), a political allegory successful on the London stage. The next year, Fleet printed a new edition of the popular New-England Primer Enlarged; five years after his death, John and Thomas, Jr., printed yet another edition of the primer (1763). It was also in 1751 that the Fleet firm printed Michael Wigglesworth's long poem, The Day of Doom. This seventh edition is noteworthy because it contains a character reference to Wigglesworth by Cotton Mather. In two years, Thomas Fleet printed three major works; of equal historical importance, perhaps, is that each of the publications is from a different discipline. The Fleet firm's strength continued to be its versatility and obvious professionalism.

The importance of the Fleets remained undiminished after Thomas's death. John, and to a lesser extent, Thomas, Jr., continued to print a variety of works. John was successful, as was his father, in attracting popular and/or influential authors. The Westminster Assembly of Divines commissioned the Fleets

167

to print The Shorter Catechism in 1759, and in the same
year the firm became involved in another venture important in printing history. As John Tebbel notes, the
Fleets "formed a connexion" with John Draper, John
Green and his partner, Joseph Russell, and the firm
of Benjamin Edes and John Gill. This conglomerate of
printers, publishers, and booksellers joined forces to
publish an enlarged edition of the ever-popular Ames
almanac. Always at the forefront of professional devel-
opments, the Fleets wisely took part in one of the first
and most carefully executed joint publishing ventures.
They, as well as the others involved, apparently recognized the benefits of acting as a cohesive group. Better planning and more influence in decision making were
possible, and more control over all phases of the project was assured the partners. The joint printing, publishing, and selling of the Ames almanac set a precedent
for the printing industry. That the Fleets were involved was not coincidental.

The 1760s found the Fleets equally successful.
Many of their notable publications in this decade were
religious in nature. In 1760, for example, they pub-
lished several of Jonathan Mayhew's sermons, and in
1762, Samuel Mather's Of the Pastoral Care. One of
Nathaniel Rogers's treatises the Fleets printed, The
Office of Gospel Ministers, in Preaching the Word of
God (1763), includes a commentary on the subject by
Michael Wigglesworth. In that year the Fleets also
printed a collection of lectures given at Harvard by
Wigglesworth's influential son, Edward. Edward
Wigglesworth, for whom the Fleets printed (with
Richard and Samuel Draper) The Doctrine of Reprobation
Briefly Considered (1763), became the first Hollis
Professor of Divinity at Harvard. He was also highly
regarded throughout New England as both author and
speaker. The Fleets' association with Rogers and
Wigglesworth is further testimony to their business
acumen and professional influence.

To these successful religious publications, the
Fleets added another accomplishment to their firm's

168

record with the 1764 printing of Thomas Hutchinson's
The History of the Colony of Massachusetts-Bay. Just
as their father had done well in printing (for Samuel
Gerrish) Samuel Penhallow's The History of the Wars of
New-England (1726), John and Thomas accurately gauged
the appeal of Hutchinson's enduring History. Hutchinson, lieutenant governor and later governor of Massachusetts, scored an immediate success with his book.
It was quickly published in London, and was republished
throughout the nineteenth century. Although dated, it
is still praised by modern historians for its thorough-
ness and accuracy. The printing of this book remains
one of the Fleets' most admirable achievements.

Although the firm continued to print a great number and variety of publications throughout the 1760s,
it collapsed with the outbreak of the Revolution. Although Tom Thumb's Folio, for Little Giants, probably
printed in 1780, bears the imprint of Thomas and John
Fleet, the postwar firm bore little resemblance to the
prewar business. Very little is known about it.

Thomas and John Fleet were among the most important printers of their time. Because the son, John,
carried on the business after his father's death, the
firm's influence spanned the greater part of the eighteenth century. Both of the Fleets stood at the forefront of the printing trade. Their shrewd insistence
on printing not only well but also diversely encouraged
the development of printing from that of a trade too
often tied to religious pamphleteering to that of a
large, profitable profession. Further, their frequent
ventures into the publishing and bookselling sides of
the industry render inaccurate any description of them
as mere printers. Certainly, their Boston Evening-Post,
the finest newspaper of its time, indicates Thomas and
John Fleet's astuteness as businessmen and their talent
as journalists. Clyde A. Duniway, for example, praises
Thomas Fleet as "the most enterprising journalist in
Boston during his long career." The Fleets' record as
printers is impressive (Evans credits each with more
than 250 publications), but their professionalism,

innovativeness, and expertise in all aspects of the
industry indicate their larger significance.

David W. Pitre

References:

Duniway, Clyde A. The Development of Freedom of
    the Press in Massachusetts. New York and London:
    Longmans, Green, 1906.

Oswald, John C. Printing in the Americas. Chicago
    and New York: Gregg, 1937; reprint edition,
    New York: Hacker Art Books, 1968.

Tebbel, John. A History of Book Publishing in the
    United States. Vol. 1. New York and London:
    Bowker, 1972.

Thomas, Isaiah. The History of Printing in America.
    Worcester, Mass.: Isaiah Thomas, Jr., 1810;
    2nd ed., revised, Albany, N.Y.: J. Munsell
    for the American Antiquarian Society, 1874;
    ed. Marcus A. McCorison, Barre, Mass.: Imprint
    Society, 1970.

Thomas Fleet, Jr.

Thomas Fleet, Jr. (1732-1797) was the son of Thomas
Fleet and brother to John Fleet. After their father's
death in 1758, the brothers conducted the T. and J.
Fleet business "at the sign of the Heart and Crown, in
Cornhill." They later announced their shop "at the
Bible and Heart." As publishers of their father's
Boston Evening-Post until 1775, they continued the
political impartiality that had been one of that news-
paper's most notable characteristics. The most signif-
icant separate title the brothers published is probably
Thomas Hutchinson's The History of the Colony of
Massachusetts-Bay (1764). Every known imprint bearing
the name of Thomas Fleet, Jr. also has John's.

Thomas Fleet, III

Thomas Fleet, III (1768-1827), a printer, was the son
of John Fleet. From 1793 to 1797 he printed alone as
Thomas Fleet, Jr., and from 1797 to 1803 he joined with
his father as John and Thomas Fleet. After his father's
retirement in 1803, Thomas continued printing by himself until 1808. Approximately seventy-five titles
bear Fleet's name in an imprint.

171

John West Folsom

John West Folsom (1758-1825), was a printer, publisher, and bookseller. He began his printing career in 1778 in partnership with Edward Draper; at least eighteen works bear their joint imprint, including a newspaper, the Independent Ledger, and American Advertiser. Their partnership ended in 1783, and Folsom continued in business alone until 1801, printing almost 100 works. He appears to have been the publisher of more than half the material he printed. Folsom's first printing shop was located "at the corner of Winter-Street" until 1785, when he moved to "the corner of Ann-Street, near the Conduit." From 1787 until 1801 his business was housed at "number 30 Union Street."

Major Authors: Hannah Adams, Isaac Backus, Abraham Weatherwise, Noah Webster, Benjamin West.

Publishers Served: Benjamin Larkin, Ebenezer Larkin, David West.

The first eight years of Folsom's career, from 1778 until 1786, appear to have been devoted largely to publishing the weekly Independent Ledger, and American Advertiser. When his partnership with co-publisher Edward Draper ended in 1783, Folsom continued to publish the newspaper alone for three years. A tax placed upon newspaper advertising was one of the major reasons he ceased publishing it in October 1786, and it was opposition to this tax that led to the earliest known example of cooperation among American printers. In the 27 July 1786 number of Peter Edes's Exchange Advertiser appears a notice signed by twelve Boston printers, including Folsom, in which they state their intention to begin printing their newspapers on a smaller scale at increased prices. It is not known

172

to what extent these printers were organized, or whether they cooperated only in the event of emergency. The tax was eventually repealed in 1788, but not before several newspapers in Massachusetts, including Folsom's, discontinued publication or changed to a magazine format.

Folsom's attention to the newspaper did not prevent his printing other works during this period, including several editions of William Billings's popular Singing Master's Assistant, or Key to Practical Music, published by Folsom and Draper beginning in 1778. Another popular work was A Narrative of Colonel Ethan Allen's Captivity (1779), which describes the author's experiences as a prisoner of the British during the three years after his capture in 1775. Revolutionary-era Americans were fascinated by this genre of prison literature, descriptive of the sufferings of those soldiers who had been captured by the enemy, and Allen's vituperative account was the most celebrated narrative of the type, going through fourteen editions before 1850. It was first published in Philadelphia in 1779, so Folsom's edition is an early one.

A more serious work is Isaac Backus's Policy, as Well as Honesty, Forbids the Use of Secular Force in Religious Affairs (1779). An itinerant Baptist preacher, Backus was also a celebrated champion of religious liberty who expressed dissatisfaction with the close association between church and state in Massachusetts. This pamphlet was written in opposition to a proposed article of the state constitution that would continue the Congregational Church as the established church of the state. Folsom also appears to have done some printing for the state of Massachusetts in 1780, 1782, and 1785, with the phrase "Printers to the Commonwealth of Massachusetts" appearing after the names Draper and Folsom in the 1782 imprint.

Most ambitious printers sought to make their establishments useful and well known to the community they served by publishing an annual almanac. Folsom

173

printed numerous almanacs, beginning in 1778 with Daniel
George's Almanack for . . . 1779, followed by the 1780
Bickerstaff's Boston Almanack. From 1784 until 1797 he
published at least one almanac annually, and occasion-
ally printed several different ones in the same year.
In 1788 he printed two editions of his own Folsom's
New Pocket Almanac.

The almanac of this period served a multitude of
purposes: calendar, weather prognosticator, textbook,
doctor, atlas and guidebook, and agricultural advisor.
It often contained scientific articles, tables of mea-
surement, essays by such literati as Pope and Dryden,
and included riddles, anecdotes, verse, and illustrations. The blank pages that were generally included
usually meant that it would do double service as a
diary and memorandum book. All of these characteristics made the almanac a familiar and popular handbook
for the entire family, so popular in fact that, in
quantity, almanacs published in the seventeenth and
eighteenth centuries outnumbered all other published
works combined, including religious works. The influence that the printer had upon the almanac was considerable, for while the author might provide the
scientific calculations to be included, it was generally the printer who provided the entertaining
fillers of essays, topical items, verse, and stories.
In no other form of American literature was his influence so pronounced in the final product.

Folsom printed two almanacs by the prolific
Benjamin West, who published numerous almanacs under
the pseudonym Isaac Bickerstaff. A Bickerstaff's
Boston Almanack was published for almost every year
from 1786 until 1793; three of these--for 1780, 1785,
and 1786--were printed by Folsom. The Bickerstaff
pseudonym became so popular and so widely used that
it is often difficult to distinguish almanacs done by
West from those done by authors who wished to capitalize on his success, a situation that annoyed him considerably. West frequently quarreled with his printers,

and appears to have done so with Folsom, for in 1785, the same year that Folsom printed West's 1786 almanac, West also published another Bickerstaff almanac by a different printer, with the word genuine inserted in the title.

Another popular series was Weatherwise's Town and Country Almanack; Folsom printed an edition for 1787. Who Abraham Weatherwise actually was, or how many people used the name, is not clear, but it was one of the most popular pseudonyms used in almanac publishing. Other almanacs printed by Folsom include one by Samuel Bullard for 1788, as well as those by Amos Pope for each year from 1792 to 1797.

Boston flourished as the center for children's book publishing in the eighteenth century, and some of the titles Folsom printed reflect the changes that occurred in this genre. Previously, American children's literature had placed great emphasis on moral teaching and very little emphasis on entertainment; it often reiterated the Puritan theme that an early death was a welcome escape for the righteous to the glories of heaven. At the same time, however, entertaining books for children were being produced in England; their importation and growing popularity finally forced American publishers to begin producing them in the eighteenth century. Publishers did not completely abandon the moralizing of earlier works for children, but they did begin to print a greater number of secular entertainment titles.

Folsom's interest in children's books came late in his career. His early efforts in this field reflected the continued emphasis on improvement of the youthful reader, as may be seen in such works as Principles of Politeness, and of Knowing the World (1791) by Philip Stanhope, the fourth Earl of Chesterfield, and in Noah Webster's popular volume of essays, The Prompter: Or a Commentary on Common Sayings and Subjects (1794). Folsom also printed the popular behavior book, A Father's Legacy to His Daughters (1791)

175

by John Gregory. Gregory, an eminent Scottish physician, prepared the work to advise his motherless daughters, and it was frequently reprinted into the middle of the nineteenth century.

Folsom printed most of his children's books in 1798. Unlike previous books of the type that he had printed, these 1798 titles emphasize entertainment. As did so many of his fellow printers and publishers, Folsom unabashedly reprinted the successes of London's Newbery publishing family, who were among the foremost publishers of children's literature in England. These English works were frequently modified by American printers to conform to the tastes of the American audience. Of the thirteen children's titles Folsom published in 1798, at least eight were reprints of Newbery titles, including The History of Tommy Titmouse, possibly Rural Felicity, or the History of Tommy and Sally, and possibly The History of Tommy Gingerbread, Who Lived upon Learning (a title slightly modified from Newbery's original, The History of Giles Gingerbread, a Little Boy Who Lived upon Learning).

While most of Folsom's energy was devoted to his newspaper, almanacs, and children's books, he did print some other items of interest, including the second edition of A View of Religions in Two Parts (1791) by Hannah Adams, an early American professional woman author. In 1794 he printed an edition of Abraham Swan's British Architect which, upon its first publication in Philadelphia in 1775, had been the first book about architecture published in America. Folsom's edition of this work has some significance since only thirteen editions of architectural books, comprising nine different works, were printed in America in the eighteenth century. Folsom may have printed an edition of Noah Webster's American Spelling Book in 1788, but no copy is known; in a letter written in August 1788, Webster mentions that Folsom has begun the spelling book.

|John West Folsom

During his twenty-three-year career John West Folsom published a newspaper, printed a considerable number of almanacs, and, in the final years, printed books for children. While very few of the individual titles he printed are of outstanding significance, taken as a whole his work is a prime example of American printing interests after the War of Independence.

Gary R. Treadway

References:

Stowell, Marion B. Early American Almanacs: The Colonial Weekday Bible. New York: Burt Franklin, 1977.

Tebbel, John. A History of Book Publishing in the United States. Vol. 1. New York and London: Bowker, 1972.

Hopestill Foster

Hopestill Foster (b. 1708) published fewer than thirty titles between 1730 and 1741 at his shop "in Cornhill." Most of his titles are religious. He published five works by Benjamin Colman, four by William Cooper, and three by John Bunyan, including a 1740 edition of Pilgrim's Progress. He also published Mather Byles's Affections on Things Above (1740).

177

John Foster

John Foster (1648-1681), printer, publisher, and almanac compiler, was the first printer in Boston, engraver of the first printed American woodcut, publisher of the first American woman author, and printer of the first medical tract in America. He printed over fifty books and broadsides, thus accounting for almost forty percent of all recorded imprints for the period from 1675 to 1681, the time he was active at his shop "over against the Sign of the Dove" in Boston.

Major Authors: Anne Bradstreet, John Eliot, William Hubbard, Increase Mather, Thomas Thacher, Samuel Willard, Roger Williams.

Publishers Served: William Avery, John Griffin, Henry Phillips, Samuel Phillips, Edmund Ranger, John Ratcliff, John Usher.

Foster was born in Dorchester, Massachusetts, in 1648. Coming from a family of some standing, he attended Harvard College. After graduating in 1667 Foster stayed on at Harvard, studying and probably tutoring younger students, until 1669, when he returned to Dorchester to accept a position as schoolmaster. From 1669 until the end of 1674 Foster's involvement in printing was confined to overseeing the printing of his engravings and, in 1674, his first almanac, which was published in Cambridge the next year. In 1674 Marmaduke Johnson, the first master printer in America, obtained a license to print in Boston and set up a shop there, but died before he could begin business. Foster, probably with the encouragement of Increase Mather, a newly appointed licenser of the press and the son of Foster's former Dorchester minister, Richard Mather, bought Johnson's

equipment and early in 1675 printed Increase Mather's
The Wicked Man's Portion, the first book printed in
Boston.

Foster was not trained as a printer, but with
friends such as Increase Mather, with skills as an
engraver and writer, and with a literary eye, his
press soon became both productive and important. It
was Foster who printed the first American collection
of Anne Bradstreet's poetry; that is all the more noteworthy because Bradstreet was a woman who wrote at a
time when women did not engage publicly in literature
or the arts. Foster's eye apparently extended to history as well, for he printed Increase Mather's Brief
History of the War with the Indians (1676) and William
Hubbard's Narrative of the Troubles with the Indians
(1677), both important accounts of King Philip's War,
the major confrontation between New England colonials
and the native population in the seventeenth century.
Science, too, concerned Foster. In addition to printing Thomas Thacher's Brief Rule . . . in the Small
Pocks or Measels in 1677, the first medical tract
printed in America, Foster also wrote in his own almanac for 1681 an essay on comets supporting the
Copernican system of celestial motion, a far from
universal notion in the third quarter of the seventeenth century.

Foster's known publishing activities extend only
to his almanacs. While in Boston, he compiled, printed,
and published one for each of the years 1676, 1678,
1679, 1680, and 1681, teaming up with Henry Phillips,
John Usher, and Samuel Phillips as co-publishers and
sellers for three of the five years. As author, printer,
and publisher, Foster was unique in the seventeenth-
century printing trade, and with respect to almanacs
this triple role would not be played again successfully
until the eighteenth century by Benjamin Franklin.
Foster's role in the publication of Hubbard's Narrative
of the Troubles with the Indians, however, went beyond
merely printing, because he engraved for it the first
map printed in the colonies. Foster's engravings

179

deserve note. His earliest extant engraving, a woodcut
portrait of Richard Mather, which appeared in Increase
Mather's Life and Death of . . . Richard Mather (1670),
was the first engraving published in America. Foster
also engraved the official seal of Massachusetts. It
first appeared in the 1672 edition of printed laws.
Foster later included it in his own publication of
Increase Mather's Brief History of the War with the
Indians.

Foster died in 1681 at the age of thirty-three.
His career was short but important, not only for the
work he printed--Bradstreet's Several Poems, Hubbard's
Narrative, and Thacher's Brief Rule--but for the various roles he played. While the printing trade became
more specialized in the eighteenth century, tradesmen
such as Benjamin Franklin, who, like Foster, combined
writing, printing, and publishing in ventures like
Poor Richard's Almanac, had an advantage over those
who did not.

Charles Wetherell

John Foster

References:

Green, Samuel A. John Foster: The Earliest American
Engraver and the First Boston Printer. Boston:
Massachusetts Historical Society, 1909.

Littlefield, George E. Early Boston Booksellers: 1642-
1711. Boston: Club of Odd Volumes, 1900; reprint
edition, New York: Burt Franklin, 1969.

Littlefield, George E. The Early Massachusetts Press:
1638-1711. Boston: Club of Odd Volumes, 1907;
reprint edition, New York: Burt Franklin, 1969.

Daniel Fowle

Daniel Fowle (1715-1787) was an author, bookseller, and one of Boston's most prolific printers and publishers. With Gamaliel Rogers as his partner, he opened his first shop in 1740 in Queen Street, "over against the South-East-Corner of the Town House." The firm of Rogers and Fowle published the short-lived Boston Weekly Magazine and, later, the American Magazine and Historical Chronicle, the first American magazine to last more than six months. In 1748 they began publishing a newspaper, the Independent Advertiser, which survived until the partnership ended in 1750. Although no copy is known to be extant, it is likely that in 1749 they printed the first English language New Testament in America. Fowle opened a bookstore in 1753 "in Ann Street, Facing the Town-Dock," and a little later moved his operation there, closing the Queen Street shop. He wrote, or had ghost written, A Total Eclipse of Liberty (1755), and, in the following year, An Appendix to the Late Total Eclipse of Liberty, both of which protest his wrongful imprisonment on suspicion of printing The Monster of Monsters, an allegorical satire attacking a recently imposed excise tax on wine and liquor. After a brief partnership with his brother Zechariah in July 1756, Daniel moved his shop to Portsmouth, where he became the first printer in that colony and the publisher of its first newspaper, the New-Hampshire Gazette, the longest running paper in American history.

Major Authors: Mather Byles, Benjamin Colman, William Douglass, Jonathan Edwards, John Locke, George Whitefield.

Publishers Served: Joshua Blanchard, Joseph Edwards, Benjamin Eliot, Samuel Eliot, Daniel Henchman, Kneeland and Green, Walter McAlpine.

181

Daniel Fowle

Fowle was born in Charlestown, Massachusetts, in October 1715, and was baptized on 16 October. His parents, John and Mary (Barrell), died in 1734, and he was placed under the guardianship of Samuel Trumbull. In approximately the same year Fowle was apprenticed to Samuel Kneeland, in whose shop he remained until he left to open his own printing house with Gamaliel Rogers and with his brother John, who acted as a silent partner. In 1751 he married Lydia Hall, who died childless a few years before him. The firm of Rogers and Fowle quickly became a business of some consequence, releasing approximately 200 imprints during the ten-year partnership. They were famed for the high quality of their work and particularly for their ink, which they manufactured themselves, an unusual practice in an age when most printing ink was imported and the laborious, sometimes hazardous process of ink making was reserved for emergencies.

Among the more important titles printed by Rogers and Fowle were the first printing of a portion of Thomas Shepard's journal (in Three Valuable Pieces, 1747); the second edition of Cotton Mather's Signatus (1748); the New-England Primer Enlarged (1746); Mather Byles's Poems. The Conflagration (1755); William Douglass's A Summary, Historical and Political, of the First Planting, Progressive Improvements, and Present State of the British Settlements in North-America (1749-1752); and three works by Jonathan Edwards: The True Excellency of a Minister of the Gospel (1744), True Saints, When Absent from the Body, Are Present with the Lord (1747), and A Strong Rod Broken and Withered (1748). They may also have surreptitiously printed, for Daniel Henchman, the first English language New Testament in America. Earlier, Bibles had been printed in other languages-- Eliot's Algonquian translation, for example, had appeared in 1663 and Christopher Sower's German translation in 1743--but the printing of English Bibles had been restricted by the Crown to a few authorized British printers, and no English Bible was printed in this country until the war cut off the supply. No copy of

the Rogers and Fowle New Testament is known to survive,
and its publication date of 1749 is conjectural.

With the exception of one false start, the firm's
ventures into serial publications were quite successful.
On 2 March 1743, they began publishing the Boston Weekly
Magazine, but the seven pages of extracts from English
magazines and one page of local news were met with in-
difference on the part of the Boston public, and it
folded after three numbers. More to the public's lik-
ing, however, was the fifty-page American Magazine and
Historical Chronicle, begun in September of the same
year and lasting until the December 1746 number. It
was edited by Jeremiah Gridley, a lawyer whose interest
in politics is reflected in the magazine's extensive
coverage of statecraft, although the politics were almost exclusively English and the word American in the
title is a misnomer. On 4 January 1748 Rogers and
Fowle started publishing the Independent Advertiser.
This weekly newspaper was continued until 5 December
1749 when it ceased as a result of the partnership
breaking up. Although it was printed by Fowle and
his partner, the paper was largely the child of Samuel
Adams, who used it to denounce the meddling of the
British government in the affairs of Massachusetts and
especially to attack William Shirley, the royal
governor.

From 1750 to 1756 Fowle operated the business
alone, and for some unknown reason his number of yearly
imprints decreased significantly, dropping from twenty-
five in 1750 to ten in 1751 and four in 1752. In 1753
Fowle opened a bookstore and later in the same year
moved his shop there. He continued to act as publisher
as well as printer, but his Ann Street publications
were few and apparently intended only to stock his
shelves. If this period in Fowle's life saw fewer imprints, it was also the time when he became a leading
if reluctant figure in the struggle to establish the
principle of freedom of the press. Fowle had never
been loathe to criticize the government by printing
titles attacking its policies, and he had already

printed a number of pseudonymous works condemning the
monetary policies of the Massachusetts government. In
1750, for example, he published and printed Vincent
Centinel's Massachusetts in Agony, lamenting the demise
of old tenor currency, and although no name appears on
the imprint, he is usually credited with the printing
of the Appendix to Massachusetts in Agony by Cornelius
Agrippa (1751). In 1748 he had, with Rogers, printed
and sold Mylo Freeman's A Word in Season to All True
Lovers of Their Liberty and Country, which is also concerned with the paper money controversy. Still earlier
in his career, Fowle, again with Rogers, had printed
for the first time in America John Locke's Letter Concerning Toleration (1743) at the behest of a group of
Yale seniors who, caught up in the religious revival
of the Great Awakening, were protesting the refusal of
President Clap to allow them to participate in nonconformist religious ceremonies.

Fowle was not penalized or reprimanded for any of
these liberties, but he was jailed briefly in 1754 as a
suspect in the printing of The Monster of Monsters, a
satire against an excise tax on wine and liquor and the
Massachusetts legislators who had authorized it. Government censorship of the press was almost nonexistent
by the middle of the eighteenth century, but on occasion the governor or the legislative body found it
convenient to try to reassert their control, usually
if the attack was too close to be comfortable or if it
made their persons seem too ridiculous to tolerate.
Such a case was The Monster of Monsters. It has been
variously attributed to Samuel Waterhouse, Benjamin
Church, and Fowle's younger brother, Zechariah, and
even though the most likely candidate is Zechariah,
the question remains unresolved. Fowle was only
alleged to have been the printer, but the authorities
ordered him arrested and a copy or copies burned by
the town hangman. Fowle was hustled away from his
dinner table, examined by a hostile group of men, and
held incommunicado for six days in the squalid city
jail. He was released with only a formal reprimand,
but his treatment deeply embittered him, and he sued

the province for £1,000 for illegal imprisonment. The
suit came to naught, and he was compelled to pay the
court costs, but in 1765, after he had moved to Portsmouth, he was awarded a refund of the court costs and,
eleven years later, was given £ 20 by the general court
for his suffering.

In 1755, still smarting from having been treated
like a criminal and angered by the strain borne by his
wife during his imprisonment, Fowle wrote, or had ghost
written, and published A Total Eclipse of Liberty to
make public the arbitrary and high-handed treatment he
received from the Massachusetts authorities. One year
later he published his sequel, An Appendix to the Late
Total Eclipse of Liberty, which similarly attacks governmental abuse of its power. As a result of imprisonment, Fowle was more than willing to listen to a group
of prominent New Hampshire citizens who approached him
about relocating to Portsmouth and becoming that province's first printer. Fowle left Boston in July 1756
and set up his press in August, releasing his first
imprint, a now lost prospectus for the New-Hampshire
Gazette, in the same month.

Fowle's importance as a printer and publisher
during his career in Boston is twofold: as a partner
in Rogers and Fowle he was a member of one of the best,
largest, and most prolific printing houses in Massachusetts, and, even more important, his unwilling clash
with the government of Massachusetts helped define the
principle of freedom of the press. It also led to two
angry but eloquent books on the injustices that can be
perpetrated by those in power if the rights of the individual are not respected, and neither the books nor the
principle were forgotten in the next two decades when
the issue became even more pronounced in the colonies.

James P. O'Donnell

|Daniel Fowle

References:

Duniway, Clyde A. The Development of Freedom of the
    Press in Massachusetts. New York: Longmans,
    Green, 1906.

Kidder, Robert W. "The Contribution of Daniel Fowle
    to New Hampshire Printing, 1756-1787." Ph.D.
    dissertation, University of Illinois, 1960.

Kobre, Sidney. The Development of the Colonial News-
    paper. Pittsburgh: Colonial Press, 1944.

Lydernberg, Harry M. "The Problem of the Pre-1776
    American Bible." Papers of the Bibliographical
    Society of America, 48 (1954).

Schlesinger, Arthur M. Prelude to Independence: The
    Newspaper War on Britain 1764-1776. New York:
    Knopf, 1958.

186

Zechariah Fowle

Zechariah Fowle (1724-1776), printer and bookseller, is remembered chiefly as the Dickensian master (and later partner) of young Isaiah Thomas, the ne'er-do-well brother of Daniel Fowle, and the sometime partner of Benjamin Mecom and Samuel Draper. Fowle's publications number approximately eighty, most of which are popular ballads, children's books, and small pamphlets. In 1757 Fowle and Mecom printed a large edition of the New-England Primer; in 1770 Fowle and Thomas founded the Massachusetts Spy, although Fowle's erstwhile apprentice bought him out after three months. In his nineteen years as a Boston printer, Fowle conducted business alternately alone and with partners. From 1751 to 1754 his printing office was in Back Street; from 1755 to 1756 he was located in Middle Street, "below the Mill-Bridge." Fowle was in partnership with his brother Daniel for part of 1756 and then with Mecom for part of 1757; when Mecom left, Fowle took on Samuel Draper "opposite the Lion and Bell in Marlborough-Street," until Draper left in 1762, at which time Fowle moved to a shop "opposite the Founder's Arms." He returned to Back Street in 1763, until his partnership with Thomas was set up in Salem Street in 1770. After their relocation in Union Street, the partnership was quickly dissolved, and Fowle returned to Back Street, "near the Mill-Bridge," until he quit the business in 1775.

Major Authors: Mather Byles, Robert Dodsley, Ebenezer and Ralph Erskine.

Immortalized in the Dictionary of American Biography as "an ignorant and shiftless printer," Fowle relied heavily upon the skills of apprentices and partners to achieve his modest success. Born at Charlestown,

187

Massachusetts, of respectable parents, Fowle learned
the printing trade from his brother, Daniel, who was
at that time in partnership with Gamaliel Rogers.
Zechariah later recounted to his own apprentice,
Isaiah Thomas, that he had worked at the press when
Rogers and Fowle clandestinely printed a New Testament
for Daniel Henchman and other booksellers. It is upon
this evidence that Thomas claims the publication of the
Baskett Bible, purportedly the first printed in this
country. When Rogers and Fowle dissolved their partnership, the printing of Pomfret's Poems was completed
by Zechariah Fowle. Published in 1751, this was the
first book to bear the name of Z. Fowle as printer.

Fowle opened his own modest printing house in
Middle Street, near Cross Street, and began printing
and selling the ballads and chapbooks that were to be
the mainstay of his career. His shop consisted of one
wooden handpress and a few worn fonts of type. In his
first near-brush with notoriety, Fowle apparently agreed
to print anonymously The Monster of Monsters (1754, by
"Thomas Thumb, Esq."), a satirical attack upon the general court and the new excise tax; he persuaded his
brother (and Daniel's employees) to help with the job.
Suspicion fell on Daniel, who was accused of printing
the pamphlet and was subsequently arrested and imprisoned. Zechariah was excused from prosecution when his
fear of arrest induced a certifiably dangerous fit of
the cholic. The brothers evidently quickly resumed a
working relationship when Daniel was released from
prison, for in 1755, many works (including Mather
Byles's Poems. The Conflagration) were "printed and
sold by D. Fowle, in Ann-Street and by Z. Fowle, in
Middlestreet." Soon, however, Daniel moved to Portsmouth, New Hampshire, and Zechariah moved to his
brother's old quarters in Ann Street.

In 1756 Fowle took on six-year-old Isaiah Thomas
as apprentice, and thus began the long, strange relationship between the older ne'er-do-well and the young
genius. When Thomas later recorded the story of his
apprenticeship in his History, he characterized Fowle

as "an indifferent hand at the press, and much worse at
the case." Fowle used the boy as a servant and ne-
glected to teach him the trade; Thomas learned instead
from Fowle's occasional partners, and, by the age of
twelve, was regarded as more competent than his master.
At Fowle's shop, now in Middle Street, the young apprentice took over increasing responsibility as his skills
grew.

After his brother Daniel, the next of Fowle's
skilled partners was Benjamin Mecom, nephew of and
former apprentice to Benjamin Franklin. Mecom, having
just arrived from Antigua in the West Indies, briefly
joined Fowle in 1757, while awaiting the delivery of
his own press and types to Boston. Thomas recounts
that Fowle had asked Mecom's help in printing a new
edition of the New-England Primer; Mecom consented,
"on condition that he might print a certain number for
himself. . . . Fowle had no help but myself, then a
lad in my eighth year. The impression consisted of
ten thousand copies." Mecom left soon thereafter to
open his own printing house in Cornhill, and Fowle
took on Samuel Draper, a trained printer, in a partnership that lasted from late 1757 to 1762.

The success of this second partnership was due
largely to Draper's skill and ambition. Fowle supplied
the capital, and Draper and Thomas performed most of
the work. Fowle and Draper, located at "the Printing-
Office opposite the Lion and Bell, in Marlborough-
Street," printed Robert Dodsley's Chronicle of the
Kings of England (1759) and a variety of sermons and
children's books, including Ebenezer and Ralph Erskine's
Sermons on Sacramental Occasions (1761) and A New Gift
for Children: Containing Delightful and Entertaining
Stories (1762).

When Draper broke up the partnership in 1762,
Fowle and his apprentice returned to smaller quarters
in Back Street, where they struggled along by printing
ballads and other popular fare. That year Fowle reprinted The New Book of Knowledge, which included

woodcuts by Isaiah Thomas, then thirteen years old.
Taught much by Draper, Thomas kept his master's business going. As John Tebbel states, Thomas, "by the
time he was sixteen . . . was for all practical purposes operating Fowle's printshop on his own." Fowle,
pleading poor health, stayed out of his own shop as
much as possible.

Frustrated by his master's indolence, Thomas
broke his indenture in September 1765. Fowle continued
printing alone. When Thomas returned after seven months
of working in other places, Fowle--having noted Thomas's
success in reviving the Portsmouth Mercury--renewed
their working relationship. The ties between these two
irritable men were further complicated in 1769, when
the widower Fowle married Thomas's widowed mother,
Rebecca Bass Thomas.

After another brief absence, Thomas returned once
again, determined to start a popular newspaper, the
Massachusetts Spy. Fowle shrewdly took Thomas as a
partner, and they set up shop in Salem Street, where
the sample edition of the Spy was published on 17 July
1770. Soon thereafter they relocated in Union Street
and began regular publication of the newspaper on 7
August 1770. On 23 October of that year, Zechariah
Fowle sold out to his erstwhile apprentice, who later
made the Spy the best-selling newspaper in New England.

Fowle once again returned to Back Street, "near
the Mill-Bridge," where he remained until 1775. The
last book bearing his name as printer is James Janeway's
A Token For Children, Being an Exact Account of the
Conversion, Holy and Exemplary Lives and Joyful Deaths
of Several Young Children in 1771. Thomas recounts
that "Fowle having on hand a considerable stock of
the small articles he usually sold, continued his shop
till 1775," although Thomas had purchased his press
and types. In that year, Fowle moved to Portsmouth,
New Hampshire, where he died at his brother's home in
1776.

|Zechariah Fowle

Zechariah Fowle's achievements, while due largely
to the skill and ambition of his extraordinary apprentice and competent partners, remain noteworthy. With
Mecom, he produced a large edition of the New-England
Primer; with Draper, Dodsley's Chronicles of the Kings
of England; with Thomas, the Massachusetts Spy. In his
twenty-four years as a printer, Fowle never paid off
his one handpress. (Ironically, the same press, purchased by Isaiah Thomas, is now a valued possession of
the American Antiquarian Society.) Chapbooks and ballads constitute most of Fowle's canon; had it not been
for his fortunate associations, Zechariah Fowle would
probably have printed little else.

Leslie Todd Pitre

References:

Oswald, John C. Printing in the Americas. Chicago:
    Gregg, 1937; reprint edition, New York: Hacker
    Art Books, 1968.

Tebbel, John. A History of Book Publishing in the
    United States. Vol. 1. New York and London:
    Bowker, 1972.

Thomas, Isaiah. The History of Printing in America.
    Worcester, Mass.: Isaiah Thomas, Jr., 1810;
    2nd ed., revised, Albany, N.Y.: J. Munsell
    for the American Antiquarian Society, 1874;
    ed. Marcus A. McCorison, Barre, Mass.: Imprint
    Society, 1970.

Wroth, Lawrence C. The Colonial Printer. New York:
    Grolier Club, 1931; revised and enlarged,
    Portland, Me.: Southworth-Anthoensen Press,
    1938; reprint edition, Charlottesville, Va.:
    University Press of Virginia/Dominion Books,
    1964.

Benjamin Franklin

Benjamin Franklin (1706-1790) is important to the history of Boston publishing because he served an apprenticeship there with his brother James Franklin, because he wrote as Silence Dogood for his brother's New-England Courant, and because his name appears, from 1723 until 1726, as printer and seller of the Courant. The paper was James's enterprise, but when the general court ordered him to cease publishing it, he continued the Courant under Benjamin's name.

References:

Brigham, Clarence S. History and Bibliography of American Newspapers: 1690-1820. Vol. 1. Worcester, Mass.: American Antiquarian Society, 1947.

Buckingham, Joseph T. Specimens of Newspaper Literature. Vol. 1. Boston: Little and Brown, 1850.

James Franklin

James Franklin (1697-1735), printer and publisher, founder of the third newspaper in Boston and fourth in the American colonies, was also the object of the last attempt at official prior censorship of the press in colonial Massachusetts. Under him, his younger brother Benjamin learned the printer's trade and got his start in satirical journalism. In 1717 Franklin opened his Boston print shop in Queen Street. In July 1724 he moved it to Union Street, where it stayed until he decided in 1726 to move to Newport, Rhode Island. Franklin's Boston imprints total about sixty, approximately half of which he published himself.

Major Authors: Benjamin Colman, William Douglass, Cotton Mather, John Wise.

Publishers Served: Samuel Gerrish, Daniel Henchman.

Franklin was born in Boston on 4 February 1697, the son of Josiah and Abiah (Folger) Franklin. His father, an immigrant from England, was a tallow maker. According to Isaiah Thomas, the son apprenticed with a printer in England as a result of his father's connections. This is at least partly confirmed by Benjamin Franklin's recollection in his Autobiography that in 1717 his brother "return'd from England with a Press and Letters to set up his Business in Boston." James Franklin's imprint appeared for the first time in 1718 when he published on his own account a reprint of Theophilus Dorrington's Familiar Guide to the Right and Profitable Receiving of the Lord's Supper and printed Thomas Prince's ordination sermon for Samuel Gerrish.

193

Of the publishers Franklin served, by far the most important numerically were Gerrish and Daniel Henchman, each of whom had Franklin print about ten books during his eight years in Boston. Both were among the seven Boston booksellers who commissioned Franklin in 1719 to print the twenty-fifth edition of Hodder's Arithmetick, first published in 1661. According to Charles Evans, this edition was "the first purely arithmetical work" published in the British American colonies. For Gerrish he printed the first edition of Thomas Walter's The Grounds and Rules of Musick Explained (1721), which contains the first engraved music printed in the colonies.

Franklin became most conspicuous as a newspaper publisher during his brief career in Boston. When William Brooker turned over to Philip Musgrave both the Boston postmastership and the Boston Gazette, the town's second newspaper, Franklin lost the job of printing the paper. He responded by deciding to risk launching yet a third Boston newspaper, the New-England Courant.

It was obvious with the first number on 17 August 1721 that the Courant would be far different from its competitors. Its saucy columns debunked the political and religious establishment, provided satirical and entertaining comment on manners and morals, and plunged at once into the burgeoning controversy over inoculating for smallpox. In opposing the new technique, the Courant and its stable of writers or "couranteers," especially Dr. William Douglass, aimed some of their sharpest darts at Increase and Cotton Mather, who were not only the most conspicuous advocates of inoculation but also the undoubted leaders of the Massachusetts ecclesiastical establishment. More important to American letters in the long run, the Courant also served as an outlet for the Silence Dogood letters and other anonymous offerings of its publisher's teen-age apprentice, Benjamin.

194

The first time the Courant's egregious assaults
on official dignity provoked a response from the government, the general court ordered James Franklin jailed
for a month until the end of its session in July 1722.
The young Benjamin continued to put out the Courant
while the offending publisher served his time. The
next time it happened, in January 1723, the general
court passed an order forbidding Franklin to publish
the Courant, or anything like it, unless each paper
was scrutinized ahead of time by the secretary of the
province. The order, however, was aimed specifically
at James Franklin. From then until James moved his
business to Newport, Rhode Island, an uncensored
Courant appeared weekly in the name of Benjamin Franklin, even after the apprentice lad ran off to Philadelphia in the autumn of 1723. When James was accused of
contempt of the general court, a grand jury declined to
indict him. The Franklin case marked the end of official attempts at prior censorship in colonial
Massachusetts.

Franklin's Newport career was as brief as it
had been in Boston, but he left as a legacy the first
printing business in the colony, which after his death
in 1735 was carried on by his widow Ann, later in partnership with his son James, Jr. James Franklin's
larger legacy includes the founding of controversial
popular journalism in America, a significant battle
in behalf of freedom of the press, and the professional
nurture of the genius of Benjamin Franklin.

Charles E. Clark

References:

Bleyer, Willard G. Main Currents in the History of
    American Journalism. Boston: Houghton Mifflin,
    1927.

Duniway, Clyde A. The Development of Freedom of the
    Press in Massachusetts. New York and London:
    Longmans, Green, 1906.

Ford, Worthington C. "Franklin's New England Courant."
    Proceedings of the Massachusetts Historical
    Society, 57 (1924).

Franklin, Benjamin. The Autobiography of Benjamin
    Franklin. Edited by Leonard W. Labaree et al.
    New Haven and London: Yale University Press,
    1964.

Thomas, Isaiah. The History of Printing in America.
    Worcester, Mass.: Isaiah Thomas, Jr., 1810;
    2nd ed., revised, Albany, N.Y.: J. Munsell
    for the American Antiquarian Society, 1874;
    ed. Marcus A. McCorison, Barre, Mass.: Imprint
    Society, 1970.

Wroth, Lawrence C. The Colonial Printer. New York:
    Grolier Club, 1931; revised and enlarged,
    Portland, Me.: Southworth-Anthoensen Press,
    1938; reprint edition, Charlottesville, Va.:
    University Press of Virginia/Dominion Books,
    1964.

Edmund Freeman

Edmund Freeman (1764-1807) printed and published in Boston from 1784 through 1791. His notable achievements were the publishing of the Boston Magazine (1784-1785), the printing of the Harvard broadsides of 1787 and 1788, and the publication of the Herald of Freedom, and the Federal Advertiser (1788-1791).

    Major Authors: Hugh Blair, Timothy Dwight, Joseph Green.

    Freeman's personal life is not well documented. He is remembered chiefly for his connection with the Boston Magazine, the leading magazine in Boston during its period of publication. Founded by John Norman and a man named White in 1783, it was directed by a distinguished editorial board composed of Boston clergy, Harvard graduates, and by professional and business men. Freeman joined Norman and White in 1784, and after a few numbers had been published by the three of them, Freeman and Thomas Greenleaf took over the magazine in July 1784.

    Until 1785 the Boston Magazine boasted a strong roster of prose contributors. It published Mather Byles's "Criticism on Nonsense" (November and December 1783) and "Essay on Flattery" (March 1784), Edward Wigglesworth's various essays on the natural sciences, and Benjamin Lincoln, Jr.'s federalistic essays. Freeman and Greenleaf, dissatisfied with the marginal profit, changed editorial policy in 1785, and began to rely on the sentimental essay and anecdotal story. The publication's quality, however, continued to surpass its competitors, the Gentlemen and Lady's Town and Country Magazine (1784) and the American Monitor (1785). John Norman, who had provided the engravings for each

197

number of the Boston Magazine after he had sold his
interest in it, complained in December 1784 that
Freeman and Greenleaf did not pay him; he suggested
further that the magazine would continue to decline
unless the publishers started paying their debts.

Freeman and Greenleaf began to rely heavily upon
popular reprints to bolster circulation. Among them
were, in 1785, Hugh Blair's literary essays, Timothy
Dwight's "Columbia," and Joseph Green's "The Poet's
Lamentation for the Loss of His Cat." Frustrated by
the low profits, Greenleaf twice offered to buy out
Freeman; after Freeman's second refusal, Greenleaf
left the partnership in September 1785. Freeman, determined to make the magazine succeed by himself, bought
new type in January 1786 and advertised his hope to
resurrect the magazine's popularity. By September it
was evident that the Boston Magazine was failing. Freeman combined the September/October and November/December
numbers, and then he discontinued the magazine.

Freeman's professional reputation did not fall
into disrepute, however. He was chosen to print the
Harvard broadsides in 1787 and 1788, and in the latter
year he also reprinted John Adams's Defence of the Constitution of the Government of the United States of
America. In the same year Freeman, in partnership with
Loring Andrews, established the Herald of Freedom, and
the Federal Advertiser as a semiweekly publication.
Freeman and Andrews published together until the close
of the second volume, when Andrews withdrew. Freeman
continued until the number of 5 April 1791. He sold
the Herald to John Howel, who continued it as the
Argus until 19 July 1791.

Freeman brought out few other publications.
Among those for which he was responsible are Hugh
Blair's Essays on Rhetoric and Candid Considerations
on Libels, both published in 1789.

Leslie Todd Pitre

198

Reference:

Richardson, Lyon N. A History of Early American News-
    papers, 1741-1789. New York: Thomas Nelson,
    1931; reprint edition, New York: Octagon, 1966.

Philip Freeman

Philip Freeman (c. 1712-1789), an Englishman, dealt in
soft leather and books in Boston. Active as a publisher
from 1749 until his death, his name appears in approximately twenty-three imprints. All of his publications
are religious. Many are specifically Baptist; nine are
by Isaac Backus. Freeman conducted business "in Union-
street next to the Corn-fields."

Reference:

Thomas, Isaiah. The History of Printing in America.
    Worcester, Mass.: Isaiah Thomas, Jr., 1810;
    2nd ed., revised, Albany, N.Y.: J. Munsell
    for the American Antiquarian Society, 1874;
    ed. Marcus A. McCorison, Barre, Mass.: Imprint
    Society, 1970.

John Gardiner

John Gardiner (1731-1793) published <u>The Speech of John Gardiner</u> in 1792. That same year he also possibly published his own <u>Gardiner on Theatre</u>, no copy of which is known to exist.

Samuel Gerrish

Samuel Gerrish (d. 1741), bookseller and publisher, published possibly the first American book sale catalogue, music book printed in bars, and Puritan Christmas sermon. Over 200 publications bear his imprint. When he began publishing in Boston in 1707, he conducted business "near the Old-Meeting House," but in 1711 he relocated at "the sign of the Buck over against the South Meeting-House" in Marlborough Street. He moved again in 1714 to the "Shop on the North Side of the Town-House" in King Street, and again in 1717 to the "Shop near the Brick Meeting House." In 1726 he reestablished "at the lower end of Cornhill," and, finally, he moved "over against the Sun-Tavern" around 1734.

<u>Major Authors</u>: John Barnard, Benjamin Colman, William Cooper, Thomas Foxcroft, Cotton Mather, Thomas Prince, Joseph Sewall, Thomas Symmes.

Gerrish was born in Wenham, Massachusetts, during the 1680s and died in 1741. In 1709 he married Mary Sewall, daughter of Samuel, who recorded his observations about them in his famous <u>Diary</u>. Mary died in

200

childbirth in 1710, and two years later Gerrish married Sarah Coney. Through his two wives he became a brother-in-law to Joseph Sewall, Thomas Foxcroft, and Ebenezer Pemberton, all illustrious men of their time.

Gerrish learned the bookselling and publishing trade as an apprentice to Richard Wilkins (and possibly Benjamin Eliot as well). When Wilkins retired at age eighty-one in 1704 (he died later that year), Gerrish assumed control of the business that he would develop into one of the most important of such firms in Boston during the first third of the eighteenth century. He began slowly as a publisher, but for the two decades after 1710 he published, on the average, ten titles per year. He published only one item in 1711; he was most active in 1727 when he published over twenty titles. His first published volume was John Williams's God in the Camp (1707), and the last to bear his imprint was a 1740 music book.

Of the authors Gerrish published, Cotton Mather was then, as now, the most important. He wrote fully a quarter of all the titles Gerrish published, and those more than fifty books constitute about twelve percent of that author's output of well over 400 works. Several of those volumes deserve special mention. The second book Gerrish published, and the only book to appear under his imprint in 1709, was Mather's The Sailours Companion. Most important of all the Mather items was the next, Bonifacius (later entitled Essays to Do Good), in 1710. This manual for good deeds so influenced Benjamin Franklin, for example, that he mentioned it in his Autobiography and wrote to Cotton's son Richard in 1779 affirming its importance to him. Gerrish's only 1711 book was Mather's Advice from Taberah, a sermon on the great Boston fire. The fire destroyed, among many other establishments, the bookselling businesses centered in Cornhill, one of which was Gerrish's. In 1712 he published Mather's Grace Defended, which was probably the earliest Puritan Christmas sermon published in America, although in it Mather rails against the growing acceptance of the pagan custom of

celebrating Christmas. In 1714 Gerrish published
Mather's The Sacrificer, a volume valuable for the
inclusion of a list of some of Gerrish's books published to that time, not all of which are recorded in
the standard bibliographies. That same year he published Maternal Consolations, Mather's eulogy of his
mother. Mather's important translation of the Psalms,
Psalterium Americanum, appeared in 1718, and Ratio
Disciplinae, his discussion of Congregational polity,
was published in 1726. Upon Mather's death in 1728,
Gerrish published eulogies of him by Mather's son
Samuel (The Departure and Character of Elijah Considered and Improved) and by Joshua Gee (Israel's Mourning
for Aaron's Death). The next year he published Samuel
Mather's The Life of . . . Cotton Mather. Gerrish also
published titles by Mather's father, Increase; his
cousin, Azariah Mather; and his nephew, Mather Byles.
Volumes by and about the Mathers--and especially
Cotton--most recommend Gerrish qua publisher.

    The Mathers were not the only authors in whom
Gerrish was interested. He published about fifteen
titles each by the divines Thomas Foxcroft and Benjamin
Colman, and he published five or more volumes by John
Barnard, Joseph Sewall, Thomas Symmes, and Thomas
Prince. The most important non-Mather title that
Gerrish published is Prince's Chronological History of
New-England in the Form of Annals (1736), many of the
ideas for which Prince gleaned from William Bradford's
manuscript that would not be published until 1856 as
History of Plymouth Plantation. Gerrish also published
Symmes' Lovewell Lamented (1725), in which the author
mourns Captain John Lovewell, who was killed in what
has become known as Lovell's Fight. Gerrish also has
the distinction of having published one of the earliest
auction sale catalogue of books in America. When his
brother-in-law Ebenezer Pemberton died in 1717, leaving
a fine library, Gerrish published A Catalogue of Curious and Valuable Books, a thirty-page pamphlet.

    In the early 1720s most New Englanders were re-
luctant to be inoculated against the ravages of

smallpox. The enlightened Cotton Mather strongly urged
inoculation, and while he met with much resistance,
Gerrish was one who shared his radical view. In 1721
he published two pro-inoculation pamphlets: Benjamin
Colman's Some Observations on the New Method of Receiving the Small-Pox by Ingrafting or Inoculating and
William Cooper's A Letter to a Friend in the Country,
a title usually attributed incorrectly to Mather. Then
in 1730 he republished a new printing of Cooper's piece
as A Reply to the Objections Made against Taking the
Small Pox in the Way of Inoculation from Principles of
Conscience and an edition of Zabdiel Boylston's An Historical Account of the Small-Pox Inoculated in New-
England, a volume first published in London in 1726.

Gerrish was also interested in the Psalms and in
music. In addition to Mather's Psalterium Americanum,
he published Isaac Watts' Honey out of the Rock (1715);
Mather's The Accomplished Singer (1721); several editions of Thomas Walter's The Grounds and Rules of
Musick Explained (first edition, 1721), probably the
first music printed in bars in America; John Tufts's
A Very Plain and Easy Introduction to the Psalms
(1721?); Walter's sermon, The Sweet Psalmist of Israel
(1722); Peter Thatcher's An Essay . . . Cases of Conscience, Concerning the Singing of Psalms (1725); and
Tufts's Introduction to the Singing of Psalm-Tunes
(1738), a book that, in its 1721 first edition, was
the earliest American music textbook.

While Gerrish was both a bookseller and a publisher, no evidence exists to suggest that he ever
printed his own books. The printer he used most frequently was Bartholomew Green, who printed Gerrish's
first book and most of the other titles bearing the
Gerrish imprint through a 1732 volume by Andrew Le
Mercier. The other printers Gerrish used were Timothy
Green, Thomas Fleet, Thomas Crump, John Allen, Samuel
Kneeland, James Franklin, and Gamaliel Rogers.

In addition to doing business with the best Boston
printers, Gerrish also joined occasionally with other

booksellers/publishers in joint-publishing ventures. As early as 1714 he and Henchman published Mather's A Monitor for Communicants; the next year he, Henchman, and Benjamin Gray published a pamphlet by Benjamin Colman. Other publishers who shared an imprint with Gerrish were Benjamin Eliot, John Edwards (these two most notably, with Henchman as well, on Mather's Psalterium Americanum), John Phillips, Nathaniel Belknap, Bennet Love, Samuel Kneeland, Thomas Hancock, and Nicholas Buttolph. Gerrish was intimately connected with and was an integral part of the Boston publishing business.

Samuel Gerrish was one of the important Boston publishers of the early eighteenth century. Others published more than he did, but he was a productive publisher whose best books are today of great literary and historical interest. Several by Cotton Mather, for example, must be considered in any examination of that great divine's work. Prince's history was one of the best and most important of such works to that time, and it remains a major document for students of early American history and culture. While Gerrish apparently wrote nothing but book catalogues for publication, his several pro-inoculation volumes suggest his own attitude in that great controversy, and his publications also indicate his interest in the Psalms and music.

References: *Samuel Gerrish*

Anon. "Samuel Gerrish." Proceedings of the Massachusetts Historical Society, 14 (1901).

Littlefield, George E. Early Boston Booksellers: 1642-1711. Boston: Club of Odd Volumes, 1900; reprint edition, New York: Burt Franklin, 1969.

Sewall, Samuel. The Diary of Samuel Sewall: 1674-1729. Edited by M. Halsey Thomas, 2 vols. New York: Farrar, Straus & Giroux, 1973.

Samuel Gerrish, Jr.

Samuel Gerrish, Jr. (1715-1751) probably published two
titles in the mid 1740s. Both John Tufts's <u>Introduction
to the Singing of Psalm-Tunes</u> (1744) and Thomas Walter's
<u>The Grounds and Rules of Musick Explained</u> (1746) bear
the name of Samuel Gerrish as publisher, and inasmuch
as Samuel Gerrish, Sr., died in 1741, the younger
Gerrish was probably the publisher of these volumes.

William Gibbons

William Gibbons (dates unknown) was partly responsible
for one known publication, Samuel Stone's <u>Short Catechism Drawn out of the Word of God</u> (1699). Gibbons
joined with Bartholomew Green and John Allen in publishing that title.

John Gill (see Benjamin Edes and John Gill)

Obadiah Gill

Obadiah Gill (1650-1700) published two known works, both by Cotton Mather. In 1685 Richard Pierce printed An Elegy on . . . Nathanael Collins for Gill, and in 1690 Gill, Joseph Browning, and James Woode had Pierce print The Way to Prosperity.

James Glen

James Glen (dates unknown), a Scot, emigrated to America in 1679. He worked for John Foster, and when Samuel Sewall became manager of the press, Glen supervised it for a few months before being succeeded in 1682 by Samuel Green, Jr. One known volume bears Glen's name as printer: Samuel Willard's Covenant-Keeping the Way to Blessedness (1682).

References:

Littlefield, George E. Early Boston Booksellers: 1642-1711. Boston: Club of Odd Volumes, 1900; reprint edition, New York: Burt Franklin, 1969.

Littlefield, George E. The Early Massachusetts Press: 1638-1711. Boston: Club of Odd Volumes, 1907; reprint edition, New York: Burt Franklin, 1969.

Thomas, Isaiah. <u>The History of Printing in America</u>.
Worcester, Mass.: Isaiah Thomas, Jr., 1810;
2nd ed., revised, Albany, N.Y.: J. Munsell
for the American Antiquarian Society, 1874;
ed. Marcus A. McCorison, Barre, Mass.: Imprint
Society, 1970.

Daniel Gookin

Daniel Gookin (1720-1752), a descendant of General
Daniel Gookin, was a bookseller from 1739 until his
death. He conducted business first "at the corner of
Water-street, Cornhill," but beginning in 1745 he announced his location as "in Marlborough-Street over
against the Old South Meeting House." He published
just under sixty titles.

<u>Major Authors</u>: John Adams, John Barnard, Mather
Byles, Charles Chauncy, Jonathan Mayhew, Thomas Shepard.

Gookin published <u>The Expectation of Man Dis-
appointed</u> in 1739 and nothing else until 1743. During
that year, however, he published three volumes, including Thomas Shepard's <u>The Saint's Jewel</u>. He more than
doubled his output the next year with seven publications, including a sermon, a poem, and a collection of
poems by Mather Byles. Gookin's most productive year
was 1745, when he published one dozen titles. Among
them are John Adams's <u>Poems on Several Occasions</u>,
Byles's <u>The Glorious Rest of Heaven</u>, and Charles
Chauncy's <u>Cornelius's Character</u>. Thereafter Gookin
published, on the average, five titles a year through
1751. During the last two-thirds of his career he published works by John Barnard, Chauncy, Andrew Le Mercier,
Jonathan Mayhew, and John Odlin.

Daniel Gookin

Despite the little that is known about Gookin, the brevity of his career, and the modest number of titles he published, his list of books published is fairly impressive. He published mainly religious works, and while he did not engage significantly in the controversies surrounding the Great Awakening, he published some of the important divines of the day. Even more impressive, however, is the poetry he saw into print. The years during which he was active might be termed America's poetic dark age, but in publishing two editions of Adams's collection of poems (1745, 1749) and Byles's The Comet (1744), as well as Collection of Poems (1744), Gookin published some of the best American poetry written after the death of Edward Taylor and before the War of Independence.

Isaiah Thomas notes that Gookin "was not largely in trade," yet the quality of the works he published testifies to his fine literary judgment, a trait not always found in more ambitious publishers.

Reference:

Thomas, Isaiah. The History of Printing in America. Worcester, Mass.: Isaiah Thomas, Jr., 1810; 2nd ed., revised, Albany, N.Y.: J. Munsell for the American Antiquarian Society, 1874; ed. Marcus A. McCorison, Barre, Mass.: Imprint Society, 1970.

Gottlieb Graupner

Gottlieb Graupner (1767-1836) was a musician who played oboe in Haydn's orchestra in his native Prussia. In America Graupner taught music with Peter A. Von Hagen at Susanna Rowson's school. He was also a composer of note. In 1795 he printed and sold, at "No. 6, Franklin Street," in Boston, Franz Kotzwara's The Battle of Prague, a sonata for pianoforte. Graupner's name appears in no other known eighteenth-century imprint.

Reference:

Vail, R. W. G. "Susanna Haswell Rowson, The Author of Charlotte Temple: A Bibliographical Study." Proceedings of the American Antiquarian Society, 42 (1932).

Benjamin Gray

Benjamin Gray (d. 1751), bookseller and publisher, concentrated on religious books and brief tracts but occasionally published civic and practical material. During his career he published, or was listed as seller of, forty-eight titles, sixteen of which he published in conjunction with others. He became involved in publishing as early as 1715; the next year he established his own shop at the upper end of King Street (north side of the Town House). From 1721 to 1746 he moved three times: to the Cornhill district (1721-1729); to No. 3,

at the head of the Town Dock (1730-1745); and to a
location near the market (1746).

Major Authors: John Bunyan, Benjamin Colman,
Cotton Mather, Increase Mather.

Isaiah Thomas lists 1719 as Gray's inaugural
year in publishing, but his name appeared in 1715 with
two of Boston's leading publishers--Samuel Gerrish and
Daniel Henchman--on funeral sermons by Benjamin Colman
and Cotton Mather. He also published Mather's Menachem
in 1716, without benefit of a joint publishing
arrangement.

After a period of apparent apprenticeship, Gray
moved into partnership with John Edwards for three
years (1719-1721). They published eight books together,
but each was free to publish other books independently.
Gray was most active in 1719, with five titles, and
1720, with seven, all of which are either civic or
religious. He published three essays on Boston, including John Colman's The Distressed State of the Town
of Boston (1720). His religious publications were
written by the Mathers. He published Cotton's A
Glorious Espousal (1719) and A Year and a Life Well
Concluded (1720). Titles by Increase are The Duty of
Parents to Pray for Their Children (1719) and Awakening Soul-Saving Truths Plainly Delivered (1720). His
joint publishing projects with Gerrish and Henchman,
his use of reputable printers to produce the books
that he published, and his ability to win minor titles
by substantial authors indicate that his career began
auspiciously.

In 1721 he produced two practical works (one an
almanac by Nathan Bowen, another a record of a Boston
town meeting), but he also became embroiled in a scandal when he published the anonymous Letter to an Eminent Clergy-man in the Massachusetts Bay. The letter
contained material that prompted an official hearing
of a government council which unanimously declared,
according to Isaiah Thomas, that the work had in it

"many Vile, Scandalous, and very Abusive Expressions, which greatly reflect on His Majesty's Government and People of this Province, and tend to disturb the Publick Peace." Since they had been unable to identify the author (it seems that even Gray did not know who the author was), the council advised the attorney general to prosecute Gray, who acknowledged having published the pamphlet. The minutes of the hearing were to appear in the local newspapers, but the report was not published. It is not clear what crime the council believed Gray to have committed or how the issue of his prosecution was resolved; Thomas reports only that the affair "was terminated by a compromise." The effect on Gray's career appears to have been considerable because he did not publish any books for six years after the incident, and when he did resume publishing, his activity was limited. Despite the promising beginning, Gray's reputation declined to the point that Thomas describes him as "not a very considerable bookseller."

From 1727 to 1736 Gray published an average of two titles per year, all of which are religious. They include funeral sermons and instructive material: John Webb's Some Plain and Necessary Directions to Obtain Eternal Salvation (1729); Jeremiah Burroughs' Rare Jewel of Christian Contentment (1731); and William Homes's Proposals of Some Things to be Done in Our Administring Ecclesiastical Government (1732). Although no copy of the book is known to exist, Gray's most notable publication of this period is Rest for a Wearied Soul (1735), for which John Bunyan is listed as the supposed author. Gray published four titles from these years with Alford Butler.

From 1736 through 1743 Gray published no books, and when he resumed activity in 1743, he published only four minor works: John Willison's Looking to Jesus (1743); possibly a New-England's Ebenezer (1745); A Short History of the Grand Rebellion in Scotland (1746); and The History of the Holy Jesus (1746). His name

211

appears as bookseller in three books during this period.
He concluded his thirty-one-year career in 1746.

Gray's most important contributions appeared
prior to the scandal in 1721, after which his career
declined sharply. He seems to have made his living
after 1721 primarily as a bookbinder and bookseller.

Richard Ziegfeld

Reference:

Thomas, Isaiah. The History of Printing in America.
     Worcester, Mass.: Isaiah Thomas, Jr., 1810;
     2nd ed., revised, Albany, N.Y.: J. Munsell
     for the American Antiquarian Society, 1874;
     ed. Marcus A. McCorison, Barre, Mass.: Imprint
     Society, 1970.

William Gray

William Gray (dates unknown) conducted business in Milk
Street. His name appears in only one known imprint,
Andrew Jones's The Black Book of Conscience, a title
Gray sold in 1742.

Bartholomew Green

Bartholomew Green (1667-1732) was the most distinguished American printer from 1690 to 1730. He printed the first number of the first continuous newspaper, the earliest printed catalogue of an academic library, and the first book in America with an illustration of its author. Alone or with John Allen he printed over 800 works. When he began printing permanently in Boston in 1692, he set up his presses in Newbury Street, at the south end of town, where he remained until his death on 28 January 1732.

Major Authors: Benjamin Colman, Cotton Mather, Increase Mather, Solomon Stoddard, Benjamin Wadsworth, Samuel Willard.

Publishers Served: Nicholas Boone, Nicholas Buttolph, Duncan Campbell, Benjamin Eliot, Samuel Gerrish, Benjamin Harris, Daniel Henchman, Samuel Kneeland, Samuel Phillip .

The grandson of Bartholomew Green (d. 1635), and the second son of Samuel Green (d. 1702), Bartholomew Green was born in Cambridge, Massachusetts, on 26 October 1667. In 1687, on ending his apprenticeship with his father, he moved to Boston, where, except for two years, he worked as a printer for the next forty-five years. In 1690 Green married Mary Short, who bore him ten children before her death in 1709. In 1710 he married Jane Toppan, by whom he had two children.

Very little is known of Green's career from 1687 to 1690, when he worked for both his father and his half-brother, Samuel Green, Jr. Green's name first appeared in 1687, along with his father's, in the

213

imprint of the second edition of John Eliot's Indian
primer. Green worked in Boston with his brother Samuel
until the latter's death from smallpox in 1690, at
which time he took over the business. In September
of that year, however, a fire destroyed most of the
building containing his brother's press. Taking with
him the parts of the press he could salvage, he returned to Cambridge to become a partner in his father's
business until 1692.

After his father's retirement in 1692, Green
returned to Boston where he printed books alone or
in conjunction with John Allen until 1704. One other
printer, Benjamin Harris, resided in Boston in 1692,
and during that year all of the Boston imprints bore
the names of Harris, Allen, or Green. The only press
in Boston from 1690 to 1692 belonged to Richard Pierce,
and after his death the executors of Pierce's estate
rented his press to these three printers. In 1693,
however, the press came into the possession of Benjamin
Harris, who was, for the first six months of the year,
the only printer whose name appeared in imprints. Sometime during these months Green went to Cambridge to get
his father's press and the salvaged portions of his
brother's press and, returning to Boston, he applied
for a license to print, which was granted on 6 June
1693 by the General Assembly of Massachusetts. Later,
in 1694, Green formed a partnership with John Allen.
Although the exact reason for their partnership is not
known, George Littlefield suggests that since Allen
had the option to buy the press of Benjamin Harris
that year, Green combined with Allen in order to avoid
competition. Green and Allen first combined in 1690
to print Samuel Lee's poem, Contemplations on Mortal-
ity, no copy of which is known to exist. However, the
bulk of their activity occurred from 1696 to 1703, during which time they printed approximately 150 titles.
After 1703 only Green's name appeared in his imprints
until 1725. From that time until his death in 1732,
Green printed a few works in conjunction with his son
Bartholomew Green, Jr., Thomas Fleet, and Samuel
Kneeland.

Green's apprenticeship and partnership with his father were beneficial not only because he learned the art of printing, but also because he learned to print in the Indian language and because he developed associations with important people that were to be profitable throughout his career. Having helped his father with John Eliot's Indian primer and having inherited his father's type, he was the only printer in Boston from 1692 until 1730 who could print books in the Indian language, printing during that time over ten such titles. Several of the more important works deserve mention. In 1690 he and his father printed, in Cambridge, John Cotton's <u>Spiritual Milk for Boston Babes</u>. In 1698 he and Allen printed Increase Mather's <u>Greatest Sinners Called</u>. This is the first book in the Indian language printed in Boston. In 1709 Green printed the <u>Massachusee Psalter</u> with Indian and English in columns on the same page. A translation of the Psalms by Experience Mayhew, this book, according to George Littlefield, is "next to the Indian Bible the most important monument of the Massachusetts language." Green was assisted by James Printer, an Indian who had learned to print under Samuel Green in Cambridge and who had worked on both editions of the Indian Bible.

Another advantage Green enjoyed in working with his father was practice in printing almanacs. Beginning with John Tulley's almanacs for 1691 and 1692, Green printed, until his death, nearly all the almanacs in New England, serving, for example, Nathan Bowen, William Brattle, Samuel Clough, Edward Holyoke, and Thomas Robie. One of the more significant works of this type is Nathaniel Ames's 1730 almanac. Green printed the work on the first paper manufactured in America, made at the town of Milton not far from Boston. Green profited as well by taking over from his father the duties of printer for Harvard College and the title of Official Printer for the acts and laws of the Massachusetts Bay Colony, duties he enjoyed until his death. In addition, he also printed the acts and laws of

Connecticut until 1702 and those of New Hampshire until
1726.

During his apprenticeship Green began to print
for Cotton Mather, the most prolific author and the
most important literary and religious figure of his
time. Mather wrote approximately 180 of the total of
more than 800 titles Green printed. Several of Mather's
works deserve mention for their historical importance.
In 1694 Green printed The Short History of New England.
In 1698 he and Allen brought out The Bostonian Ebenezer,
an eighty-two-page, 3 x 5 inch volume which is the first
history of Boston. Decennium Luctuosum, a history of
New England's war with the Indians from 1688 to 1698,
appeared in 1699. In 1710 he printed Mather's
Bonifacius (later entitled Essays to Do Good), a manual for good deeds that later greatly influenced
Benjamin Franklin. In 1712 Grace Defended appeared.
Although in it Mather rails against the growing acceptance of pagan customs in celebrating Christmas, this
work is probably the earliest Puritan Christmas sermon
printed in America. Green also printed approximately
forty titles by Increase Mather. Green's association
with the Mathers and with the government of Massachusetts provided him with over half of his total output.

In 1700 Green involved himself even more directly
in a religious controversy. A year earlier Benjamin
Colman had returned from England to become minister of
the Brattle Street Church, a new church in Boston dif-
fering from the three already in existence in that it
advocated doing away with the recital in public of a
personal religious experience in favor of the reading
of the Bible and reciting of the Lord's Prayer.
Increase Mather, who opposed these innovations, criticized the Brattleites in his The Order of the Gospel
(1700). Soon thereafter, several of Colman's followers
applied to Green to print a pamphlet entitled Gospel
Order Revived, Being an Answer to a Book Lately Set
Forth by the Reverend Mr. Increase Mather. Although
Mather's book had been unlicensed, Green, who was a
follower of the Mathers, declined to print the reply

216

to Mather before it had been submitted to the licensers of the press, to which its authors would not consent. After denying his services, Green printed a handbill justifying his stand.

Green also printed other works of historical and religious significance. In 1696 he and Allen printed Joshua Scottow's Massachusetts or the First Planters of New-England. Containing the first publication of Thomas Dudley's famous letter of 1630 to the Countess of Lincoln, this is one of the most valuable books connected with the early history of the Massachusetts Bay Colony. In 1700 Green and Allen printed Samuel Sewall's The Selling of Joseph, a three-page pamphlet that is perhaps the first antislavery document in America. In 1701 he and Allen printed the ninth edition of Michael Wigglesworth's The Day of Doom, a visionary apocalyptic poem of God's frightening justice. This is the earliest extant complete edition of the poem.

In addition to printing almanacs, government documents, histories, sermons, and poems, Green printed textbooks and an occasional humorous work. For example, he printed Nathaniel Strong's England's Perfect Schoolmaster; or Directions for Spelling, Reading . . . (1710), Ezekiel Cheever's Short Introduction to the Latin Tongue (1724), and an anonymous book entitled Epitome of English Orthography (1697).

Green is also important for having made several technical innovations in printing. In 1696 he and Allen printed Increase Mather's Angelographia. In this book on the nature and power of angels, a portrait of the author appears, said to be the first engraved on metal in America. The 1698 ninth edition of the Bay Psalm Book contains a few pages of music incidental to the text and thus marks the first appearance of pages of woodcut music. In 1717 Green was responsible for an advance in American book illustration when he printed an edition of Hugh Peter's A Dying Father's Last Legacy, which contains a woodcut frontispiece of the author, copied from an unsigned line engraving extracted from London editions of the book appearing in 1660 and 1661.

Green made significant contributions to the history of book cataloguing and book selling. In 1723 Green printed Catalogus Librorum Bibliothecae Collegij Harvardini and in 1725 a Continuatio Supplementi. Compiled by Joshua Gee and John Hancock respectively, these two volumes constitute the first printing of a catalogue for an American public library.

Green is also important in the history of American journalism. In 1704 he began printing for John Campbell the Boston News-Letter, the first newspaper continuously published in America. Except for the period from 10 November 1707 to 8 October 1711, when John Allen printed it, Green printed every number of the paper until his death. He bought the newspaper from Campbell in 1722, and in 1727 he changed its name to the Weekly News-Letter, returning it to its former title in 1730. After Green's death, John Draper, his son-in-law, took over duties of printing the paper.

In 1726 Green was involved in the largest publication project of its kind in the first half of that century when he and Samuel Kneeland combined their presses to bring out Samuel Willard's A Compleat Body of Divinity, a posthumous compilation and publication of Willard's work undertaken by Joseph Sewall and Thomas Prince. Printed for Daniel Henchman and Benjamin Eliot, this 927-page work was the first folio volume, other than acts and laws, and the largest work up to that time, printed in America.

In addition to the magnitude of his many accomplishments, Green is significant for the number of fine early American printers he produced. Gamaliel Rogers, John Draper, Samuel Kneeland, Bartholomew Green, Jr., and Timothy Green all apprenticed under him.

Bartholomew Green was the most important printer in New England during the first quarter of the eighteenth century. No one else printed as many works or as many historically significant titles. Known for his piety, industry, and discretion in never printing anything light or damaging to another's reputation, he contributed to the development of printing, bookselling, and book cataloguing in America.

Mark S. Shearer

References:

Kiessel, William C. "The Green Family: A Dynasty of Printers." New England Historical and Genealogical Register, 104 (1950).

Littlefield, George E. Early Boston Booksellers: 1642-1711. Boston: Club of Odd Volumes, 1900; reprint edition, New York: Burt Franklin, 1969.

Littlefield, George E. The Early Massachusetts Press: 1638-1711. Boston: Club of Odd Volumes, 1907; reprint edition, New York: Burt Franklin, 1969.

McMurtrie, Douglas C. "The Green Family of Printers." Americana, 26 (1932).

Thomas, Isaiah. The History of Printing in America. Worcester, Mass.: Isaiah Thomas, Jr., 1810; 2nd ed., revised, Albany, N.Y.: J. Munsell for the American Antiquarian Society, 1874; ed. Marcus A. McCorison, Barre, Mass.: Imprint Society, 1970.

Bartholomew Green, Jr.

Bartholomew Green, Jr. (1699-1751) served an apprenticeship with his father before beginning as a printer on
his own in 1724. Other than printing Thomas Symmes's
Lovewell Lamented (1725), Green is most important as
the printer of the Boston Gazette from 1727 until 1736.
From 1736 to 1743 he was in partnership with Bezoune
Allen and John Bushell. In 1751 Green established the
first press in Halifax, Nova Scotia, but he died before
he could begin operating it. Bushell succeeded him at
that press.

Mark S. Shearer

References:

Kiessel, William C. "The Green Family: A Dynasty of
    Printers." New England Historical and Genea-
    logical Register, 104 (1950).

McMurtrie, Douglas C. "The Green Family of Printers."
    Americana, 26 (1932).

Thomas, Isaiah. The History of Printing in America.
    Worcester, Mass.: Isaiah Thomas, Jr., 1810;
    2nd ed., revised, Albany, N.Y.: J. Munsell
    for the American Antiquarian Society, 1874;
    ed. Marcus A. McCorison, Barre, Mass.: Imprint
    Society, 1970.

John Green

John Green (dates unknown) was evidently not John Green (1731-1787), the son of Bartholomew Green, Jr. This other Green was in partnership with John Bushell in 1743 and 1744, and with Bushell and Bezoune Allen from 1745 to 1747. Green's name appears in fewer than twenty imprints.

John Green

John Green (1731-1787) was a member of the Boston loyalist printing firm, John Green and Joseph Russell. The two were known primarily for their printing ties to the American Board of Customs there. Probably as a result of their government income, they gave the government party at least pedestrian support in their newspaper, the Massachusetts Gazette and Boston Post-Boy. In 1755 Green was located opposite Mr. Church's Vendue House, and later that year he and Russell, after a brief stay on Tremont Street, established their "Printing Office near the Custom House and next to the Writing School on Queen Street." In 1757 they were opposite the Probate Office in Queen Street (or at the east corner of Dorset's Alley), where they remained.

Major Authors: East Apthorp, Andrew Eliot, Edmund Quincy, William Wood.

Publishers Served: Edes and Gill, the Drapers, the Fleets.

221

Green, the son of Bartholomew Green, Jr., and the great-grandson of Samuel Green of Cambridge, the second printer in the colonies, was born in Boston and attended the Boston Public Latin School. He was apprenticed to John Draper, a prominent government party printer, and married Draper's daughter, Rebecca. They were childless, and so John signified the end of his line of the Green printing dynasty, the first in the colonies. Isaiah Thomas describes Green as "a man of steady habits, true to his engagements, and well respected." He died in Boston in November 1787.

Although Green was in business for himself from time to time, the most significant portion of his printing career was as a partner in Green and Russell. The firm was established in 1755 and continued until the War of Independence. Isaiah Thomas records that Green managed the printing business while Joseph Russell operated an auction house. They shared the profits of both enterprises. After the Revolution began, Green became interested in the Independent Chronicle, published by Powars and Willis, but Green's name never appeared on the masthead.

Rather than publishing books, Green and Russell earned their major income as government printers. As their government income increased, the two became more obnoxious to Bostonians and their general printing business declined still more. The Post-Boy publishers printed about sixteen to twenty-five percent of all that was published in Boston before 1767. That year their share of total Boston printing (excluding newspapers) dropped to four percent and then to zero prior to the War of Independence. Most Boston printers depended on religious printing for over half of their total printing volumes; Green and Russell, on the average, showed less than five percent of their total printing volume as religious works. In this, they were unique among the Boston printers.

Even before the American board of Customs was established in Boston, Green and Russell had the major

share of general government printing there. In 1763
they unseated Samuel Kneeland as printer to the Assembly;
a few years later the two loyalists were accorded the
same treatment by Edes and Gill, appointed in June 1769
as printers to the Massachusetts General Assembly dominated by a popular party. With the exception of printing
for the General Assembly, the most substantial government
work in Boston, based on volume, was printing the perpet-
ual and temporary laws of Massachusetts. From 1763
through 1765, Green and Russell virtually monopolized
that printing. Four hundred copies were printed each
time at 2d a sheet (the printers charged twice that for
copies on better quality paper that were sent to the
English ministry). About 1765, however, Green and
Russell were caught in the midst of friction between
the governor and the Council over the allocation of this
printing. The governor won, and Green and Russell had
to share the printing of the laws with the Draper firm
until the Revolution. During all this time, the income
from this printing remained the same despite the inflation scholars claimed was so rampant in the colonies.
This, together with other evidence, suggests that such
printing may have been prestigious but not particularly
profitable. For example, the government required only
400 copies of each edition of the laws while as many as
2,000 copies of a single religious essay might be printed.
In addition, religious publications generally contained
more pages per publication than the supplements to the
laws. Evidence also shows that printers probably received more gross income from religious printing than
from government printing. But to Green and Russell,
this government income was essential for survival.

The two printers, however, attributed their
financial success and their financial ruin to their
appointment as printers to the Board of Customs Commissioners, established in Boston in 1767. The board's
business was a lucrative source of income, a political
plum, but it meant the loss of other business and certainly of reputation in a city dominated by the popular
party. Therefore, once involved, Green and Russell
clung to their customs appointment which fast became

their major source of income. Unlike the printing for
the council or assembly when printers were paid for
actual work, some customs board payments appeared to be
pure subsidy. Green and Russell received the appointment, Governor Francis Bernard wrote, because they were
"well affected to Government." Their newspaper gave at
least tempered support to the government party in return
for the continued appointment. However, as soon as John
Mein began attacking the popular party and nonimportation in his Chronicle, Green and Russell began to lose
their grip on the cherished appointment. The board apparently seized the opportunity to subsidize a more
fearless supporter of the government party than Green
and Russell and gradually began shifting business to
Mein in 1769. When Green and Russell felt the winds of
change, they wrote to Governor Thomas Hutchinson, who,
in turn, wrote the lords of the treasury in 1771, cau-
tioning them against dismissing Green and Russell from
customs service:

> I wish Mr. Mein may have the favour of Govern-
> ment in some way or other, but it will certainly
> hurt the Board & the cause of Government if
> Green & Russell are laid aside. They have been
> sufferers and lost almost all their other cus-
> tomrs by refusing to comply with the demands of
> the late seditious leaders and it will discour-
> age others from adhering to Government if they
> should be rewarded in this manner for their
> services they have done. I think nothing more
> is necessary for their security than to have
> the true state of the case made known.

Instead of reassurances from the board, Green and Russell
lost the stationery contract and heard in early April
1772 that Fleeming had been offered both printer and
stationer appointments by the board. (John Fleeming
continued publishing and printing in Boston after his
partner John Mein fled for his life to England.) Green
and Russell wrote directly to England to protest. They

complained that earlier when the board gave the stationery contract to Fleeming's partner, John Mein, they ap-
pealed that decision because they had a large supply of
the special government stationery on hand. Valued at several hundred pounds sterling by Green, the stationery was
imperial quality and therefore could not be sold to
Bostonians for common business purposes. Green and
Russell predicted it would "lay dead on their
hands. . . ." According to Green, the customs board
responded "as it was the pleasure of the Board to
appoint Mr. Mein Stationer, and as we [Green and
Russell] were appointed printers, and, without a doubt,
would always be continued as such, he [spokesman for
the board] would advise us not to mention anything further about it." Green concluded with the appeal that
the board at least continue to retain them as printers.
As a result, the board withheld Fleeming's official
appointment as printer and stationer in keeping with
Lord North's recommendation.

While Green and Russell and Mein and Fleeming
were in the good graces of the customs board, funds
flowed freely. According to customs records, Green and
Russell were paid more than £2,400 from 1769 through
1775, while Mein and Fleeming received more than £1,500
for the same period. These were rather tidy sums for
colonial printers. Even for the central office of the
customs service in America, almost £4,000 spent on stationery and printing for five or six years was an in-
credibly large sum. Customs board officials considered
this was well spent for public service, probably for the
propaganda the printers' newspapers provided for the
government party. In addition, over the years, Green
and Russell received a total of £806 from their printing for the governor, council, and assembly.

During this time, the Post-Boy barely paid for
itself through advertising and subscription income.
The newspaper was begun 22 August 1757 as the Boston
Weekly Advertiser and finally became the Massachusetts
Gazette, and Boston Post-Boy and Advertiser. On 23 May
1768, the newspaper began bearing the government's royal

225

arms. Green and Russell often printed on Monday the same government news that was published on Thursday in Richard Draper's News-Letter. Perhaps because of this and the general dullness of the newspaper, circulation remained small. In addition, their advertising dropped from more than half of the column space in their newspaper in the early 1760s to between twelve and twenty percent when the Revolution was at its height. During the latter period, the Post-Boy only had about ten to twelve percent of the total advertising in all Boston newspapers.

The only other major publication for which Green and Russell were known was their one-fourth interest in the Ames almanac. The loyalist printer Margaret Draper wrote that the total circulation of the almanac was 50,000 to 60,000 per year and that one-fourth interest amounted to £50 annual income.

Although John Green did not flee Boston with the other loyalists when the British troops left the city, life was not particularly pleasant for him. Even though John Adams wrote that Green and Russell continued to publish the Post-Boy in their "peaceable, quiet harmless, dovelike, inoffensive Manner," the printers nevertheless incurred the wrath of the townspeople for refusing to publish the Farmer's Letters (popular party columns). After that, Green wrote they "soon lost the largest part of the Subscribers of those that then took our Newspaper." They also lost their Assembly printing because they were loyalists, and, as Green continued, "with no Expectation of ever being able to regain our former Employment here. . . ." The printer reported threats on his life and property. At one point, the customs commissioners retreated to Castle William for safety and Green and Russell visited them or sent messages almost daily to inform the officials of Boston events. One of their letters to the commissioners, Green and Russell wrote, later was reprinted in the Boston newspapers among the letters to the English Ministry from the governor and customs board. Perhaps if the popular party had known Green and Russell were the authors of

226

that letter, the two printers would not have been able to remain in Boston. As it was, Green bitterly complained of the business harassment that occurred despite Governor Bernard's implied promise that Green would prosper, when Bernard said: "Mind Green, who will get most at the winding up of Affairs, Edes & Gill, or you."

When Green's will was probated in 1788, it indicated a modest estate. His furniture, horse, chaise, sulkey, red greatcoat, and a dozen assorted waistcoats were valued at £327/4/3 and reflected a man who enjoyed possessions and who might have been the slightest bit vain. There was a house and land on Newbury Street valued at £600 and half a brick house and half a wood store on Court Street valued at £350. Green's pew at the Reverend Clark's Meeting House was valued at £15. Also, there was a notation that Green's annual income from a share in Adams and Nourse's printing operation was unknown. Thus, Green's total estate was £1,292/4/3, a modest one for a printer of the day. The notes also indicate that although Green's major printing activity occurred before the War of Independence, he was at least an investor in some printing operations after that time.

Green's place in history, however, was won because of his role as printer and stationer for the American Board of Customs in Boston, infamous though that agency was. Green's politics did not suit most Bostonians, but they remembered him nevertheless as a good printer who used good type.

MaryAnn Yodelis Smith

References:

Boston. Public Library. John Adams Notes.

Cambridge. Houghton Library, Harvard University.
    Francis Bernard Papers, 1763-1770.

Thomas, Isaiah. The History of Printing in America.
    Worcester, Mass.: Isaiah Thomas, Jr., 1810;
    2nd ed., revised, Albany, N.Y.: J. Munsell
    for the American Antiquarian Society, 1874;
    ed. Marcus A. McCorison, Barre, Mass.: Imprint
    Society, 1970.

Yodelis, MaryAnn. Who Paid the Piper? Publishing
    Economics in Boston, 1763-1775. Journalism
    Monographs, 38. Lexington, Ky.: Association
    for Education in Journalism, 1975.

Jonas Green

Jonas Green (1712-1767) was the youngest of Deacon
Timothy Green's five sons. He served an apprenticeship
with his father in New London before working with his
brother Timothy and Samuel Kneeland in Boston during
1734 and 1735. Jonas's name appears in two known Boston
imprints. In 1735 he printed Judah Monis's Grammar of
the Hebrew Tongue, the first Hebrew grammar published in
America. In 1734 he printed a broadside in which he
proposed printing the grammar by subscription. Green
moved to Philadelphia where he worked with both Benjamin
Franklin and Andrew Bradford in the mid 1730s. In 1738
he moved to Annapolis where he established the Maryland
Gazette (1745) and printed Bacon's Laws of Maryland
(1765). Lawrence C. Wroth notes that the Bacon project
was "one of the small group of notably fine typographical
productions of colonial America."

References:

Demeter, Richard L. Primer, Presses, and Composing
     Sticks: Women Printers of the Colonial Period.
     Hicksville, N.Y.: Exposition Press, 1979.

McMurtrie, Douglas C. "The Green Family of Printers."
     Americana, 26 (1932).

Thomas, Isaiah. The History of Printing in America.
     Worcester, Mass.: Isaiah Thomas, Jr., 1810;
     2nd ed., revised, Albany, N.Y.: J. Munsell
     for the American Antiquarian Society, 1874;
     ed. Marcus A. McCorison, Barre, Mass.: Imprint
     Society, 1970.

Wroth, Lawrence C. The Colonial Printer. New York:
     Grolier Club, 1931; revised and enlarged,
     Portland, Me.: Southworth-Anthoensen Press,
     1938; reprint edition, Charlottesville, Va.:
     University Press of Virginia/Dominion Books,
     1964.

Nathaniel Green

Nathaniel Green (1710-1758), son of Deacon Timothy
Green, published Arthur Browne's The Excellency of
the Christian Religion in 1738. No other Boston
volume is known to bear his imprint.

Samuel Green

Samuel Green (1615-1702) was the Harvard College printer for forty-three years and printer to the Massachusetts general court. He printed the first Bible in America, an Algonquian version translated by John Eliot (1663); the first original nonreligious work, Nathaniel Morton's New-Englands Memoriall (1669); the first and last of Eliot's Indian tracts; the first Connecticut law book, the Book of the General Lawes (1673); the first Connecticut election sermon (1674); the earliest extant Massachusetts election sermon (1663); and the earliest surviving Thanksgiving proclamation (1676).

Publishers Served: Joseph Browning (or Brunning), Society for the Propagation of the Gospel in New England, and the Parts Adjacent in America (the New England Company), Benjamin Harris, Harvard College, Massachusetts General Court, Samuel Sewall, Hezekiah Usher, John Usher.

Green was born in England and emigrated with his parents in 1633, quite probably aboard the Griffin, which also carried John Cotton and Thomas Hooker. His occupations before being appointed to the press were varied: a sergeant in the militia (he rose through the ranks and was made a captain in 1686), a land speculator, and doorkeeper to the Massachusetts House of Deputies. In 1649 Harvard President Henry Dunster chose Green to succeed Matthew Day as the college printer, even though he had no training in the craft. His first known imprint is the cornerstone of American Congregationalism, The Platform of Church Discipline (1649), but it is likely that the 1649 almanac by Urian Oakes is also his. The press, which was the first in the colonies and had been brought from England by Jose Glover, was then operating on the first floor of the president's residence,

230

but in March 1655 it was relocated in the recently completed Indian College. It was there that Green worked
until he retired in 1692.

For most of his career Green made only a marginal living from printing, and he often augmented his
income by selling textbooks and paper to the college
students and by cutting their hair. He was further
compensated for his work by being appointed town clerk
of Middlesex County in 1652, and in 1658 he was awarded
300 acres of land in Haverhill by the general court.
The financial pressures apparently did not daunt him;
he had nineteen children by two wives, and he reared
three of his sons in the craft. Green was responsible
for some 275 imprints during his tenure at Harvard, and
his most productive period was from 1660 to 1674 when he
had the assistance of Marmaduke Johnson. After 1675 he
lost much of his business to the Boston printers; in
1679, for example, Green printed but six titles, most
of which were done for either Harvard or the general
court, while the Boston-based John Foster released
fourteen imprints. Green's last imprint was Cotton
Mather's Ornaments for the Daughters of Zion (1692),
an admonition to Massachusetts women to live more godly
lives by shunning the profane dangers of dancing, cos-
metics, and immodest clothing. Green died on 1 January
1702, but the Harvard press had died ten years earlier
when he retired, and, with the exception of a few months
during the Revolution when the British occupied Boston,
no more printing was done in Cambridge until the nineteenth century.

Green was not an enterprising printer and for
the most part was content to print what was ordered by
his two major employers, the Boston booksellers and the
New England Company. A large number of his imprints
are topical and ephemeral, examples of which are the
yearly Quaestiones and Theses for Harvard; announcements
for fasts, days of thanksgiving, and other orders for
the general court; and almanacs, primers, and catechisms for the booksellers. But he also printed more
substantial titles, including a number of important

historical and literary documents. Among these are
Michael Wigglesworth's The Day of Doom (1662) and his
Meat out of the Eater (1670); the frequent supplements to
the laws, culminating in the revised second and third edi-
tions of The Book of the General Lawes and Libertyes (1660
1672); Urian Oakes's Elegy upon the Death of the Reverend
Mr. Thomas Shepard (1677); John Cotton's Discourse about
Civil Government (1663) and Spiritual Milk for Boston
Babes in Either England (1656); Increase Mather's The
Life and Death of That Reverend Man of God, Mr. Richard
Mather (1670); and the Daily Meditations of Philip Pain
(1670).

One group of titles that gave Green steady employment for a time were the Eliot Indian tracts, translations into Algonquian of the Bible, Psalms, catechisms,
and selected sermons to be used as teaching aids in con-
verting the Indians. These were ordered and paid for by
the New England Company, and include the pamphlets now
known as the Indian primer (1654), the Christian Cove-
nanting Confession (1660?), and the Psalter (1663). The
most significant of these translations was the complete
Bible released in 1663. Green had begun with Genesis
and had completed it in 1655, but his experience with
this and the primer had taught him the difficulty of
composing in a non-Indo-European language that he did
not understand. Compounding Green's problems was the
need for an unusually high number of k, q, and o sorts,
which his fonts did not supply. To help speed the work,
Green petitioned the general court in June 1658 for
more type, and in December of the same year Eliot asked
Governor Endicott to request the New England Company to
send over additional supplies as well as a journeyman
printer to assist Green. The company complied, and in
1659 Green received paper, another press, the second in
the colonies, and a specially cast font of type with a
ligatured double o and ample quantities of the needed
sorts.

Although the requisite material supplies were
now at hand, the untrained Green still needed an experienced assistant to help in the composing, but when

Marmaduke Johnson arrived in the summer of 1660, Green must have considered it a mixed blessing. Johnson's training was invaluable to Green, but the two men did not get along well together, perhaps due to Johnson's attempt to woo one of Green's daughters while still having a wife in England. They did, however, work well together, averaging approximately one sheet a week on the Bible for three years. The Bible finished and his contract completed, Johnson returned to England in 1664, but he permanently emigrated the following year, bringing with him type, paper, and a press, the third in Massachusetts, with which he started a rival printing house in Cambridge. Johnson's return also meant that Green lost the income provided by the Indian tracts, for while in England Johnson had been appointed to replace Green as the New England Company's official printer, a move made probably at the instigation of John Eliot, who appreciated the younger man's quickness and skill. When Johnson died in 1674, Green resumed printing for the Company, completing another edition of the Bible in 1685 and also printing the last of the Indian tracts done in Eliot's life, a translation of Thomas Shepard's The Sincere Convert (1689).

The importance of Samuel Green in the history of American publishing appears to be primarily a matter of accident. He was in the right place at the right time, and as the only printer in Massachusetts for much of his career he printed many of the historically important documents in the developing colony. His craftsmanship, slight in the beginning, steadily improved, and his later work shows that he developed a sound eye for typographical layout and design. But through his sons and their descendants he became the progenitor of a dynasty of printers that helped spread the craft throughout New England and the middle colonies for almost 200 years.

James P. O'Donnell

233

Samuel Green

References:

Kiessel, William C. "The Green Family: A Dynasty of
    Printers." New England Historical and Genea-
    logical Register, 104 (1950).

Littlefield, George E. The Early Massachusetts Press:
    1638-1711. Boston: Club of Odd Volumes, 1907;
    reprint edition, New York: Burt Franklin, 1969.

McMurtrie, Douglas C. "The Green Family of Printers."
    Americana, 26 (1932).

Morison, Samuel Eliot. Harvard College in the Seven-
    teenth Century. Vol. 1. Cambridge: Harvard
    University Press, 1936.

Winship, George P. The Cambridge Press: 1638-1692.
    Philadelphia: University of Pennsylvania
    Press, 1945.

Samuel Green

234

Samuel Green, Jr.

Samuel Green, Jr. (1648-1690), a printer and publisher, worked in Boston from 1681 to 1690. He printed the first publication approaching an American newspaper, Increase Mather's Present State of the New-English Affairs (1689), and the first work on military science in the colonies, James Fitzroy's Abridgement of the English Military Discipline (1690). He worked initially under Samuel Sewall, the manager of the Boston press, but in 1684 Sewall resigned his position and Green was awarded a license to print in Boston by the general court. His first shop was probably located in the same place John Foster worked in, "over against the Sign of the Dove," and around 1687 he moved to Milk Street, "over against the South-Meeting-House." Green printed or published fewer than 100 titles during his eight years in Boston.

Major Authors: Ezechiel Carré, John Cotton, William Hubbard, Cotton Mather, Increase Mather, John Tulley, Samuel Willard.

Publishers Served: Joseph Browning (or Brunning, Benjamin Harris, Samuel Phillips, John Usher.

Green was born in Cambridge in 1648, son of the Harvard printer Samuel Green and his first wife, Jane (Banebridge) Green. He was apprenticed to his father, but after he received his freedom sometime between 1670 and 1675 he discovered that there was no room in Massachusetts for another printer. There were only three presses in the colony at the time; two were being used by his father and the third, the one brought over in 1665 by Marmaduke Johnson, was owned by Boston's John Foster, and there was not sufficient work to keep

even these busy. As a result, Green was forced to abandon his craft. He moved to Hartford, where he opened a
general store. In 1677 he married Hannah Butler, and
shortly afterwards they moved to New London where he
again operated a store. When John Foster died in 1681,
Samuel Sewall was appointed the manager of the Boston
press, but having no training in the practical side of
the business, he asked Green to return to the city and
assist him. Green agreed, and arrived with his family
in December 1681.

Sewall resigned from his post late in 1684, and
Green assumed full control of the press even though he
had no official permission to print in Boston. He petitioned the general court for a license, and it was
awarded him in 1685. Like the rest of the Green family,
Samuel was an industrious workman, but his hard work at
the press did not bring in an adequate income to support
his family and he was forced to resume selling groceries
to the colonists as a sideline to his printing business.
In his Life and Errors (1705), the London bookseller
John Dunton fondly recalls Green, praising him for his
good sense and good humor and especially complimenting
Hannah Green as the perfect mother. But the Greens also
had their share of grief; of their three known children
only one lived to maturity, and Green and his wife died
while still young, both succumbing to the smallpox epidemic that swept through Boston in July 1690.

The majority of Green's imprints were, as might
be expected, religious in nature. The Calvinistic tracts
printed or published by Green--such as William Perkins's
The Foundation of Christian Religion Gathered into Six
Principles (1682), William Hubbard's The Benefit of a
Well-Ordered Conversation (1684), reprints of John
Cotton's God's Promise to His Plantations (1686) and
Spiritual Milk for Boston Babes in Either England (1690),
and Solomon Stoddard's The Safety of Appearing at the Day
of Judgment (1687)--were staples of the Massachusetts
reading public during the period.

Green was also the printer of fifteen titles by Increase and Cotton Mather. For the elder Mather he printed, among others, <u>Practical Truths Tending to Promote the Power of Godliness</u> (1682), <u>Some Important Truths about Conversion</u>, and <u>An Essay for the Recording of Illustrious Providences</u>, both in 1684. Green released Cotton Mather's second title, <u>The Boston Ephemeris</u> (1683) and a number of others, including <u>Work upon the Ark</u> (1689), <u>A Companion for Communicants</u> (1690), and <u>The Wonderful Works of God Commemorated</u> (1690).

In addition to religious titles, Green printed for the Massachusetts government in 1689 and 1690, but more important are his political titles after the Glorious Revolution. In 1689, for example, he published a broadside calling for the surrender of the despotic Governor Andros; in the same year he reprinted Gilbert Burnet's <u>Sermon Preached before the House of Commons, on the 31st of January 1688</u> for Samuel Phillips; and for Benjamin Harris he reprinted the 1628 Massachusetts charter. This last came at a time when Increase Mather had gone to England to secure a new charter for the colony that would allow them to continue their theocracy. Also in 1689 Green printed Increase Mather's <u>The Present State of the New-English Affairs</u>, the first approximation of a newspaper in the colonies. Bearing scant resemblance to a modern newspaper or even to the contemporary English papers, it does, however, offer two letters from Mather and a brief news account describing his trials in finding a way through the maze of the English bureaucracy.

Samuel Green, Jr., was neither as prolific a printer as his two half-brothers, Bartholomew and Timothy, nor was he as historically important as his father. Yet he was not insignificant. He printed some of the most important religious titles of his time, and his work for the Mathers further enhances his claim to our attention. His political titles are few, but they are instructive for the information they provide on how closely the colonists kept an eye on their mother country. Green was a hard-working,

237

careful craftsman, and it seems clear that he would have made a greater contribution to American printing had not an untimely death cut short his career.

James P. O'Donnell

References:

Dunton, John. The Life and Errors of John Dunton. London: Malthus, 1705; reprint edition, New York and London: Garland, 1974; edited by John B. Nichols, London: Nichols, 1818; reprint edition, Burt Franklin, 1969.

Kiessel, William C. "The Green Family: A Dynasty of Printers." New England Historical and Genealogical Register, 104 (1950).

Littlefield, George E. Early Boston Booksellers: 1642-1711. Boston: Club of Odd Volumes, 1900; reprint edition, New York: Burt Franklin, 1969.

Littlefield, George E. The Early Massachusetts Press: 1638-1711. Boston: Club of Odd Volumes, 1907; reprint edition, New York: Burt Franklin, 1969.

McMurtrie, Douglas C. "The Green Family of Printers." Americana, 26 (1932).

Roden, Robert F. The Cambridge Press: 1638-1692. New York: Dodd, Mead, 1905; reprint edition, New York: Burt Franklin, 1970.

Winship, George P. The Cambridge Press: 1638-1692. Philadelphia: University of Pennsylvania Press, 1945.

238

Timothy Green

Timothy Green (1679-1757) was a printer, publisher, and bookseller operating in Boston from 1700 to 1714. His shop was located "at the Lower End of Middle Street," and he often added to his imprints "at the North Part of Town" to distinguish his shop from that of his brother, Bartholomew. He printed or published about ninety titles, including Increase Mather's <u>The Blessed Hope</u> (1701), some copies of which contain the first American copperplate, a portrait of Mather engraved by Thomas Emmes. In 1714 he relocated to New London, where he became that colony's second printer and where he remained for the rest of his life.

<u>Major Authors</u>: John Danforth, Obadiah Gill, James Janeway, Cotton Mather, Increase Mather, Samuel Moodey (or Moody), William Secker.

<u>Publishers Served</u>: Nicholas Boone, Nicholas Buttolph, Benjamin Eliot, Samuel Gerrish, Daniel Henchman, Samuel Sewall, Jr.

Green was born in Boston in 1679, son of Samuel Green and his second wife, Sarah (Clark) Green. His father was the Cambridge printer from 1649 to 1692 and founder of a dynasty of printers who helped spread the craft throughout New England and the middle colonies for nearly 200 years. He began his apprenticeship in approximately 1690, but it is not clear under whom he served; perhaps with his father until his retirement and then with his older brother Bartholomew. Green opened his first shop in 1700, and his first imprint was probably Cotton Mather's <u>Reasonable Religion</u>, which he printed that year for Benjamin Eliot.

239

Timothy Green

On 28 January 1702, Green married Mary Flint in
a ceremony performed by his patron, Cotton Mather. They
maintained the Green family tradition of large families
by having eight children. Of his six surviving sons,
five became printers: Timothy II, Samuel III, John,
Nathaniel, and Jonas, while Thomas became a Boston pew-
terer. In 1707 Green was invited to move to New London,
Connecticut, by Connecticut Governor Gurdon Saltonstall,
but he refused, declining to leave an established business for the hazards of starting a new one. Saltonstall
next approached Thomas Short, brother-in-law of Bartholomew Green, who agreed. When Short died in 1712, Green
was again asked to relocate, and this time he agreed,
but only after the Connecticut General Assembly sweet-
ened the offer by appointing him the government printer
at a salary of £50 , the same sum paid to the deputy
governor. He moved in 1713, and his family followed
the next year.

During his fourteen years in Boston, Timothy
Green printed or published in only one branch of the
trade--religious works. He was a pious, devout man,
and his piety earned him the sobriquet of Deacon
Timothy. But Isaiah Thomas tells us that he was
neither a bigot nor gloomy; he was a kindly man,
much given to jokes, none of which, unfortunately,
Thomas records. Perhaps the most significant feature
of Green's years in Boston is his allegiance to Increase
and Cotton Mather. He printed or published close to
seventy works by this prolific father and son team, and
their writings comprise close to three-quarters of his
total number of imprints. This concentration can be
explained by Green's affiliation with the same stamp
of Congregationalism as the Mathers. Green was firmly
in the Mather camp, and he demonstrated his loyalty by
not printing any of the tracts that attacked them in
the factional disputes that occurred with increasing
frequency in the early years of the eighteenth century.

240

Increase Mather had been the major power in
Boston ever since the 1660s when he became the pastor
of the North Church and, later, President of Harvard.
By 1700, however, his leadership was becoming increasingly resented and his conservatism increasingly irk-
some to those who wished to modify some of the
Congregational principles set down in the Cambridge
Platform of 1649. One such dispute was the doctrinal
quarrel that led to the formation of the Brattle Street
Church. The dispute had started when William and
Thomas Brattle, Solomon Stoddard, Ebenezer Pemberton,
and John Leverett had begun urging some changes in
church polity. The changes they advocated--such as
not requiring a public narration of the conversion
experience of prospective church members and allowing
all adult baptized members of the church who contributed toward the minister's maintenance to have a voice
in selecting him rather than just the full communicants--
were regarded by the Mathers as dangerous innovations.
The elder Mather fired the first salvo with his The
Order of the Gospel Professed, printed by Bartholomew
Green in 1700. In the following year the revisionists
replied with The Gospel Order Revived, printed by
William Bradford in New York. Timothy Green entered
the fray in 1701 by publishing a defense of the Mather
position, A Testimony, to the Order of the Gospel, by
John Higginson and William Hubbard, and, in the same
year, by selling Cotton Mather's Collection of Some of
the Many Offensive Matters Contained in a Pamphlet Entitled the Order of the Gospel Revived. It is not certain who printed the latter piece, but perhaps it was
Green or his brother.

The squabble flared for a time, but it quickly
died down after the dissenting members seceded from the
North Church and founded the Brattle Street Church with
the newly ordained Benjamin Colman as its minister.
Apart from the doctrinal considerations, the most interesting aspect of the quarrel was the accusation in The
Gospel Order Revived that Increase Mather held the city
of Boston and its printers in thrall and that the printers dared not release anything contrary to his wishes;

241

therefore the revisionists could not have their pamphlet printed in the city. Bartholomew Green replied to this charge by printing a rebuttal, stating that he agreed to print the tract, but because the revisionists wanted it to be anonymous he would first submit it to the lieutenant governor for approval, a customary procedure. When the authors refused this offer, only then did he decline to print the pamphlet. In support of his brother's contention, Green and John Allen filed a deposition, also printed by Bartholomew, confirming his brother's account, noting that they had been in the shop at the time. This secondary dispute is interesting because it suggests that despite the censorship laws still in effect, the practice of submitting copy to licensers of the press was becoming less common and took place only in unusual circumstances. In short, prior restraint of the press, even when it was voluntary, was becoming the exception rather than the rule.

That controversy was not the only occasion on which Green aligned himself with the Mathers. In 1701 he printed Some Few Remarks, upon a Scandalous Book, against the Government and Ministry of New-England. The scandalous book was Robert Calef's More Wonders of the Invisible World (London, 1700), an attack on the 1692 witch trials, on Cotton Mather, whom Calef wrongly accuses of being one of the chief witch hunters, and on Mather's allegedly trying to rekindle the flames with his manuscript, "Another Brand Pluckt Out of the Burning," an account of the possession of Margaret Rule. The Few Remarks was edited by Obadiah Gill and a committee at Mather's church. To their defense they attached a letter by Mather, quite correctly noting that it was he who had argued against allowing the testimony of spectral evidence as grounds for conviction, thus helping to bring the madness of the trials to a close.

Not all of Green's books and pamphlets were quite so controversial, however. Most were, in fact, quite unexceptional and standard Congregationalist fare. He printed, for example, James Janeway's Token

for Children (1700), a series of memorials on the blessed
deaths of several children, including Cotton Mather's son
Nathaniel; William Secker's Wedding Ring Fit for the Fin-
ger (1705); the Serious Call to the Quakers, Inviting
Them to Return to Christianity (1709) by George Keith, a
Quaker turned Episcopalian; Josiah Dwight's Bright Side
of a Dark Providence (1710); The Mind at Ease (1712) by
Thomas Bridge (for whom Cotton preached his funeral sermon and later published it as Benedictus in 1715); John
Danforth's The Blackness of Sin against Light (1710);
and Jeremiah Burroughs's Preparation for Judgment (1713).

These titles appear to be almost afterthoughts
to Green's real business of printing or publishing the
works of the Mathers. While Green did not print the
most important works of either man, such as Increase's
biography of his father and Cotton's Christian Philosopher or his Bonifacius, he did print a good many of
those in the second rank. For Increase he did Ichabod
(1702), a jeremiad on the gradual decline of religious
rigorousness in Massachusetts; The Voice of God, in
Stormy Seas (1704), a sermon occasioned by the storm of
7 and 8 April of that year; Meditations on Death (1707);
A Discourse Concerning Faith and Fervency in Prayer
(1710), for which Green joined with four other publishers in hiring his brother to do the printing; and A
Sermon Concerning Obedience and Resignation (1714), a
dignified and melancholy sermon on the death of Mariah,
Increase's wife of fifty-two years. Green's work for
Cotton Mather included The Great Physician (1700), a
sermon Green heard him preach and liked so well that he
asked Mather his permission to print it; The Armour of
Christianity (1704); A Faithful Monitor (1704), an abstract of Massachusetts laws; Lex Mercatoria (1705), on
the role and duties of merchants in a theocracy; Christianity Demonstrated (1710); a catechism, The A, B, C,
of Religion (1713); and What Should Be Most Tho't Upon
(1713), which contains a spirited defense by Mather of
his frequent publications.

Timothy Green's publishing career was neither
the most varied nor the most interesting among publishers

243

in Boston. His religious fervor dictated the titles he published, so that his religiosity sometimes got the better of his business sense. Whenever he heard a sermon he liked, or when one was recommended to him, he more often than not printed it without first considering whether anyone would buy it. When he died, these unsold products of his zeal were placed in bushel baskets and sold by the pound as waste paper. Not all his Boston imprints, however, were quite so inconsequential. His allegiance to the Mather family resulted in his printing a substantial number of their writings; that friendship with the Mathers and publishing of their works make his fourteen years in Boston significant.

James P. O'Donnell

References:

Kiessel, William C. "The Green Family: A Dynasty of Printers." New England Historical and Genealogical Register, 104 (1950).

Littlefield, George E. Early Boston Booksellers: 1642-1711. Boston: Club of Odd Volumes, 1900; reprint edition, New York: Burt Franklin, 1969.

Littlefield, George E. The Early Massachusetts Press: 1638-1711. Boston: Club of Odd Volumes, 1907; reprint edition, New York: Burt Franklin, 1969.

McMurtrie, Douglas C. "The Green Family of Printers." Americana, 26 (1932).

Thomas, Isaiah. The History of Printing in America. Worcester, Mass.: Isaiah Thomas, Jr., 1810; 2nd ed., revised, Albany, N.Y.: J. Munsell for the American Antiquarian Society, 1874; ed. Marcus A. McCorison, Barre, Mass.: Imprint Society, 1970.

Timothy Green II

Timothy Green II (1703-1763), printer and publisher, conducted business in partnership with Samuel Kneeland in Boston from 1726 to 1752. Kneeland and Green printed more than 400 works at the "Printing House over against the Prison in Queen Street," making their shop the leading printing house in Boston in the second quarter of the eighteenth century. Their output made up more than twenty percent of all recorded imprints in the period. Kneeland and Green printed the first religious periodical in America, all the major theological works of Jonathan Edwards, and two of the seven newspapers published in Boston from 1726 until 1752. For many years they were printers to the Massachusetts House of Representatives, and they printed all Massachusetts laws for more than a decade.

Major Authors: Nathaniel Appleton, Benjamin Colman, Jonathan Dickinson, Jonathan Edwards, Thomas Foxcroft, Israel Loring, Thomas Prince, Joseph Seccombe, George Whitefield, William Williams.

Publishers Served: Joseph Edwards, Samuel Eliot, Hopestill Foster, Samuel Gerrish, Thomas Hancock, Daniel Henchman, John Phillips, Nathaniel Proctor.

Green was born in Boston on 12 December 1703 to Timothy and Mary Flint Green. As a Green, Timothy was heir to a great tradition in printing. His grandfather was Samuel Green, the Cambridge printer. Both his father Timothy and uncle Bartholomew Green were Boston printers. Samuel Kneeland, a cousin, was his future partner, and his brother Jonas and cousin Thomas Green would also participate in the colonial trade. Indeed, the Green family has deservedly been called a dynasty of printers.

245

In 1713 Timothy's father accepted an invitation
from Connecticut Governor Gurdon Saltonstall to move to
New London; the only printer to have worked in that
colony, Thomas Short, had died the year before. Green's
family followed in 1714. It was in New London that
young Timothy learned the trade. His father had an
ample number of potential apprentices in Timothy and
his brothers Samuel, Nathaniel, and Jonas, all of whom
would become printers. In 1724 Timothy II returned to
Boston to work in the shop of his uncle, Bartholomew
Green. Timothy may have returned to New London in 1726,
but only briefly, for in that year he formed a partnership in Boston with his cousin Samuel Kneeland. Green
thus began a career that would make him and Kneeland the
leading Boston printers for the next quarter century.

In 1727 Boston had two newspapers, the Boston
News-Letter, published by Bartholomew Green, and the
Boston Gazette, which Kneeland had printed from 1720 to
1726 and which Bartholomew Green, Jr., took over in 1727.
That there was room for a third Boston newspaper was
clear from the success of James Franklin's New-England
Courant, which had been published from 1721 to 1726.
When Franklin went to Newport, Rhode Island, at the end
of 1726, Kneeland moved quickly to establish the New-
England Weekly Journal in an attempt to fill the gap
left by the Courant, a paper devoted to literary and
political commentary rather than conventional news.
The Weekly Journal failed to attain the level of wit
exhibited by the Courant, but it did not give its readers standard newspaper fare, filling its columns instead
with essays from London papers. It was Timothy Green
who, according to Isaiah Thomas, had complete charge of
its printing. Kneeland and Green continued to publish
the Weekly Journal until 1741. In 1736 they also assumed
the job of printing the Boston Gazette, first for John
Boydell, and on his death in 1739, for his widow Hannah
Boydell. Kneeland and Green acquired full ownership of
the Gazette when Hannah Boydell died in 1741; in October
they incorporated the Weekly Journal into the Gazette,.
which they published continuously until Green left Boston
in 1752.

During the first decade of their partnership Kneeland and Green printed primarily religious works, published largely by Samuel Gerrish and Daniel Henchman, including Jonathan Edwards's first publication, God Glorified in the Work of Redemption (1731). In 1736 Kneeland and Green printed for Samuel Gerrish the first volume of Thomas Prince's monumental Chronological History of New-England, one of the first colonial histories to employ documentary evidence.

In the decade after 1736, New England was struck by a wave of religious enthusiasm, part of a continental phenomenon known as the Great Awakening. Its leading spokesman was George Whitefield, but in New England Jonathan Edwards was its guiding spirit. And it was Edwards's account of the revivals in the Connecticut River Valley in A Faithful Narrative of the Surprising Work of God, printed by Kneeland and Green in 1738, that marked the beginning of the Great Awakening in New England.

The Great Awakening split the New England ministry into two camps, pro and con. Kneeland and Green aligned themselves with the supporters, as their record of printing suggests. In addition to printing more of Whitefield's works than did any other firm in town, Kneeland and Green printed the first religious periodical published in America, Thomas Prince's Christian History (1743-1745), which chronicled the Awakening. And they printed all of Jonathan Edwards's major theological writings that gave theoretical foundation, with a blend of Calvinism and Lockean philosophy, to the Great Awakening. Edwards's Sinners in the Hands of an Angry God (1741) is typical of the language of the revivals, and his Treatise Concerning Religious Affections (1746) ranks among the major theological works in American religious history.

Kneeland and Green also received official patronage in the form of government business. From 1732 to 1748 they were, jointly, printers to the Massachusetts House of Representatives, printing the Journals

247

of its proceedings. Kneeland alone was printer to the House after 1748, but since Green was still his partner, Green's efforts in the printing of the House Journals seem likely. From 1742 until 1752, when Green left Boston for New London, Kneeland and Green printed all Massachusetts laws which, excluding broadsides bearing no colophon, totaled more than seventy imprints.

Kneeland and Green were the leading printers in Boston by virtue of the volume of imprints produced. Assuming that Green helped Kneeland print those works on which only Kneeland's name appears, their imprints account for nearly twenty-two percent of all Boston imprints for which printers are known. From 1732 to 1752 they printed almost a quarter of Boston imprints every year. That proportion reached forty percent in 1738, more than any other firm printed while Green was in Boston. Kneeland and Green printed mainly religious works. Isaiah Thomas states that they printed the first complete English Bible in America, the so-called Baskett Bible of 1752, but no copy exists.

Kneeland and Green dissolved their partnership in 1752. Green moved to New London, Connecticut, where, as the oldest son, he assumed management of the business his father had built and from which he was retiring. Green continued to print in New London for another ten years before his death on 3 October 1763. In his Boston career he headed the leading printing house in town, published two newspapers, and printed the most important theological works of the Great Awakening. In New London he maintained the continuity of the Green family, which would supply both Connecticut and Vermont with printers for the remainder of the eighteenth century.

Charles Wetherell

References:

Brigham, Clarence S. History and Bibliography of Amer-
     ican Newspapers: 1690-1820. Vol. 1. Worcester,
     Mass.: American Antiquarian Society, 1947.

Kiessel, William C. "The Green Family: A Dynasty of
     Printers." New England Historical and Genea-
     logical Register, 104 (1950).

Thomas, Isaiah. The History of Printing in America.
     Worcester, Mass.: Isaiah Thomas, Jr., 1810;
     2nd ed., revised, Albany, N.Y.: J. Munsell
     for the American Antiquarian Society, 1874;
     ed. Marcus A. McCorison, Barre, Mass.: Imprint
     Society, 1970.

William Green

William Green (d. 1787) was active in Boston from 1778
to 1786 "at Shakespeare's Head." All ten Boston works
bearing his name as publisher are practical; not one is
of great significance.

Joseph Greenleaf

Joseph Greenleaf (1720-1810) conducted business in Boston for two years after 1773. He announced his printing office "in Hanover-Street" and "opposite the Conduit, near the Market." Most of the fewer than twenty-five titles Greenleaf printed and sold are insignificant, but he did print works by John Cotton, Samuel Cooper, and Joseph Warren (his 1775 Oration). Greenleaf is most important as the author of pseudonymous pro-patriot pieces in the Massachusetts Spy and as publisher, succeeding Isaiah Thomas, of the Royal American Magazine from July 1774 through March 1775, when it ceased publication. Frank Luther Mott characterizes Greenleaf's numbers of the Magazine as "badly printed with poor type and ink on inferior paper."

References:

Mott, Frank Luther. A History of American Magazines: 1741-1850. New York and London: Appleton, 1930; Cambridge: Harvard University Press, 1938; Cambridge: Belknap Press of Harvard University Press, 1957.

Thomas, Isaiah. The History of Printing in America. Worcester, Mass.: Isaiah Thomas, Jr., 1810; 2nd ed., revised, Albany, N.Y.: J. Munsell for the American Antiquarian Society, 1874; ed. Marcus A. McCorison, Barre, Mass.: Imprint Society, 1970.

250

Newspaper
Publishers'
Devices

Used by the *Polar Star*

Used by the *Independent Advertiser*

Used by the *Boston Gazette*, the *Boston Weekly Post-Boy*, and the *Boston Weekly Advertiser*

Used by the *Boston Gazette, Or, Weekly Advertiser*

Used by the *Massachusetts Mercury*

Used by the *Massachusetts Centinel: And the Republican Journal*

Used by the *Independent Chronicle*

Used by the *Massachusetts Spy*

Used by the *Massachusetts Spy*

Used by the *Federal Orrery*

Used by the *Independent Ledger, and American Advertiser*

Printers' Marks

Mark of John Russell

Mark of Belknap & Hall

Oliver Greenleaf

Oliver Greenleaf (c. 1777-1843) was in business with David West from 1799 until 1805. During their first two years together they and several others published two editions of The Psalms of David, Imitated (1799) and two Isaiah Thomas almanacs (1799, 1800). Greenleaf and West also joined with John West in publishing George Walker's novel The Vagabond (1800). Greenleaf was active as a Boston bookseller from 1805 until his death.

Thomas Greenleaf

Thomas Greenleaf (1755-1798) was in partnership with Edmund Freeman in 1784 and 1785. They published the Boston Magazine at their shop "north side the Market." After Freeman twice refused to let him buy the business, Greenleaf moved to New York in 1785.

William Greenough

William Greenough (1772-1860) printed approximately
twenty titles from 1793 to 1795. He was in business
alone in 1793, the year he printed his most significant
work, the first volume of the first American edition of
Fanny Burney's Cecilia (he printed the second volume in
1794). In 1794 he formed a partnership with Ezra W.
Weld; they continued together into 1795 at "No. 42,
Cornhill" or "No. 49, State-Street." Greenough and
Weld printed the Federal Orrery and edited, with the
engraver Samuel Hill, the Massachusetts Magazine. He
served as a printer in Boston as late as 1834.

References:

Brigham, Clarence S. History and Bibliography of Amer-
    ican Newspapers: 1690-1820. Vol. 1. Worcester,
    Mass.: American Antiquarian Society, 1947.

Mott, Frank Luther. A History of American Magazines:
    1741-1850. New York and London: Appleton,
    1930; Cambridge: Harvard University Press,
    1938; Cambridge: Belknap Press of Harvard
    University Press, 1957.

John Griffin

John Griffin (d. 1686) was an English bookseller who came to America for religious reasons. He published four known titles between 1678 and 1685, none of great significance. His importance rests with his probable relationship with Benjamin Harris. George E. Littlefield proposes that Griffin was Harris's agent and correspondent in America, and that when Harris came to America in 1686 and found Griffin dead, he moved into Griffin's shop "at the south corner of State and Washington Streets," one of the choicest locations.

Reference:

Littlefield, George E. Early Boston Booksellers: 1642-1711. Boston: Club of Odd Volumes, 1900; reprint edition, New York: Burt Franklin, 1969.

James Davenport Griffith

James Davenport Griffith (dates unknown) conducted business "a few doors east of the Green-Dragon" for two
years after 1785. His name appears in the imprints of
only four known volumes, two of which are Weatherwise
almanacs. In 1785 Griffith bought John Gill's printing
materials and the rights to Gill's Continental Journal.
Griffith published the Journal from mid 1786 until it
folded, according to Clarence S. Brigham, "because of
the State tax on advertisements," in June 1787. That
year Griffith moved to Keene, New Hampshire, where he
published newspapers into 1792.

References:

Brigham, Clarence S. History and Bibliography of Ameri-
    can Newspapers: 1690-1820. Vol. 1. Worcester,
    Mass.: American Antiquarian Society, 1947.

Thomas, Isaiah. The History of Printing in America.
    Worcester, Mass.: Isaiah Thomas, Jr., 1810;
    2nd ed., revised, Albany, N.Y.: J. Munsell
    for the American Antiquarian Society, 1874;
    ed. Marcus A. McCorison, Barre, Mass.: Imprint
    Society, 1970.

Benjamin Guild

Benjamin Guild (1749-1792), minister and occasional college tutor, succeeded Ebenezer Battelle as proprietor of the Boston Book Store, to which he added a circulating library. He had William P. Blake as a partner and Lemuel Blake as an apprentice; upon Guild's death the former succeeded him in the business. Guild's name appears in the imprints of only eight known titles, three of which are his own catalogues (1788, 1789, 1791).

Reference:

Tebbel, John. A History of Book Publishing in the United States. Vol. 1. New York and London: Bowker, 1972.

Peter Albrecht Von Hagen

Peter Albrecht Von Hagen (d. 1803), a violinist and organist, was also a music publisher with his son and their silent partner Benjamin Crehore from 1797 to 1800. They published at least twenty-two pieces of sheet music during those years.

Peter Albrecht Von Hagen, Jr.

Pete. Albrecht Von Hagen, Jr. (1781-1837), a pianist, was also a music publisher with his father (until 1800) and silent partner Benjamin Crehore (until 1803). From a shop in Cornhill, the firm published at least twenty-two pieces of sheet music through 1800.

Reference:

Lehmann-Haupt, Hellmut. The Book in America. New York: Bowker, 1939; revised and enlarged, New York: Bowker, 1951.

Ebenezer Hall

Ebenezer Hall (1749-1776) learned printing from his
brother Samuel. Ebenezer's name appears in fewer than
ten Boston imprints, all with Samuel. The brothers
published the Essex Gazette in Salem from 1772 to 1775,
and when they moved to Cambridge in the latter year
they continued the newspaper as the New-England Chronicle. The Halls printed in Harvard's Stoughton Hall.

References:

Brigham, Clarence S. History and Bibliography of Amer-
     ican Newspapers: 1690-1820. Vol. 1. Worcester,
     Mass.: American Antiquarian Society, 1947.

Buckingham, Joseph T. Specimens of Newspaper Litera-
     ture. Vol. 1. Boston: Little and Brown, 1850.

Thomas, Isaiah. The History of Printing in America.
     Worcester, Mass.: Isaiah Thomas, Jr., 1810;
     2nd ed., revised, Albany, N.Y.: J. Munsell
     for the American Antiquarian Society, 1874;
     ed. Marcus A. McCorison, Barre, Mass.: Imprint
     Society, 1970.

Prince Hall

Prince Hall (dates unknown) conducted business "opposite the Quaker Meeting-House, Quaker-Lane." His name appears in only one known imprint, his own Charge, Delivered to the African Lodge, June 24, 1797, at Menotomy (1797).

Samuel Hall

Samuel Hall (1740-1807), editor, bookseller, printer, and publisher, is remembered primarily as a publisher of children's books. More than 450 publications from Boston and Salem bear his imprint. He established the first printing house in Salem in April 1768, "nearly opposite the late Rev. Mr. Huntington's Meeting House," which is later cited as "a few doors above the Town-House" or "near the Exchange." He was joined by his brother Ebenezer in 1772. In 1775 the Hall brothers moved to Cambridge, establishing their press at Harvard's Stoughton Hall. Ebenezer died in February 1776. In April, Samuel moved to Boston where he located his press in School Street. In October 1781 he reestablished his press in Salem, this time "near the Court House," where he remained until 1785. Hall next relocated in State Street in Boston. In 1787 he moved to 53 Cornhill on Publishers' Row where he remained until his retirement in 1805, when he sold the establishment to Thomas Emands and Ensign Lincoln.

Major Authors: John Allyn, Jeremy Belknap, Caleb Bingham, Jedidiah Morse, William Perry, William Symmes, Peter Thacher, Nathaniel Thayer, Noah Webster.

267

Hall was born on 2 November 1740, the son of Jonathan and Anna (Fowle) Hall of Medford, Massachusetts. After serving an apprenticeship with his uncle, Daniel Fowle, the publisher of the New-Hampshire Gazette, Hall, in 1762, entered into partnership with Ann Franklin. Isaiah Thomas notes that Hall married Ann Franklin's daughter, although no record of the marriage exists. Ann Franklin and Hall printed the Newport Mercury, in Rhode Island, and some government publications. After her death in 1763, Hall continued in Newport until March 1768, when he sold the Mercury to Solomon Southwick and moved to Salem, Massachusetts, to establish his printing house there. Hall remained in Massachusetts until his death on 30 October 1807.

Hall developed his publishing business slowly. He published only 117 titles in his first twenty years at the trade in Massachusetts, and nearly half of them are sermons. In Salem, Hall, first alone and later with his brother Ebenezer, printed the Essex Gazette, which was founded to promote "a due sense of Rights and Liberties of our Country." At this time they also printed a few books, including an edition of the New-England Primer Improved and political books and pamphlets. When Isaiah Thomas, publisher of the Massachusetts Spy, was forced to move from Cambridge, the provincial congress persuaded the pro-Whig Hall brothers to accommodate it and the army by moving to that city. Under the imprint of S. and E. Hall, they published at Harvard a few books and the New-England Chronicle: or, Essex Gazette. When Samuel moved to Boston after Ebenezer's death, he published the New-England Chronicle from February to June 1776. During the War of Independence, Hall published few titles--four in 1776, one in 1777, none from 1778 to 1780, two in 1781, and four in 1782. Most of them concern the Revolution, including Bills Pending before Parliament Concerning Massachusetts Bay (1774); Grand American Congress (1774); Timothy Pickering's Easy Plan of Discipline for a Militia (1775, 1776), which was first printed in Hall's Essex Gazette; Rules and Regulations for the Massachusetts Army (1775); and a 1781 broadside telling of the surrender of General Cornwallis. Joseph T.

Buckingham notes that "the country had no firmer friend, in the gloomiest period of its history, as well as in the days of its young and increasing prosperity, than Samuel Hall."

In 1781 Hall reestablished his printing house in Salem where he published the Essex Gazette and fewer than ten titles per year. However, three books published at this time were textbooks: a new edition of the New-England Primer Improved (1784) and two Latin grammars (1783, 1785). In 1785 he moved back to Boston where he published books and the Massachusetts Gazette. After the sale of the newspaper, and because of Hall's poor health, he relocated his publishing house and book store at 53 Cornhill. Except for a short period from April to October 1789, when he published in French the Courier de Boston, Hall confined himself to his publishing and bookselling business.

After publishing Noah Webster's American Magazine in 1787 and 1788, Hall devoted himself to publishing children's books, both for school and for entertainment. The yearly output of his press increased; he published over 300 titles from 1789 to 1800, seventy-five percent of all the publications of the Massachusetts presses. In 1795 alone he published approximately sixty titles. One-third of these publications are for children, one-third are sermons, and the rest are almanacs and a few books of science and literature.

Hall's juvenilia include, possibly, James Janeway's Token for Children (1793), which had been first published in 1694. Hall released the expected plethora of catechisms, including those by Joseph Priestly, Shippie Townsend, Isaac Watts, and that of Cotton Mather, which was included in the New-England Primer Improved. Since moralistic chapbooks were popular, the Hall press published The Entertaining History of Honest Peter (1794) and Richard Johnson's Hermit of the Forest (1789).

269

With the didactic view of books for children so prevalent in the eighteenth century, such as entertaining book as The Big Puzzling Cap (1793?) was justified as being intellectually stimulating. One riddle book by John-the-Giant-Killer, Esq. is entitled Food for the Mind (1798?). Hall, however, did not publish only English juvenilia. He published two translations: Arnaud Berquin's Looking-Glass for the Mind, translated from the French by Samuel Cooper (1795), and Karl von Bogatzky's Golden Treasury for the Children of God, translated from the German (1796).

Hall's most significant contribution is in the field of children's educational books. He published such beginners' books (primers, picture books, and easy-to-read books) as The Royal Alphabet (1793) and The Good Child's Delight (1793?). The latter of these promises "short entertaining lessons of one and two syllables"; Tom Thumb's Little Book (1795?) proposes "a new and pleasant method to allure little ones in the first principles of learning." For older children Hall published books of guidance and etiquette, one of which is Eleazar Moody's The School of Good Manners (1790).

Hall published numerous textbooks. In 1794 copyright was given to Hall for A Short and Easy Guide to Arithmetick, which was designed "for use of schools and private families." He later published the first and second editions of Samuel Temple's Concise Introduction to Practical Arithmetic (1796, 1798) and sold the revised and corrected New and Complete System of Arithmetic (1797) by Nicholas Pike. He, with others, contracted with Manning and Loring the first American edition of Alexander Adam's Rudiments of Latin and English Grammar (1799), and Hall published the first edition of English grammars by Caleb Alexander (1792) and Benjamin Dearborn (1795). He published the first two editions of Caleb Bingham's spelling book, The Child's Companion (1792), and several editions of Bingham's Astronomical and Geographical Catechism beginning in 1795. He published William Perry's spelling book and sold Perry's Royal Standard Dictionary (1796).

Hall published sermons by John Allyn, William Symmes, and by Congregationalist ministers Jeremy Belknap, Jedidiah Morse, and Peter Thacher. Historian Belknap and patriot Thacher were also founders of the Massachusetts Historical Society, and Hall published several volumes of the Society's Collections (1795, 1798) and its Catalogue of Books (1796). Morse, the father of American geography, used the Hall press for some of his sermons as well as for the first edition of The American Gazetteer (1797). Hall published a sermon by Nathaniel Thayer, Boston financier and philanthropist. Church literature was also an important part of Hall's trade. He published numerous editions of Isaac Watts's hymnbooks under various titles, church histories, and proceedings of church conventions.

In other areas Hall contracted with Manning and Loring to print William Cheselden's Anatomy of the Human Body (1795) and John Holliday's tract on yellow fever (1796). Hall's own press published a dissertation on puerperal fever (1789) and the first Boston edition of James Sims's Observations on the Scarlatina Anginosa (1796). In the field of literature Hall published primarily British fiction, including works by Daniel Defoe, Henry Fielding, and Samuel Richardson. Hall was responsible for the first Boston editions of Richardson's The History of Sir Charles Grandison (1794) and Clarissa (1795).

Hall also published captivity narratives by Jackson Johnnet and Mary Rowlandson and a half-dozen pieces of execution literature, such as Levi Ames's Last Words (1773), "published at his desire as a solemn warning to all, more particularly young people," and Ezra Ripley's sermon Love to Our Neighbor (1800), delivered the day "on which Samuel Smith was executed for burglary."

Despite Hall's many publications, few were first editions. His juvenilia are important largely for his innovations in making the books attractive. Although he published the first Boston editions of two of Samuel Richardson's novels, he did not publish the works of

271

American writers except for textbooks and historic and
scientific works. Hall is remembered primarily as a
publisher of children's books and as an early supporter
of the War of Independence.

Sue Cunha-Cheesman

References:

Buckingham, Joseph T. Specimens of Newspaper Litera-
     ture. Vol. 1. Boston: Little and Brown, 1850.

Halsey, Rosalie V. Forgotten Books of the American
     Nursery. Boston: Charles E. Goodspeed, 1911;
     reprint edition, Detroit: Singing Tree Press,
     1969.

Thomas, Isaiah. The History of Printing in America.
     Worcester, Mass.: Isaiah Thomas, Jr., 1810;
     2nd ed., revised, Albany, N.Y.: J. Munsell
     for the American Antiquarian Society, 1874;
     ed. Marcus A. McCorison, Barre, Mass.: Imprint
     Society, 1970.

Thomas Hall (see Joseph Belknap and Thomas Hall)

Thomas Hancock

Thomas Hancock (1703-1764) was a bookseller and publisher of sermons and other devotional literature. Although more heavily engaged in general commerce than in publishing, more than forty publications bear his imprint. Throughout his publishing career (1724-1742), Hancock's shop was located "in Ann-Street, near the Draw-Bridge"; around 1730 he named it "the Bible and Three Crowns."

Major Authors: Benjamin Colman, William Cooper, Cotton Mather, Thomas Prince, Samuel Willard.

Hancock was born in Cambridge Farms (later Lexington), Massachusetts, on 13 July 1703. In 1717 he was apprenticed for seven years to Samuel Gerrish in Boston. Upon the expiration of his apprenticeship in 1724, Hancock opened his own shop in Ann Street and rapidly progressed as a bookseller and publisher. He became a close friend of Daniel Henchman, one of Boston's foremost booksellers, and they united in joint publishing ventures on several occasions from 1728 to 1731. In 1729 Hancock, Henchman, and others built the first paper manufactory in Massachusetts. Hancock's marriage to Henchman's daughter in 1730 marked a turning point in his career: during the years prior to his marriage he had published three-fourths of the works that would ultimately bear his imprint. After his marriage he used the prestige and wealth of his alliance with Henchman to expand rapidly his commercial interests beyond bookselling into domestic and foreign trade, profiteering, and smuggling. Consequently, only eleven items bear his imprint during the twelve years after 1730, and these appear with great irregularity. Before his death Hancock amassed a considerable fortune, becoming one of the most prominent Bostonians of his era and one of the wealthiest

273

merchants in New England. He willed approximately
£50,000 to his nephew, John Hancock.

With only a few exceptions, all of Hancock's
publications are of a religious nature, either sermons,
tracts, spiritual essays, or catechisms. He published
many of the great divines of the period, including
Cotton Mather. It was Mather's Tela Praevisa that
launched Hancock in his publishing career in 1724. In
1726 he published another Mather sermon, The Choice of
Wisdom, as well as Mather's last major work, Manuductio
ad Ministerium (1726), completed two years before the
divine's death. Intended as a manual of directions for
a candidate to the ministry, Manuductio contains the
most characteristic expression of Mather's later philosophical development. When Mather died in 1728, Hancock
published one of the three commemorative funeral sermons,
Benjamin Colman's Holy Walk and Glorious Translation of
Blessed Enoch.

Over the years Hancock published at least ten
other sermons by Colman, as well as ones by such prominent clergymen as William Cooper, Samuel Mather, Samuel
Willard, and William Williams. Some measure of his stat-
ure as a publisher may be ascertained from the fact that
he published four election sermons from 1728 to 1732.
Each year, upon the election of a new council, a prominent minister was requested to preach a sermon before
the colony's governing body; these election sermons frequently dealt with the rights of Englishmen and the
responsibilities of the magistrates. Heard by large
audiences, and usually printed by order of the assembly,
they were widely distributed throughout the colony, and
became for the colonists what Justin Winsor calls the
"text-books of politics." The preachers were not above
lecturing the assembly, as did Jeremiah Wise in his 1729
election sermon, published by Hancock (Rulers the Ministers of God for the Good of Their People): "God has not
subjected, the Lives, Liberties or Properties of a People
to the Pleasure of their Superiors." Such admonitions
were to be heard with greater frequency as the century
progressed. The remaining election sermons that Hancock

published are Robert Breck's <u>The Only Method to Promote</u> <u>the Happiness of a People and Their Posterity</u> (1728), Benjamin Colman's <u>Government the Pillar of the Earth</u> (1730), and John Swift's sermon of 1732.

Other devotional works published by Hancock include a commonly used catechism of that era, Thomas Vincent's <u>Explicatory Catechism</u> (1729), and two editions of <u>The Psalms, Hymns, and Spiritual Songs of the Old and</u> <u>New-Testament</u> (1740, 1744), originally published in 1640 and known as the <u>Bay Psalm Book</u>. Hancock's 1744 edition of this work was the last publication bearing his imprint.

One of the few nonreligious works Hancock pub- lished was Isaac Greenwood's <u>Arithmetick, Vulgar and</u> <u>Decimal</u> (1729), the first school textbook written by a colonist. He also published Thomas Prince's <u>Vade Mecum</u> <u>for America</u> (1731), a potpourri of useful information for the traveler. Nor did he refrain from engaging in the inoculation controversy, publishing three pro- inoculation works in 1730, when Boston was threatened by a smallpox epidemic. Zabdiel Boylston's <u>Historical</u> <u>Account of the Small-Pox Inoculated in New-England</u> (1730) describes Boylston's successful inoculations in Boston at the beginning of the 1720s. Two 1730 publica- tions by William Douglass, <u>A Practical Essay Concerning</u> <u>the Small-Pox</u> and <u>A Dissertation Concerning Inoculation</u> <u>of the Small-Pox</u>, are surprising in their support of inoculation, since Douglass had been one of the fiercest opponents of the practice in the bitter controversy of the previous decade.

Thomas Hancock's importance rests not so much on the works he published as on the authors he published. For though he published only a few works of renown, many of his authors were among the most prominent and influ- ential clergymen of Massachusetts, men whose ideas con- tributed to the intellectual history of that time and place.

Gary R. Treadway

275

| Thomas Hancock

References:

Allan, Herbert S. John Hancock, Patriot in Purple.
    New York: Beechhurst Press, 1953.

Baxter, W. T. The House of Hancock: Business in
    Boston, 1724-1775. New York: Russell and
    Russell, 1965.

Winsor, Justin. The Memorial History of Boston.
    Vol. 3. Boston: Osgood, 1881.

Benjamin Harris

Benjamin Harris (c. 1673-1716) was the foremost publisher
and bookseller in seventeenth-century America; he produced possibly the nation's first newspaper. Born in
London, he began as a publisher and bookseller there
until his political activities sent him to jail. Shortly
after his illegal release, he came to America in 1686,
where in Boston he resumed publishing and bookselling
"by the Town Pump near the Change." In 1694 he moved
from "over-against the old-Meeting-House," where he had
been in business with John Allen, to "the Sign of the
Bible, over-against the Blew Anchor." His most notable
Boston publication is the New-England Primer, one of
the most important books in publishing history. In his
peak year, 1690, he published nine, possibly ten, of the
fifteen books published in Boston that year. After
eight years in Boston, he returned to London and resumed
his publishing career until his death.

Major Authors: John Tulley, probably the
Mathers, and himself, as the supposed author of the
Primer.

Frank Luther Mott, the historian of American
journalism, notes that "the too frequent occurrence of
the ridiculous in the career of Ben Harris prevents our
making a hero of him." Most of Harris's vagaries occurred in London, however, and during his eight years in
America, if he was not a hero, he at least made a pro-
found impact on the cultural life of the colonies.

From the beginning he was a figure of controversy. At the start of his career, as a printer in
Bell Alley, London, his first book in 1673 was an
antipapist tract, and he followed this with others
attacking the Catholics and the Quakers. Associating

277

himself with Lord Shaftesbury and the Whigs, he started a party newspaper that was ultimately suppressed in 1681. Joining Titus Oates, he exposed the imaginary conspiracy known as the Popish Plot. In 1679 Harris published a seditious pamphlet that brought him a fine of £500 and a sentence to stand in the pillory. Failing to pay the fine, he was sent to King's Bench prison, from which he was illegally discharged with forged papers. Free again, he resumed pope-baiting in his coffeehouse, where he sold books, patent medicines, and playing cards whose backs contained antipapist propaganda.

Harris was forced to flee England after the accession of James II when he published, in 1686, a book entitled English Liberties, in an edition of 5,000 copies that were immediately seized by the authorities. In the fall of that year, complaining that England was an "uneasie . . . Place for honest men," he arrived in Boston, where he believed his Anabaptist faith would be more welcome. He brought with him his son, Vavasour, and a stock of books that he installed in a shop on the south corner of State and Washington Streets, in an enclave of seven booksellers. There he published his first American book in 1687, John Tulley's almanac for that year, printed for him by Samuel Green.

Having established himself, Harris returned briefly to England for more stock, and to see his wife, returning in January 1688 to find that his son had kept the business prosperous; a second edition of Tulley's almanac had been published while he was gone. Later that year, in November, he made another trip to London but soon returned to publish an edition of the new charter, which proved to be highly profitable. He was already the richest bookseller in Boston, and in 1690 he became the town's leading coffeehouse proprietor as well. His London Coffee House was simply an expansion of the bookstore, made by building a counter from which he dispensed coffee, tea, and chocolate to a few tables. It was a place so respectable that Boston ladies, denied access to the taverns, came to sip the beverages, talk, and buy books, rubbing elbows with such local celebrities

as the Mathers, some of whose prolific book output was
published by Harris.

Overconfident as usual, on 25 September 1690
Harris published Publick Occurrences Both Foreign and
Domestick, which, depending on one's definition of newspaper, was either the first or second American newspaper.
It contained indiscreet stories about the French king,
and news about the Mohawks that the government wanted to
suppress. The chief complaint, however, was that Harris
had failed to obtain a license to print it, and so the
paper was suspended permanently four days after it
appeared, and citizens were warned again that no one
could print without a license.

It was only a minor setback for Harris, since
he had published earlier that year the New-England
Primer, one of the most remarkable volumes in publishing history, sometimes called the Little Bible of New
England, which continued to sell for nearly two centuries and influenced profoundly the minds of generations
of Americans. Its origin was in a book Harris had published in London in 1679, The Protestant Tutor, intended
to teach spelling to children along with antipapist,
pro-Protestant propaganda. The Primer borrowed its
thesis from the Tutor but omitted the propagandizing.

That year, 1690, was a climactic time for Harris.
Under the Primer's impetus, he set up a print shop in
1691, with John Allen, another refugee from London who
had previously printed several of Increase Mather's
works. Apparently the partnership was even more successful than Harris's previous association with Green
and Richard Pierce, who had printed Harris's first books,
because their first year's list of nine (possibly ten)
books was three-fifths of Boston's total output. Briefly,
in 1692, the partners became official printers to the
governor, a position of distinction more than profit,
but they lost the post a year later to Green. Possibly
for this reason the partners ended their relationship
that year. Harris moved his shop in 1694 from quarters

"over-against the old-Meeting House" to a new location
"at the Sign of the Bible, over-against the Blew Anchor."

After only a year in that location, Harris decided, for reasons that remain a mystery, to give up
Boston and return to England, which he did early in 1695,
leaving Vavasour to close out the business. Back in
London, he returned to publishing newspapers, in which
he quarreled with various London notables, including
Jonathan Swift and his old friend, John Dunton. The
last number of his London Post appeared in 1716, and
apparently he died in that year, although the exact date
is not known.

Harris won a place for himself in publishing history by publishing one of America's first newspapers,
and by compiling (if, in fact, he did) and publishing
the New-England Primer, which laid the foundation for
children's literature in America. Coming to Boston as
an immigrant stranger, Harris left it eight years later
as Boston's leading bookseller and coffeehouse proprietor. He lacked much in personal character, but made up
for it in enterprise, energy, and sheer intelligence.
He has been termed, correctly, the seventeenth century's
foremost American bookseller.

John Tebbel

References:

Ford, Worthington C. The Boston Book Market: 1679-
    1700. Boston: Club of Odd Volumes, 1917;
    reprint edition, New York: Burt Franklin,
    1972.

Littlefield, George E. Early Boston Booksellers:
    1642-1711. Boston: Club of Odd Volumes, 1900;
    reprint edition, New York: Burt Franklin, 1969.

Mott, Frank Luther. American Journalism, A History: 1690-1960. Third edition. New York: Macmillan, 1962.

Tebbel, John. A History of Book Publishing in the United States. Vol. 1. New York and London: Bowker, 1972.

Vavasour Harris

Vavasour Harris (dates unknown) conducted business "over-against the Old-Meeting-House" or "at the sign of the Bible, over-against the Blew Anchor" in 1695. He came to America in 1686 with his father Benjamin Harris, and when Benjamin returned to London in late 1794 or early 1795, he left his business with Vavasour and the responsibility of superintending the printing contracts with John Allen. The 1695 books printed by the Harris press therefore bear the names of Vavasour Harris and John Allen in the imprints. Two of the three known titles bearing Vavasour Harris's name are by Cotton Mather.

References:

Littlefield, George E. Early Boston Booksellers: 1642-1711. Boston: Club of Odd Volumes, 1900; reprint edition, New York: Burt Franklin, 1969.

Littlefield, George E. The Early Massachusetts Press: 1638-1711. Boston: Club of Odd Volumes, 1907; reprint edition, New York: Burt Franklin, 1969.

281

Charles Harrison

Charles Harrison (d. c. 1745) was born in England. In
Boston he was active as a bookseller and binder from
1738 to 1745 "over-against the Brazen Head in Cornhill."
Seven of his twenty-two known titles are by George
Whitefield, three are by Gilbert Tennent, and two are
by Cotton Mather. He possibly published only one secular book, Samuel Richardson's Pamela (1744).

Reference:

Thomas, Isaiah. The History of Printing in America.
     Worcester, Mass.: Isaiah Thomas, Jr., 1810;
     2nd ed., revised, Albany, N.Y.: J. Munsell
     for the American Antiquarian Society, 1874;
     ed. Marcus A. McCorison, Barre, Mass.: Imprint
     Society, 1970.

J. Hastings

J. Hastings (given name and dates unknown) was one of
the sellers of Noah Webster's American Magazine in 1788.

Aaron Hawes

Aaron Hawes (dates unknown) was responsible for only one known publication. In 1771 he had Isaiah Thomas print John Owen's Eschol.

Joseph Hawkins and
Daniel Tillotson (or Tillotsen)

Joseph Hawkins (b. 1772) and Daniel Tillotson (or Tillotsen) (dates unknown) conducted business at "no. 39, Cornhill." In 1800 they published The Columbian Phenix and Boston Review from January through July, at which time it ceased publication.

Reference:

Mott, Frank Luther. A History of American Magazines: 1741-1850. New York and London: Appleton, 1930; Cambridge: Harvard University Press, 1938; Cambridge: Belknap Press of Harvard University Press, 1957.

Thomas Hazard

Thomas Hazard (dates unknown) printed The Merry Fellow's Pocket Companion in 1799.

Daniel Henchman

Daniel Henchman (1689-1761) was the leading bookseller and publisher in Boston during the first half of the eighteenth century. More than 300 publications by at least 116 authors bear his imprint. He published sermons and theological lectures by many of the most eminent divines, including the first published work of Jonathan Edwards. Throughout his career his shop was located in Cornhill at the south corner of State and Washington streets (later King Street), a site alternately described as "over against the Brick Meeting-House" and "on the south-side of the Town-House."

Major Authors: Benjamin Colman, Jonathan Edwards, Cotton Mather, Thomas Prince, Joseph Sewall, Solomon Stoddard, Gilbert Tennent, Nathaniel Ward, George Whitefield, Samuel Willard.

Henchman, son of Abigail and Hezekiah Henchman of Boston, was born 21 January 1689 and died 25 February 1761. In addition to being a prominent bookseller, he was a citizen of some standing in Boston, taking an active part in military and civil affairs. An officer in the Boston regiment of militia and twice captain of the Ancient and Honourable Artillery Company, he served also as justice of the peace for Suffolk, overseer of the poor, and deacon of the Old South Church.

Little is known of Henchman's early life. If he served the conventional seven-year apprenticeship, he may have set up as an independent bookseller as early as 1710. This estimate is strengthened by evidence provided by Henchman's oldest surviving ledger, dated 1712, which contains references to an earlier volume. In 1713 he opened his shop in Cornhill, and in the same year married Elizabeth Gerrish of Boston, daughter of

John Gerrish, a prominent general trader. This association, and subsequent associations formed through the
marriage of his daughter Lydia to Thomas Hancock, helped
to cement Henchman's position in the community.

Henchman was most active as a religious publisher.
Almost all of the approximately 300 titles he published
can be classified under the rubric theology. Of that number the majority are transcripts of lectures or sermons,
including ordination and funeral sermons, weekly lecture sermons such as those delivered at the Thursday
Lectures in Boston, discourses on the duties of government preached before the governor and the council on
election day, and sermons of the artillery company.
Doctrinal writings such as official synod platforms and
catechisms, works of pure theology, and various editions
of the Old Testament and Psalms comprise the remainder
of Henchman's religious canon.

Henchman launched his publishing career in 1712
with a sermon by Cotton Mather entitled A Town in Its
Truest Glory. Until his death in 1728, Mather continued
to be one of Henchman's major authors, contributing a
total of twenty-eight titles. With the exception of the
Psalterium Americanum (1718), Mather's translation of
the Psalms for use in singing, these titles are not
among Mather's most celebrated. They do, however, serve
as reminders of the tragedy that it was his lot to over-
come. A common theme in the works published by Henchman
is the necessity of early piety. Nine of Mather's fifteen children died young. It is hardly surprising then
that in such works as Golgotha, subtitled A Lively Description of Death (1713), and The City of Refuge (1716),
Mather impassionedly urges early piety as a means of
attaining heavenly refuge. That early piety was a
common concern among ministers of the day is further
evidenced by Henchman's publication in 1721 of A Course
of Sermons on Early Piety, including, in addition to
Mather's contribution, lectures by eight of the United
Ministers of Boston.

Henchman published such other eminent writers as Benjamin Colman (sixteen titles), Thomas Prince (fifteen titles), and Joseph Sewall (thirteen titles), three of the most learned and influential theologians residing in the colonies at the time. One of Colman's most famous works is his Humble Discourse on the Incomprehensibleness of God, published separately by Henchman and Samuel Gerrish in 1715, with a second edition by Henchman appearing in 1740. This document was a principal vehicle for the popularization of the new science. As further testimony to Colman's scientific enlightenment, Henchman also might have published, in 1730, his pro-inoculation work entitled Narrative of the Success and Method of Inoculating the Small Pox in New-England.

Thomas Prince and Joseph Sewall, colleagues at the Old South Church, shared Colman's interest in the observation and interpretation of natural phenomena. In 1719 Prince described an aurora borealis in An Account of a Strange Appearance in the Heavens. In a more somber vein, the great earthquake of 1727 inspired both Prince and Sewall, who viewed the event as God's judgment upon an errant people. Prince's work, with the running title God Shakes the Earth Because He is Wroth, offered the diagnosis, while Sewall's Repentance the Sure Way to Escape Destruction promised the cure. Other notable titles by Prince that Henchman published include The Departure of Elijah Lamented (1728), a sermon occasioned by the death of Cotton Mather, and Extraordinary Events the Doings of God (1745), a thanksgiving sermon following the capture of Louisburg on Cape Breton, Nova Scotia. The latter work, republished by Henchman in 1747, went through five London editions.

It is not quantity of titles alone that grants an author a major place in a publisher's canon. Although Henchman published only four titles by Jonathan Edwards, one of these, Edwards's first published work, lends Henchman just fame. On Thursday, 8 July 1731, Edwards, grandson and heir apparent of Solomon Stoddard, the "pope" of Northampton, was invited to give the public

lecture in Boston. Having increasingly taken on the
character of a professional exhibition rather than a
mere theological lecture, the Thursday Lecture was to
be Edwards's testing ground. His invitation to speak
was in the nature of a challenge: would he prove himself, as his grandfather before him, to be an ecclesiastical force to be contended with by the New England
clergy? The answer was affirmative. In recognition of
the fact, the Harvard community, through the agency of
Daniel Henchman, published Edwards's sermon under the
title God Glorified in the Work of Redemption, by the
Greatness of Man's Dependence upon Him, in the Whole
of It. The work is a landmark in ecclesiastical history. A protest against reliance on moral effort to
achieve salvation, it helped to usher in the revivalist
movement by giving voice to a still nascent call for
renewed orthodoxy.

In the decade following Edwards's lecture, New
England was once again embroiled in religious controversy. As enthusiasm for a general revival grew, the
clergy began to align itself with pro- or antirevivalist factions. It is testimony to Henchman's centrality
as a publisher (as well as to his business acumen) that
he could count among his published authors the major per-
sonalities of each group, although he did not often publish their most decisive works.

Among the prorevivalists published by Henchman,
Gilbert Tennent and George Whitefield rank with Edwards
as creators of the Great Awakening. Tennent was a New
Jersey Presbyterian noted (and disliked) for his search-
ing examinations into the experiences of professing
Christians. His spiritual exposé, A Solemn Warning to
the Secure World from the God of Terrible Majesty
(running-title: The Presumer Detected) was published
by Henchman in 1735. In 1741, when Tennent returned
to the same theme in a sermon preached at the Evening
Lecture in Boston, Henchman produced The Righteousness
of the Scribes and Pharisees Considered. Titles published for Whitefield, while less dramatically phrased,
are equally important as documents of that feverish

287

time. In 1740 and 1741 Henchman produced both an autobiography of the early life of Whitefield and several
of Whitefield's sermons.

Antirevivalist sentiment is best represented
among Henchman's publications in Edward Wigglesworth's
Seasonable Caveat against Believing Every Spirit: With
Some Directions for Trying the Spirits, Whether They Are
of God (1735). In the two Harvard lectures comprising
the work, Wigglesworth addresses the problem of false
prophets, denying the peculiar gift of God to
evangelists.

The majority of Henchman's titles are not so
partisan. Funeral orations alone account for approximately one-eighth of his publishing output, the greater
number being elegies in honor of members of the clergy.
Titles such as Precious Treasure in Earthen Vessels
(Joseph Sewall on Ebenezer Pemberton, 1717) and Faithful
Pastors Angels of Churches (Benjamin Colman on Peter
Thacher, 1739) were common, as the clergy turned out to
honor their own. Henchman's connection with the Ancient
and Honourable Artillery Company also served to enhance
his career. Pursuant to its aim of being "a nursery of
good soldiers," the company annually invited a renowned
minister to preach on the duty of soldiers. Thomas
Symmes's Good Soldiers Described and Animated (1720)
and Nathaniel Walter's Character of a Christian Hero
(1746) are typical of the ministry's response.

Two other of Henchman's religious publications
also bear mention. The first is Samuel Willard's Compleat Body of Divinity (1726), a transcription of 250
lectures in which Willard systematically surveys the
entire field of theology. Published twenty years after
Willard's death at the instigation of Thomas Prince and
Joseph Sewall, the ponderous volume has the double honor
of being the largest book printed in America to that
time and one of the first subscription books ever published. Its importance at the time of publication was
signified by a rubricated title page, an expensive and
therefore relatively rare distinction. Henchman is

also alleged to have published, in 1752, the first English language Bible printed in America. The story orig-
inates with Isaiah Thomas who claims to have heard of
the project from those who "had assisted at the case and
press in printing this Bible." As it was illegal at
that time to print the Bible in the colonies without a
royal patent, Henchman's Bible, printed by Kneeland and
Green, bore the London imprint of the Bible from which
it was reprinted, viz., "London: Printed by Mark
Baskett, Printer to the King's Most Excellent Majesty."
Because no copy of the pirated Baskett Bible has been
discovered, it is impossible to substantiate the story.

Henchman's nonreligious publications are few,
but in several cases they are outstanding. In 1713 he
published the first American edition of Nathaniel Ward's
Simple Cobler of Aggawam in America (1731), originally
published in London in 1647. Other titles of interest
are Thomas Prince's Vade Mecum for America, America's
first guidebook, providing gazetteer information, tables
of commodities, and rates of interest for the use of
traders and travelers; and, in a more macabre vein,
Samuel Penhallow's History of the Wars of New-England
with the Eastern Indians (1726), a work described in the
Dictionary of American Biography as "a volume stating
harrowing facts with no attempt to soften the ghastly
deeds of the savage."

Because of the volume and the ambitiousness of
Henchman's publishing ventures, he was a central figure
in the Boston book trade. He maintained accounts with
a number of prominent Boston printers, among them
Bartholomew Green, Samuel Kneeland, Thomas Fleet, and
John Draper. On occasion, Henchman entered into coop-
erative ventures with other publishers, most notably
Samuel Gerrish, with whom he published a number of his
early sermons. Several of Henchman's most important
works were the result of collaborative efforts. In
1718 Gerrish, Henchman, Benjamin Eliot, and John
Edwards produced Mather's Psalterium Americanum. Later,
in 1726, Eliot was involved in the publication of Samuel
Willard's Compleat Body of Divinity. Henchman's

son-in-law, Thomas Hancock, also worked with him from time to time, Prince's Vade Mecum for America being one product of their collaboration.

Daniel Henchman's reputation as a publisher would be secure if only his most famous publications were considered. His position is further enhanced, however, by several other of his contributions to the publishing field. First, he was instrumental in establishing the first paper mill in New England. In 1728 the provincial government passed an act to encourage the manufacture of paper. A patent was granted to Daniel Henchman, Benjamin Faneuil, Gillam Phillips, Thomas Hancock, and Henry Dering, and in 1729 the plant was built near Milton Lower Falls, a little distance from Boston. Although the mill was only moderately successful, it represents an earnest effort on the part of Boston tradesmen to alleviate their dependency on foreign manufactures. In addition, Henchman's bookshop served as a training ground for young publishers. John Phillips, Nathaniel Belknap, Henry Knox, Thomas Hancock, and Samuel Webb have been cited as Henchman's apprentices. Of these, only Hancock's apprenticeship has been disputed; his papers of indenture to Samuel Gerrish seem to support the dissenting view.

Henchman's final contribution to the history of publishing was, perhaps, inadvertent. Several of his account books survive, detailing his various business dealings, including his publishing ventures. From these ledgers it is possible to gain a sense of how the publishing business was conducted in colonial times. Among other innovations, Henchman's records reveal the beginnings of a reciprocal author-publisher relationship. Although author royalties did not commence until the early nineteenth century, the records show that Henchman gave author's copies, as many as fifty to a single author.

Daniel Henchman was as progressive in his business dealings as he was prolific as a publisher. In view of his great accomplishments, he seems to be deserving of Isaiah Thomas's panegyric: "the most eminent and enterprising bookseller that appeared in Boston, or, indeed, in all British America, before that year 1775."

Donna Nance

References:

Baxter, William T. "Daniel Henchman, A Colonial Bookseller." Essex Institute Historical Collections, 70 (1934).

Silver, Rollo G. "Publishing in Boston, 1726-1757: The Accounts of Daniel Henchman." Proceedings of the American Antiquarian Society, 66 (1956).

Thomas, Isaiah. The History of Printing in America. Worcester, Mass.: Isaiah Thomas, Jr., 1810; 2nd ed., revised, Albany, N.Y.: J. Munsell for the American Antiquarian Society, 1874; ed. Marcus A. McCorison, Barre, Mass.: Imprint Society, 1970.

John Hicks (see Nathaniel Mills and John Hicks)

Samuel Hill

Samuel Hill (c. 1766-1804) was probably the best Boston
engraver of his time. He also published, in 1792,
Andrew Ellicott's map, Plan of the City of Washington,
and in 1800 he published the first American edition of
Batty Langley's The Builder's Jewel. He published the
Massachusetts Magazine with William Greenough and Ezra W.
Weld in 1794 and 1795. Hill conducted business at
"no. 2, Cornhill."

References:

Mott, Frank Luther. A History of American Magazines:
    1741-1850. New York and London: Appleton,
    1930; Cambridge: Harvard University Press,
    1938; Cambridge: Belknap Press of Harvard
    University Press, 1957.

Tebbel, John. A History of Book Publishing in the
    United States. Vol. 1. New York and London:
    Bowker, 1972.

William Hilliard

William Hilliard (1778-1836) began his printing career "at the Cambridge Press" in 1800. That year his name appeared in seven known imprints, and he printed Harvard theses, the first to be printed in a century. Hilliard's important accomplishments came well after 1800, however. John Tebbel notes that Hilliard "left his mark on publishing, not only with his books but because his house fathered the Old Corner, the Boston Type and Stereotype Foundry, and Little, Brown." In 1825 he helped Thomas Jefferson build the University of Virginia library.

Reference:

Tebbel, John. A History of Book Publishing in the United States. Vol. 1. New York and London: Bowker, 1972.

Robert Hodge

Robert Hodge (c. 1746-1813), a Scot, worked first in Philadelphia before moving to Baltimore in 1772. Later that year he located in New York City where he was a partner with Frederick Shober until 1775. At the outbreak of the Revolution Hodge moved to the country, and he next printed in Norwich, Connecticut, in 1778. He established his Boston printing office "in Marshall's Lane, near the Boston Stone" in 1779. In 1781 and 1782 he was in partnership with Nathaniel Coverly "in Newbury Street, near the Sign of the Lamb," but in the latter year the partnership dissolved and Hodge returned to Marshall's Lane. The sixteen known Boston titles bearing Hodge's name are undistinguished. With the end of military hostilities he moved once again to New York City where he continued in business at least into 1796.

Reference:

Thomas, Isaiah. The History of Printing in America. Worcester, Mass.: Isaiah Thomas, Jr., 1810; 2nd ed., revised, Albany, N.Y.: J. Munsell for the American Antiquarian Society, 1874; ed. Marcus A. McCorison, Barre, Mass.: Imprint Society, 1970.

294

John Hodgson

John Hodgson (d. c. 1781), a Scot, was a bookseller and
binder in Boston. His name appears in the imprints of
only three known volumes. In 1765 he published an edition of A New Version of the Psalms of David. After he
gave up his shop in 1768, Hodgson worked with John Mein
and, according to Isaiah Thomas, sold a few books.

Reference:

Thomas, Isaiah. The History of Printing in America.
    Worcester, Mass.: Isaiah Thomas, Jr., 1810;
    2nd ed., revised, Albany, N.Y.: J. Munsell
    for the American Antiquarian Society, 1874;
    ed. Marcus A. McCorison, Barre, Mass.:
    Imprint Society, 1970.

John Homes

John Homes (dates unknown) apparently operated a book
and stationery store "Opposite the North Door of the
State House, State Street." Charles Evans records that
Homes published a catalogue of his books for sale in
1797, but there is no known copy.

Joseph Hovey

Joseph Hovey (dates unknown) conducted business at "No. 47, Marlboro' Street" (or "No. 39, Cornhill"). His name appears in only one known imprint, a Weatherwise almanac. He possibly published Poor Richard's <u>Massachusetts Almanack</u> in 1789.

Job How

Job How (dates unknown) worked, with his brother John How and possibly John Allen, for Samuel Green, Jr. Job's name appears in only one known imprint, James Allen's <u>Neglect of Supporting and Maintaining the Pure Worship of God</u> (1687). He and John Allen printed that volume for Green.

References:

Littlefield, George E. <u>Early Boston Booksellers: 1642-1711</u>. Boston: Club of Odd Volumes, 1900; reprint edition, New York: Burt Franklin, 1969.

Littlefield, George E. <u>The Early Massachusetts Press: 1638-1711</u>. Boston: Club of Odd Volumes, 1907; reprint edition, New York: Burt Franklin, 1969.

Thomas, Isaiah. The History of Printing in America.
Worcester, Mass.: Isaiah Thomas, Jr., 1810;
2nd ed., revised, Albany, N.Y.: J. Munsell
for the American Antiquarian Society, 1874;
ed. Marcus A. McCorison, Barre, Mass.: Imprint
Society, 1970.

John Howe

John Howe (1754-1835) printed in Boston in 1775 and 1776.
A Tory, he printed pro-British documents, most of which
are broadsides. During late 1775 and early 1776 he
printed the Massachusetts Gazette for Margaret Draper
"in Newbury-Street."

References:

Brigham, Clarence S. History and Bibliography of American Newspapers: 1690-1820. Vol. 1. Worcester,
Mass.: American Antiquarian Society, 1947.

Thomas, Isaiah. The History of Printing in America.
Worcester, Mass.: Isaiah Thomas, Jr., 1810;
2nd ed., revised, Albany, N.Y.: J. Munsell
for the American Antiquarian Society, 1874;
ed. Marcus A. McCorison, Barre, Mass.: Imprint
Society, 1970.

297

John Howel

John Howel (dates unknown) was active in Boston in 1791.
That year he bought from Edmund Freeman the <u>Herald of
Freedom, and the Federal Advertiser</u>, a semi-weekly newspaper. In July he changed the name to the <u>Argus</u> and published it into October. That year he also printed, for
Ebenezer Larkin, Jean Paul Rabaut, Saint-Étienne's address to the English people.

References:

Brigham, Clarence S. <u>History and Bibliography of American Newspapers: 1690-1820</u>. Vol. 1. Worcester,
Mass.: American Antiquarian Society, 1947.

Buckingham, Joseph T. <u>Specimens of Newspaper Litera-
ture</u>. Vol. 1. Boston: Little and Brown, 1850.

William Hoyt

William Hoyt (1759-1812) was in partnership with
Nathaniel Coverly in 1789 "at the corner of Back-
Street." From April through September they printed
and sold the Gentlemen and Ladies Town and Country
Magazine. Charles Evans notes that "this magazine
terminated its execrable typographical existence . . .
with the questionable distinction of having been, prob-
ably, the worst-printed magazine that ever was issued."
Hoyt and Coverly also printed the Minutes of the Warren
Association in 1789.

References:

Brigham, Clarence S. History and Bibliography of Ameri-
    can Newspapers: 1690-1820. Vol. 1. Worcester,
    Mass.: American Antiquarian Society, 1947.

Mott, Frank Luther. A History of American Magazines:
    1741-1850. New York and London: Appleton, 1930;
    Cambridge: Harvard University Press, 1938;
    Cambridge: Belknap Press of Harvard University
    Press, 1957.

Nathaniel Hurd

Eldad Hunter

Eldad Hunter (dates unknown) was active in Boston in 1774, although his name appears in only one known imprint. He printed and sold a sermon by Samson Occom.

Nathaniel Hurd

Nathaniel Hurd (1730-1777) was, with Paul Revere, the most significant American book-plate engraver before the War of Independence. Two broadsides--Sperma-Ceti Candles (1770, 1775)--bear Hurd's name as engraver. A Caricatura, another broadside by Hurd, was advertised in 1765, but no copy is known to exist.

References:

Anon. "Early American Artists and Mechanics," New England Magazine, 3 (1832).

Brigham, Clarence S. "Report of the Librarian." Proceedings of the American Antiquarian Society, 24 (1914).

Vail, R. W. G. "Report of the Librarian." Proceedings of the American Antiquarian Society, 47 (1937).

Ellis Huske

Ellis Huske (d. 1755) succeeded John Boydell as post-master in October 1734. He was unable to persuade Boydell to give up the Boston Gazette, so Huske established the Boston Weekly Post-Boy. It appeared under his name from 1734 to 1754.

References:

Brigham, Clarence S. History and Bibliography of American Newspapers: 1690-1820. Vol. 1. Worcester, Mass.: American Antiquarian Society, 1947.

Thomas, Isaiah. The History of Printing in America. Worcester, Mass.: Isaiah Thomas, Jr., 1810; 2nd ed., revised, Albany, N.Y.: J. Munsell for the American Antiquarian Society, 1874; ed. Marcus A. McCorison, Barre, Mass.: Imprint Society, 1970.

Winsor, Justin. The Memorial History of Boston. Vol. 2. Boston: Ticknor, 1881.

Benjamin Indicott (or Endicott)

Benjamin Indicott (or Endicott) (dates unknown) conducted business at "No. 10 on the Town Dock." In 1730 he published Edmund Massey's Sermon against the Dangerous and Sinful Practice of Inoculation.

302

Henry G. Jenks

Henry G. Jenks (dates unknown) printed one known volume, <u>The Curiosities of London, and Westminster Described</u> (1787).

Marmaduke Johnson

Marmaduke Johnson (c. 1628-1674) was the first journey-man printer in America. He established the first private press in the colonies, serving as both printer and publisher. He helped print the first Bible and the first original, non-religious American work, and he was also the first licensed Boston printer. He produced close to sixty books, either alone or in conjunction with Harvard printer Samuel Green. In 1674 Johnson received permission to move his shop from Cambridge to Boston, but he died before printing a book there.

<u>Major Authors</u>: John Eliot, Increase Mather, Timothy Rogers, Thomas Vincent, Samuel Wakeman.

<u>Publishers Served</u>: Society for the Propagation of the Gospel in New England, Joseph Farnham, Edmund Ranger, Hezekiah Usher, John Usher.

Johnson was born in Rothwell, England, son of a tailor. He was apprenticed to John Field on 9 January 1646 for the conventional seven years, and he gained his freedom on 4 October 1652. Though little has been discovered of his London years, it is known that he was jailed for debt and that he penned the anonymous <u>Ludgate,</u>

<u>What It Is: Not What It Was</u>, a condemnation of the debtor's prison system printed by his brother Thomas in 1659. In 1660 he was brought to America by the Society for the Propagation of the Gospel in New England (also known as the New England Company), to assist Harvard College printer Samuel Green in the printing of John Eliot's Algonquian translations of the Bible, Psalms, and noteworthy sermons. He was fined £5 in 1662 for gaining the affections of Green's daughter while still having a wife and child in England, and for making threats against any man who should pay his addresses to her, he was ordered to keep the peace. Johnson subsequently absented himself from work for six months. The Massachusetts Commissioners complained to the New England Company about the delay in getting the Indian Bible printed, but Johnson had powerful friends in John Eliot and Harvard President Charles Chauncy, and when his term was up in May 1663, he was hired for an additional year. Johnson returned to England in August 1664, but he permanently emigrated the following May, this time as the company's sole authorized printer. He carried with him a new font of nonpareil type for the company's works, as well as a press and fonts of his own with which he opened the first privately owned press in America.

Johnson's relations with the Cambridge authorities were at best uneasy, and matters were not improved when he returned as the company's printer and also announced his intention to start a private, competing press. The reluctance of Massachusetts officials to lose the revenues derived from printing money necessary to support the college led to the first long-lived American press licensing act. In 1662 the Massachusetts General Court had appointed Daniel Gookin and Jonathan Mitchel as licensers of the press, but the act was repealed in 1663. When Johnson reappeared in the colony, the court reestablished the licensing act and, in a move aimed specifically at him, further stipulated that no press could be operated outside Cambridge. Johnson complied with the order and located his shop in the center of town. He continued to work in tandem with Green, but he also released books under his own imprint.

304

In 1668 he was fined £5 for printing The Isle of Pines
without authority. In 1670 he married the widow Ruth
Cane, his first wife having died in 1662, and in 1673
he became a constable of Cambridge. He petitioned the
general court in 1674 to be allowed to remove to Boston,
pleading the need better to support his family, and the
court granted his petition. There is, however, no extant Boston imprint of Johnson's; his last book, Samuel
Torrey's An Exhortation unto Reformation (1674), bears
a Cambridge imprint. Johnson died in Boston on 25 December 1674. His will reveals him to have been a substantial man of property, thus belying his earlier reputation
as a profligate and ne'er-do-well.

In December of 1658, John Eliot petitioned the
New England Company for a trained printer to assist
Green in completing the immense Algonquian Bible, the
first printed in America. Eliot had completed his translation early in 1658, but because of the special complex-
ities of composing in an unfamiliar, non-Indo-European
language and the need for an unusually high number of k
and q sorts, work had proceeded very slowly. To facili-
tate composition, Eliot ordered from England, through
the Boston bookseller Hezekiah Usher, a special font,
a bourgeois face on a brevier body, with additional
sorts and a special ligatured double o, which was delivered in 1659. By the time Johnson arrived in 1660,
only one sheet of Matthew had been worked off, but with
his expert help the schedule was soon a sheet a week.
When both presses, the company's and the college's,
were available, four chases were worked simultaneously,
and some 75,000 sorts were in use at any one time. The
completed Bible contained between 145 and 150 sheets
(many were intended as presentation copies and had added
English title pages, half titles, dedications, and tables
of contents), representing approximately thirty-eight
months of labor for the thousand copies of the Old Testament and 1500 copies of the New.

The Indian Bible was not the sole production
Johnson had a hand in from 1660 to 1663. Almanacs for
1661, 1663, and 1664 were published under the imprint

305

of both men, but the 1662 almanac bears only the name of
Green. The most famous book printed in this period was
Michael Wigglesworth's The Day of Doom (1662), an apocalyptic dream vision poem in ballad stanzas which was so
thoroughly read that not one of the 1800 copies of the
first edition survives. Because of the heavy burden of
the Bible, other press jobs were necessarily short. The
longest was John Davenport's eighty-seven page Another
Essay for the Investigation of the Truth (1663). Still
shorter were John Norton's A Brief Catechism (1660), a
reprint of Eliot's A Primer or Catechism in the Massachusetts Indian Language (1662), which was designed to
be bound with the Indian Bible, and John Cotton's A Discourse about Civil Government (1663).

The working relationship between Johnson and
Green was strained after Johnson's affair with Green's
daughter, and the latter complained repeatedly to the
authorities about the man nominally under him. The dis-
sension did not keep them from working together, however;
economic necessity and, probably, Green's recognition
that Johnson was the superior printer and therefore valuable to keep the shop running smoothly kept them working
together. In 1664, the fourth year of Johnson's term,
the two men printed six titles, among them another translation by the indefatigable Eliot, this time of Richard
Baxter's Call to the Unconverted (Wehkomaonganoo Asquam
Peantogig, Kah Asquam Quinnuppegig), John Allin's Animadversions upon the Antisynodalia Americana, John
Norton's Three Choice and Profitable Sermons, and A
Defence of the Answer by Richard Mather and Jonathan
Mitchel.

When Johnson returned to Cambridge in 1665, the
two men continued to work jointly whenever it proved
expedient or profitable or both. From 1665 to 1671,
when their professional relationship was at last dissolved, they had printed fourteen books, the majority
being such standard sectarian fare as John Davenport's
A Catechism Printed for the Use of the First Church in
Boston (1669), no copy of which is known; Thomas Walley's
Balm in Gilead (1669); William Stoughton's New Englands

True Interests (1760); Samuel Danforth's A Brief Recognition of New Englands Errand into the Wilderness (1671); and Jonathan Mitchel's Nehemiah on the Wall (1671).

The years 1669 to 1671 were of special significance to American publishing, for in those three years Johnson and Green printed four books which have become important for their historical and literary associations. In 1669 they produced Nathaniel Morton's New-England's Memoriall, the first original work, not religious in character, penned in America. The book is a history of the Plymouth Colony and relies almost exclusively for its material on the manuscript chronicle of the Plymouth Plantation that was written by Morton's uncle, Governor William Bradford. It is quite possibly the most handsome book printed in America to that time. Johnson used his new and largely undamaged type font, the impressions are crisp, and the typography is clear and easy to read. Two volumes of poetry were put out for sale in 1670: Michael Wigglesworth's Meat out of the Eater, a lengthy tribute to the benefits of afflictions, and Philip Pain's Daily Meditations. The latter had been printed in 1668 by Johnson alone, but no copy is extant. The 1670 edition contains a poetical postscript by Johnson. The fourth and certainly the most important book printed by the two men was Increase Mather's excellent biography of his father, The Life and Death of That Reverend Man of God, Mr. Richard Mather (1670).

When Johnson set up his own press in 1665 he became the first private printer in America. In his capacity as the company's designated printer he continued to print Eliot's translations, including The Indian Grammar Begun (1666), The Indian Primer (1669), Indian Dialogues (1671), and The Logick Primer (1672). Religious exhortations and homilies remained the staple of Johnson's own business as well, and he printed Increase Mather's Wo to Drunkards (1673), Samuel Wakeman's pious A Young Man's Legacy to the Raising Generation (1673), and Samuel Danforth's The Cry of Sodom Enquired Into (1674).

307

There were signs, however, that the public was becoming interested in lighter, more topical books. In 1667 Green printed Thomas Vincent's God's Terrible Voice in the City of London, describing the ravages of the great fire and plague in that city. It was evidently well received, for in 1668 Johnson published it under his own imprint, causing Green once again to complain to the Cambridge authorities. In 1669 both men collaborated on A True and Exact Relation of the Late Prodigious Earthquake & Eruption of Mount Aetna by Heneage Finch. Johnson's efforts to cater to the public's wants received a setback in 1668 when he was fined £5 for the unauthorized printing of The Isle of Pines. This book, which was extraordinarily popular in England, is a short, mildly erotic, fictional account of a group of shipwreck survivors who populate their deserted island with Adamic abandon and without benefit of clergy. More palatable to the leaders of the colony was Johnson's printing of John Dod's Old Mr. Dod's Sayings (1673), a collection of humorous maxims in which the humor is kept secondary to the moralizing.

|Marmaduke Johnson's contributions, both as a printer and publisher, make him a significant figure in the development of American publishing. Although his output was small, the books he printed either by himself or with Samuel Green are important historically and for the information they provide about the changing reading habits of the New England colonists. Johnson's own life might also serve as an example of an American success story, a rise from rags to, if not riches, then at least sturdy independence. Johnson brought with him to Massachusetts the technical knowledge of printing that was so sorely needed to make publishing take root here and flourish, and his rise marks the upward swing of American publishing.

James P. O'Donnell

Marmaduke Johnson

References:

Littlefield, George E. The Early Massachusetts Press:
    1638-1711. Boston: Club of Odd Volumes, 1907;
    reprint edition, New York: Burt Franklin, 1969.

Roden, Robert F. The Cambridge Press: 1638-1692.
    New York: Dodd, Mead, 1905; reprint edition,
    New York: Burt Franklin, 1970.

Winship, George P. The Cambridge Press: 1638-1692.
    Philadelphia: University of Pennsylvania
    Press, 1945.

309

Thomas Johnston

Thomas Johnston (1708-1767), painter, japanner, organ builder, and one of the earliest Boston engravers, had a shop "in Brattle-Street." He printed and sold his own engravings, including editions of Thomas Walter's The Grounds and Rules of Musick Explained, in 1755 and 1766, and several maps.

References:

Coburn, Frederick W. "The Johnstons of Boston." Art in America, 21 (1933).

Downs, Joseph. "American Japanned Furniture." Bulletin of the Metropolitan Museum of Art, 28 (1933).

Jones, Matt B. "Bibliographical Notes on Thomas Walter's 'Grounds and Rules of Musick Explained.'" Proceedings of the American Antiquarian Society, 42 (1932).

Hitchings, Sinclair. "Thomas Johnston," in Boston Prints and Printmakers: 1670-1775. Boston: Colonial Society of Massachusetts, 1973.

Shipton, Clifford K. "Report of the Librarian." Proceedings of the American Antiquarian Society, 59 (1949).

Wroth, Lawrence C. "The Thomas Johnston Maps of the Kennebeck Purchase." In Tribute to Fred Anthoensen Master Printer. Portland, Me.: Anthoensen Press, 1952.

Daniel Kneeland

Daniel Kneeland (1725-1789) was a printer, publisher, and bookseller active in the fifteen years before the American Revolution. In 1759 he opened his first shop with his brother John in a corner of his father's printing house in Queen Street. The partnership ended in 1765, and Daniel continued there alone until 1769, when he opened a printery in "Hanover-Street, a little below Concert-Hall." In 1770 he returned to Queen Street, working alone until 1772, when he associated himself with Nathaniel Davis in the firm of Kneeland and Davis. This partnership ended in 1774, and Kneeland remained in business for another year, his last known imprint appearing in 1775. Kneeland printed approximately ninety titles, and about a third of these were published and sold by him.

Major Authors: Joseph Alleine, Nathaniel Ames, Charles Chauncy, George Cooke, Andrew Croswell, Thomas Dilworth, Benjamin Grosvenor, Nathaniel Low, Isaac Watts.

Publishers Served: Nicholas Bowes, Joseph Edwards, Philip Freeman, Thomas Leverett, John Perkins, Samuel Webb, John Wharton, Joshua Winter.

Kneeland was born in Boston in 1725, son of Samuel and Mary (Alden) Kneeland. Through his paternal grandmother he was related to the numerous and widespread Green family of printers, and through his mother to the Alden family, whose most famous American ancestors were John and Priscilla Alden. He was apprenticed to his father, the proprietor of one of Boston's largest printing houses, and was trained in printing and bookbinding. Instead of striking out for himself after taking up his freedom, as was customary, he remained in his father's

311

shop, most likely acting as a bookbinder and assistant to his father; his name consequently did not appear on the titles he helped print. He may have worked on Samuel's 1752 edition of the first English language Bible in America. In 1759 he set up a shop with his brother John in a part of their father's establishment and released his first known title, Sin, Thro' Divine Interposition, An Advantage to the Universe, by Samuel Hopkins, in the same year. The firm of D. and J. Kneeland began promisingly enough, producing ten titles in 1760 and nine in 1761, but their business quickly fell off. They produced eight imprints in 1762, seven in 1763, four the following year, and only two in 1765. The partnership ended in 1765, and John left to open another printery with Seth Adams. Daniel continued in the Queen Street shop until 1769, when he opened his own printing firm in Hanover Street.

In December of 1769 Kneeland's father died, and Daniel moved back to the Queen Street location soon thereafter. His business improved slightly in 1770, when he published nine titles, but it quickly deteriorated again. He released five in 1771 and only three in 1772. Apparently hoping to make a better go of it by adding another pair of hands, Kneeland formed a partnership with Nathaniel Davis in 1772. Kneeland and Davis did slightly better for a time, publishing approximately a dozen titles. When Davis left in 1774, however, Kneeland again had difficulty finding enough work, printing only four items in 1775, the four chapters of The First Book of the American Chronicles of the Times, which are also his last known imprints. From 1775 to May 1789, when he died, nothing more is known of him. He appears to have been sympathetic to the independent cause, and he may have served in the war in some capacity, although by that time he was well into his middle years. After the war he may have gone to work for another printer or he may have retired. Charles Evans lists a 1783 edition of the Brady and Tate New Version of the Psalms printed by Kneeland and his brother, but no copy is known and it may be a ghost, the result of an error by Evans in recording the 1763 edition

Isaiah Thomas informs us that the Kneeland brothers got their start in business as a result of a disagreement between the booksellers and the printing houses of John Draper, Green and Russell, and the Fleet brothers. It had been the practice of the printers each to print one of the three sheets of the best selling Ames almanac and sell them to the booksellers on a proportional basis, according to their costs, but in 1759 they decided to publish the almanac themselves and to charge a higher, set price. The booksellers retaliated by equipping Daniel and John Kneeland with a press, type, and supplies, with which they reprinted the 1760 almanac as soon as it appeared. The booksellers continued to subsidize the Kneelands for a time, but after six years, the other printers perhaps becoming more tractable, they withdrew their sponsorship and divided the equipment and supplies among themselves. The firm then broke up, and Daniel bought the press and some of the type and set up for himself, remaining in his father's Queen Street location.

Compared with his father, Daniel was not very successful in his craft, and one indication of why he made only a marginal living from the press might be found in the marked difference between the titles he printed for other publishers and those he published himself. Among the items he was hired to print were the New-England Primer Enlarged (1761); the Westminster Shorter Catechism (1762); Thomas Dilworth's often reprinted New Guide to the English Tongue (1764); Benjamin Grosvenor's misleadingly titled Health, An Essay on its Nature, Value, Uncertainty, Preservation, and Best Improvement (1761), which is neither a medical book nor a guide to health improvement but a treatise on the moral utility of good health; the eighth edition of A Short Introduction to the Latin Tongue (1761); and the several reprintings of The Youth's Instructor and George Cooke's The Complete English Farmer (1770, 1772). All were popular titles and all sold well.

But of those titles that he published himself, and consequently those that he chose to print because he believed they might prove profitable, almost all are undistinguished, even when they are by otherwise popular authors. With the exception of the yearly almanacs by Nathaniel Low, most of Kneeland's publications have a fairly limited appeal. Among these are Andrew Croswell's Letter to the Reverend Alexander Cumming (1762) and his Comfort in Christ (1767); the anonymous and hackneyed moralizing of A Letter from a Solicitous Mother, to Her Only Son (1763); John Cleaveland's Essay, to Defend Some of the Most Important Principles in the Protestant Reformed System of Christianity (1763); Isaac Backus's True Faith Will Produce Good Work (1767); and Charles Chauncy's Trust in God, The Duty of a People in a Day of Trouble (1770).

One area in which Kneeland did achieve considerable success, but one in which he did not reap the monetary rewards, was in printing Psalters and hymnbooks for other publishers. In 1764, for example, he printed The New-England Psalter for Samuel Webb and for Wharton and Bowes. He printed subsequent editions in 1770 and 1771. Far more popular, however, were his printings of Nicholas Brady and Nahum Tate's New Version of the Psalms and several titles by Isaac Watts. The polished and elegant Brady and Tate translation of the Psalms had been well received ever since it had first appeared in 1696, and numerous editions had been printed in England and America. In 1760 Kneeland used the sheets printed by his father in the same year, changing only the name on the imprint, and released two issues of it. In 1762 he printed his first true edition of this title, and in 1763 he printed another, with four issues for four booksellers. Three more editions followed in 1766, 1769, and 1773. Kneeland also printed several titles by Isaac Watts, one of the most popular authors and writers of hymns of his time, including editions of The Psalms of David, Imitated in 1761, 1763, 1770, and 1773; the fifteenth edition of the Divine Songs (1765), the first children's hymnbook; two editions of the Hymns and Spiritual Songs (1771, 1773); and, in 1772, Horae Lyricae, a book of religious poems of such

314

exceptional merit that they earned a place for Watts in Dr. Johnson's Lives of the English Poets.

In the decade before the Revolution, Kneeland, like virtually every other Boston printer and publisher, began printing an increasing number of political titles. Kneeland's position in the controversy seems clearly on the side of the Whigs. In 1769, for example, he published the sixth edition and quite possibly the seventh of the anonymous Brittania's Intercession for the Deliverance of John Wilkes. Wilkes, a bitter enemy of Lord Bute and co-founder of the North Briton, was commonly if not entirely accurately known as a defender of democratic principles against the authoritarianism of George III, and as such he had much support in the colonies. And in 1769 Kneeland reprinted and sold Robert Livingston's Address to the New York Assembly in support of his right to the seat to which he had been elected, despite the refusal of the conservative province legislators to seat him because of his advocacy of American independence.

The most successful of Kneeland's political publications were the Oration, on the Beauties of Liberty (1773) and The American Alarm (1773), both attributed to Isaac Skillman but actually written by John Allen, and four of the five parts of the anonymous First Book of the American Chronicles of the Times (1774-1775). The Alarm is a strongly worded protest against Governor Hutchinson's announcement in 1772 that henceforth the salaries of the governor and judges would be paid by the crown, thus making them less likely to be sympathetic to the colonists. The Oration is a similarly passionate indictment of the British investigation of the Gaspee, but even more important it sets forth the religious justifications for liberty. If these are somewhat conventional political tracts of the time, the American Chronicles are most decidedly not. First published in Philadelphia in five chapters, the Chronicles are a prose, mock-epic narration of contemporary events couched in a parody of scriptural phraseology. The references to Thomas the Gageite, Mordecai the Benjamite,

315

and the ascription of the colonists' troubles to the king setting up a heathen god--a tea chest--must have been both titillating to a people saturated in the Bible and a welcome relief from the intensity and earnest doggedness of most of the pre-Revolutionary political writings.

Daniel Kneeland's role in Boston publishing is a comparatively minor one. As a printer he was not prolific and as a publisher he was not, with a few exceptions late in his career, successful. He made several promising beginnings, first with his brother and later with Nathaniel Davis, but both, for one reason or another, quickly grew sour. Little is known of his private life, and one intriguing question is his disappearance from 1775 until his death in 1789. He was, in short, an unimportant member of his craft, a surprising fate for one who had the advantages of having a father well established in the trade and one who apparently assisted his son all he could.

James P. O'Donnell

References:

Bumsted, John M. and Charles E. Clark. "New England's Tom Paine: John Allen and the Spirit of Liberty." William and Mary Quarterly, 21 (1964).

Thomas, Isaiah. The History of Printing in America. Worcester, Mass.: Isaiah Thomas, Jr., 1810; 2nd ed., revised, Albany, N.Y.: J. Munsell for the American Antiquarian Society, 1874; ed. Marcus A. McCorison, Barre, Mass.: Imprint Society, 1970.

316

John Kneeland

John Kneeland (1729-1795), printer, publisher, and bookseller, was active from 1759 to 1775 and is responsible
for approximately 150 imprints. His first venture into
business was with his older brother Daniel, the firm of
D. and J. Kneeland being located in a corner of their
father's printing office in Queen Street. In 1765 he
went into partnership with Seth Adams, and they continued to work out of Kneeland's father's shop for a few
months before moving to a location "next to the Treasurer's office in Milk Street." The firm of Kneeland
and Adams continued for seven years, at which time Adams
left. Kneeland continued alone until 1775, when the
British army occupied Boston.

Major Authors: Amos Adams, Charles Chauncy,
Andrew Croswell, Thomas Dilworth, Jonathan Edwards,
Moses Hemmenway, Samuel Hopkins, Nathaniel Low, Jonathan
Mayhew, Samuel Phillips, Isaac Watts.

Publishers Served: Nicholas Bowes, Joseph
Edwards, Philip Freeman, Daniel Henchman, Thomas
Leverett, John Perkins, Samuel Webb, John Wharton,
Joshua Winter.

Kneeland was born in Boston in 1729, son of
Samuel and Mary Kneeland. He had impressive family
connections: his mother was descended from John and
Priscilla Alden and he was related to the Green dynasty
of printers through his grandmother, Mary (Green) Kneeland. His father was head of one of Boston's largest
printing houses, and he served his apprenticeship under
him. After taking up his freedom he apparently remained
with his father until the opportunity arose to strike
out for himself, a chance that came in 1759 as the result of a dispute between the booksellers and the three
firms that printed the three sheets of the popular Ames

317

almanac. John Draper, Green and Russell, and Thomas and
John Fleet had previously printed one sheet apiece of the
almanac and sold them to the booksellers on a prorated
basis, but in 1759 the printers decided to charge a higher
set price for the sheets. The booksellers parried by band-
ing together and setting up the Kneeland brothers in business in a part of their father's shop, providing them with
the press, type, and supplies with which they reprinted
the 1760 almanac as soon as it appeared. The booksellers
continued to subsidize the Kneelands until 1765, when they
decided there was no further need for their services.
They divided the equipment among themselves and the firm
of D. and J. Kneeland came to an end.

After his partnership with his brother was dissolved, Kneeland immediately started another printing
house with Seth Adams, who had also been an apprentice
in Samuel Kneeland's shop. This partnership also survived only a few years, Adams leaving to become a post
rider in 1772. Kneeland continued the Milk Street shop
alone until 1775, when the British army occupied Boston
and a number of printers, including, apparently, Kneeland, either fled the city or closed down. His last
known title was Andrew Croswell's Mr. Murray Unmask'd,
two editions of which he printed in 1775. Nothing more
is heard of Kneeland before his death in March 1795,
although Evans records a 1783 Kneeland edition of the
Brady and Tate New Version of the Psalms. This imprint
is, however, probably a ghost; no copy is known and it
is likely an error for the 1763 edition.

Although the printing of the Ames almanac was
the initial reason for their existence, the firm of D.
and J. Kneeland stayed in business for six years largely
as printers of Psalters and hymnbooks for other publishers, and they remained a staple in Kneeland's later
career as well. The one Psalter that they most frequently printed was the Nicholas Brady and Nahum Tate
New Version of the Psalms. First published in 1696,
this neat and graceful translation was more to the
taste of the eighteenth century than the fine but
rugged Sternhold and Hopkins Old Version or the accurate

but awkward Bay Psalm Book, and it was often reprinted both in England and the colonies. The first appearance of the Kneeland brothers on a New Version imprint was in 1760, when they used the sheets printed by their father for his edition in the same year. Their first true edition came in 1762, and in 1763 they printed another edition for four booksellers. With Seth Adams, Kneeland printed another edition in 1765. In addition to the Brady and Tate translation, the Kneelands were also the printers of the twenty-fourth edition of The Psalms of David (1763) and the fifteenth edition of the Divine Songs, Attempted in Easy Language (1765), both by Isaac Watts, and an edition of the New-England Psalter (1764). Kneeland also printed Watts's freely paraphrased Psalms of David, Imitated in 1761, 1763, 1767, and 1773; his Hymns and Spiritual Songs (1767); Andrew Law's Select Number of Plain Tunes Adapted to Congregational Worship (1767); and the Hymns and Spiritual Songs of James Humphrey in 1774.

One of the most curious aspects of Kneeland's career is that he remained relatively untouched by the changes that were radically altering Massachusetts. In a time of increasing secularism, of intense political feeling and animosity, and of religious revisionism, he printed few secular titles, even fewer political works, and only a few religious tracts that could not have been printed a century or more earlier. He appears to have been a cautious businessman, preferring either to be hired by a publisher and make a small but safe profit, or, for his own publications, restricting himself to the most predictably salable titles or waiting until an item had proven itself in the marketplace before reprinting it.

A good example of his wary approach to publishing is his printing of textbooks and titles on self-improvement, a well-established and remunerative branch of the Boston book trade. Education had always been placed at a premium by the Puritans; the New-England Primer, for example, had admonished the student that "He who ne'er learns his ABC, forever will a blockhead be." Education was not confined to children. Tradesmen, shopkeepers, and apprentices often formed clubs and societies within which they tried to further their education, the most famous but certainly not the only one of these being Benjamin Franklin's Junto Club. Both textbooks for children and self-help books for adults were profitable items in the book trade. Yet Kneeland all but ignored the possibilities of this market and contented himself with waiting until he was hired by a publisher before printing in this branch of the trade. In 1760 the Kneeland sons' names appear in the imprint of The Youth's Instructor, a speller which they, for Thomas Leverett, used the sheets already printed by their always obliging father for his edition. In 1761 they printed for Joshua Winter the New-England Primer Enlarged, and for Wharton and Bowes A Short Introduction to the Latin Tongue in the same year. For a number of publishers they reprinted Thomas Dilworth's popular grammar and speller A New Guide to the English Tongue in 1764, and Kneeland reprinted it again in 1768 and 1773. In 1768 Kneeland and Adams printed the New-England Primer Improved for Leverett, and after seeing that it sold well, Kneeland made his first venture into textbook publishing by reprinting and selling it for himself in 1771.

Kneeland also printed several political titles, but he did far fewer than most of his colleagues and those he did print he was hired to print. In 1766 he was employed by Philip Freeman to print Good News from a Far Country, by Samuel Stillman, pastor of the First Baptist Church, on the repeal of the Stamp Act. In the same year, for Thomas Leverett, Kneeland printed Charles Chauncy's Discourse on "The Good News from a Far Country," and in 1773 he released Samuel Mather's patriotic if misguided Attempt to Shew, That America Must Be Known to the Ancients for Leverett and Bowes.

Nor did Kneeland take many risks in his printing of religious works. Most of his titles in this area are quite conventional Calvinistic tracts, examples of which include Eli Forbes's The Good Minister (1761) and Samuel Langdon's A Summary of Christian Faith and Practice

320

(1768). Kneeland did print a few religious titles of
more enduring significance, but, typically, they are
all reprints. For the booksellers he reprinted the
Westminster Shorter Catechism in 1762, and for himself
he reprinted Isaac Watts's The First Set of Catechisms
and Prayers (1770), Jonathan Edwards's The Justice of
God in the Damnation of Sinners (1773) and his Sinners
in the Hands of an Angry God (1772).

Kneeland was not completely without initiative,
however. In 1759 he printed and sold Sin, Thro' Divine
Interposition, An Advantage to the Universe by Samuel
Hopkins, a friend, disciple, and biographer of Jonathan
Edwards. Hopkins was not as fiercely Calvinistic as his
mentor, and his teachings on disinterested benevolence
led to the first American missionaries to Asia. Kneeland
also chanced becoming involved in controversy on one
occasion. When Jonathan Mayhew and John Cleaveland began squabbling over the doctrine of Christ's atonement,
Kneeland published both Mayhew's 1763 Two Sermons, em-
phasizing God's goodness and relegating God the Law-Giver
to a lesser position, and Cleaveland's Essay to Defend
Some of the Most Important Principles in the Protestant
Reformed System of Christianity (1763), which accuses
Mayhew of heresy in denying the necessity of Christ aton-
ing for man's sins. The dispute flared for a time, with
some tracts being exchanged, but it quickly sputtered
out after a few years. Kneeland, perhaps characteristi-
cally, did not publish any of the succeeding pamphlets,
evidently choosing to remove himself from the fray after
it began to heat up.

Late in his career Kneeland also gingerly tested
the waters of religious toleration, although his two
tracts in this area would scarcely make him a leader in
the Age of Reason. Freedom of religion had been repug-
nant to the settlers of Massachusetts, and this attitude
had been inherited by a good many of their descendants.
Consequently, although the idea was not as offensive as
it would have been a hundred years earlier, Kneeland's
printing of two titles urging religious freedom took
some courage, but it was not something he plunged into

headlong. His first title was Amos Adams's <u>Religious
Liberty an Invaluable Blessing</u> (1768), but he was only
its printer, having been hired by Thomas Leverett. In
1774, however, he printed and sold for himself Barnabas
Binney's Rhode Island College valedictory address, <u>An
Oration . . . Being a Plea for the Right of Private
Judgment in Religious Matters.</u>

    John Kneeland was a competent and serviceable,
if undistinguished, Boston printer and publisher. He
appears to have inherited little of his father's drive
and talent, but he was certainly more successful than
his older brother and his two other brothers who never
established shops of their own. He was evidently well
regarded as a craftsman by his peers, and, indeed, he
seems to have preferred the small but safe profits of
working for a publisher to gambling with the larger but
uncertain gains to be made by publishing titles for himself. Those titles he did publish for himself were,
with a few exceptions, either quite conventional or confined to reprints. As a result, few of Kneeland's imprints are historically important. He was, in short,
an unexceptional man in an exceptional age.

    James P. O'Donnell

Reference:

Thomas, Isaiah. <u>The History of Printing in America.</u>
    Worcester, Mass.: Isaiah Thomas, Jr., 1810;
    2nd ed., revised, Albany, N.Y.: J. Munsell
    for the American Antiquarian Society, 1874;
    ed. Marcus A. McCorison, Barre, Mass.:
    Imprint Society, 1970.

Samuel Kneeland

Samuel Kneeland (1697-1769) was a printer, publisher, bookseller, and partner in the firm of Kneeland and Green. He printed the first English language Bible in America (1752); the first American edition of the first sermon preached in America, Robert Cushman's The Sin and Danger of Self-Love (1724); the first American religious journal, Thomas Prince's Christian History (1743-1745); and the first folio volume of divinity in the colonies, which is also one of the earliest American examples of title-page rubrication, Samuel Willard's Compleat Body of Divinity (1726). He was at first the printer and later the publisher of the Boston Gazette, the second newspaper in America, and in 1727 he began printing the New-England Weekly Journal, the fourth American newspaper. For his entire career his shop was "the Printing House over against the Prison in Queen Street." In 1727 he opened a bookstore "in King Street, next door to the Post Office," but he abandoned it after a few years. Kneeland retired in 1765 with almost 900 imprints bearing his name.

Major Authors: Joseph Alleine, Richard Baxter, Mather Byles, Charles Chauncy, Benjamin Colman, Jonathan Dickinson, Thomas Foxcroft, Cotton Mather, Increase Mather, Jonathan Mitchel, Samuel Moodey (or Moody), Thomas Prince, Samuel Sewall.

Publishers Served: Nathaniel Belknap, Joseph Edwards, Benjamin Eliot, Samuel Gerrish, Benjamin Gray, Thomas Hancock, Daniel Henchman, Thomas Lewis, Massachusetts House of Representatives, Philip Musgrave.

Kneeland was born in Boston on 31 January 1697, son of John and Mary Kneeland. His mother was the daughter of Samuel Green, Cambridge printer from 1649 to 1692

323

and patriarch of a dynasty of printers that for nearly
200 years was instrumental in spreading the craft
throughout New England and the middle colonies. He
served his apprenticeship under his uncle, Bartholomew
Green, and in 1721 he married Mary Alden, great-
granddaughter of John and Priscilla Alden, by whom he
had five sons and six daughters. All four of his surviving sons served as apprentices to their father, and
two of them, John and Daniel, later became Boston
printers with shops of their own.

Kneeland opened his printing office in 1718 and
began printing the Boston Gazette in 1719. When the
Gazette was taken from him in 1727, he immediately
started the New-England Weekly Journal, which was noted
for its high literary quality. In the same year he
opened his bookstore in King Street with his partner
and cousin Timothy Green II. For the years of the
store's existence, Kneeland chose to leave the printing
to his partner while he sold books. In 1722 he became,
with his former master, printer to the Massachusetts
House of Representatives and was responsible for the
printing of their Journal. When Bartholomew Green died
in 1732, Kneeland and Timothy Green became the official
House printers, a job that they, and later Kneeland
alone, held until 1761. Timothy Green left the firm in
1752 to return to New London, Connecticut, and assist
his aged and ailing father, and Kneeland continued the
business alone. Kneeland retired in 1765 and died four
years later, on 14 December 1769.

In eighteenth-century Massachusetts few printers
could afford the luxury of specializing in a particular
branch of the trade. The competition among the printing
houses was too intense, the cost of supplies too high,
and the margin of profit too slight to permit the loss
of even a small number of the jobs that specialization
would entail. Yet if any printer could be described as
having a speciality, Samuel Kneeland's abiding interest
in religious matters comprises one. Of Kneeland's 900
recorded imprints, an overwhelming number are devoted to
theology and religion. His first imprint was possibly

324

Cotton Mather's Proposals for Printing the Psalterium
Americanum (1717), which was followed in the next year
with an edition of the Psalter. From 1717 until 1728
Kneeland printed or published some thirty-five titles
by this prolific divine, including Desiderius (1719),
An Heavenly Life (1719), The Tryed Professor (1719),
Coheleth (1720), The Right Way to Shake Off a Viper
(1720), Genuine Christianity (1721), Coelestinus (1723),
Light in Darkness (1724), Religious Societies (1724),
A Good Old Age (1726), and Boanerges (1727).

In addition to printing Mather, Kneeland further demonstrated his piety by printing the first English language Bible in America and printing or publishing
the twenty-first (1726), twenty-fourth (1737), and twenty-
sixth (1744) editions of the Bay Psalm Book as well as
the 1758 edition; the New-England Primer Enlarged in
1727, 1735, and 1752; the Westminster Shorter Catechism
in 1739 and 1762; and the Westminster Confession of
Faith, Together with the Larger Catechism in 1724. He
printed, moreover, a substantial number of the books and
pamphlets that brought the religious revival of the Great
Awakening to the attention of Massachusetts readers. For
George Whitefield, whose theatrical oratory was a key
factor in the spread of the Great Awakening, Kneeland
printed The Duty and Interest of Early Piety (1739), The
Indwelling of the Spirit (1739), and several parts of
Whitefield's journal. For Gilbert Tennent, another of
the leading advocates of the Great Awakening, Kneeland
printed A Solemn Warning to the Secure World from the
God of Terrible Majesty (1735), Two Sermons Preached at
New-Brunswick (1742), and The Necessity of Holding Fast
the Truth (1743). And for Jonathan Dickinson he printed
The Reasonableness of Christianity (1732) and published
The True Scripture-Doctrine Concerning Some Important
Points of Christian Faith (1741), for which he hired
Daniel Fowle to do the printing. Kneeland also printed
Thomas Prince's Christian History, an eight-page weekly
religious journal that ran from 5 March 1743 to 23 Febru-
ary 1745 and was chiefly devoted to essays in praise of
the Great Awakening.

But among all the religious titles Kneeland printed during his forty-seven year career, those he did for Jonathan Edwards must rank among his most valuable. Kneeland either printed or had published fifteen titles by Edwards, and among the most important of these are his first, God Glorified in the Work of Redemption (1731), A Faithful Narrative of the Surprising Work of God in the Conversion of Many Hundred Souls (1737); A Divine and Supernatural Light (1734); Sinners in the Hands of an Angry God (1741); Some Thoughts Concerning the Present Revival of Religion in New-England (1742); A Treatise Concerning Religious Affections (1746), a work so popular that the unusually large press run of 1,300 copies fell far short of the number of potential buyers; A Careful and Strict Inquiry into the . . . Freedom of the Will (1754), his monumental rebuttal of Arminianism; The Great Christian Doctrine of Original Sin Defended (1758); and the posthumous Two Dissertations (1765), which was also one of Kneeland's last imprints.

The secular side of his trade was not so extensive, but it, too, had its highlights. In 1744 he released Mather Byles's Poems on Several Occasions, and in 1736 he printed, for Samuel Gerrish, Thomas Prince's Chronological History of New-England in the Form of Annals, a well-written history of the settling of Massachusetts noteworthy for its unpartisan judiciousness. He also printed Increase Mather's enlightened defense of smallpox inoculation, Several Reasons Proving That Inoculation or Transplanting the Small Pox is a Lawful Practice (1721), a broadside of signal importance in American medical and social history.

Another branch of Kneeland's secular printing was his work for the Massachusetts House of Representatives, whose Journal and acts and laws he printed, with Bartholomew Green, from 1723 to 1728. In 1729 they lost the profitable House business to Thomas Fleet but regained it three years later. Bartholomew Green died in December of 1732 and the House then awarded its printing orders to Kneeland and Timothy Green. After his partner left the firm in 1752, Kneeland continued

326

to print for the House alone until 1761, when he lost
the contract to Edes and Gill, who had probably under-
bid him. Besides the Journal and acts and laws, the
House members also on occasion authorized other titles
to be printed, especially sermons they considered note-
worthy. These supplemental printing orders resulted in
Kneeland printing, among others, William Welsteed's
Dignity and Duty of the Civil Magistrate (1751) and
Samuel Dunbar's The Presence of God with His People,
Their Only Safety and Happiness (1760).

Newspaper publishing was yet another area in
which Kneeland succeeded. In August 1720, he began
printing the Boston Gazette for William Brooker, the
Boston postmaster who had taken the printing job away
from James Franklin to give it to Kneeland. Kneeland
continued to print the Gazette under a number of post-
masters until 1727, when Henry Marshall replaced him
with Bartholomew Green. On 11 October 1736 Kneeland
and his partner regained the printing of the Gazette
under John Boydell. When Boydell died in December 1739,
his heirs tried to continue publishing it, but after
two years they gave up, selling the rights to Kneeland
and Green, who became the paper's publishers as well
as printers with the number for 19 October 1741.

When Kneeland lost the Gazette to Bartholomew
Green in 1727, he immediately began a rival newspaper,
the New-England Weekly Journal, the first number appearing on 20 March 1727. The time was auspicious, for
James Franklin's New-England Courant had folded just
the year before. The Courant, which Franklin had
started after being replaced by Kneeland in the printing of the Gazette, was modeled after the more literary
London papers like the Spectator and the Guardian, and
hence was more polished and self-consciously literate
than any other contemporary American newspaper. When
the Courant ceased after Franklin left for Rhode Island,
Kneeland continued the literary tradition with his
Journal, although he did not follow Franklin's lead
in taunting the authorities. The paper was a success,
despite its higher than customary rates of sixteen

shillings a year or twenty if sealed, and the reason may be the caliber of its contributors, who included Increase Mather, Thomas Prince, Mather Byles, Judge Danforth, and Governor William Burnet. Kneeland devoted a goodly amount of space to bookish concerns, frequently printing poetry, criticism, and, beginning on 14 February 1732, he took the unusual step of serially reprinting The London Merchant, George Lillo's edifying domestic tragedy.

The Journal ran until 1741 when Kneeland and Green bought the rights to the Gazette and combined it with the Journal on 20 October 1741, forming the Boston Gazette, Or New England Weekly Journal, the first newspaper merger in the American colonies. When Green left the firm, Kneeland changed the title to the Boston Gazette, Or, Weekly Advertiser with the 3 January 1753 number and continued printing and publishing it on his own. Apparently the weekly deadlines were too taxing for only one man, for Kneeland soon sold it to Edes and Gill, who changed the name to the Boston-Gazette, Or, Country Journal and began printing it with the 7 April 1755 number.

Samuel Kneeland was neither the most important nor the most prolific Boston printer and publisher in the middle years of the eighteenth century, yet his influence was substantial. The apprentices he trained dispersed, set up their own shops, and continued his tradition of careful and correct workmanship. His two sons, John and Daniel, for example, were at first partners and afterwards each opened his own shop; the important Benjamin Edes and John Gill possibly served apprenticeships with Kneeland; Daniel Fowle was a member of Rogers and Fowle and later became the first New Hampshire printer; Seth Adams became a partner in Kneeland and Adams with John Kneeland. Samuel Kneeland's lifelong interest in religion led him to print a sizeable number of the most important religious tracts of his time, and his sound literary judgment helped him recognize and print some titles of permanent importance to literary history. His New-England Journal was

328

instrumental in bringing belles-lettres to Massachusetts
and helped foster a growing sophistication in literary
matters.

James P. O'Donnell

References:

Kobre, Sidney. The Development of the Colonial Newspaper. Salem: Salem Press, 1944.

Lydenberg, Harry M. "The Problem of the Pre-1776
American Bible." Papers of the Bibliographical
Society of America, 48 (1954).

Mott, Frank Luther. A History of American Magazines:
1741-1850. New York and London: Appleton,
1930; Cambridge: Harvard University Press,
1938; Cambridge: Belknap Press of Harvard
University Press, 1957.

Mott, Frank Luther. American Journalism, A History:
1690-1960. Third edition, New York: Macmillan,
1962.

Silver, Rollo G. "Government Printing in Massachusetts-
Bay, 1700-1750." Proceedings of the American
Antiquarian Society, 68 (1958).

Silver, Rollo G. "Government Printing in Massachusetts,
1751-1801." Studies in Bibliography, 16 (1963).

Henry Knox

Henry Knox (1750-1806) had a brief but successful career as a Boston bookseller before becoming a military leader during the War of Independence. He served an apprenticeship with John Wharton and Nicholas Bowes from 1761 to 1766, and he finally left Bowes in 1771 to operate the London Bookstore "opposite Williams's Court." In 1772 he moved "next to the Sign of the Three Kings, a little to the Southward of the Town-House, in Cornhill." His name appears in nine known imprints from 1771 through 1774. One of his publications is his 1773 catalogue of books for sale.

References:

Ford, Worthington C. "Henry Knox and the London Book-Store in Boston: 1771-1774." Proceedings of the Massachusetts Historical Society, 61 (1928).

Thomas, Isaiah. The History of Printing in America. Worcester, Mass.: Isaiah Thomas, Jr., 1810; 2nd ed., revised, Albany, N.Y.: J. Munsell for the American Antiquarian Society, 1874; ed. Marcus A. McCorison, Barre, Mass.: Imprint Society, 1970.

John Langdon

John Langdon (1747-1793) served an apprenticeship with John Wharton and Nicholas Bowes. From 1770 to 1774 he was in business for himself "opposite the Post-Office in Cornhill." His name appears in only five known imprints, none of any consequence. He quit the book business with the outbreak of the War of Independence.

Reference:

Thomas, Isaiah. The History of Printing in America. Worcester, Mass.: Isaiah Thomas, Jr., 1810; 2nd ed., revised, Albany, N.Y.: J. Munsell for the American Antiquarian Society, 1874; ed. Marcus A. McCorison, Barre, Mass.: Imprint Society, 1970.

331

Benjamin Larkin

Benjamin Larkin (1754-1803) was a bookseller and publisher who conducted business from 1781 to 1803 at
"No. 46 Cornhill." He published, either alone or in
collaboration with others, approximately fifty titles.

Major Authors: Jonathan Edwards, James Relly,
Isaac Watts.

Larkin did most of his publishing in collaboration with other Boston booksellers and publishers. Only
one-third of his titles were published by him exclusively.
He began slowly in the business, publishing, on the
average, one title each year from 1781 through 1789.
Even in his most active years (1790-1797) he averaged
only five titles a year, peaking in 1794 with seven.
During the last two years of his career he published
only one title.

One-fourth of Larkin's titles are songbooks,
eight of which are by Isaac Watts. He also published
James Relly's Hymns Used in the Universal Churches
(1791) and Solomon Howe's Worshipper's Assistant (1799).

Almanacs were another Larkin staple. He published David Fenning's The Ready Reckoner (1785),
Isaiah Thomas's almanacs (1794-1797), various Bickerstaff almanacs (1796-1798), and his own Larkin's Pocket
Register (1795).

With the exception of two literary works--
Mrs. Burke's Ela, or the Delusions of the Heart (1790)
and Ann Radcliffe's The Romance of the Forest (1795)--
most of Larkin's other titles are a miscellany of
religious and instructional works. Most notable of

332

them is Jonathan Edwards's <u>Treatise Concerning Religious Affections</u> (1794).

Benjamin Larkin, about whom little is known, was a minor Boston publisher at the end of the eighteenth century.

Marta Paul Johnson

Ebenezer Larkin

Ebenezer Larkin (c. 1769-1813), publisher and wholesale and retail bookseller, entered business in a small way in 1789 by publishing two titles. His firm was then located at 50 Cornhill. His shop and his publishing activities expanded rapidly. In 1792 he began to sell stationery items, and in 1795, his most active year as a publisher, his name appeared in twenty-five imprints. In 1796 he moved his shop to 47 Cornhill, where he remained in business with one brief interruption until his death on 24 December 1813. In the course of his twenty-four years as a prosperous publisher and bookseller, Larkin came into contact with most of the important men in the book trade, both in Boston and other major centers of publication, and he published a number of titles of special historical interest. He published the first New England edition of Milton's Paradise Lost in 1794, a reprint of the famous Newton text, and in 1793 he published the first American edition of Fanny Burney's novel Cecilia, or Memoirs of an Heiress.

Major Authors: John Quincy Adams, Joseph Addison, Fanny Burney, William Cowper, John Locke, John Milton, Hannah More, Elizabeth Singer Rowe, Isaac Watts, George Whitefield, William Wilberforce.

Surprisingly little is known about the Larkin family even though four members--Benjamin, Ebenezer, Isaac, and Samuel--were all active in the book trade in eighteenth-century Boston. Of them Ebenezer was probably the most important and influential. In his obituary in the Columbian Centinel for 29 December 1813 and in the various notices of the sale of his estate, he is referred to as "Ebenezer Larkin, Esq.," implying that at least by that time he had achieved the status of a substantial gentleman. A conservative businessman

334

throughout his career, Larkin was willing to stock and
publish only titles and authors with a proven sales
value. The distinctly biblical names of his family
suggest a rather conservative Puritan background, and
that taste appears in the titles he published and sold.
He specialized in divinity, law, medicine, and education.
The titles of lasting literary value with which he dealt
are clearly didactic in nature and in a small minority.

If Larkin's conservative approach did little to
encourage a taste for the belles-lettres, it certainly
seems to have been a sound business practice. The ad-
ministrator's notice of the sale of Larkin's stock which
appeared in the Independent Chronicle for 17 February
1814, informed the public that it included over 15,000
volumes, largely in law, theology, and medicine. A further notice printed in the Chronicle for 27 October 1814
mentions that the sale of an additional 1,000 volumes
"just received from Philadelphia" was part of Larkin's
estate, most of which were theological in nature. These
apparently were volumes ordered from Philadelphia before
his death. The reason for this large stock is that
Larkin was a wholesaler as well as a publisher and re-
tailer. In 1795 Larkin published John Willison's The
Afflicted Man's Companion, a household medical text
that was printed exclusively for Larkin by William
Greenough. At the end of the volume appears a six-page
list of "New American Editions" consisting of slightly
more than 200 titles that were available from Larkin's
shop both "wholesale and retail." In the same advertisement Larkin declares that he can furnish everything
a businessman needs to set up a country bookshop.

During his career Larkin published three sale
catalogues dated 1793(?), 1798, and 1810. The one for
1798 is most readily available and indicates the kind
of shop he had. It lists items for sale on fifty-two
pages. Two pages list stationery items, blank account
books, printing paper, sealing wax, and so on. A page
and a half are devoted to children's books and chapbooks. One page lists plays, operas, and farces. A
list of maps occupies three and one-half pages. The

335

remaining forty-four pages contain a single list of approximately 1,200 titles in what then passed for alphabetical order. The large majority of these are in divinity, law, medicine, and education. Many of the titles Larkin advertised were printed outside of Boston, indicating that he had business connections well beyond that town. In 1796, for example, Larkin was one of only four booksellers in Massachusetts to stock A Vindication of Mr. Randolph's Resignation. In 1795 Edmund J. Randolph resigned his position as attorney general of the United States under complicated circumstances that stirred considerable public interest. Randolph wrote his Vindication to clear his character and had the volume printed by Samuel Harrison Smith in Philadelphia. Smith sent 550 copies of the title to Massachusetts: 200 to Thomas and Andrews, 150 to David West, 150 to William Spotswood, and 50 to Larkin. By this time Larkin's firm clearly ranked among the largest in Boston.

Although political titles are not numerous in Larkin's sale catalogue, there is some evidence that he was willing on occasion to lend his firm's support to a political cause. In 1801, for example, Timothy Pickering, in a letter to Governor James Sullivan, attacked the political principles of John Quincy Adams. When the first printing of Adams's reply quickly sold out, Larkin placed himself at the head of a coalition of democratic publishers and printers who took it upon themselves to publish another large edition.

Larkin's business affiliations with his various relatives are rather entangled. During 1793 and 1794 one imprint each year records that the title was published for E. Larkin and for E. and S. Larkin in State Street. Apparently during those years Ebenezer and his brother Samuel were in a formal partnership and maintained a shop in State Street at the same time that Ebenezer had his shop at 50 Cornhill. It was a short-lived enterprise, for nothing more is heard about the shop in State Street after 1794, and no further imprints bear the names of the two brothers in conjunction until 1799, when two titles appeared bearing the E. and S. Larkin imprint.

In 1800 one of the three titles bearing their imprint in partnership indicates that their business was located at 47 Cornhill, the location to which Ebenezer had moved his shop in 1796. The brothers' partnership was publicly announced in the Columbian Centinel for 16 July 1800, and in 1802 there appeared a Catalogue of Books, for Sale by E. and S. Larkin, No. 47 Cornhill. However, the Independent Chronicle for 27 September 1802 announced the dissolution of the business which Ebenezer then carried on at the same location. That seems to have been the end of the partnership.

Ebenezer continued in business alone until 1805, when the Columbian Centinel for 22 June and the Independent Chronicle for 20 June announced that Ebenezer's business had been taken over by Joseph Larkin and moved to 48 Cornhill. This seems to have been a short-lived arrangement, however, for one year later, on 25 June 1806, the Centinel announced that Joseph and Ebenezer were once again in business in partnership at the old location of 47 Cornhill. Then two years later, the Chronicle for 30 June and the Centinel for 25 June 1808 announced the dissolution of the partnership and Ebenezer's continuation of the business at 47 Cornhill. In September of that year Joseph opened his own shop at 43 Cornhill, and Ebenezer continued his business undisturbed by partners at 47 Cornhill until his death in 1813.

During the course of his career, Larkin's name appeared in imprints along with those of a great many printers and other publishers. Many of the titles he published or helped publish came from the presses of Joseph Bumstead, John W. Folsom, and the large firm of Thomas and Andrews. He also commonly published through the Apollo Press of Belknap and Young, Samuel Etheridge, William Greenough, John Howel, Manning and Loring, William Spotswood, and Alexander Young. In 1791 he also began publishing titles through Isaiah Thomas, and thereafter Larkin's name appears as publisher on many titles Thomas printed, especially the almanacs. Surprisingly, however, Thomas says nothing

337

about the Larkins in his famous <u>History</u>. Larkin's name
appears in imprints as co-publisher with a long list of
other publishers both in Boston and elsewhere. Among
those with whom he most commonly cooperated were John
Boyle, Thomas and Andrews, and, most frequently, David
West.

A conservative businessman with conservative
literary tastes, Larkin was not remarkable for innova-
tion, for handling literary titles, or for publishing
important first editions, although his edition of
Milton's <u>Paradise Lost</u> is an exception to this general-
ization. His business was based on his specialization
in titles dealing with divinity, law, medicine, and
education. That his stock totaled more than 15,000
volumes at the time of his death is convincing testimony
of his success and of the financial resources that he
brought to bear on the publishing business in Boston.

C. R. Kropf

References:

Anon. "Milton's Impress on the Provincial Literature of
New England." <u>Proceedings of the Massachusetts
Historical Society</u>, 42 (1908-1909).

Ford, Worthington C. "The Recall of John Quincy Adams
in 1808." <u>Proceedings of the Massachusetts
Historical Society</u>, 45 (1911-1912).

Silver, Rollo G. "The Boston Book Trade, 1800-1825."
<u>Bulletin of the New York Public Library</u>, 52
(1948).

Isaac Larkin

Isaac Larkin (1771-1797) was Thomas Adams's partner
from 1793 to 1797. Together they served as printers
to the Massachusetts General Court and as printers and
publishers of the Independent Chronicle: and the Universal Advertiser. Aside from the semiweekly numbers
of the Chronicle, over fifty state documents bear the
Adams and Larkin imprint. Their printing office was
located "opposite the New Court-House" in Court Street.

Major Authors: Samuel Adams, John Hancock.

Publishers Served: The Massachusetts General
Court.

Other than the date of his death, 4 December
1797, at age twenty-six, and his activities as a
printer, little is known of Larkin. Virtually all of
his printing was done with Thomas Adams, who took him
as partner in 1793, filling the vacancy left by his
previous partner, John Nourse, who had died in 1790.
As printers to the Massachusetts General Court, Adams
and Larkin printed over fifty documents for the state,
including speeches, proclamations, resolves, and acts
and laws. Their most ambitious project for the court
was the first volume of the Laws of the United States
of America (1795). They also printed the Massachusetts
Constitution (1795) and speeches and proclamations by
John Hancock (1793) and Samuel Adams (1795-1796).

As did most other printers, Adams and Larkin
printed their share of sermons. In 1794 they printed
and sold A Discourse on the Rise and Fall of Papacy by
Robert Fleming, and a sermon preached before Lieutenant
Governor Samuel Adams by Samuel Deane. In 1795 they
printed The Nature and Manner of Giving Thanks to God

339

by Ebenezer Bradford and, reflecting an issue of the day, The Altar of Baal Thrown Down: or, The French Nation Defended, against the Pulpit Slander of David Osgood by James Sullivan.

As a partner in printing and publishing the Independent Chronicle, Larkin had a hand in producing a newspaper that enjoyed a long and distinguished career. Throughout the period of ardent party politics following the American Revolution, this newspaper, which began as a continuation of the New-England Chronicle in September 1776, was, according to Frank Luther Mott, "the leading New England representative of the Republican party, as the Centinel was of the Federalists." And, again according to Mott, "neither was 'weasel mouthed' when the situation seemed, according to the scurrilous custom of early American political journalism, to call for gibes and insults." The views expressed in the Chronicle doubtless reflected Larkin's own political beliefs. Adams, who with Nourse began publishing the Chronicle in 1784, continued publishing it after Larkin's death.

Although Isaac Larkin died only four years into his partnership with Thomas Adams, on 4 December 1797, he printed one of America's longest lived and politically active newspapers while at the same time serving as printer to the general court. Thus, although his output was relatively small, it has some historical significance.

Marta Paul Johnson

References:

Brigham, Clarence S. History and Bibliography of American Newspapers: 1690-1820. Vol. 1. Worcester, Mass.: American Antiquarian Society, 1947.

Mott, Frank Luther. American Journalism, A History. 3rd edition. New York: Macmillan, 1962.

Samuel Larkin

Samuel Larkin (1773-1849) was in business in "State-Street" with his brother Ebenezer Larkin in 1793 and 1794 and again from 1799 to 1802. Samuel's name appears in the imprints of nine known works, the most notable of which is The Poetical Works of John Milton (1794).

Daniel W. Laughton

Daniel W. Laughton (c. 1775-1799) was in partnership with Ebenezer Rhoades in "Court-Street." They printed three known titles, all in 1798. Two are sermons by Joseph Russell and Peter Thacher; the third is John West's Boston Directory.

Richard Lee

Richard Lee (1747-1823) printed and published a 1793 broadside. He also conducted business in Warren, Rhode Island; Stockbridge, Massachusetts; and Rutland, Vermont.

341

John Leverett

John Leverett (1727-1777) conducted business "in Corn-hill" from 1754 to 1758. His name appears in six known imprints, all with his brother Thomas Leverett. Half of their publications are the first three numbers of Thomas Prince's Annals of New-England, volume one.

Martha Leverett

Martha Leverett (dates unknown) was active as a book-seller between 1778 and 1782, although her name appears in only three known imprints. After succeeding her hus-band Thomas in business, she published James Hervey's Meditations and Contemplations in 1778, The Psalms of David, Imitated in 1781, and Isaac Watts's Hymns and Spiritual Songs in 1782.

Thomas Leverett

Thomas Leverett (1730-1778) was a bookseller, binder, stationer, and a general merchant dealing in English goods. In 1752 and 1753 he conducted business alone "in Cornhill," but from 1754 until 1758 he was a part-ner with his brother John Leverett. After 1758 Thomas Leverett was once again in business for himself. He is announced as bookseller in approximately fifty-five texts by several printers, including John Draper, Edes and Gill, and Daniel Kneeland. Thirty-two of those volumes are either sermons or collections of hymns and Psalms. He sold two of the most popular Psalters in the colonies, Brady and Tate's New Version of the Psalms of David, Imitated (five editions after 1754) and Isaac Watts's Psalms of David (two editions after 1759). Among the various authors Leverett sold, the most important one is Charles Chauncy, whose name appears in Twelve Sermons (1765) and A Compleat View of Episcopacy (1771), among other Chauncy volumes. He also sold Thomas Prince's Annals of New-England (1754, 1755), almanacs by Roger Sherman and Nathaniel Ames, the New-England Primer Improved (1768, 1771), several grammars by Henry Dixon and others, and occasional political, scientific, and legal tracts. The last text bearing Leverett's name is a sermon by Samuel Cooks on the British attack at Lexington (1777). His wife Martha succeeded him in business.

Michael Clark

Reference:

Thomas, Isaiah. The History of Printing in America. Worcester, Mass.: Isaiah Thomas, Jr., 1810; 2nd ed., revised, Albany, N.Y.: J. Munsell for the American Antiquarian Society, 1874; ed. Marcus A. McCorison, Barre, Mass.: Imprint Society, 1970.

343

Thomas Lewis

Thomas Lewis (c. 1695-1727) succeeded Philip Musgrave as postmaster, and because of that position he published the Boston Gazette from May 1725 to April 1726.

References:

Brigham, Clarence S. History and Bibliography of American Newspapers: 1690-1820. Vol. 1. Worcester, Mass.: American Antiquarian Society, 1947.

Buckingham, Joseph T. Specimens of Newspaper Literature. Vol. 1. Boston: Little and Brown, 1850.

John S. Lillie

John S. Lillie (d. 1842) served as apprentice to
Benjamin Sweetser. In 1800 Lillie bought the Constitutional Telegraphe from Samuel S. Parker and published
that newspaper until March 1802, at which time he was
convicted of libel and imprisoned for three months.

References:

Brigham, Clarence S. History and Bibliography of Amer-
    ican Newspapers: 1690-1820. Vol. 1. Worcester,
    Mass.: American Antiquarian Society, 1947.

Buckingham, Joseph T. Specimens of Newspaper Litera-
    ture. Vol. 2. Boston: Little and Brown, 1850.

Ensign Lincoln

Ensign Lincoln (1779-1832) was a nineteenth-century
printer who began in business in 1800 on "Water-Street."
That year he printed one known title, Thomas Baldwin's
The Approved Workman.

Francis Lindley and
John Moore

Francis Lindley (dates unknown) and John Moore (dates
unknown) were partners in bookselling and printing in
1798 at "No. 19, Marlborough-Street." Their names
appear in only two known imprints: they sold songs by
James Davenport and Robert Treat Paine.

James Loring (see William Manning and James Loring)

Bennet Love

Bennet Love (b. 1703), a binder, was active as a publisher in 1727 and 1728. His name appears in only a
few imprints. He joined with others in publishing
works by Samuel Checkley (1727), Cotton Mather (1727),
and Ebenezer Gay (1728).

Reference:

Thomas, Isaiah. <u>The History of Printing in America</u>.
    Worcester, Mass.: Isaiah Thomas, Jr., 1810;
    2nd ed., revised, Albany, N.Y.: J. Munsell
    for the American Antiquarian Society, 1874;
    ed. Marcus A. McCorison, Barre, Mass.:
    Imprint Society, 1970.

346

Macclintock

Macclintock (given name and dates unknown) established the Times: or the Evening Entertainer with Thomas Hall in October 1794. Macclintock stayed with the newspaper for one month. His name appears in only one other known imprint, a broadside that he and Hall published in 1794.

Reference:

Brigham, Clarence S. History and Bibliography of American Newspapers: 1690-1820. Vol. 1. Worcester, Mass.: American Antiquarian Society, 1947.

William Manning and James Loring

William Manning (1767-1849) and James Loring (1770-1850), printers and booksellers, ran the chief bookmaking establishment in Boston at the end of the eighteenth century. They printed over 200 publications from 1793 to 1800, including several with color illustrations and plates and one of the first books printed in the French language in America. They were major printers for the Baptists of New England in a period of denominational growth and organization. A record of their imprints gives a good overview of the various types of material published in Boston during this period. They occupied their first office in Quaker Lane from 1793 to 1795. In 1795 they relocated to Spring Lane where the business remained until 1798. In 1798 the firm moved again to No. 2

347

Cornhill, "near the Old South Meeting House," where they had a bookshop as well as a printing operation.

Major Authors: Thomas Baldwin, Caleb Bingham, George Minot, Sarah Wentworth Morton, Robert Treat Paine, Susanna Rowson, Robert Southey, Samuel Stillman.

Publishers Served: Most of the Boston publishers and booksellers.

Manning was born on 15 April 1767 in Providence, Rhode Island; he died on 25 July 1849 in Cambridgeport, Massachusetts. He married Lydia Brown in 1794, and after her death in 1812 he married the widow Lydia Wyer Keith. Manning was the father of sixteen children. During most of his long life he was involved in printing and publishing activities. Following his apprenticeship in the office of Bennett Wheeler of Providence, Manning worked as a journeyman for Isaiah Thomas in Worcester, Massachusetts, and Boston. In 1793 he formed a partnership with James Loring; thus began the firm of Manning and Loring. In 1795 Thomas and his partner Ebenezer Andrews hired Manning as manager of their Boston print shop. Manning managed this shop with its five presses for the duration of his eight-year contract. He continued to manage the Thomas and Andrews shop for one additional year, but then left to devote more attention to his own firm. During the years 1793 to 1800, then, William Manning was employed in two shops; as Joseph Buckingham, one of the apprentices in the Thomas and Andrews shop, notes, Manning was "frequently absent [from Thomas and Andrews] to attend to the business of his partnership."

Much of the day-to-day running of Manning and Loring must have been left to the printer, James Loring. Loring was born in Hull, Massachusetts, on 22 July 1770. His longevity nearly equaled that of his partner; he died at the age of eighty on 9 July 1850. Loring was educated in the printing offices of Powars and Willis and Benjamin Russell. He was for fifty-five years a printer and bookseller in Boston. By 1800 Manning and Loring employed four journeymen and three apprentices

348

in their office. Two of their apprentices, Ensign
Lincoln and Thomas Edmands, later formed a firm of
their own, Lincoln and Edmands (1805).

Manning and Loring were principally printers;
book manufacture was their main occupation. Half of
their imprints from 1793 to 1800 indicate that they were
printed by Manning and Loring for another firm. The volume of their work was substantial; they printed for most
of the major Boston publishers and booksellers of the
time. Some of their titles were printed for publishers
who also had their own printing operations, such as
Thomas and Andrews, William Spotswood, and Samuel Hall.
They also printed for publishers and booksellers who had
no in-house printing operation. David West, John West,
James White, William P. and Lemuel Blake, Caleb Bingham,
Ebenezer Larkin, and Joseph Nancrede were some of those
in the latter category.

Technically their printing was probably above
average and they were among the first to try new techniques. Their 1795 printing of Samuel Rogers's The
Pleasures of Memory was, according to Charles Evans,
"printed with an elegant new type, on a wire wove vel-
lum paper, hot pressed, and interspersed with some very
elegant copper plate prints." Hot pressing was a fad
of short duration, but the attention Manning and Loring
gave to the appearance of their books continued. Evans
notes that their printing of a plan of the city of Boston (1796) was "handsomely coloured" on "fine paper."
Plates, engravings, and illustrations often appear in
their volumes. In 1797 they printed Duncan MacKintosh's
Essai Raisonné sur la Grammaire et la Prononciation
Angloise in French, complete with diacritical marks.
This work shows a mastery of printing techniques well
above the average.

Since they printed for so many different firms,
it is not surprising that Manning and Loring imprints
cover a wide range of subjects. Approximately forty-
five percent of their publications are in the field of
religion; education, literature, and the social sciences

were also important, with approximately twelve percent
of their imprints devoted to each. They printed several
titles in the natural sciences as well as almanacs, directories, broadsides, and minutes of organization meet-
ings. The range of their publications is representative
of the Boston press of the period.

Most of the items Manning and Loring printed and
sold which were not commissioned by other booksellers
concerned religious topics. Manning and Loring were
Baptists, and Joseph T. Buckingham has noted that they
were "men of strong religious tendencies and conscientious observers of all religious times and services."
At this time part of the Baptist denomination in New
England had departed from its separatist origins and
was becoming institutionalized. The creation of the
Warren Baptist Association in 1767 brought separatist
Baptists into the mainstream of Baptist life. The
Warren Association, which, though based in Rhode Island,
consisted largely of Massachusetts churches, became a
center of Baptist organization comparable to the Philadelphia Association and remained a unifying and sustain-
ing force among Baptists. Manning and Loring regularly
printed the minutes of the Warren Association's yearly
meeting. They also did the first printing of the Baptist Catechism in America (1795). They printed several
sermons delivered by Samuel Stillman, long the pastor
of the First Baptist Church in Boston, and Thomas
Baldwin, pastor of Boston's Second Baptist Church.
William G. McLoughlin notes that these men were "the
acknowledged leaders of the denomination." They were
establishment Baptists, men interested in making the
Baptist denomination respectable. While their sermons
contained few new ideas and made no lasting literary
or theological contribution, these men were effective
publicists for their faith, and Manning and Loring
helped in this effort.

Although Manning and Loring were devoted Baptists,
they did not hesitate to print religious items from
other denominations; for example, they printed the
Episcopal Book of Common Prayer (1794) and a collection

of hymns used in Roman Catholic worship (1800). After
the death of George Washington in 1799 they were much
occupied with printing eulogies for the departed president. They printed seventeen separate Washington eulogies, many given by local Boston worthies as well as
copies of those given in other areas of the country.
They also printed a collection of Washington eulogies
and did a printing of Washington's will.

Manning and Loring also did a large volume of
business in the field of education. They had a long
association with Caleb Bingham, the author of school
texts whose books were constant companions of the Bible
and the Psalms in the New England schools. They printed
approximately half the editions of Bingham's books in America and stocked Bingham's own bookstore and others with
such titles as The American Preceptor and The Columbian
Orator. They also printed the first American edition
of English Grammar, Adapted to the Different Classes of
Learners (1800) by Lindley Murray, the Scottish-American
grammarian who has been called the father of English
grammar. Numerous other texts in all fields of study
were printed by Manning and Loring. Their firm, after
various transformations, became the educational firm of
Benjamin H. Sanborn & Co. in the nineteenth century.

Manning and Loring were also active in the field
of literature. They printed first editions of some
American authors of note and first American editions
of several works first published in England. Sarah
Wentworth Morton was an American poet of contemporary
fame, although her reputation endured largely because
she was mistakenly assumed to have written the first
American novel, The Power of Sympathy. She did write
poetry in rhyming couplets, and produced an unfinished
epic of the American Revolution. Manning and Loring
printed for her the two completed volumes of this
effort, Beacon Hill (1797) and The Virtues of Society
(1799). The author published these two volumes under
the pseudonym "Philenia, a lady of Boston." Mrs.
Morton's fame was aided by her beauty and charm of

manner and the fact that few women of the time were writing verse at all.

Manning and Loring had a lesser association with another woman author, Susanna Rowson. Mrs. Rowson, a writer and actress who also established a successful school for girls in Boston, wrote popular novels. Manning and Loring printed for David West the first edition of her Reuben and Rachel (1798), an historical novel tracing the lives of some of the descendants of Columbus.

Robert Treat Paine, a poet and critic whose notoriety was enhanced by his eccentricities and his satirical attacks on important personages of the day, had one of his best known poems, The Ruling Passion (1797), printed by Manning and Loring. This poem was first delivered as a Phi Beta Kappa address at Harvard. The historian and jurist George Richards Minot was another of Manning and Loring's customers. They printed his Continuation of the History of the Province of Massachusetts Bay from the Year 1748 (1798). This work was a continuation of Thomas Hutchinson's famous history, and was somewhat eclipsed by the posthumous publication of Hutchinson's own continuation. Manning and Loring also printed two editions of Minot's oration on the death of Washington (1800).

Imprints done by Manning and Loring illustrate the variety of material first published in England that was of interest to Americans at the time. Since they printed for several publishers and booksellers, their list becomes representative of the entire book world in Boston. Literature, science, and history are some of the major fields in which Americans eagerly bought books first produced abroad.

The well-known British poet Robert Southey was published in America by Joseph Nancrede. Manning and Loring printed several editions for Nancrede, including the first American editions of Southey's epic Joan of Arc (1798) and his Poems (1799). The firm also printed several first American editions of other well-known works. They printed

352

the first Boston edition of Fanny Burney's novel Camilla
(1797), and the first American editions (for David West)
of two volumes of Essays (1798, 1799) by Sir Benjamin
Thompson, Count of Rumford, a well-known physicist and
adventurer. The Anatomy of the Human Body (1795) by
William Cheselden, an English surgeon and writer, was
printed in its first American edition by Manning and
Loring, as was Scottish novelist Henry MacKenzie's Man
of the World (1795). They also printed the first American editions of George Chalmers's Life of Thomas Paine
(1796) and The History of the Destruction of the Helvetic
Union and Liberty (1799) by the Swiss journalist Jacques
Mallet du Pan.

Manning and Loring also printed those staples of
the early American press, almanacs and directories. They
printed Robert Bailey Thomas's Farmer's Almanack annually
from 1797 to 1801. In 1796 they printed the second Boston directory. In 1800 they began printing the Massachusetts Register and United States Calendar, a continuation
of Fleet's Register, which contained a record of state
and county officers, merchants, and manufacturers. There
is no evidence that they printed any newspapers or other
serial publications, even though both Manning and Loring
became active in this respect after 1800.

Both partners continued their careers in the printing world after 1800. Items appeared with the Manning
and Loring imprint as late as 1815, although Manning
went to Worcester in 1814 as publisher of the Massachusetts Spy, a prominent weekly newspaper. Loring was
the founder and first editor of the Christian Watchman
(1819-1848), a national Baptist paper.

The firm of Manning and Loring made several contributions to the Boston publishing world. By printing
a large quantity of high-quality items and by using
sophisticated techniques, they advanced standards of
book production. Their specialization in book production also encouraged the development of publishing and
bookselling as separate endeavors in late eighteenth-
century Boston. Since they worked for so many publishers

353

and booksellers, Manning and Loring's imprints provide
a view of the wide range of publishing activity that
was occurring in Boston at that time. And finally,
when they followed their own interests and printed for
their faith, Manning and Loring were important to the
development of the Baptist denomination in America.

Jane Isley Thesing

References:

Anon. "Loring, James," New England Historical and
    Genealogical Record, 4 (1850).

Buckingham, Joseph T. Personal Memoirs and Recollec-
    tions of Editorial Life. Vol. 1. Boston:
    Ticknor, Reed, and Fields, 1852.

Manning, William H. The Genealogical and Biographical
    History of the Manning Families of New England
    and Descendants. Vol. 1. Salem, Mass.: Salem
    Press, 1902.

McLoughlin, William G. New England Dissent, 1630-1883:
    The Baptists and the Separation of Church and State.
    Vol. 2. Cambridge: Harvard University Press, 1971.

Silver, Rollo G. The American Printer, 1787-1825.
    Charlottesville, Va.: University Press of
    Virginia, 1967.

Tebbel, John. A History of Book Publishing in the
    United States. Vol. 1. New York and London:
    Bowker, 1972.

Francis Marriott

Francis Marriott (dates unknown) possibly printed one volume, The Land We Live In; or Death of Major André. No copy of that work is known to exist; Charles Evans assumed its publication from a copyright entry.

Henry Marshall

Henry Marshall (d. 1732) was, by reason of his position as postmaster, publisher of the Boston Gazette from 1727 until his death.

References:

Brigham, Clarence S. History and Bibliography of American Newspapers: 1690-1820. Vol. 1. Worcester, Mass.: American Antiquarian Society, 1947.

Buckingham, Joseph T. Specimens of Newspaper Literature. Vol. 1. Boston: Little and Brown, 1850.

Alexander Martin

Alexander Martin (c. 1777-1810) began his career in Fayetteville, North Carolina, in 1792. After a brief stay in New York he moved to Boston, where he edited the Massachusetts Magazine from October 1795 until June 1796. In the latter year he printed the Federal Orrery, and in 1796 and 1797 he printed the Polar Star. He announced his shop variously as "at the Magazine and Orrery Office, Quaker Lane, immediately opposite the Quaker Meeting-House," "at the Printing-Office, over Major Hawes's Shop, Quaker-Lane," and "No. 71, State-Street, opposite the Custom-House." He relocated in Baltimore in 1798.

References:

Brigham, Clarence S. History and Bibliography of American Newspapers: 1690-1820. Vol. 1. Worcester, Mass.: American Antiquarian Society, 1947.

Buckingham, Joseph T. Specimens of Newspaper Literature. Vol. 2. Boston: Little and Brown, 1850.

Mott, Frank Luther. A History of American Magazines: 1741-1850. New York and London: Appleton, 1930; Cambridge: Harvard University Press, 1938; Cambridge: Belknap Press of Harvard University Press, 1957.

356

John Mary

John Mary (dates unknown) sold his own <u>New French and English Grammar</u> in 1784. The next year he sold the second edition as <u>A New Grammar, English and French</u>. His name appears in no other known imprint.

Walter McAlpine

Walter McAlpine (dates unknown), a Scot, was a bookseller who learned binding from his brother, William M'Alpine. He announced his business as "in Union-Street" and "near the Mill-Bridge." His name appears in seven known imprints from 1743 to 1745, only one of which is significant: Jonathan Edwards's <u>The True Excellency of a Minister of the Gospel</u> (1744).

Reference:

Thomas, Isaiah. <u>The History of Printing in America</u>. Worcester, Mass.: Isaiah Thomas, Jr., 1810; 2nd ed., revised, Albany, N.Y.: J. Munsell for the American Antiquarian Society, 1874; ed. Marcus A. McCorison, Barre, Mass.: Imprint Society, 1970.

William M'Alpine

William M'Alpine (d. 1788) had a three-fold business in printing, bookbinding, and bookselling in Boston during the American Revolution. His Tory sympathies, however, eventually forced his departure when the British troops evacuated Boston. Indeed, his politics probably caused his business to diminish rather than continue to flourish during the early 1770s. He conducted business in Marlborough Street opposite the Old South Church, midway between the governor's and Dr. Gardiner's, and possibly other locations on that street as well. His printing is recognized generally by the reversed qs used to substitute for scarce bs.

Major Authors: Andrew Croswell, Samuel Hopkins, Aaron Hutchinson, David Macgregore, Jonathan Parsons, John Porter.

Publishers Served: Andrew Barclay, John Perkins.

A Scotsman by birth, M Alpine learned bookbinding from his family and came to Boston as a young man. There he established a binding shop, as well as a book shop, on Marlborough Street, opposite the Old South Church. He imported books from Glasgow and attempted to expand his business by distributing books for other Boston printers.

Apparently because of a dispute with the printers and booksellers in Boston who handled the Ames almanac, probably the most popular in the colonies, M'Alpine sent to Edinburgh for a press and type, as well as a foreman to be superintendent of printing. The dispute over which printers and booksellers would control the printing and sales of the almanac continued for years. Inclusion in

this group was important to M'Alpine because from 60,000
to 70,000 copies of Ames were sold annually in Boston
and throughout the other colonies, according to Margaret
Draper, another Boston printer. There were frequently
bitter charges, traceable to M'Alpine, in the Boston
newspapers, that independent printers were kept from
sharing in the Ames business. Generally, the almanac
was printed by the combined efforts of the Drapers,
Green and Russell, the Fleets, and Edes and Gill. After
Ames died and the printing combination hired a young
Harvard scholar to write the copy, the almanac bore the
name of the author, Benjamin West. However, in that
year, 1767, the newspapers and other publications carried some undercurrent of complaint by the printers
about M'Alpine, who also printed an Ames almanac.
The next year, the combination publicly rebuked
M'Alpine for publishing a counterfeit edition:

> The Public are advertised that some of the
> Almanacks published for the Year 1769, contain
> above Twenty Errors in the Sitting of the
> Courts;--that a Counterfeit Ames's Almanack
> has been pointed out agreeable to the Original
> Copy with the Name of Wm. McAlpine at the
> Bottom: Therefore whoever is desirous of
> having the true genuine correct Ames's Alma-
> nack, are requested to take Notice. That at
> the Bottom of the Outside Title, is, BOSTON,
> Printed and Sold by the Printers and Book-
> sellers, &c. and no particular Name thereto.

This did not discourage M'Alpine, however, from continuing his printing.

In general, M'Alpine had a small portion of the
total Boston printing business. He built his business
to a high of fifteen percent of the total Boston printing in 1765 and eighteen percent in 1767. However,
during the other years, his business averaged about
five percent of the total printing in Boston. It

appears that about 1768 John Mein's growing image of the obnoxious Scotsman printer, an enemy of the popular party, also hurt M'Alpine. Mein's partner, John Fleeming, had been connected with M'Alpine's printing business for about a year, and even this may have been enough for Bostonians to mark M'Alpine as a distrusted loyalist. M'Alpine, desirous of expanding his business, did not hesitate, however, at printing political sermons that praised the popular party. Even this did not bolster his steadily declining business, and he left Boston with the retreating British troops in 1775. He died in Glasgow, Scotland, in 1788.

MaryAnn Yodelis Smith

References:

Thomas, Isaiah. The History of Printing in America. Worcester, Mass.: Isaiah Thomas, Jr., 1810; 2nd ed., revised, Albany, N.Y.: J. Munsell for the American Antiquarian Society, 1874; ed. Marcus A. McCorison, Barre, Mass.: Imprint Society, 1970.

Yodelis, MaryAnn. Who Paid the Piper? Publishing Economics in Boston, 1763-1775. Journalism Monographs, 38. Lexington, Ky.: Association for Education in Journalism, 1975.

John Douglass M'Dougall

John Douglass M'Dougall (d. 1787) came to America from
Ireland. He began selling books in Philadelphia in
1774, and he relocated in Providence in 1775. In 1777
he moved to Boston where he was active through 1781.
His name appears in ten known Boston imprints, with
Lord Chesterfield's Letters . . . to His Son (1779)
being his only significant publication. M'Dougall
announced his business as "opposite the Old South
Meeting-House" and "two doors south of the Treasurer's
Office."

Benjamin Mecom

Benjamin Mecom (1732-c. 1776) was a printer, bookseller,
and newspaper publisher active in Antigua, Boston, New
York, New Haven, Philadelphia, and Burlington, New
Jersey. Approximately forty-five Boston imprints bear
his name. He learned the printing business as an apprentice to James Parker in New York City in a shop Parker
owned in partnership with Benjamin Franklin. In 1752
Franklin appointed Mecom to manage his printing shop in
St. John's, Antigua, West Indies. In 1756 Mecom resigned the position, bought the equipment from Franklin,
and moved to Boston where he opened the New Printing
Office in early 1757 in Cornhill, opposite the Old
Brick Church near the Court House. He closed that
shop in 1762, and in 1763 opened the Modern Printing-
Office in New York City in Rotten-Row. This business
soon failed. Mecom stored his press and stock as security for the debts he had contracted with his old

361

employer Parker and moved to New Haven where he rented
a printing shop from Parker at the post office near
Hay-market in early 1765. Plagued by financial problems, Mecom moved to Philadelphia in 1767, where he
opened a printing shop in Arch Street opposite the
Presbyterian Meeting House. When this business failed
in 1770, Mecom found employment in the printing shop
of William Goddard. In 1774 Mecom moved his business
to Burlington, New Jersey, where he ended his career
as an employee in the printing shop of Isaac Collins.

Major Authors: Benjamin Franklin, James Janeway,
Isaac Watts.

Publishers Served: Green and Russell, Thomas
Johnston.

Born 29 December 1732, Mecom was the third of
twelve children of Edward Mecom and Janet, the youngest
sister of Benjamin Franklin. Although Franklin took an
interest in Mecom's career, the younger man was plagued
by two problems throughout his life. He was a poor
business manager; his first and major project in
Boston, for example was a 30,000-copy edition of the
New-England Psalter (1758). The project took him
nearly two years to complete, and he sold the copies
at such a low price that he made no profit. Eventually
Parker, with Franklin's reluctant consent, had to sell
Mecom's press and stock to pay the debts Mecom had contracted. In addition, Mecom seems to have been eccen-
tric if not mentally unstable. Isaiah Thomas reports
seeing him work at press wearing a powdered bob wig,
gloves, and ruffles. The last that is known of Mecom
appears in a letter that William Smith of Burlington
wrote to Franklin on 19 July 1776 reporting that Mecom
had taken leave of his senses and asking that he be
restrained as a dangerous person.

Whatever his personal failings, Mecom is important
to the history of the book trade for several reasons.
Perhaps most significant, he was the printer of the
famous and extremely rare first separate edition of his

362

uncle's Father Abraham's Speech to a Great Number of People (1758), the collection of the sayings of Poor Richard. As Charles Evans notes, this work has probably been translated and reprinted more often than any other work by an American author. Mecom's most active year was 1760 while he was in Boston; at least eighteen imprints from that year bear his name. He reprinted two editions of Franklin's The Interest of Great Britain Considered (1760) and another edition of Father Abraham's Speech (1760?), three titles by the popular English divine James Janeway, and an assorted collection of the usual sermons, political tracts, and educational texts. Mecom was also the first printer to experiment with stereotype printing. Sometime around 1775 he cast several pages of the New Testament in stereotype, but by this date he was experiencing serious mental problems and nothing came of the experiment.

In the course of his career Mecom printed five periodicals, of which two are important. In Antigua he revived the weekly Antigua Gazette in November 1752. In January 1755, he began printing it on a triweekly basis and continued it until he left his position there. At the time it was the only newspaper on the islands and is therefore a valuable resource. In Boston he printed the New-England Magazine, which appeared in only three numbers between August 1758 and March 1759. In New York City, in 1763, another experiment with a periodical, the New-York Pacquet, also failed after only six numbers. He was more successful in New Haven where he revived the Connecticut Gazette, which appeared with his imprint from 5 July 1765 to 19 February 1768. Finally in 1769, in Philadelphia, Mecom tried to establish a newspaper, the Penny Post, but it appeared in only nine numbers between 9 and 27 January.

Had Mecom been blessed with the business acumen of his famous uncle, his career would doubtless deserve more attention. As an early experimenter with stereotype printing he was working on an idea that would eventually revolutionize the printing industry. As it

363

is, he is best remembered as the printer of the first separate edition of Franklin's Father Abraham's Speech.

C. R. Kropf

References:

Eames, Wilberforce. "The Antigua Press and Benjamin Mecom, 1748-1765." Proceedings of the American Antiquarian Society, 38 (1928).

Thomas, Isaiah. The History of Printing in America. Worcester, Mass.: Isaiah Thomas, Jr., 1810; 2nd ed., revised, Albany, N.Y.: J. Munsell for the American Antiquarian Society, 1874; ed. Marcus A. McCorison, Barre, Mass.: Imprint Society, 1970.

John Mein

John Mein (dates unknown), bookseller, publisher, and
editor, established the first Boston lending library
and published the first American editions of works by
Oliver Goldsmith and Laurence Sterne. He edited the
Boston Chronicle, the first semiweekly newspaper in
that city. In 1766 he offered what was, to that time,
the largest number of books for sale in America. He
also established, in 1769, a foundry for casting type.
He set up business as a bookseller in Marlborough
Street, "nearly opposite to Bromfield's Lane," but he
relocated at the London Book Store, "on the North side
of King Street," in November 1765. A year later, he
and John Fleeming established a printing shop in Wing's
Lane, and they expanded in 1767 to Newbury Street,
"almost opposite the White-Horse Tavern." Mein published over fifty volumes.

   Major Authors: John Dickinson, Thomas Dilworth,
Oliver Goldsmith, William Knox, Laurence Sterne, Isaac
Watts, Benjamin West.

   Mein emigrated to Boston from Edinburgh, where he
probably had been a bookseller, in October 1764. He
established a Boston shop briefly with his fellow Scot
George (or Robert) Sandeman; in late 1765 he formed a
partnership with another countryman, John Fleeming,
that lasted until Mein fled Boston for London in November 1769. Even though Mein was in Boston for only five
years, and even though he was, to quote John Alden, "the
outstanding American publisher of the day both in the
number and in the quality of the books he issued," he
was a controversial figure more noted for his politics
than for the quality of his business.

365

S P E C I M E N

OF

MEIN and FLEEMING's Printing Types.

Rempublicam, Quirites, vitamque omnium veſtrum, bona, fortunas, conjuges, liberoſque veſtros, atque hoc domicilium clariſſimi imperii, fortunatiſſimam pulcherrimamque urbem hodierno die, deorum immortalium ſummo erga vos amore, laboribus, conciliis, periculis meis, ex flamma atque ferro, ac pae-

REMPUBLICAM, Quirites, vitamque omnium veſtrum, bona, fortunas, conjuges, liberoſque veſtros, atque hoc domicilium clariſſimi imperii, fortunatiſſimam pulcherrimamque urbem hodierno die, deorum immortalium ſummo erga vos amore, laboribus, conciliis, periculis meis, ex flamma atque ferro, ac paene ex faucibus fati ereptam, ac vobis conſervatam ac reſtitutam videtis. Et ſi non mi-

Rempublicam, Quirites, vitamque omnium veſtrum, bona, fortunas, conjuges, liberoſque veſtros, atque hoc domicilium clariſſimi imperii, fortunatiſſimam pulcherrimamque urbem hodierno die, deorum immortalium ſummo erga vos, amore, laboribus conciliis periculis meis, ex flamma atque ferro, ac paene ex faucibus fati ereptam, ac vobis conſervatam ac reſtitutam videtis. Et ſi non

Rempublicam, Quirites, vitanque omnium veſtrum, bona, fortunas, conjuges, liberoſque veſtros, atque hoc domicilium clariſſimi imperii, fortunatiſſimam pulcherrimamque urbem hodierno die, deorum immortalium ſummo erga vos amore, laboribus, conciliis, periculis meis, ex flamma atque ferro, ac paene ex faucibus fati ereptam, ac vobis conſervatam ac reſtitutam videtis. Et ſi non minus nobis jucundi atque illuſtres, ſunt ii dies, quibus conſervamur, quam illi quibus naſcimur: quod ſalutis certa letitia eſt, naſcendi incerto conditio: et quod ſine ſenſu naſcimur, cum voluptate ſervamur: profecto, quoniam illum, qui hanc urbem condidit, ad deos immortales benevolentia famaque ſuſtulimus: eſſe apud vos poſteroſque veſtros in honore debebit is, qui eandem hanc ur-

Rempublicam Quirites vitamque omnium veſtrum, bona, fortunas, conjuges, liberoſque veſtros, atque hoc domicilium clariſſimi imperii, fortunatiſſimam pulcherrimamque urbem hodierno die, deorum immortalium ſummo erga vos amore, laboribus, conciliis, periculis meis, ex flamma atque ferro, ac pæne ex faucibus fati ereptam, ac vobis conſervatam ac reſtitutam videtis. Et ſi non minus nobis jucundi atque illuſtres, ſunt ii dies, quibus conſervamur, quam illi quibus naſcimur: quod ſalutis certa letitia eſt, naſcendi incerto conditio: et quod ſine ſenſu naſcimur, cum voluptate ſervamur: profecto, quoniam illum, qui hanc urbem condidit, ad deos immortales benevolentia famaque ſuſtulimus: eſſe apud vos poſteroſque veſtros in honore debebit is, qui eandem hanc urbem conditam amplificatamque ſervavit, nam toti urbi, templis, delubris, tec-

Rempublicam, Quirites, vitamque omnium veſtrum bona, fortunas, conjuges, liberoſque veſtros, atque hoc domicilium clariſſimi imperii, fortunatiſſimam pulcherrimamque urbem hodierno del, deorum immortallum ſummo erga vos amore, laboribus, conciliis, periculis meis, ex flamma atque ferro, ac pæne ex faucibus fati ereptam ac vobis conſervatam ac reſtitutam videtis. Et ſi non minus nobis jucundi atque illuſtres ſunt ii dies, quibus conſervamur, quam illi, quibus naſcimur: quod ſalutis certa letitia eſt, naſcendi incerta conditio: et quod ſine ſenſu naſcimur, cum voluptate ſervamur: profecto, quoniam illum, qui hanc urbem condidit, ad deos immortales benevolentia famaque ſuſtulimus: eſſe apud vos poſteroſque veſtros in honore debebit is, qui eandem hanc urbem conditam amplificatamque ſervavit. Nam toti urbi, templis, delubris, tectis ac moenibus omnibus ſubjectos prope jam ignes circumdatoſque reſtinximus: iidemque gladios in rempub. deſtrictos retudimus, mucronuſque eorum a jugulis veſtris dejecimus. Quae quoniam in ſenatu illuſtrata, patefacta, compertaque ſunt

☞MEIN and FLEEMING execute all ſorts of PRINTING WORK in the beſt and moſt reaſonable manner, and with the utmoſt expedition.

Upon his arrival in America Mein established the
first lending library in Boston. As a result of that
enterprise, he published, in 1765, a catalogue of his
library's holdings, and that got him started in the
publishing business. His first printer was William
M'Alpine, whose work may be identified by the inverted
q used for the scarce b. John Fleeming did all the
rest of Mein's printing after they became partners in
1766.

Mein's two most important publications, at least
from a literary point of view, are the first American
editions of Oliver Goldsmith's The Vicar of Wakefield
(1767), of which there is no known copy, and Laurence
Sterne's A Sentimental Journey through France and Italy
(1768). Five years passed before the first title was
republished in America; the next American edition of
Sterne's book was in 1770. Mein also published Joseph
Addison's Cato (1767) and John Dickinson's Letters from
a Farmer in Pennsylvania and possibly his The Liberty
Song, both in 1768. From 1767 until 1770 he published
the first four annual volumes of Benjamin West's
Bickerstaff's Boston Almanack, a series that continued
until the middle of the nineteenth century. Among the
numerous religious works bearing the Mein imprint are
A New Version of the Psalms of David (1767, 1770),
Chandler Robbins's The Ways of God Vindicated (1767),
and Isaac Watts's Hymns and Spiritual Songs (1766, 1769).
Mein, knowing how to exploit the market, also published
some titles with false London imprints. He thought that
London editions would sell better than American ones.

Mein is probably better known for his politics
than he is as a publisher. He was a Tory who antagonized Bostonians in general and the merchants in particular by opposing the nonimportation movement that
was intended to protest the Townshend Acts. He and
Fleeming established the Boston Chronicle, modeled on
the London Chronicle, in December 1767, a newspaper
that soon became the first semiweekly in Boston.
(Joseph T. Buckingham has noted that the Chronicle,
"in its mechanical experimenting, far surpassed any

paper that had appeared before it.") As editor, Mein
used the pages of the Chronicle to praise the crown and
ridicule many of the eminent Boston Whigs. As a result,
subscriptions declined and Mein became one of the most
hated men in town. The Whigs so despised Mein that in
November 1769, they carried an effigy of him with the
following acrostic attached to it:

I nsulting Wretch, we'll him expose--
O 'er the whole world his deeds disclose;
H ell now gapes wide to take him in;
N ow he is ripe--O lump of Sin!
M ean is the man--M--n is his name;
E nough he's spread his hellish fame;
I nfernal furies hurl his soul,
N ine million times, from pole to pole!

After fighting with some Bostonians, on 17 November 1769
Mein left America, never to return.

As a political figure Mein is remembered, to use
John Alden's phrase, as a "scourge of patriots." As a
publisher, however, he should be thought of highly.

References:

Alden, John E. "John Mein, Publisher: An Essay in
    Bibliographic Detection." Papers of the Biblio-
    graphical Society of America, 36 (1942).

Alden, John E. "John Mein: Scourge of Patriots."
    Publications of the Colonial Society of Massa-
    chusetts, 34 (1943).

John Mein

Thomas, Isaiah. The History of Printing in America.
    Worcester, Mass.: Isaiah Thomas, Jr., 1810;
    2nd ed., revised, Albany, N.Y.: J. Munsell
    for the American Antiquarian Society, 1874;
    ed. Marcus A. McCorison, Barre, Mass.: Imprint
    Society, 1970.

Wroth, Lawrence C. The Colonial Printer. New York:
    Grolier Club, 1931; revised and enlarged,
    Portland, Me.: Southworth-Anthoensen Press,
    1938; reprint edition, Charlottesville, Va.:
    University Press of Virginia/Dominion Books,
    1964.

John Mein

369

Nathaniel Mills and John Hicks

Nathaniel Mills (1749-c. 1785) and John Hicks (1750-1794) were minor loyalist printers and newspaper publishers in Boston during the American Revolution, publishing the Massachusetts Gazette and Boston Post-Boy for two years. Unlike the other Tory printers, however, Hicks was a convert from the popular party and later, he even became a loyalist spy. Hicks was in business alone through 1772 next to the Cornfield on Union Street. He and Mills established their partnership on School Street next to Cromwell's Head Tavern in 1773. In 1775 they left for two years in England. They reestablished in New York City, where they remained until they ended their partnership in 1783 and went their separate ways.

Major Authors: Samuel Cooper, Samuel Dunbar, Oliver Noble, Benjamin West.

Publishers Served: Cox and Berry, Edes and Gill.

Mills and Hicks completed their printing apprenticeships about the same time and so were ripe to be persuaded, Isaiah Thomas records, to purchase the Post-Boy and give some revitalized support to the government party. Their partnership was comparatively short lived (1773-1783), their fame merely modest, and their financial success reportedly substantial, but undocumented.

History has given John Hicks the label of turncoat. He was born in Cambridge where his boyhood home still stands on Boylston Street near the Charles River. Apparently a zealous Whig, Hicks reportedly was one of the young men who attacked the British soldiers in the Boston Massacre in 1770. His father was a martyr to the patriot

370

cause during the retreat from Lexington on 19 April 1775. Hicks's politics changed, however, and he posed as a patriot while gathering valuable information for the British General Gage regarding American troops at Cambridge. Hicks's contemporaries claimed that he then "traitorously" returned to the "tyrants" with the information.

Much less is known of Hicks's partner, Nathaniel Mills. Born near Boston, he was John Fleeming's apprentice. Called a "sensible, genteel young man" by Isaiah Thomas, Mills had "principal charge" of the Post-Boy.

Mills and Hicks's brief tenure as publishers of the Boston Post-Boy accounts for their most significant contribution to publishing history. John Green and Joseph Russell, perhaps under severe pressure from royal government that was thoroughly dissatisfied with the Post-Boy's weak support, sold the paper to Mills and Hicks on 26 April 1773. The two purchased John Fleeming's printing office on School Street at that time. Isaiah Thomas notes that "the British party handsomely supported the paper of Mills and Hicks, and afforded pecuniary aid to the printers." No other records, however, indicate the financial arrangements Mills and Hicks may have made to purchase the printing office and the publishing rights to the Post-Boy. In fact, records show that Green and Russell had been more financially favored with government printing than their successors. When Mills and Hicks assumed control of the Post-Boy, of course, they restored some of the other printing business lost because Green and Russell printed for the hated Board of Customs, but not to the level enjoyed by Green and Russell in 1763 and 1764 before the Revolution reached intensity. Mills and Hicks made graphic changes in the Post-Boy that clearly signified new proprietors, but they did not make sweeping content changes. For example, the new publishers allowed more space between advertisements, added column rules (which did little to improve the paper's appearance), and enlarged the emblems in the masthead. In general, however, the content remained dull and did not overwhelmingly support the mother country; in fact, there were a few

371

criticisms of the government party. Nevertheless, after the Boston Tea Party, Mills and Hicks did publish the strongest arguments in Boston against nonimportation as a means of retaliation against the British. They warned that the property of the Boston merchants would be destroyed, that other colonies would not be sympathetic, and that redcoats would be installed permanently in Boston as a result. This sporadic support of the government party continued until Mills and Hicks stopped printing the newspaper on 17 April 1775 and fled Boston with the British troops.

While Mills and Hicks were Boston publishers, they estimated that their combined printing and stationery business brought £ 300 annually, a comparatively modest income for a printer. As was the case for most colonial publishers, the newspaper barely paid for itself through advertising and subscription income, and any substantial profit for the firm came from job printing, as well as from some stationery sales. Economic evidence indicates that the Post-Boy contained only sixteen percent of the total newspaper advertising in Boston from 1773 through 1775 and that newspaper circulation was low. In fact, Mills and Hicks wrote that the popular party eventually prevented the news carriers "from circulating their Papers." Further, Mills and Hicks produced only eight percent of the total printing, excluding newspapers, in Boston during that period. This occurred in part because the two did not inherit the customs board printing that Green and Russell found so lucrative. In 1773 and 1774, only an average of fourteen percent of Mills and Hicks's total printing was for government; they printed nothing for government in 1775. On the other hand, during the same two years of 1773 and 1774, an average of sixty-three percent of their printing was religious; about thirty-six percent of the 1775 printing was religious. (Most Boston printers devoted about half of their efforts to religious printing.) Also, political pamphlets accounted for only a small portion of Mills and Hicks's total printing volume. Although they did print more loyalist than patriot propaganda, Mills and Hicks were either pressured by the popular

372

party or moved by their own desire to make money and so printed patriot materials. They also printed Mills and Hicks' Register, an almanac.

In the end, the Boston experience probably was an economic loss for Mills and Hicks. They attempted to sell their "Compleat Sett of Printing Materials" before they left Boston with the retreating British, but they apparently were not successful. A British Public Record Office memorial reads: "at the commencement of the late War in America they [Mills and Hicks] were settled in Boston New-England, where they published a Weekly News Paper, and were in good Business. . . . That when the British Army evacuated Boston they were obliged to leave a great part of their Property in that Town, not having an opportunity to get it brought off for want of Shipping." However, nothing indicates that the British government compensated them for those losses.

Few records of Mills and Hicks's activities after they left Boston are extant. According to Isaiah Thomas, the two spent two years in England and then sailed to New York, which was controlled by the British at the time. Mills and Hicks apparently opened a stationery store there and completed some printing for the Royal Army and Navy. In time, they joined Alexander and James Robertson in publishing the Royal American Gazette in New York from 1 January 1782 through 31 July 1783. After the property was sold at auction, Mills and Hicks went to Halifax, Nova Scotia, and dissolved their partnership. Thomas reports that Mills eventually lived at Shelburne, Nova Scotia; there is no evidence that he continued printing. Hicks returned to Massachusetts. Thomas records that Hicks had acquired "considerable property" during the war and purchased a handsome estate in Newton where he lived until his death. Joseph Buckingham verifies that the two printers "acquired wealth," but no hard evidence of this can be found. (Hicks's will cannot be located in the Middlesex County Probate Records.)

373

Thus, Mills and Hicks did their part to insure that a diversity of voices during the American Revolution would include that of the government party, dull and uninspired though that voice was. And for that contribution to the traditions underlying the formulation of the First Amendment, Mills and Hicks should be remembered fondly.

MaryAnn Yodelis Smith

References:

American Antiquarian Society. Mills and Hicks Letterbook, 1774-1780.

Buckingham, Joseph T. Specimens of Newspaper Literature. Vol. 1. Boston: Little and Brown, 1850.

Thomas, Isaiah. The History of Printing in America. Worcester, Mass.: Isaiah Thomas, Jr., 1810; 2nd ed., revised, Albany, N.Y.: J. Munsell for the American Antiquarian Society, 1874; ed. Marcus A. McCorison, Barre, Mass.: Imprint Society, 1970.

Yodelis, MaryAnn. Who Paid the Piper? Publishing Economics in Boston, 1763-1775. Journalism Monographs, 38. Lexington, Ky.: Association for Education in Journalism, 1975.

Thomas Minns (see Alexander Young and Thomas Minns)

Judah Monis

Judah Monis (1683-1764) composed and sold, "at his house in <u>Cambridge</u>," <u>A Grammar of the Hebrew Tongue</u>. Jonas Green printed that first American Hebrew grammar in 1735.

John Moore (see Francis Lindley and John Moore)

Seth H. Moore

Seth H. Moore (c. 1776-1831) conducted business in Boston in 1797. That year he printed <u>The Rules and Regulations of the Friendly Fire Society</u>. He moved to Haverhill, Massachusetts, in 1798, returned to Boston by 1803, and finally located in Roxbury around 1818.

Jedediah Morse

Jedediah Morse (1761-1826), Congregational minister, author, and father of American geography, published one known title. In 1796 he joined with others in publishing Richard Cecil's <u>Friendly Visit to the House of Mourning</u>, a volume he published again in Charlestown in 1803.

Reference:

Winsor, Justin. <u>The Memorial History of Boston</u>.
    Vol. 3. Boston: Osgood, 1881.

Philip Musgrave

Philip Musgrave (d. 1725), postmaster, published the <u>Boston Gazette</u> from September 1720 until July 1725.

References:

Brigham, Clarence S. <u>History and Bibliography of American Newspapers: 1690-1820</u>. Vol. 1. Worcester, Mass.: American Antiquarian Society, 1947.

Buckingham, Joseph T. <u>Specimens of Newspaper Literature</u>. Vol. 1. Boston: Little and Brown, 1850.

Joseph Nancrede

Joseph Nancrede (1761-1841), Franco-American bookseller and publisher, was influential in introducing French literature and thought to the young republic through his publications at a time when the interchange of ideas between France and America had important political and cultural consequences. He published approximately thirty titles in various editions, of which the most significant were the first American editions of the writings of Bernardin de Saint-Pierre. In 1795, in partnership with Thomas Hall, he began business under the style of Hall and Nancrede, establishing a French and English bookstore "on the north side of the State-house." In 1796 he set up independently at 49 Marlborough Street. For various individual enterprises he entered into temporary partnerships with William Spotswood (1796 and 1797) and Barnard B. Macanulty of Salem (1801). In 1803 part of his stock was taken over by Dyer and Eddy, and Nancrede moved to 24 State Street. The remainder of his stock was auctioned in 1804 when his publishing career ended.

Major Authors: François de Salignac de La Mothe Fénelon, Jacques Mallet du Pan, Jacques Henri Bernardin de Saint-Pierre.

Nancrede was born Paul Joseph Guérard in Hericy, near Fontainebleau, France, in 1761, and died in Paris in 1841. Reared by his grandfather, he entered military service in 1779 and was a member of the French expeditionary force in the American Revolution. He was present at the siege of Yorktown. After a sojourn in France (1783-1785) he returned to America, taking the name of Paul Joseph Guérard de Nancrede, later simply Joseph Nancrede. In 1787 he became French instructor at Harvard College, a position he retained for a decade.

His teaching experience drew to his attention the striking need for French texts in America. In 1788 he married Hannah Dixey by whom he had nine children. Also in
1788 he translated De la France et des Etats-Unis by
Brissot de Warville and Etienne Clavière, and extracts
of the translation were published in the Massachusetts
Centinel and the Independent Chronicle. From 1789 until
1794 he taught French privately. In 1789 he established and edited the Courier de Boston, a French newspaper published by Samuel Hall that ran for six months
and adopted the motto: "L'Utilite des deux Mondes."
In 1791 he translated Brissot de Warville's Discours
sur la Question. Si le Roi Peut être Jugé, published
by Belknap and Young (1791). The following year the
same firm published Nancrede's important compilation,
L'Abeille Françoise, ou Nouveau Recueil, De morceaux
brillans, des auteurs François les plus celebres, the
first anthology used as a French textbook in this
country. In 1793 Nancrede wrote an anonymous pamphlet,
Les Citoyens Francois, in which he attacked the consular
system. His experience as teacher, editor, compiler,
and translator were all put to use when he entered the
bookselling and publishing business.

Setting up in 1795 as bookseller with Thomas Hall,
Nancrede stocked mainly imports from abroad, especially
the writings of French authors and French authors in
English translation: Voltaire and Rousseau, Brissot de
Warville and Condorcet, Condillac and Raynal, Molière
and Mirabeau, Montesquieu and Scarron. His wares made
a pointed appeal to French emigrés settled in Boston as
well as to American citizens who were becoming more and
more aware of the infiltration of French thought into
American mores.

Nancrede varied and amplified his stock by means
of exchanges with colleagues in America with whom he
established business relations, some friendly, some
less so. In 1795 he visited Médéric-Louis-Elie Moreau
de Saint-Méry, Philadelphia bookseller-stationer-
publisher, exchanging books with him and becoming correspondent for Moreau de Saint-Méry's Courrier de la

France et des Colonies. In 1796 Nancrede received supplies of periodicals from Joseph Dennie, editor of the
Farmer's Museum in Walpole, New Hampshire. Having imported fifty copies of Bowditch's New American Navigator,
Nancrede was in 1802 threatened with a lawsuit for in-
fringement of copyright by Edmund March Blunt of Newburyport, Massachusetts, whose bookstore was headquarters for
American nautical publications. In later years Nancrede
supplied consignments of stock to William Cobbett, the
pamphleteer, who became a bookseller in Philadelphia.

Between 1796 and 1800 Nancrede's name appeared in
the imprint of fourteen different works as one of the
sellers of books published by others: Thomas Hall,
Isaiah Thomas, the Russells of Quaker Lane. These works
include Oulton's Wonderful Story-Teller, a Pilgrim's
Progress, Surr's George Barnwell, and L'Estrange's version of Seneca's Morals.

In 1795 Nancrede began his brief but significant
career as a Boston publisher. While still in partnership with Thomas Hall he published a bilingual edition
(with French and English texts on facing pages) of the
Projet de Constitution pour La République Française
which he himself had translated, and Treaties with
France, Great Britain, and the United States, a work
containing Alexander Dallas's study of Jay's Treaty and
Noah Webster's "Vindication of that Instrument."

As an independent publisher, Nancrede published
in 1796 a reprint in French of the French constitution
proposed to the people of France by the National Con-
vention, which was also published under a second title:
Procès-verbal de l'assemblée . . . pour prendre
connoissance de la constitution.

Between 1796 and 1797 Nancrede undertook his
most ambitious and most influential publishing project,
the introduction to this country of the major works of
Bernardin de Saint-Pierre. This project involved multivolume sets, engraved illustrations, elaborate prefaces,
a dedication to George Washington, and bilingual editions.

379

Joseph Nancrede

For any long-established publisher this would have been
a major undertaking; for a young and comparatively inex-
perienced publisher it was extremely demanding.

On 30 September 1796, Nancrede announced (in his
Catalogue of Books) as "This Day Published" in a pocket-
size volume, Paul and Virginia, Saint-Pierre's master-
piece, a narrative set in an exotic land whose tenets
reaffirm Rousseau's doctrine. In addition to that English edition, Nancrede published the work in French and
in a two-volume bilingual edition. For all these editions he entered into a temporary partnership with
William Spotswood.

The following year Nancrede independently published Saint-Pierre's Studies of Nature in several versions, including a three-volume edition with engravings
by Samuel Hill of Boston and William Rollinson of New
York. The work which, according to Nancrede's advertisement of 24 July 1797, "established beyond the power
of contradiction, the doctrine of a Universal Providence," introduced to this country the philosophic
romanticism of a distinguished French writer. Cogni-
zant of the significance of his undertaking, Nancrede
dedicated Studies of Nature to President George Washington in the "belief that the general intention and
execution . . . will coincide with your views, . . .
Such a belief is the natural consequence of his
[Nancrede's] opinion that the work is calculated to
interest the Philosopher, by presenting ingenious and
useful speculation . . . the Philanthropist, by excit-
ing 'A WARMER INTEREST IN FAVOUR OF SUFFERING HUMAN-
ITY' . . . the Friend of Religion and Morals, by
illustrating the being and providence of DEITY . . .
and the Lover of Nature, by displaying the harmony
and proportion . . . that mark her productions."

Nancrede also published A Vindication of Divine
Providence in two volumes (compiled from the portions
of Studies of Nature that relate to religion), and
Botanical Harmony Delineated, a translation of the
eleventh of Saint-Pierre's Studies of Nature. All

380

these editions were printed for Nancrede, as was Studies of Nature, by Isaiah Thomas's firm.

Also in 1797--an annus mirabilis for Nancrede--he published Fénelon's Telemachus (Les Aventures de Télémaque Fils d'Ulysse), edited and corrected by the publisher himself, in French, in English, and in a two-volume bilingual edition. Telemachus was dedicated "To the American Youth of Both Sexes."

In 1798 Nancrede published an English translation of Claude Rulhière's History, or Anecdotes of the Revolution in Russia in the Year 1762, advertised in his Catalogue of Books Just Imported from London (1798) as printed on "fine paper, with an elegant Portrait of the late Empress of Russia, neatly bound and lettered," priced at seventy-five cents.

Nancrede's publications of 1799 reflect the collapse of pro-French feeling in America. Mallet du Pan's History of the Destruction of the Helvetic Union and Liberty, purportedly concerned with Switzerland, is actually a denunciation of the French Republic. La Harpe's Du Fanatisme dans La Langue Révolutionnaire is a study of fanaticism. Vittorio Barzoni's The Romans in Greece, in English translation, compares the French to the ancient Romans who plundered the Greeks.

While Nancrede emphasized in his publications books that would explain French politics, literature, and thought to American readers, his list was not exclusively of Franco-American interest. From the beginning it had included works that would serve non-French readers as well, especially students, theologians, merchants, politicians, and farmers.

A few of Nancrede's publications were directed to the specific needs of Harvard University. In 1795 Hall and Nancrede published a folio broadside in Latin listing the theses in the various faculties of the University, and two years later Nancrede published Joseph Perkins's

381

Oration upon Genius, Pronounced at the Anniversary Commencement of Harvard University.

Several Nancrede imprints were designed for students of literature and language: Robert Southey's epic
poem Joan of Arc (1798); the first American edition of
Southey's Poems (1799); the first American edition of
Lindley Murray's English Grammar (1800). Toward the
end of his publishing career he published a poem entitled Boston by Winthrop Sargent (1803).

Other Nancrede publications were geared to the
needs of theologians: Thomas Cogan's Letters to William
Wilberforce . . . on the doctrine of Hereditary Deprav-
ity (1799) and The Pulpit Orator (1804), an anthology of
sermons and discourses by English and French orators
directed to a clerical readership.

For merchants and sailors, Nancrede, in the course
of his temporary partnership with Spotswood, published
John Malham's The Naval Gazetteer; or, Seaman's Complete
Guide (1797), a two-volume illustrated geography in first
American edition.

The deliberations of statesmen and politicians
fascinated Nancrede. One of his earliest publications,
when he was still in partnership with Thomas Hall, was
Peter Porcupine's (William Cobbett's) "A Little Plain
English" addressed to the people of the United States
on the Treaty and on the Conduct of the President (1795).
Nancrede followed this the next year with John Gardner's
Brief Consideration of the Important Services and Distinguished Virtues and Talents, which Recommend Mr. Adams
for the Presidency of the United States. In 1800, when
patriotic publishers were releasing pamphlets bordered
in black in memory of George Washington, Nancrede added
three eulogies to the collection: one by Josiah Dunham,
a captain in the Sixteenth United States Regiment; one
by Major-General Henry Lee, member of Congress from
Virginia; and one by John Miller Russell. One of his
last publications was an anthology he himself had compiled: The Forum Orator; or the American Public

Speaker, including orations from the British Parliament and the United States Congress (1804).

For American farmers Nancrede provided the first American edition of Charles Marshall's Introduction to the Knowledge and Practice of Gardening (1799). For those in search of health he published Lectures on Diet and Regimen (1800) by A. F. M. Willich, declaring in the publisher's advertisement that epidemics might be caused by "the vicious diet and incautious regimen peculiar to the Americans . . . we find all foreigners, who visit this country, . . . exclaiming against our copious and everlasting dinners."

Since Nancrede was never active as a printer, he engaged for his presswork the services of colleagues in the printing trade, especially printers of the French language: Isaiah Thomas's firm for his ambitious Saint-Pierre project; Manning and Loring for many publications including Mallet du Pan's History of the Destruction of the Helvetic Union; Belknap and Hall; and others.

In order to advertise his own publications as well as his stock as bookseller, Nancrede published between 1796 and 1803 four major catalogues: Catalogue of Books in the Various Branches of Literature; Lately Imported from London, Dublin, Paris, and other Capitals of Europe (1796); Joseph Nancrede's Catalogue of Books Just Imported from London (1798) and two Fixed-Price Catalogues (1803).

Not all of Nancrede's publishing ambitions were realized. His negotiations with the Vermont lawyer and author Royall Tyler for publication of a book of moral tales for American youth proved fruitless. A grandiose plan to publish a multivolume system of universal geography involved Nancrede in a temporary partnership with Barnard B. Macanulty of Salem, an agreement with the author James Tytler, a journey abroad to obtain books and maps, and several pamphlets outlining the proposed work--but the plan came to nothing.

383

The failure of that enterprise may have played a part in Nancrede's decision to abandon his trade as publisher and, for a time, his adopted country. (He had been naturalized in 1799). On 15 June 1803 the Columbian Centinel announced that Dyer and Eddy, sellers of watches, fancy goods, jewelry, and books, had taken over "the store, and greater part of the stock lately owned by Mr. Joseph Nancrede." According to the Centinel of 20 August 1803, Nancrede "removed his books to No. 24, State Street, corner of Kirby-Street, over Sam'l Bradford's Auction store." In February 1804 the remainder of Nancrede's stock was auctioned by Bradford. His career as Franco-American publisher had ended.

Separated from his wife, Nancrede took his children abroad to be educated, and during the latter part of his life he became a dabbler in books and politics. He resided in France from 1804 to 1812, in Philadelphia from 1812 to 1825, and again in France from 1825 until his death in 1841.

Nancrede's brief period as bookseller-publisher in Boston was significant. Despite the paucity of his imprints, he was a productive publisher who was responsible for the first American editions of several important works. From 1795 to 1804, through the books he imported for sale and through his own publications, he helped introduce French thought to America. During a decade of crisis in Franco-American affairs, he effectively interpreted the one country to the other.

Madeleine B. Stern

References:

Stern, Madeleine B. "A Salem Author and a Boston Publisher: James Tytler and Joseph Nancrede." New England Quarterly, 47 (1974).

Stern, Madeleine B. "Saint-Pierre in America: Joseph Nancrede and Isaiah Thomas." Papers of the Bibliographical Society of America, 68 (1974).

Stern, Madeleine B. "Joseph Nancrede, Franco-American Bookseller-Publisher, 1761-1841." Papers of the Bibliographical Society of America, 70 (1976); reprinted in Books and Book People in 19th-Century America, by Madeleine B. Stern, New York and London: Bowker, 1978.

Edmund Negus

Edmund Negus (dates unknown) was a stationer and bookseller from 1719 to 1730. His name appears in two 1719 imprints, Cotton Mather's Genethlia Pia and the twenty-fifth edition of James Hodder's Arithmetick.

Francis Nichols

Francis Nichols (dates unknown) was active as a bookseller in Boston, Philadelphia, and New York from 1797 to 1820. His name appears in only three known Boston imprints through 1800. He published Richard Johnson's Juvenile Trials for Robbing Orchards (1797), the first American edition of Richard Watson's Address to Young Persons after Confirmation (1797), and William Bell's Practical Enquiry into . . . the Lord's Supper (1800).

385

Jonathan Nichols

Jonathan Nichols (dates unknown) was a printer whose name appears in only one known imprint. In 1799 he printed a song, Damon's Soliloquy, as a broadside.

John Norman

John Norman (c. 1748-1817) was an engraver, bookseller, and printer. He published Boston's first city directory, music, maps, and some of the earliest books on architecture to appear in America. In 1783 his shop was located in "Marshall's Lane, near the Boston Stone." He relocated "near Oliver's Dock" in 1788, and in 1790 he moved to "no. 75, Newbury-Street."

Major Authors: William Billings, Jacob French, Abraham Swan, Timothy Swan.

Born in England, Norman was first mentioned in America in May 1774, when he advertised himself in Philadelphia's Pennsylvania Journal as "John Norman, Architect and Landscape Engraver, from London," offering his services as engraver to "booksellers in any part of America." Three months later, he and a partner, styling themselves as "Engravers and Drawing Masters," advertised an evening drawing school. Norman remained in Philadelphia until 1780, serving as an engraver and publishing only a few books.

In 1781 he was in Boston, where he worked as an engraver before beginning to print in 1783. His

386

engravings from this period include the title-piece and
music for William Billings's Psalm-Singer's Amusement
(1781) and portraits of military heroes in An Impartial
History of the War in America between Great Britain and
the United States (2 vols., 1781-1782). His ability as
a portrait engraver was not marked; in fact the engravings he produced for An Impartial History were blister-
ingly denounced for their poor quality. In the field of
architecture, music, and maps, however, Norman's work
seems to have been more acceptable to his contemporaries;
throughout his career as a publisher he engraved many of
the works he printed, in addition to engraving works with
which he had no connection as a printer or publisher,
including Isaiah Thomas's 1791 two-volume folio Bible.

Norman appears to have begun his Boston publishing
career in 1783 when he served as one of several printers
for the Boston Magazine, which began in November 1783,
and ceased in October 1786. It was published by a
"Society for Compiling a Magazine in the Town of Boston,"
many of whose members later founded the Massachusetts
Historical Society. One of the society's main objects
in publishing the magazine was to produce a Massachusetts geographical gazetteer, which appeared as a supplement to certain issues and which attempted to give
an account of every town in the commonwealth. He
printed the periodical with a man named White until
1784, when they were joined by Edmund Freeman. Norman's
name was dropped from the imprint in July 1784, after an
apparent disagreement. During his association with the
Boston Magazine, Norman illustrated it with his engravings, including a "Plan of Boston" in the first volume.

Although he printed a few almanacs, grammars, and
religious items, Norman's most numerous and significant
publications were in the realm of architecture, music,
maps, and navigational aids, all of which were acceptable vehicles for his continued interest in engraving.
In 1786 he printed and engraved his own architecture
book, The Town and Country Builder's Assistant, which
consisted of material taken from English sources and
which was illustrated by "upwards of 200 examples."

Intended for the less well-to-do builder, this was the
first book on architecture compiled in America. In 1792
he printed the first American edition of William Pain's
The Practical Builder. This was followed by Abraham
Swan's British Architect; or, the Builder's Treasury of
Stair-Cases, which Norman published in 1794. He had
originally printed this British work in Philadelphia in
1775, at which time it had been the first book of architecture published in this country. Norman's output in
this genre is significant when one considers that only
thirteen editions of nine different works in architecture were published in eighteenth-century America.

Because he was an engraver, it is not surprising
that Norman published a number of music collections,
beginning in 1784 with The Massachusetts Harmony, a work
attributed to William Billings, a prominent Boston singing master, choir director, and America's first native
composer. Norman published an additional Billings work,
The Suffolk Harmony, in 1786. Although not as prominent
as Billings, Timothy Swan was another native American composer of some popularity whose Federal Harmony Norman
published in 1788, 1790, 1792, and 1793. A third New
England composer, Jacob French, had his New American
Melody published by Norman in 1789. In addition to
local talent, Norman also printed the music of the
famous English hymn writer, Isaac Watts, whose Psalms
of David, printed by Norman in 1789, was a staple volume in hymn production. Watts's Hymns and Spiritual
Songs was printed by Norman in that same year.

Throughout his career Norman published various
maps and navigation charts. In 1791, 1792, and 1793
he published his own American Pilot, Containing the
Navigation of the Sea Coast of North America; this
work is a compendium of useful data for the navigator,
including information on tides and currents, depth of
water and anchorage in principal harbors and rivers,
and courses and distances between places on the coast.
One of his most significant publications was the Boston
Directory (1789), Boston's first city directory. Illustrated with a map of the city, the directory includes

388

such items as lists of merchants' and traders' shops, banks and their hours of business, and the offices of physicians and attorneys.

Although the quantity of titles published by Norman was relatively small, his significance rests on the areas in which he published.   In architecture he printed the first architectural book compiled in America, his own Town and Country Builder's Assistant (1786), as well as other titles whose importance rests on the scarcity of books published in architecture in eighteenth-century America.   In music he printed some of the nation's first native composers.   And finally, he published the first city directory of Boston.   Many of the works he printed contain his engravings as illustrations.

Gary R. Treadway

References:

Green, Samuel A.   "Remarks on the Boston Magazine, the Geographical Gazetteer of Massachusetts, and John Norman, Engraver." Proceedings of the Massachusetts Historical Society, 2nd series, 18 (1904).

Hitchcock, Henry-Russell.   American Architectural Books, A List of Books, Portfolios, and Pamphlets on Architecture and Related Subjects Published in America Before 1895.   Minneapolis: University of Minnesota Press, 1962.

Stauffer, David M.   American Engravers upon Copper and Steel.   New York: Grolier Club, 1907; reprint edition, New York: Burt Franklin, 1964.

William Norman

William Norman (d. 1807), son of John Norman, was a bookseller in Boston from 1794 until his death. His name appears in eleven known imprints through 1800; he regularly published, on the average, two volumes a year from 1794 through 1799. He sold religious, practical, and musical works. He also sold, with others, Osgood Carleton's Accurate Map of the District of Maine (1795). Norman conducted his business "at his Book-Store, No. 75, Newbury-Street, nearly opposite the Sign of the Lamb."

John Nourse

John Nourse (c. 1762-1790) was in partnership, from 1783 until his death, with Thomas Adams. No known imprint bears Nourse's name without that of Adams. Adams and Nourse were editors of the Independent Chronicle from 1784 through 1789, and as such they helped disseminate the voice of Jeffersonian Republicanism. They were also printers for the Massachusetts General Court, for whom they offered to print the acts and resolves at no charge in order to secure the right to all other government printing. That, as Rollo G. Silver has shown, was an unsound financial arrangement for Adams and Nourse.

Reference:

Silver, Rollo G. "Government Printing in Massachusetts, 1751-1801." Studies in Bibliography, 16 (1963).

John Parker

John Parker (d. 1738) was a cutler and grocer who also sold books "at the head of the Town-Dock." His name appears in only one known imprint, Thomas Foxcroft's Elisha Lamenting after the God of Elijah (1737).

Reference:

Thomas, Isaiah. The History of Printing in America. Worcester, Mass.: Isaiah Thomas, Jr., 1810; 2nd ed., revised, Albany, N.Y.: J. Munsell for the American Antiquarian Society, 1874; ed. Marcus A. McCorison, Barre, Mass.: Imprint Society, 1970.

Luther Parker

Luther Parker (1781-1849) was a printer who was responsible for only one known book through 1800, Isaiah Parker's Funeral Discourse (1800).

Samuel Stillman Parker

Samuel Stillman Parker (1776-1811) published the semi-weekly <u>Constitutional Telegraphe</u> from its inception in October 1799 until he sold it to Jonathan S. Copp in July 1800.

References:

Brigham, Clarence S. <u>History and Bibliography of American Newspapers: 1690-1820</u>. Vol. 1. Worcester, Mass.: American Antiquarian Society, 1947.

Buckingham, Joseph T. <u>Specimens of Newspaper Literature</u>. Vol. 2. Boston: Little and Brown, 1850.

William Pelham

William Pelham (1759-1827) sold books at "No. 59, Cornhill." Of the seven known titles bearing his name published from 1796 to 1800, he was solely responsible for only two, John C. Cross's musical drama <u>The Purse; or, Benevolent Tar</u> and William Saunders's <u>Treatise on the . . . Liver</u>, both in 1797.

392

John Pemberton

John Pemberton (1708-c. 1759), bookseller and binder
from 1730 until his death, conducted business "in Cornhill." He published religious titles by Nathaniel
Appleton (1730), John Flavel (1731), and his father
Ebenezer Pemberton (1744).

Reference:

Thomas, Isaiah. The History of Printing in America.
    Worcester, Mass.: Isaiah Thomas, Jr., 1810;
    2nd ed., revised, Albany, N.Y.: J. Munsell
    for the American Antiquarian Society, 1874;
    ed. Marcus A. McCorison, Barre, Mass.: Imprint
    Society, 1970.

Elkanah Pembroke (see Elkanah Pembrooke)

Elkanah Pembrooke (or Pembroke)

Elkanah Pembrooke (or Pembroke) (d. c. 1706) possibly
worked for John Allen and clerked for William Avery
before opening his own shop "near the Head of the Dock"
in 1689. He published only one known title, Richard
Alleine's Heaven Opened. Bartholomew Green and John
Allen printed that work for Pembrooke in 1699.

References:

Ford, Worthington C. The Boston Book Market: 1679-1700.
    Boston: Club of Odd Volumes, 1917; reprint edition,
    New York: Burt Franklin, 1972.

Littlefield, George E. Early Boston Booksellers: 1642-
    1711. Boston: Club of Odd Volumes, 1900; reprint
    edition, New York: Burt Franklin, 1969.

John Perkins

John Perkins (c. 1739-1783) was an apprentice to Joshua
Winter and succeeded him in business. Perkins located
first "near the Mill-Bridge"; in 1762 he moved to "Union-
Street near the Market," where he remained for the rest
of his career. He published fewer than forty titles in
fifteen years. His most productive year was 1771 when
he released seven titles; he published nothing in 1763
or 1766. His publications were, with one exception,
undistinguished. He published thirteen Psalters, six

394

editions of the New-England Primer, three almanacs, and three items by Isaac Watts. His most significant publication was Christoph Wieland's The Trial of Abraham (1764), the earliest American edition of any of that German author's works.

Although Perkins never had a partner, a few of his early volumes were joint publishing ventures. He shared imprints with Daniel Henchman, John Phillips, Joseph Edwards, Thomas Leverett, William M'Alpine, Michael Dennis, Joshua Winter, and Samuel Webb. He joined with more notable publishers for the 1766 Ames almanac: the Drapers, Edes and Gill, Green and Russell, and the Fleets. Few of the books Perkins published alone bear the name of a printer, but the printers who are known to have done work for him are Daniel Kneeland, John Kneeland, Seth Adams, Edes and Gill, Isaiah Thomas, John Boyle, Joseph Greenleaf, and possibly William M'Alpine.

Perkins was a minor Boston publisher whose sole importance is that he was the first American to publish Christoph Wieland.

Reference:

Wright, Wyllis E. "A Newly Discovered Edition of Wieland's Trial of Abraham." Modern Language Notes, 65 (1950).

Joanna Perry

Joanna Perry (1665-1725) was a cousin to Samuel Phillips and the wife of Michael Perry. After Michael's death in 1700, she carried on his bookselling business. Her shop was destroyed in the 1711 fire, and she relocated "in King Street on the North Side of the Town House." Her name appears in three known imprints. She published sermons by Henry Harris (1712) and Benjamin Colman (1714); in the latter year she also published Cotton Mather's Pascentius.

Reference:

Littlefield, George E. Early Boston Booksellers: 1642-1711. Boston: Club of Odd Volumes, 1900; reprint edition, New York: Burt Franklin, 1969.

Michael Perry

Michael Perry (1666-1700), bookseller and publisher, was
a cousin to Benjamin Eliot and, through his wife Joanna,
to Samuel Phillips, with whom Perry probably served an
apprenticeship. Perry began in the business in 1694
"under the west-end of the Town-House" (or "under the
Exchange") when Phillips transferred the lease of his
shop to him. Perry's name appears in approximately
twenty-four imprints from 1694 to 1700, one-third of
which are by Cotton Mather, including Johannes in Eremo
(1695). Perry also published works by John Cotton,
Increase Mather, Solomon Stoddard, and Samuel Willard.
Samuel Sewall, Jr., worked for Perry briefly in 1694.
Joanna Perry continued her husband's business after his
death.

References:

Ford, Worthington C. The Boston Book Market: 1679-
    1700. Boston: Club of Odd Volumes, 1917; re-
    print edition, New York: Burt Franklin, 1972.

Littlefield, George E. Early Boston Booksellers: 1642-
    1711. Boston: Club of Odd Volumes, 1900; reprint
    edition, New York: Burt Franklin, 1969.

Phillips

Phillips (given name and dates unknown), a printer, was in business during 1776 and 1777 with Edward Draper "at the new Printing-Office, next door but one to the Sign of the Lamb Tavern, in Newbury-Street." Phillips's name appears in only three known imprints, two 1777 almanacs (1776) and Samuel Cooke's The Violent Destroyed (1777).

Eleazer Phillips

Eleazer Phillips (1682-1763), nephew to Samuel Phillips, was active as a Boston bookseller from 1709 to 1715. He announced his business variously as "in Corn-Hill," on "the south side of the Town-House," "under the Town-house in Kings Street," and "at the sign of the Eagle in Newbury Street." Phillips's name appears in sixteen known imprints. He published works by Cotton and Increase Mather, Peter Thacher, and Nehemiah Walter. Phillips's son, Eleazer, Jr., introduced printing to South Carolina in 1730.

Reference:

Littlefield, George E. Early Boston Booksellers: 1642-1711. Boston: Club of Odd Volumes, 1900; reprint edition, New York: Burt Franklin, 1969.

Gillam Phillips

Gillam Phillips (1695-1770), bookseller, was the son of
Samuel Phillips, with whom he served his apprenticeship.
Gillam established his own business in 1711 and announced
his shop variously as "over against the west end of the
Town-House," "in King-Street," "at the Three Bibles and
Crown in King-Street," and "over against the South side
of the Town-House." Phillips's name appears in only
five known imprints from 1717 to 1732, the most signif-
icant of which is perhaps his first, Cotton Mather's
Brief Account of the State of the Massachusetts-Bay
Province (1717). With Daniel Henchman, Thomas Hancock,
and others, Phillips established the first New England
paper mill at Milton Lower Falls in 1729. He married
Mary Faneuil, Peter Faneuil's sister.

References:

Littlefield, George E. Early Boston Booksellers: 1642-
    1711. Boston: Club of Odd Volumes, 1900; reprint
    edition, New York: Burt Franklin, 1969.

Park, Lawrence. "Joseph Blackburn--Portrait Painter."
    Proceedings of the American Antiquarian Society,
    32 (1922).

399

Henry Phillips

Henry Phillips (1656-1680), bookseller, probably served
his apprenticeship with Hezekiah Usher before opening
his own shop "in the west end of the Exchange" in 1677.
His name appears in only three known imprints, all of
which were printed by John Foster. In 1677 Phillips
published Increase Mather's Renewal of Covenant the
Great Duty Incumbent on Decaying or Distressed Churches;
in 1679 and 1680 he published Foster's almanacs.
Phillips had his brother Samuel Phillips as an
apprentice.

Reference:

Littlefield, George E. Early Boston Booksellers: 1642-
    1711. Boston: Club of Odd Volumes, 1900; reprint
    edition, New York: Burt Franklin, 1969.

Temporary

ACTS and LAWS

Of His Majesty's

PROVINCE

OF THE

Massachusetts-Bay

IN

NEW-ENGLAND.

BOSTON; NEW-ENGLAND:

Printed by Order of His EXCELLENCY the GOVERNOR,
COUNCIL and House of REPRESENTATIVES :
And Sold by GREEN and RUSSELL in Queen-Street.
MDCCLXIII.

Representative Title pages (Courtesy William L. Clement's Library, University of Michigan)

Two

SERMONS,

Preached unto a

NEW-ASSEMBLY,

of CHRISTIANS

at 𝔅𝔯𝔦𝔡𝔤𝔴𝔞𝔱𝔢𝔯.

On, 14 d. VI. m. 1 7 1 7.

A Day of PRAYER kept by them,

at their Entring into the

NEW-EDIFICE,

Erected for the

Worſhip of G O D

among them.

The Firſt, By *JAMES KEITH,*

Paſtor of the Church in *Bridgwater.*

The Second,

By *SAMUEL DANFORTH,*

Paſtor of the Church in *Taunton.*

With a Preface of Dr. *Increaſe Mather,*

and Dr. *Cotton Mather.*

BOSTON: Printed by *T.* Crump, for *Samuel Phillips,* and Sold at his Shop in King-Street 1717.

Patriotism and Religion.

A SERMON,

PREACHED ON THE 25th OF APRIL,

1799,

THE DAY RECOMMENDED

BY THE PRESIDENT OF THE UNITED STATES,

TO BE OBSERVED AS A

NATIONAL FAST.

BY John Lathrop, D. D.

MINISTER OF A CHURCH IN BOSTON.

Published by Desire.

BOSTON:

PRINTED BY JOHN RUSSELL.

1799.

TWELVE

SERMONS

On the following seasonable and important Subjects.

Juſtification impoſſible by the Works of the Law.

The Queſtion anſwered, "wherefore then ſerveth the Law"?

The Nature of Faith, as juſtifying, largely explained, and remarked on.

The Place, and Uſe, of Faith, in the Affair of Juſtification.

Human Endeavours, in the uſe of Means, the way in which Faith is obtained.

The Method of the Spirit in communicating the "Faith, by which the Juſt do live".

The Inquiry of the young Man in the Goſpel, "what ſhall I do that I may have eternal Life"?

With interſperſed Notes, in Defence of the Truth; eſpecially in the Points treated on, in the above Diſcourſes.

By CHARLES CHAUNCY, *D. D.*

And one of the Paſtors of the firſt Church of Chriſt in BOSTON.

BOSTON; NEW-ENGLAND:
Printed by D. and J. KNEELAND, for THOMAS LEVERETT, in Corn-hill. MDCCLXV.

PIETAS

ET

GRATULATIO

COLLEGII CANTABRIGIENSIS

APUD NOVANGLOS.

BOSTONI-MASSACHUSETTENSIUM

TYPIS J. GREEN & J. RUSSELL.

MDCCLXI.

John Phillips

John Phillips (1701-1763) published approximately fifty
titles from 1717 to 1760. He succeeded his father
Samuel Phillips in business. He was located "on the
south side of the Town-House" until 1730, when he reestablished at the shop of his father-in-law, Nicholas
Buttolph, "at the Stationer's Arms, No. 1. Next door
to Mr. Dolbeare's Brazier, near the Town Dock."

Major Authors: Benjamin Colman, Cotton Mather.

After an apprenticeship with Daniel Henchman,
Phillips published, on the average, one volume a year
during his forty-three-year career. He was most active
from 1726 to 1732 when he published all but ten of his
total number of publications. He published nothing in
the ten years after 1742 or from 1754 to 1759.

Although Phillips published little during his long
if sporadic career, about one-quarter of his publications are by two of the most significant clergymen of
that time, Cotton Mather and Benjamin Colman. He published six titles by each of them. After what was possibly Phillips's first publication, the sixth edition of
John Hill's Young Secretary's Guide (1717), his next
three and four of his next six publications were by
Mather. Mather's The Pure Nazarite was Phillips' only
1723 publication, and Mather's Baptistes and Religious
Societies were all that he published in 1724. Of
Phillips's three 1725 publications, one is Mather's
Zalmonah. Phillips published Pietas Matutina and Terra
Beata, his last Mather titles, in 1726, two years before
the great divine died. Not one of these six is among
Mather's most important works, however.

406

While 1726 was the last year Phillips published Mather, it was the first year he published Colman. After It is a Fearful Thing to Fall into the Hands of a Living God, Phillips published one Colman title annually through Dying in Peace in a Good Old Age in 1730. The only exception was in 1728 when he published two of Colman's volumes, Death and the Grave without Any Order and The Holy Walk and Glorious Translation of Blessed Enoch.

Most of Phillips's publications are religious. In addition to titles by Mather and Colman, he published works by such less significant divines as Samuel Phillips, Benjamin Bass, William Cooper, John Barnard, Ebenezer Gay, Matthew Henry, William Williams, Thomas Foxcroft, Isaac Clancy, and Israel Loring.

Phillips used the major printers of the day. Samuel Kneeland printed seven of his titles; Timothy Green, Bartholomew Green, and Thomas Fleet did five each; and Daniel and John Kneeland jointly printed one Phillips title. Phillips also teamed with others in joint publishing efforts. Thomas Hancock's name appears with Phillips's in nine publications, Daniel Henchman's in five, Samuel Gerrish's in two, John Eliot's in two, and Bennet Love's in one. One of the publications Phillips shared with Gerrish is William Cooper's Reply to the Objections Made against Taking the Small Pox in the Way of Inoculation from the Principles of Conscience (1730), a central document in the inoculation controversy of the day.

Phillips succeeded his father in business and continued his modest record as a publisher. John Phillips published two important theologians--Cotton Mather and Benjamin Colman--but none of their most important work bears his name. He published primarily religious volumes. He worked with the best Boston printers and frequently shared a publishing project with another minor publisher, Thomas Hancock.

407

John Phillips

References:

Littlefield, George E. Early Boston Booksellers: 1642-
    1711. Boston: Club of Odd Volumes, 1900; reprint
    edition, New York: Burt Franklin, 1969.

Tebbel, John. A History of Book Publishing in the United
    States. Vol. 1. New York and London: Bowker,
    1972.

Thomas, Isaiah. The History of Printing in America.
    Worcester, Mass.: Isaiah Thomas, Jr., 1810;
    2nd ed., revised, Albany, N.Y.: J. Munsell
    for the American Antiquarian Society, 1874;
    ed. Marcus A. McCorison, Barre, Mass.: Imprint
    Society, 1970.

Samuel Phillips

Samuel Phillips (1662-1720), bookseller and publisher, published approximately ninety titles from 1681 to 1720. He advertised his shops variously as "at the west end of the exchange," "at the west end of the Town-House," "near the south-east end of the Exchange, by the Rose & Crown Tavern," "at the Brick Shop, at the west end of the Exchange," "at the Brick-shop near the Town-House," "at the Brick Shop near the Old Meeting-house," and "on the South-Side of the Town-House in King-street." Married to Hannah Gillam, daughter of the almanac compiler Benjamin Gillam, their son Gillam Phillips apprenticed with Samuel and later became a publisher in his own right.

Major Authors: Cotton Mather, Increase Mather, Solomon Stoddard, Samuel Willard.

In 1681, after serving an apprenticeship with his brother Henry Phillips, Samuel Phillips published two titles, an almanac and a religious piece. Practical and spiritual volumes would remain the staples of his business; they reflected the readers' concerns. One other aspect of his business was governmental: he published seven volumes of the Massachusetts Bay Province's acts and laws (1693-1694). In 1720, the year he died, Phillips participated in a joint publishing effort for only the second time; together with Nicholas Buttolph, Benjamin Eliot, and Daniel Henchman (and his nephew Eleazer Phillips in Charlestown) he published the second edition of Mary Rowlandson's captivity tale that became so popular that it inspired many similar efforts in that genre.

Phillips' most noteworthy publications are by divines, especially Increase and Cotton Mather. He

409

published four titles by the father: A Discourse Concerning the Uncertainty of the Times of Men (1697), The Surest Way to the Greatest Honour (1699), A Discourse Concerning the Grace of Courage (1710), and Several Sermons (1715). He published seventeen volumes by the son, beginning in the early 1690s and continuing through The Man of God Furnished in 1708. Perhaps Phillips's most important title is Cotton Mather's Wonders of the Invisible World (1693). The Mathers accounted for about one-quarter of all the titles Phillips published. Among his other religious volumes are seven works by Samuel Willard, including Israel's True Safety (1704), and four items by Solomon Stoddard, with the last, The Duty of Gospel-Ministers (1718), being the last religious title that Phillips published. Other theologians he published include Thomas Bridge (his 1705 Artillery Company Sermon), John Danforth, Benjamin Keach, and Benjamin Wadsworth.

Phillips, like most publishers, dealt in almanacs. His first is his most important. Either the first or second title he published was John Foster's almanac for 1681. Foster, one of the most important men in early American publishing, printed the volume himself; he died that same year. Phillips published three almanacs by John Tulley and one each by his father-in-law Benjamin Gillam, William Williams, Christian Lodowick, and William Brattle. He also published An Almanack (1707) and three volumes of the N. England Kalendar (1704-1706).

Phillips used the best printers available to him. Of the nine he employed, Bartholomew Green printed over half of his publications, while John Allen accounted for twenty (most in conjunction with Green), Samuel Green did sixteen, and Thomas Fleet printed four. John Foster, Richard Pierce, Benjamin Harris, Vavasour Harris, Nicholas Buttolph, and Benjamin Eliot also printed for Phillips.

Phillips had a long career as a publisher; it spanned the last two decades of the seventeenth century and the first two of the eighteenth. Although he published the most influential men of his time--the Mathers--he published none of their major works. His publications nonetheless reflect the temper of the times, and his edition of Mary Rowlandson's captivity, in the year he died, hints at the growing secularism that became one of the new century's most pronounced characteristics.

References:

Littlefield, George E. Early Boston Booksellers: 1642-1711. Boston: Club of Odd Volumes, 1900; reprint edition, New York: Burt Franklin, 1969.

Tebbel, John. A History of Book Publishing in the United States. Vol. 1. New York and London: Bowker, 1972.

Thomas, Isaiah. The History of Printing in America. Worcester, Mass.: Isaiah Thomas, Jr., 1810; 2nd ed., revised, Albany, N.Y.: J. Munsell for the American Antiquarian Society, 1874; ed. Marcus A. McCorison, Barre, Mass.: Imprint Society, 1970.

Richard Pierce

Richard Pierce (d. c. 1965) was the fifth printer to conduct business in Boston. He printed primarily for the
booksellers, and most notably for Joseph Browning.
Pierce printed <u>Publick Occurrences</u>, probably the second
attempted newspaper in the English colonies, and the
first edition of the <u>New-England Primer</u>. His name
appears in the imprints of thirty-seven titles.

   <u>Major Authors</u>: Cotton Mather, Increase Mather,
Richard Steere.

   <u>Publishers Served</u>: Joseph Browning (or Brunning),
Nicholas Buttolph, James Cowse, Obadiah Gill, Benjamin
Harris, John Usher.

   Almost nothing is known of Pierce's life before
1680, when he married Sarah Cotton and affiliated himself with the family of John Cotton of Boston (Cotton's
eldest son, Seaborn, was Sarah's father). It is im-
probable that a London printer named Richard Pierce
(last recorded in 1679) was Richard Pierce of Boston.
Pierce came to Boston and served his apprenticeship
under John Foster. After Foster's death, he was employed by Samuel Green, Jr., and remained with him
until the retirement of Samuel Sewall, the manager of
the press, presented him with the opportunity to open
his own press. Backed by the Dudley, Cotton, and
Bradstreet families--Sarah was related to all of them--
Pierce was able to obtain a license to print and opened
his offices in 1684.

   Pierce printed most frequently for Joseph Browning;
the books he printed were sold at Browning's shop "at
the corner of Prison-Lane next the Exchange." Twenty-
one of the Mathers' books published from 1682 to 1691

bear Browning's imprint, a number fully rivaling the
Mather titles published by Samuel Green during the same
period. The majority of Browning's Mather volumes--
seventeen in all--were printed by Pierce, beginning with
Increase's The Doctrine of Divine Providence Opened and
Applyed (1684) and continuing through to Cotton's Memorable Providences Relating to Witchcrafts and Possessions (1689) and Addresses to Old Men, and Young Men,
and Little Children (1690), the first known book to bear
Nicholas Buttolph's imprint.

Pierce proved himself to be as active in the printing community as was his old master, Samuel Green. Among
the important volumes he printed, other than works by
the Mathers, were Richard Steere's Monumental Memorial
of Marine Mercy (1684) and the fourth edition of Michael
Wigglesworth's Meat out of the Eater (1689). Pierce's
most significant job was printing the first edition of
the New-England Primer for Benjamin Harris in 1690.
That same year Harris published and Pierce printed
Publick Occurrences Both Foreign and Domestick. This
newspaper had but one number; it was unlicensed and so
was suppressed by the governing council of the colonies.
While often referred to as America's first newspaper,
it was inspired by Samuel Green's single-sheet printing
of The Present State of the New English Affairs (1689),
containing Increase Mather's foreign correspondence.
After Publick Occurrences, the next true news publication in America was not until 1704, with The Boston News-
Letter.

Richard Pierce became part of Boston's printing
industry at a time when the market began its first expansion. His career was not long, only seven years in
all, but he was able to produce over thirty-five titles
during that time and to challenge the city's accepted
masters. Certainly the attention given his work by the
Mathers stands as testimony to his craftsmanship. The
New-England Primer is his most renowned production;

413

the educational stimulus that grew from its circulation
pervaded the colonies for more than a century.

Phyllis A. Smith

References:

Littlefield, George E. Early Boston Booksellers: 1642-
    1711. Boston: Club of Odd Volumes, 1900; reprint
    edition, New York: Burt Franklin, 1969.

Littlefield, George E. The Early Massachusetts Press:
    1638-1711. Boston: Club of Odd Volumes, 1907;
    reprint edition, New York: Burt Franklin, 1969.

Thomas, Isaiah. The History of Printing in America.
    Worcester, Mass.: Isaiah Thomas, Jr., 1810;
    2nd ed., revised, Albany, N.Y.: J. Munsell for
    the American Antiquarian Society, 1874; ed.
    Marcus A. McCorison, Barre, Mass.: Imprint
    Society, 1970.

Edward Eveleth Powars
and Nathaniel Willis

Edward Eveleth Powars (dates unknown) and Nathaniel
Willis (1755-1831), printers and publishers, were in
business as partners from 1776 through 1779, "opposite
the New Court-House in Queen-Street," and again from
1784 to 1786. In 1786 they conducted business on the
"north side of State-Street." They were primarily newspaper publishers, although during their first years of
partnership they were "Printers to the honorable House
of Representatives" of Massachusetts.

Major Authors: Isaac Backus, Aaron Burr, Charles
Chauncy, Nathaniel Low.

Powars and Willis began a partnership in 1776 in
order to publish a newspaper. That year they bought the
New-England Chronicle from Samuel Hall, changed its title
to the Independent Chronicle, and continued publishing
it until March 1779, at which time Powars withdrew from
the partnership; Willis continued the Chronicle until he
sold it to Adams and Nourse in 1784. In October 1781
Powars established the Boston Evening-Post. He changed
the title to the American Herald in January 1784, and
in April he and Willis resumed their partnership and
published the Herald through July 1786, when Willis withdrew. Powars continued publishing the Herald through
June 1788, at which time he moved it to Worcester, Massachusetts. Two years later, in July 1790, Powars established the Saturday Evening Herald in Boston; it ceased
publication five months later. In October 1791 he
assumed control of the Argus and published it into
June 1793.

Other than newspapers, Powars and Willis, as partners, printed or published approximately thirty titles.
Most significant is the work they did for the

Massachusetts House of Representatives. Rollo G. Silver has noted that they were contracted in October 1776, to print the Journal of the 1776-1777 session. By December they had printed few sheets, but after some debate the House decided to permit them to continue with the job. Powars and Willis might also have printed Peter Whitney's American Independence Vindicated, the first published address on the Declaration of Independence.

Powars published and printed little other than newspapers during his years without Willis. Perhaps his most significant title is a reprint of Aaron Burr's The Supreme Deity of Our Lord Jesus Christ, Maintained (1791). Willis, on the other hand, was fairly active alone in Boston from 1780 through 1784, during which time he was responsible for approximately sixteen publications. He printed and published four annual volumes of Nathaniel Low's Astronomical Diary, but his most important work was done as "Printer to the honorable General Court," in which capacity he printed four annual volumes of the court's resolves.

Powars was a compositor in Charlestown for Samuel Etheridge in 1803, and after that he was a messenger to the Massachusetts governor and council. Later, as a bookseller he traveled west, where he died. Willis, a participant in the Boston Tea Party and grandfather to Nathaniel P. Willis, continued publishing newspapers after he left Boston. In 1790 he moved to Winchester, Virginia, after which he moved to Shepherdstown and then Martinsburg, in what is now West Virginia. In 1800 he located in Chillicothe, Ohio, where he lived until his death in 1831.

References:

Brigham, Clarence S. History and Bibliography of American Newspapers: 1690-1820. Vol. 1. Worcester, Mass.: American Antiquarian Society, 1947.

Buckingham, Joseph T. Specimens of Newspaper Litera-
        ture. Vol. 1. Boston: Little and Brown, 1850.

Silver, Rollo G. "Government Printing in Massachu-
        setts, 1751-1801." Studies in Bibliography,
        16 (1963).

William Price

William Price (c. 1685-1771) was America's first art
dealer. He kept a shop for fifty years at 219 Washington Street that he described as "against ye Town House"
and "at ye King's Head & Looking Glass in Cornhill, near
the Town House." His name appears in the imprint of
only one known title, but it is an important one. In
1722 he sold, with John Bonner, Bonner's map of Boston.
Thereafter Price controlled the plate and published it,
with additions and corrections, several times through
1769.

References:

Barton, Edmund M. "Report of the Librarian." Proceed-
        ings of the American Antiquarian Society, 15
        (1902).

Whitehill, Walter M. Boston: A Topographical History.
        Cambridge: Belknap Press of Harvard University
        Press, 1959.

Thomas Prince, Jr.

Thomas Prince, Jr. (1722-1748) edited and published the
Christian History from March 1743 to February 1745.   It
was, Frank Luther Mott has noted, "less a magazine than
a chronicle of the 'Great Awakening.'"   Prince was the
son of Thomas Prince, the famous historian and Congregationalist minister.

References:

Moore, John W.   Moore's Historical, Biographical, and
     Miscellaneous Gatherings.   Concord, N.H.:
     Republican Press, 1886; reprint edition,
     Detroit: Gale Research, 1968.

Mott, Frank Luther.   A History of American Magazines:
     1741-1850.   New York and London: Appleton, 1930;
     Cambridge: Harvard University Press, 1938;
     Cambridge: Belknap Press of Harvard University
     Press, 1957.

Thomas, Isaiah.   The History of Printing in America.
     Worcester, Mass.:   Isaiah Thomas, Jr., 1810;
     2nd ed., revised, Albany, N.Y.:   J. Munsell
     for the American Antiquarian Society, 1874;
     ed. Marcus A. McCorison, Barre, Mass.:   Imprint
     Society, 1970.

James Printer

James Printer (dates unknown) was the first American Indian to become a printer. His name was James, but he became known as James the printer and finally as James Printer. He learned English at the Indian School in Cambridge, and he worked under Samuel Green from 1659 to 1675. Because he and John Eliot were the only ones who could read both the Indian and English languages, Printer was indispensable in helping print Eliot's Indian Bible. Printer's name appears in only one known imprint. In 1709 he and Bartholomew Green printed the Massachusee Psalter for the Society for the Propagation of the Gospel in New England.

References:

Littlefield, George E. The Early Massachusetts Press: 1638-1711. Boston: Club of Odd Volumes, 1907; reprint edition, New York: Burt Franklin, 1969.

Moore, John W. Moore's Historical, Biographical, and Miscellaneous Gatherings. Concord, N.H.: Republican Press, 1886; reprint edition, Detroit: Gale Research, 1968.

Thomas, Isaiah. The History of Printing in America. Worcester, Mass.: Isaiah Thomas, Jr., 1810; 2nd ed., revised, Albany, N.Y.: J. Munsell for the American Antiquarian Society, 1874; ed. Marcus A. McCorison, Barre, Mass.: Imprint Society, 1970.

Winterich, John T. Early American Books & Printing.
    Boston and New York: Houghton Mifflin, 1935;
    reprint edition, Detroit: Gale Research, 1974.

James Printer [signature]

Nathaniel Procter (see Nathaniel Proctor)

Nathaniel Proctor (or Procter)

Nathaniel Proctor (or Procter) (d. 1766), bookseller and
binder, published approximately twenty volumes from 1730
to 1744. He published titles by Mather Byles, Jonathan
Edwards, Cotton Mather, and Samuel Mather. He apparently
published nothing after 1744 until 1765 when he published
two books, one of which is John Taylor's Verbum
Sempiternum, a book known as the Thumb Bible because it
is smaller than two inches square. Proctor conducted
business "in Fish Street" for approximately a decade
before relocating "at the Bible and Dove in Ann-street,
near the Draw-Bridge." He published Taylor's Bible
"near Scarlett's-Wharffe."

420

Thomas Ran (see Thomas Rand)

Thomas Rand

Thomas Rand (1721-1791), bookseller and binder, conducted business "in Cornhill." His name appears in eight known imprints from 1744 to 1756. He published religious ti-tles, including two by Thomas Prince and one by Thomas Foxcroft. In 1766 William M'Alpine printed an edition of The Psalms of David, Imitated for Thomas Ran. Ran was probably Rand.

Edmund Ranger

Edmund Ranger (d. 1705) succeeded his rival John Ratcliff as the foremost Boston binder of the day. Ranger's name appears in only four known imprints. He published works by William Dyer (1672), Increase Mather (1673, 1678), and James Allin (1679).

References:

Holmes, T. J. "The Bookbindings of John Ratcliff and Edmund Ranger, Seventeenth Century Boston Bookbinders." Proceedings of the American Antiquarian Society, 38 (1928).

Holmes, T. J. "Additional Notes on Ratcliff and Ranger Bindings." Proceedings of the American Antiquarian Society, 39 (1929).

Land, William G. "Further Notes on Ratcliff and Ranger Bindings." Proceedings of the American Antiquarian Society, 39 (1929).

Lehmann-Haupt, Hellmut. The Book in America. New York: Bowker, 1939; revised and enlarged, New York: Bowker, 1951.

Wroth, Lawrence C. The Colonial Printer. New York: Grolier Club, 1931; revised and enlarged, Portland, Me.: Southworth-Anthoensen Press, 1938; reprint edition, Charlottesville, Va.: University Press of Virginia/Dominion Books. 1964.

John Ratcliff (or Ratcliffe)

John Ratcliff (or Ratcliffe) (dates unknown) came to
America in 1663 to bind John Eliot's Indian Bible. He
was probably the first professional binder in America,
and he had no competition until Edmund Ranger began his
business in 1771. Ratcliff was also a bookseller and
publisher whose name appears in four known imprints. He
published The Narrative of the Most Dreadful Tempest
(1674); a work by Increase Mather (1679); Cotton Mather's
first publication, A Poem (1682); and Joseph Rowlandson's
The Possibility of Gods Forsaking a People (1682).

References:

Holmes, T. J. "The Bookbindings of John Ratcliff and
    Edmund Ranger, Seventeenth Century Boston Book-
    binders." Proceedings of the American Anti-
    quarian Society, 38 (1928).

Holmes, T. J. "Additional Notes on Ratcliff and
    Ranger Bindings." Proceedings of the American
    Antiquarian Society, 39 (1929).

Land, William G. "Further Notes on Ratcliff and
    Ranger Bindings." Proceedings of the American
    Antiquarian Society, 39 (1929).

Lehmann-Haupt, Hellmut. The Book in America. New
    York: Bowker, 1939; revised and enlarged,
    New York: Bowker, 1951.

|John Ratcliff (or Ratcliffe)

Wroth, Lawrence C. The Colonial Printer. New York:
    Grolier Club, 1931; revised and enlarged,
    Portland, Me.: Southworth-Anthoensen Press,
    1938; reprint edition, Charlottesville, Va.:
    University Press of Virginia/Dominion Books,
    1964.

John Ratcliffe (see John Ratcliff)

Paul Revere

Paul Revere (1735-1818) appeared in the imprints of
fewer than a dozen titles from 1764 to 1796. Primarily
he was the engraver, printer, and/or seller of engravings, although he printed and sold, with the author,
Josiah Flagg's Collection of the Best Psalm Tunes (1764).
Revere's most famous engraving is of the Boston Massacre
(1770).

Reference:

Brigham, Clarence S. Paul Revere's Engravings.
    Worcester, Mass.: American Antiquarian Society,
    1954.

425

Ebenezer Rhoades

Ebenezer Rhoades (c. 1775-1818) printed the Independent Chronicle from May 1799 until 1817. His name also appears in the imprints of at least five titles published from 1798 through 1800, including the 1798 Boston Directory.

References:

Brigham, Clarence S. History and Bibliography of American Newspapers: 1690-1820. Vol. 1. Worcester, Mass.: American Antiquarian Society, 1947.

Buckingham, Joseph T. Specimens of Newspaper Literature. Vol. 1. Boston: Little and Brown, 1850.

Gamaliel Rogers

Gamaliel Rogers (1704-1775) was a printer and, in a minor way, a publisher operating his own shop in Long Lane from 1727 to 1729. After that date his name disappears from any known imprints until 1740, when he went into partnership with the young Daniel Fowle. The firm of Rogers and Fowle was located in Queen Street, "over against the South-East-Corner of the Town House," or, in later imprints, "next to the prison in Queen Street, near the Town House." The association of the two men was successful, resulting in slightly over 200 imprints and three serials: the quickly abandoned Boston Weekly Magazine; the more popular American Magazine and Historical

Chronicle, the first magazine in America to last more than six months; and a newspaper, the *Independent Advertiser*. They may also have printed, in 1749, the first English New Testament in America, although no copy has survived to confirm this. Rogers left the firm in 1750, when he is supposed to have opened another printery, which apparently also quickly failed. In his old age he began yet another store, where he sold liquor, groceries, and the remnants of his book stock. Rogers died in 1775 in Ipswich, Massachusetts, where he had gone to live with one of his daughters.

Major Authors: Charles Chauncy, Benjamin Colman, George Whitefield.

Publishers Served: Joshua Blanchard, Michael Dennis, Joseph Edwards, Samuel Eliot, Hopestill Foster, Samuel Gerrish, Thomas Hancock, Daniel Henchman, John Phillips, Nathaniel Proctor.

Little is known of Rogers, but a sketchy picture can be pieced together from the record of his imprints and Isaiah Thomas's reminiscence of him. He was apprenticed to Bartholomew Green and served for an unknown time before opening his own printing house in Long Lane in 1727. His business started slowly and quickly grew even worse; he printed four titles in 1727, five in 1728, and a mere two in 1729. No imprints bear his name again until 1740, and it is likely that he went to work for another printer for those eleven years, perhaps with his former master or with Samuel Kneeland, where he could have met Daniel Fowle. In 1740 he associated himself with Fowle, and the firm of Rogers and Fowle almost immediately became one of the leading printing houses in Boston. They were noted for the high quality of their work and especially for their ink, which they manufactured themselves, an unusual practice in an age when most printers were content with ink imported from Britain and one that indicates a painstaking attention to detail.

The partnership was dissolved in 1750, and Rogers is supposed to have moved to New Boston, in the western

part of the city, where he opened another shop by himself. Thomas says that he remained there for several
years before fire destroyed his press and type in 1752
or 1753, effectively ending his career as an independent
printer. No imprints of his from this period survive,
however; probably he printed only a very few and those
have now been lost. In his old age Rogers opened yet
another shop across the street from the Old South Church,
where he sold groceries, liquor, and the remaining copies
of the stock from his printing days. Rogers was one of
the infirm and aged who received permission in 1775 to
leave occupied Boston, and he journeyed to Ipswich, apparently to live with one of his daughters, who had married a minister there. He died in Ipswich in the autumn
of the same year.

Although Thomas fondly recalls the advice Rogers
gave him on the value of industry and application, apparently the older man was speaking with the wisdom of hind-
sight rather than describing the principles that guided
much of his own career. If the number of his imprints is
any indication, Rogers was not among the most ambitious
or aggressive of Boston printers. From 1727 to 1729 they
number only eleven. These include Thunder and Earthquakes
(1727) by James Allen (or Allin); Thomas Foxcroft's Discourse Preparatory to the Choice of a Minister (1727);
the Westminster Shorter Catechism (1728); Samuel Mather's
The Departure and Character of Elijah (1728); and two
pamphlets by Benjamin Colman, Prayer to the Lord of the
Harvest for the Mission of Labourers into His Harvest
(1727) and An Argument for and Persuasive unto the Great
and Important Duty of Family Worship (1728). Rogers may
not be entirely at fault for his failures, however. The
Boston book trade was already overcrowded, and the always
chancy affair of opening a new business was further complicated by the progressively worsening inflation and
the currency problems that had plagued Boston since the
opening of the century.

After eleven years of silence, Rogers again reappeared in 1740 as a partner in Rogers and Fowle, and
his fortunes took an immediate turn for the better. It

428

is not certain why the partnership succeeded so well; perhaps Fowle supplied the initiative and drive while Rogers supplied the experience. But in any event, prosper they did, especially in the field of serial publications. In March 1743 the two men began the Boston Weekly Magazine, which lasted for only three numbers, but when they switched to a monthly format in September of the same year, with the American Magazine and Historical Chronicle, they met with more success. The Chronicle lasted slightly more than three years, ending with the December 1746 number, and it owed much of its popularity to being closely modeled after the famous London Magazine. Their venture into newspaper publishing was equally well received. The Independent Advertiser was first released on 4 January 1748, and was still doing well when the last number appeared on 5 December 1749, just before the partnership ended. Part of the reason for the paper's success may be due to its editor, the fiery and controversial Samuel Adams, who used it as a platform from which to denounce the meddling of the British government into the affairs of Massachusetts and particularly to assail Royal Governor William Shirley.

In the early years of the firm the partnership seems to have been a loose one, and although the two men released imprints with both their names, they also printed titles independently of each other. In 1740, for example, they collaborated on seven titles while they each separately released two; in 1741 they shared twelve imprints, with Rogers printing thirteen others by himself and Fowle five; and in 1742 they shared thirty-one titles and each printed four others. This practice was customary in the New England printing houses, especially when one partner lacked a press, type, or the money to buy supplies. The one without equipment would agree to pay the other for the use of his materials, and they would then share the fee paid by the bookseller who had ordered the title. As their business grew and the partnership became more firmly established, Rogers and Fowle gradually abandoned the practice. In 1743 both men worked on twenty-four titles while Rogers reserved only one to himself and Fowle two, and from 1744 to 1749 they shared all the imprints and did not resume separate printing until the firm was breaking up in 1750, when Rogers printed two titles by himself, Fowle five, and they shared seven.

Of the books and pamphlets printed solely by Rogers from 1740 to 1744, a substantial number concern the religious revival of the Great Awakening. In 1727 and 1728 Rogers had printed two titles by Benjamin Colman, an early and influential advocate of the revival and a defender of George Whitefield, the English minister who helped ignite the Great Awakening with his theatrical oratory and showmanship. When he joined with Fowle, Rogers continued to print tracts favorable to the movement under his own imprint. In 1740 he released A Letter from the Reverend Mr. George Whitefield to the Reverend Mr. John Wesley, and 1741 saw Whitefield's The Indwelling of the Spirit and a part of Whitefield's journal. Rogers also printed a number of sermons by other proponents of the Great Awakening, including The Sin and Danger of Quenching the Spirit (1741) by William Cooper, an associate of Colman's at the Brattle Street Church; Benjamin Lord's Believers in Christ (1742); and Jonathan Dickinson's The True Scripture-Doctrine Concerning Some Important Points of Christian Faith (1741), which tries to constrain the fervor of the revival by placing it within the confines of the classical stages of the conversion process.

With the assistance of Fowle, Rogers printed still more tracts urging the spread of the Great Awakening. Among these are Colman's Souls Flying to Christ Pleasant and Admirable to Behold (1740); Whitefield's Lecture on the Prodigal Son (1742) and his Free Grace Indeed! (1741); and several tracts by the quarrelsome Andrew Croswell, including A Letter from the Revd Mr. Croswell to the Revd Mr. Turell (1742) and Mr. Croswell's Reply to a Book Lately Published, Entitled A Display of God's Special Grace (1742), the last being a shrill denunciation of Jonathan Dickinson's more temperate and judicious appreciation of the religious revival.

Given the evidence of these and additional titles favoring the Great Awakening, it would be tempting to

430

conclude that Rogers was an eager and zealous partisan of the movement. Yet such a conclusion seems unwarranted. He also printed The New Creature Describ'd (1741), The Gifts of the Spirit to Ministers Consider'd in Their Diversity (1742), and The Wonderful Narrative (1742), all written by Charles Chauncy, the chief spokesman of the Old Lights, a group hostile to the enthusiasm of the revival. Moreover, nearly all of these were ordered and paid for by the Boston publishers, chiefly Joseph Edwards and Samuel Eliot, thus eliminating much of the element of choice in Rogers's imprints.

The career of Gamaliel Rogers is an interesting if comparatively minor chapter in the history of Boston publishing before 1800. His is mainly a chronicle of misfortune and mystery; the causes of his repeated failures, his whereabouts for those eleven hidden years, and his occupations from 1752 to 1775 are questions that need to be answered before his place in the Boston printing community can be fully assessed. Yet he also had his successes. As a partner in Rogers and Fowle his role in magazine and newspaper publishing is a significant one, and the other imprints he shared with Fowle, including the probable publication in 1749 of the first American New Testament in English; the first printing of a portion of Thomas Shepard's journal in Three Valuable Pieces (1747); and an edition of the New-England Primer Enlarged (1746), are important enough to be a part of any discussion of colonial life and letters.

James P. O'Donnell

References:

Buckingham, Joseph T. Specimens of Newspaper Literature. Boston: Little and Brown, 1850.

Kobre, Sidney. The Development of the Colonial Newspaper. Pittsburgh: Colonial Press, 1944.

Mott, Frank Luther. A History of American Magazines:
    1741-1850. New York and London: Appleton, 1930;
    Cambridge: Harvard University Press, 1938;
    Cambridge: Belknap Press of Harvard University
    Press, 1957.

Mott, Frank Luther. American Journalism, A History:
    1690-1960. Third edition. New York: Macmillan,
    1962.

Thomas, Isaiah. The History of Printing in America.
    Worcester, Mass.: Isaiah Thomas, Jr., 1810;
    2nd ed., revised, Albany, N.Y.: J. Munsell
    for the American Antiquarian Society, 1874;
    ed. Marcus A. McCorison, Barre, Mass.: Imprint
    Society, 1970.

Susanna Haswell Rowson

Susanna Haswell Rowson (1762-1824), popular novelist,
joined with others to sell her Reuben and Rachel in 1798.

Benjamin Russell

Benjamin Russell (1762-1845) was the leading newspaper
editor and publisher in New England during the politically
turbulent decade of the 1790s and for some time into the
nineteenth century. From printing offices first for a
brief time in 1784 at No. 9, Marlborough Street in Boston
and then in State Street opposite the east corner of the
State House (now called the Old State House) over "Mr. E.
Battelle's book-store," Russell moved easily and authori-
tatively within the community in which he was a prominent
and influential citizen. Russell was one of a new breed
of politically minded printer-editors who came to prominence in the 1790s. Within his printing and publishing
enterprise, his newspaper, the Massachusetts (later
Columbian) Centinel, was paramount. The publication of
separate imprints--books, pamphlets, and broadsides--was
for Russell but a minor adjunct to what was clearly a
journalistic operation. From 1784 to 1800, Russell's
shop produced only about thirty nonnewspaper imprints
that are known to have survived.

Major Authors: Christopher Gore, Stephen Higginson,
Harrison Gray Otis, Phillis Wheatley.

Publishers Served: Militia companies, Masonic
lodges, and other civic, trade, patriotic, and fraternal
organizations.

Russell was born in Boston on 13 September 1762 of
a mechanic family with roots in New England extending
back to some of the earliest migrations in the 1630s.
Benjamin was the first but not the last of his family
to enter the book trades; his brothers John and Joseph N.
Russell also became printers, as did his son-in-law
James Cutler prior to his marriage to Russell's daughter.
Benjamin Russell received some formal schooling, which

Benjamin Russell (Courtesy American Antiquarian Society)

was interrupted in April 1775, by the outbreak of the American Revolution. In September Russell was taken by his father to Worcester, Massachusetts, to be apprenticed to the ardent patriot printer Isaiah Thomas, the publisher of the Massachusetts Spy. Russell's apprenticeship with Thomas was twice interrupted by military service: for a month in 1777 and for six months in 1780, the latter tour possibly in substitution for his master. Perhaps because of this favor, Thomas in 1782 gave Russell his early release from apprenticeship, but Russell stayed on in the Worcester printing shop as a journeyman for another year.

By November 1783 Russell had moved back to Boston, determined to establish a newspaper in the metropolis. To that end, he formed a partnership with William Warden, a young Bostonian, the firm being called Warden and Russell. After experiencing some difficulty in procuring type, the pair published, on 24 March 1784, the first number of their semiweekly paper, the Massachusetts Centinel: And the Republican Journal. The Centinel was at first a tiny sheet, measuring only about 8 1/2 x 11 inches when folded.

Russell managed and edited the Centinel alone after Warden died on 18 March 1786, and began to increase its size (to about 9 x 15 inches), advertising patronage, circulation, and influence. He never took on another partner. In 1790 (effective with the number of 16 June) Russell changed the name of his paper to the Columbian Centinel. & Massachusetts Federalist. In so doing he made formal his identification with the new national government, a policy that remained the hallmark of his paper's political stance throughout the decade. His allegiance to the federal government was rewarded with his appointment in June 1790 as printer for the eastern states, a post he had actively sought. When partisan movements developed during the 1790s, Russell allied himself with the Federalist cause and became its leading journalistic exponent in New England.

435

There must have been little commercial significance
to most of the items among Russell's relatively meager
output of published separates. Rather, most were patronage items, but not in the usual sense of political patronage. Instead they were publications sponsored by militia
companies, Masonic lodges, and other organizations to
which Russell--inveterate joiner that he was--belonged
or aspired. In this vein, he printed election sermons of
the Ancient and Honourable Artillery Company preached by
David Osgood (1788), Thomas Barnard (1789), and Jonathan
Homer (1790); Masonic orations by Josiah Hussey (1793)
and John Mellen (1793); and Fourth of July orations by
Harrison Gray Otis (1788) and Joseph Blake (1792).

Some of the more important items among Russell's
slender output are several timely tracts of political or
social commentary. One of these, Sans Souci. Alias Free
and Easy (Warden and Russell, 1785), is a satire on the
Tea Assembly, a recently formed club of prominent young
Boston socialites that had been the object of attack in
the newspaper for its alleged unvirtuous, unrepublican
excesses. Warden and Russell claimed that a member of
the Tea Assembly had threatened to kill them if they went
ahead with publication, but they were not deterred. Another work, Stephen Higginson's The Writings of Laco
(1789), is a series of essays reprinted from the Centinel
that played an important role in the process of political
polarization in Boston. Others are Christopher Gore's
Manlius (1794) and a Review of the Administration of the
Government of the United States (1797).

Outside the political mainstream of Russell's works
are the almanacs he published: Weatherwise's Genuine
Almanack and Bickerstaff's Genuine Almanack, both for
the year 1798. Probably the only real literary work
Russell published is Phillis Wheatley's Liberty and Peace
(Warden and Russell, 1784).

Russell's distinguished career as a newspaper editor and publisher continued well into the nineteenth century, during which time he held numerous political or

436

civic offices in Boston and in the Commonwealth of Massachusetts. He retired from business in 1828 and died in Boston on 4 January 1845.

John B. Hench

References:

Baylies, Francis. Eulogy on the Hon. Benjamin Russell, Delivered Before the Grand Lodge of Free and Accepted Masons . . . March 10, 1845. Boston: Office of the Freemasons' Magazine, 1845.

Buckingham, Joseph T. Specimens of Newspaper Literature. Vol. 2. Boston: Little and Brown, 1850.

Hench, John B. "The Newspaper in a Republic: Boston's Centinel and Chronicle, 1784-1801." Ph.D. dissertation, Clark University, 1979.

437

Ezekiel Russell

Ezekiel Russell (1743-1796), printer and publisher, produced approximately 139 titles during his career. With
the exception of a few poems and essays, almanacs, and
one short-lived journal, Russell's productions have nothing significant about them save the common, lurid, and
macabre. He began printing in Boston as an apprentice
to his brother, Joseph, around 1758. In 1765 he moved
to Portsmouth, New Hampshire, as an apprentice to Thomas
Furber and soon became a partner in the short-lived firm,
Furber and Russell. By 1767 Russell had moved back to
Boston, but in 1768 he located in Providence, Rhode
Island. He returned again to Boston in 1769, purchased
a press and a few types, and set up his shop in a house
near Concert Hall. During the next decade his address
changed rapidly. In 1770 and 1771 Russell's address was
Queen Street; in 1771 and 1772, Marlborough Street; and
in 1772 and 1773, Union Street next to the cornfield.
Russell was absent from Boston during the years from
1775 to 1780 while attempting to set up business in
Salem and Danvers. While in Salem Russell published a
newspaper, the Salem Gazette, which was the second paper
in that town. It was discontinued for want of support.
After printing in Danvers from 1777 to 1780, Russell
returned to Boston and established a shop in Essex
Street near either the Liberty Stump, Pole, or Square.

Major Authors: Benjamin West, Phillis Wheatley.

Russell was born in Boston in 1743 and died there
in 1796. Little is known about his life outside of his
publishing and printing activities. He learned his trade
from his brother, Joseph, who was the partner of John
Green. Isaiah Thomas relates that Ezekiel's wife was
"an help meet for him" and aided him in the business.
Russell was frequently in need of money, a condition

that is reflected in the progression of titles bearing his imprint. The sum of Russell's publications (both as a publisher and printer) fall into three broad groups that seem to reflect his various strategies for earning money. The categories are: the extraordinary but respectable, that is, works representing legitimate concerns, such as sermons, poems, and essays that had some unusual appeal to buyers; the almanacs, including many by Isaac Bickerstaff that were guaranteed to sell; and the depraved, especially from 1785 on.

One example of the first category is Russell's publication in 1770 of Phillis Wheatley's Elegiac Poem. Perhaps Russell felt that he had discovered a worthy poet whose verse should be brought to the public eye, but Russell's more likely design is betrayed by the listing of the author's name as "Phillis, A servant girl of 17 years of age, . . . who has been but 9 years in this country from Africa." Phillis Wheatley's poems are not remarkable except for the facts of her situation, and Russell no doubt felt bound to capitalize upon them. Four years after Wheatley's poem, Russell printed an essay by Cotton Mather on education, Corderius Americanus. Since the essay was a funeral sermon upon Ezekiel Cheever, the well-known master of the free-school in Boston, it no doubt attracted an automatic readership. Ten years later, in 1784, Russell printed another Wheatley poem, and, consistent with his taste, it was another dirge, this time upon Dr. Samuel Cooper. The only other short piece of importance by Russell was a George Whitefield hymn, printed in 1790; it was (appropriately) designed to be sung at the author's own funeral.

Despite Russell's morbid nature, he did print one publication of undeniable importance, the ill-fated magazine the Censor, which was a political magazine in the style of the Tatler or Spectator. Russell's involvement with it is ironic because the magazine was founded as a mouthpiece for British sympathizers while, seven years earlier, Russell's first full-fledged business venture had been an attempt to publish a Whig newspaper with Thomas Furber. Russell's politics were

439

clearly contingent on profit. The first number of the
Censor came out on Saturday, 23 November 1771, and although it lasted only until the following April, it did
contribute some of the most articulate and persuasive
arguments for British rule. Several prominent politicians contributed articles, including Lieutenant Governor
Oliver, who made the most important statements of Tory
principles at the time. These essays were submitted
under the signature, A Freeman. In addition, Russell
himself is thought to have written some of the copy. As
the Censor's circulation failed, Russell attempted to
save the magazine by transforming it into a newspaper by
adding local news and advertisements. He failed. However, its Tory bias, not Russell's incompetence, doomed
the Censor.

The second broad group of Russell's publications
comprised his various almanacs, including those by
Nathaniel Ames (1772-1774); Benjamin West, including
the "genuine" Bickerstaffs (1783-1793, 1797, with many
years having two or more editions); Daniel George
(1784); and Abraham Weatherwise (1797). Almanacs were,
of course, important publications, and Russell must have
made considerable profit from them. Perhaps the most
important almanac in America at the time was Benjamin
West's. West had become interested in astronomy through
Bishop Berkeley's library, and he was certainly qualified
to make precise astronomical calculations. He took the
A.M. from Harvard in 1770 and the LL.D. from Brown in
1792. In 1763 he wrote his first almanac, and the name
Bickerstaff, chosen from Dean Swift, was on his title
page by 1768. West's almanacs were accurate and illustrated, and they were so popular that they attracted a
hoard of disreputable imitators who counterfeited the
name and discouraged him from publishing any more almanacs after 1779. However, when Ezekiel Russell began
publishing them in 1782, West once again became interested and, until he died in 1793, furnished the astronomical data exclusively for Russell's almanacs. Other
almanacs published by Russell were less important and
were known for other features. Abraham Weatherwise's,
for example, were best known for their elaborate

440

illustrations. Nathaniel Ames's almanacs were plagued
with the same kind of piracy problems as West's. Ames's
almanacs were written by father and son until 1776 when
the son quit in despair, writing that the printers in
Boston "are all knaves, liars, and villains."

The third, and largest, category of Russell's work
is well characterized by R. W. G. Vail, who describes
Russell as "one of the smart printers of the eighteenth
century who made good money by catering to . . . depraved
taste." The majority of Russell's titles fall into the
category of the depraved. A quick survey will reveal that
the tabloid is not the exclusive invention of the twentieth century. The first hint of an incremental interest
in the lurid and bizarre came in 1785 when Russell printed
a sermon by Timothy Hilliard on the execution of three
criminals "with an appendix exhibiting some account of
their conversation and behavior in prison." The following year Russell published and printed an account by
James Buckland of A Wonderful Discovery of a Hermit who
told his tale of woe at the modest age of 227 years. In
the same year he produced the Narrative of Mrs. Scott and
Capt. Stewart's Captivity, which told, among other things,
"a particular detail of the horrid, barbarous and cruel
massacre of her husband, Mr. Scott, and four children and
a lad named Ball, who were most inhumanely murdered by
the blood-thirsty savages. . . ." In addition, sometime
during his career, Russell invented, with the help of his
wife, a logo which was, not surprisingly, a row of coffins. Death was Russell's greatest resource. The cul-
mination came, perhaps, in 1792, when he published and
printed A True and Particular Narrative of the Late Tremendous Tornado, or Hurricane decorated with no fewer
than twenty coffins and nine exclamation marks (seven in
a row) on the title page. At least twenty-one of Russell's
titles from 1785 until his death deal directly with the
horrors of murder or execution, including The Prisoner's
Magazine, subtitled Malefactor's Bloody Register. Others
were unabashedly fraudulent, such as the title printed by
Russell's wife shortly after his death: A Copy of a Letter Written by Our Blessed Lord and Saviour . . . Found
under a Great Stone, 65 Years after His Crucifixion.

441

(Russell had printed and published a similar letter, <u>To King Agbarus</u> in 1792.)

Russell's work as a publisher and a printer is thus most significant as a reflection of certain eighteenth-century tastes. His main concern seems to have been with what would make him financially secure; he showed no scruples about working for either Whig or Tory, did not shy away either as a printer or a publisher from the horrible or unlikely, and seemed to have a curious predilection for subjects dealing with death. His work may be interesting, but it is not, ultimately, memorable.

Thomas Goldstein

References:

Nichols, Charles L. "Notes on the Almanacs of Massachusetts." <u>Proceedings of the American Antiquarian Society</u>, 22 (1912).

Richardson, Lyon N. <u>A History of Early American Magazines, 1741-1789</u>. New York: Nelson, 1931; reprint edition, New York: Octagon, 1966.

Thomas, Isaiah. <u>The History of Printing in America</u>. Worcester, Mass.: Isaiah Thomas, Jr., 1810; 2nd ed., revised, Albany, N.Y.: J. Munsell for the American Antiquarian Society, 1874; ed. Marcus A. McCorison, Barre, Mass.: Imprint Society, 1970.

Vail, R. W. G. "Report of the Librarian." <u>Proceedings of the American Antiquarian Society</u>, 46 (1936).

John Russell

John Russell (c. 1764-1831) was a printer, bookseller, and editor of the Federalist newspaper, the <u>Boston Gazette</u>. The first text bearing his name was printed by "brothers Benjamin and John Russell" in 1793, but from 1795 to 1797 John and his brother Joseph N. Russell printed and sold several volumes from their shop over Major Hawes's Work-Shops, in Quaker Lane near State (later Water) Street in Boston. Joseph left his brother in 1797 and established his own printing business with Henry Hoskins in Wiscasset, Maine. John remained in Quaker Lane and in 1799 engaged one of his apprentices, James Cutler, as a partner. Shortly after the War of 1812, Russell engaged another young man, Simon Gardner, as another partner under the name of "Russell, Cutler, & Co." After Cutler died on 18 April 1818, Gardner and Russell continued the firm until 1823, when John followed his brother to Maine. The terms of these partnerships are unknown, but of the approximately sixty publications bearing Russell's name, only the newspaper and those works printed for the state of Massachusetts bear either Cutler's or Gardner's name.

<u>Major Authors</u>: August Friedrich von Kotzebue, Robert Treat Paine, Thomas Paine, George Washington.

During the first two years of Russell's career, most of his printing and selling was confined to works bearing some relation to his and Joseph N. Russell's first paper, the <u>Boston Price-Current and Marine-Intelligencer</u>. As that paper grew more political, however, the firm's interests broadened as well, and from 1798 to 1800 over half of the publications bearing Russell's name were essays, novels, poems, and plays, including works by Robert Treat Paine, John Mason Williams, George Walker, Joseph Story, and translations

443

of the popular German author August Friedrich von
Kotzebue. Most of the other publications were polit-
ical tracts, including letters and essays by George
Washington and Thomas Paine.

The most remarkable technical achievement accomplished by Russell is certainly the special edition of
Washington's letter "Declaring His Acceptance of the
Command of the Armies of the United States," printed on
silk in 1800, but Russell printed several other interesting texts. In addition to works printed for the
state of Massachusetts and addresses before the Phi
Beta Kappa Society of Harvard, he printed and sold
Jonathan Carver's Three Years Travels through the In-
terior Parts of N. America (1799), a travel narrative
that includes a dictionary of Chippewa and Naudowessie
languages; the Boston Directory (1800), that was made
from the 1796 survey by Osgood Carlton; and the Constitution of the Associated Mechanics and Manufacturers of
the Commonwealth of Massachusetts (1800).

Russell was best known, however, for his newspaper.
On 5 September 1795 he and Joseph N. Russell began publishing the Boston Price-Current, a small quarto published
on Monday and Thursday and containing matter strictly rel-
evant to its title. On 7 March 1796 it was increased to
crown folio and continued in this size and form until 7
June 1798. At that time it was enlarged to the size of
the three other Boston papers and retitled Russell's
Gazette; Commercial and Political. Announcing this
change, Russell said that "the portentious aspect of
our political horizon . . . designate[s] the present
period as one, which loudly calls for the virtuous
energies of all good citizens; and ought to inspire, in
the breast of every man, a solicitude to contribute his
efforts in support of the cause of virtue, freedom, and
independence." He then goes on to explain that for this
reason he is deviating from the hitherto strictly commercial nature of the paper "to afford an opportunity of
rendering it an important and useful vehicle of political
information." "To the friends and supporters of the constitution," says Russell, he "declares his paper

444

exclusively devoted. To the enemies of either he avows
himself an enemy."

The tone of Russell's announcement is characteristic of the virulent Federalism expressed in the pages
of the paper, which was retitled the Boston Gazette
after Russell engaged Cutler as his partner because of
ill health. "It presented itself, twice a week," says
Joseph T. Buckingham, "charged to the muzzle, with argument, invective, and ridicule, against the French Directory, Napoleon, Jefferson, Madison, The Chronicle, the
Aurora, and all the host of Jacobins, Democrats, Repub-
licans, or by whatever name the adversaries of Federalism chose to be called." Accompanying the politics, the
Gazette also included a considerable number of reviews,
announcements, and advertisements about the plays then
being produced in Boston. Much of Robert Treat Paine's
best work appeared first in the Gazette, and in addition
to printing the play-bills, Russell himself contributed
several reviews of a less vituperative nature than his
political writing. Russell was also attracted to British
writers, and he usually placed a short quotation above
each column of advertisements that he published, a practice that apparently attracted considerable attention.

Russell continued publishing the Gazette until
1823, when he resigned his interest in the paper in a
farewell address in which he looked back on the great
"experiment in political history" that was the American
Revolution and the growth of a nation so remarkable that
"it seems as it were a dream." It was a time, says
Russell, in which "the gristle has become bone, the youthful muscle gained strength and hardihood, and the whole
colossal body adorned with manly grace and comeliness."
Furthermore, Russell notes with pride, it was a period
in which "philosophy has been brought down to the common
business of life," a remark that summarizes as well the
ambitions and accomplishments of Russell's own career.

Michael Clark

John Russell

Reference:

Buckingham, Joseph T. Specimens of Newspaper Literature.
    Vol. 2. Boston: Little and Brown, 1850.

Joseph Russell

Joseph Russell (1734-1795) was a printer, bookseller, and one of the most prominent book auctioneers in New England. With his partner John Green, Russell printed over 150 titles. Green and Russell first worked from a house on Tremont Street, near the head of Court Street in Boston, but this building was razed to make way for Scollay's Buildings. They spent most of their career, until 1774, in Queen Street, opposite the Probate Office. When Russell later introduced auctioneering as one of the firm's activities, they reserved a room for this purpose, and Green and Russell remained there until the dissolution of their partnership in 1774. Russell's name never appeared as a printer after that, but in 1774 he engaged Samuel Clap as his partner, and together they continued as booksellers and auctioneers in Boston until Russell's death. From 1755 until 1763 Green and Russell printed approximately eighty titles, including samples of virtually every kind of literature imaginable at the time, although they seldom printed more than one work by any one author. Their most important book was Harvard's Pietas et Gratulatio (1761), but they also printed an annual edition of Nathaniel Ames's almanac and a weekly newspaper. After 1763 they continued to publish the almanac and the newspaper, but their appointment as printers to the British commissioners confined most of their other work to government forms and publications, most notably numerous editions of the Temporary Acts and Laws of His Majesty's Province, the Journal of the House of Representatives, and the Acts of Parliament.

Major Authors: Mather Byles, Charles Chauncy, Samuel Cooper, Andrew Eliot, Thomas Foxcroft, John Gill, Jonathan Mayhew, Samuel Webster.

447

Russell was born in Boston on 8 September 1734 and died there on 29 November 1795. He served his apprenticeship with Daniel Fowle, with whom he lived until 1775. In July of that year, an antigovernment tract appeared in Boston, The Monster of Monsters. Although it bears no printer's name, the House of Representatives rightly suspected Daniel Fowle and his brother Zechariah to be its printers, and in October the House brought into custody Royall Tyler, who was arrested and then released; Daniel Fowle, who was imprisoned briefly; and Russell, who was questioned and then released. (Zechariah Fowle became ill upon hearing of his brother's arrest and was unable to appear before the House.) Daniel Fowle, disgusted with the treatment of himself and his brother, left for New Hampshire in 1755. His brother took over his printing house, and Russell entered into partnership with John Green.

The connection with Green involved Russell with the oldest family of printers and booksellers in New England. John Green was the great-grandson of Samuel Green, who had taken over Stephen Day's Cambridge press in 1649, and the son of Bartholomew Green, Jr. The firm of Green and Russell also had several apprentices who went on to establish their own businesses in Boston: John Boyle became the partner of Richard Draper and then continued as a printer and bookseller in Boston; John Hicks later joined with Nathaniel Mills and together they bought Green and Russell's paper in 1773; and Ezekiel Russell, Joseph's younger brother, worked briefly as a printer and auctioneer and then founded the Censor, a Loyalist journal that flourished briefly before the war. Ezekiel was the only member of Russell's immediate family involved in the printing business, but after the war another branch of the Russell family became prominent among Boston printers. Benjamin Russell, born in Boston in 1762 and apprenticed to Isaiah Thomas, became the printer and editor of the influential Columbian Centinel, and Benjamin's brother John published the paper eventually known as the Boston Gazette, one of the most vehement of the Federalist journals. Benjamin Russell did not begin printing until the 1780s, long after Joseph had turned from printing to

448

auctioneering, but Benjamin did acknowledge his kinsman in the Centinel after his death. Although no mention is made of Joseph Russell's career as printer, newspaper editor, or auctioneer, an obituary of 2 December 1795 does praise his devotion to God, his generosity and good will, and his conscientious attention to his duties as treasurer of Boston, a post he held at his death.

In their first eight years together, Green and Russell printed and sold a wide range of material including various sermons and religious tracts, captivity narratives, descriptions of natural disasters, accounts of military exploits, and a few long poems. During their first year, most of their texts had been published earlier elsewhere, such as A Platform of Church-Discipline and the Confession of Faith, two of the most important seventeenth-century documents regarding church government, and Samuel Pike and Samuel Hayward's Some Important Cases of Conscience Answered, a popular collection of homilies and confessional narratives first published in London. But by their third year they had printed a sermon by Thomas Foxcroft, another by Charles Chauncy, Henry Dixon's Youth's Instructor in the English Tongue, and Brady and Tate's collection of Psalms and hymns, complete with several plates of music. In 1757 Green and Russell began publishing a newspaper every Monday, and in 1758 they printed the first of their annual editions of Ames's almanac. After 1763, however, only twelve titles appeared in addition to their almanac, newspaper, and government work. Seven of these are religious works by East Apthorp, Andrew Croswell, and Andrew Eliot, and the rest are the same congeries of scientific and occasional texts that characterized much of the earlier work. Throughout their career Green and Russell apparently printed whatever was available and would sell. Few authors appear more than once, and there are no clear patterns in the subject matter they printed except for the work commissioned by the British authorities. Like the work of most printers of their period, the range of material they published reflects the variety of taste among the public rather than an effort to influence that taste in a specific direction.

449

Among the generally unremarkable collection of material printed by Green and Russell, one text stands out. In 1761 the faculty and students of Harvard College decided to follow their British counterparts and compile a collection of poems on the occasion of the death of George II, and they chose Green and Russell to print the book. Unlike most such collections, the Pietas et Gratulatio Collegii Cantabrigiensis Apud NovAnglos was conceived, as Moses Coit Tyler notes, to "represent to Europe the progress thus far made, in the new world, in the most elegant studies." In this book, says Tyler, Harvard "deposited the evidence of the mechanical expertness then attained in America in the manufacture of books and of poetry," and Charles Evans calls it the "handsomest specimen of the printer's art produced in the American Colonies." Several copies were printed on thick paper for presentation to the royal family, and a specially bound copy was presented to King George III. The poetry itself has little historical importance, but one of the poems is printed in Greek type and is the earliest extended use of Greek letters in the colonies. The types had been presented to Harvard College in 1726 by Thomas Hollis of London and did not belong to Green and Russell, but they were the only printers ever to use them because the types were destroyed when the college library burned in 1764.

Although the Pietas was a magnificent achievement, to their contemporaries Green and Russell were primarily known through their weekly newspaper. Two years after entering into their partnership, Green and Russell revived Ellis Huske's Boston Weekly Post-Boy, a paper that had originated in Huske's activities as Postmaster and had not been published since 1754. They retained one of the devices used by Huske—a post-boy riding a horse and blowing a horn—renamed the paper the Boston Weekly Advertiser, and published their first number on 22 August 1757. In a prefatory paragraph from "The Printers to the PUBLIC," Green and Russell proclaim their ambition "to promote knowledge, Vertue, and innocent Amusement," and note that they will "always be obliged to any Gentleman, that will favor us with Pieces of Speculation, provided they are wrote in a manner consistent with Decency and Public Peace." The cautiously eclectic tone of this introduction is borne out by the contents of the paper, which, in addition to a long, mutually complimentary exchange between the Massachusetts Council and the new governor, include the usual assortment of local news, reports on events in England reprinted from British papers, and the printers' own advertisement of their willingness to do "all sorts of Printing Work . . . at a Moderate rate, with Care and Dispatch."

On 1 January 1759 the title of the paper was changed to Green and Russell's Post Boy and Advertiser and the second device used by Huske--a ship--was added to the masthead. On 30 May 1763 the note "Printers to the Honourable House of Representatives" was also added just below the title. Throughout the period the format and content of the paper remained unchanged. Early in 1768, however, an event occurred that altered the paper significantly and provides an example of the difficulties that were beginning to emerge between the British author-ity and the increasing sense of identity and place that was emerging in the colonies. On 29 February 1768 the Boston Gazette published a virulent attack on Governor Bernard, and although directed to respond by the gover-nor, both Houses of the Massachusetts Legislature refused to do so. Four days later, however, the records of the Council announced that "Messrs. Draper and Green & Russell be appointed Printers of the Massachusetts Ga-zette." While the details of this appointment are un-clear, Albert Matthews notes that the Massachusetts Gazette seems thus to have been instituted in Boston as the voice of the British authorities, a move gener-ated by the governor's inability to control the Boston press. Beginning on 23 May 1768, Green and Russell responded to this appointment by simply adding the Gazette to the Post-Boy and publishing both papers every Monday, usually on the same sheet of paper. (Richard Draper, the other printer named in the appoint-ment, also added the Gazette to his own paper, the Boston News-Letter, and published them both every Thurs-day.) Both devices were dropped from the Post-Boy and

451

the size of its title was reduced, but the <u>Gazette</u> bore
the royal arms as its device and the notice "Published
by Authority." This arrangement lasted through 25
September 1769. On 2 October of that year, Green and
Russell combined the two papers, changed the title to
the <u>Massachusetts Gazette, and the Post-Boy Advertiser</u>,
and assumed the royal arms as their device. (Richard
Draper, meanwhile, combined his two papers and changed
the title to the <u>Massachusetts Gazette; and the Boston
Weekly News-Letter</u>.) On 26 April 1773 the <u>Gazette . . .
and Advertiser</u> carried the announcement that Green and
Russell had sold the paper to Nathaniel Mills and John
Hicks, and with the support and encouragement of the
British government, Mills and Hicks increased circulation
and turned the paper into one of the more energetic prewar journals. After selling the paper, Green and Russell
printed nothing except government documents, usually in
conjunction with Richard Draper. The last imprint bearing their name appeared in 1774.

Joseph Russell's success as a printer and bookseller and his later prominence as an auctioneer grew
out of the necessarily wide range of interests and abilities that typified the American printer before 1800.
Throughout their career, Green and Russell printed and
sold virtually every kind of text read at the time, although most of their publishing after 1763 was restricted
to their newspaper and to government documents. Among
the list of forgotten authors and routine publications
that came from their press, the magnificent cultural and
technical achievement of the <u>Pietas et Gratulatio</u> stands
out as perhaps the most significant single text printed
in America before the <u>Declaration of Independence</u>. Conceived and executed as the demonstration of the colonies'
cultural maturity, the <u>Pietas</u> also demonstrated that the
American printer--as represented by Green and Russell--
was capable of matching the finest work of his British
counterpart. Most of Russell's responsibilities in that
partnership, however, lay in his activities as an auctioneer, and after taking Samuel Clap as a partner he

went on to popularize the sale of new books through auction in the latter part of the eighteenth century.

Michael Clark

References:

Ayer, Mary F. Check-List of Boston Newspapers: 1704-
    1780. Publications of the Colonial Society of
    Massachusetts. Vol. 9. Boston: The Society,
    1907.

Buckingham, Joseph T. Specimens of Newspaper Literature.
    Vol. 1. Boston: Little and Brown, 1850.

Lehmann-Haupt, Hellmut. The Book in America. New York:
    Bowker, 1939; revised and enlarged, New York:
    Bowker, 1951.

Russell, Gurdon W. An Account of Some of the Descendants
    of John Russell. Boston: Case, Lockwood &
    Brainard, 1910.

Thomas, Isaiah. The History of Printing in America.
    Worcester, Mass.: Isaiah Thomas, Jr., 1810;
    2nd ed., revised, Albany, N.Y.: J. Munsell
    for the American Antiquarian Society, 1874;
    ed. Marcus A. McCorison, Barre, Mass.: Imprint
    Society, 1970.

Tyler, Moses Coit. A History of American Literature.
    Vol. 2. New York: G. P. Putnam's Sons, 1878.

Joseph N. Russell

Joseph N. Russell (c. 1775-c. 1810) was a printer whose name appears in ten known imprints from 1795 to 1797, every one of which he printed with his brother John Russell. They were brothers to Benjamin Russell. Their most important effort was printing the weekly Boston Price-Current and Marine Intelligencer that eventually became the Boston Gazette. Joseph N. and John Russell began the Price-Current in September 1795 and Joseph withdrew in June 1796. The brothers conducted business "at their Printing-Office over Maj. Hawes's work-shops, Quaker-Lane."

References:

Brigham, Clarence S. History and Bibliography of American Newspapers: 1690-1820. Vol. 1. Worcester, Mass.: American Antiquarian Society, 1947.

Buckingham, Joseph T. Specimens of Newspaper Literature. Vol. 2. Boston: Little and Brown, 1850.

Sarah Hood Russell

Sarah Hood Russell (1749-1806) continued the printing business of her husband Ezekiel after his death in 1796. In 1797 she printed and sold, "at Russell's office," Eunice Smith's Dialogue or, Discourse between Mary & Martha.

William Selby

William Selby (c. 1739-1798), a musician, published his own Two Anthems for Three and Four Voices in 1782.

Samuel Sewall

Samuel Sewall (1652-1730) managed the Boston press for three years after the death of John Foster in 1681. Sewall hired Samuel Green, Jr. to do the printing, and Green in turn succeeded Sewall as manager of the press. Sewall's name appears in the imprints of sixteen known works, six of which are by Increase Mather.

References:

Jones, Matt B.   "The Early Massachusetts-Bay Colony Seals." Proceedings of the American Antiquarian Society, 44 (1934).

Littlefield, George E.   Early Boston Booksellers: 1642-1711. Boston: Club of Odd Volumes, 1900; reprint edition, New York: Burt Franklin, 1969.

Littlefield, George E.   The Early Massachusetts Press: 1638-1711. Boston: Club of Odd Volumes, 1907; reprint edition, New York: Burt Franklin, 1969.

Samuel Sewall

Sewall, Samuel. <u>The Diary of Samuel Sewall: 1674-1729</u>.
    Edited by M. Halsey Thomas. Vol. 1. New York:
    Farrar, Straus & Giroux, 1973.

Samuel Sewall, Jr.

Samuel Sewall, Jr. (1678-1751), son of the famous diarist
and manager of the Boston press, was active as a bookseller and publisher from 1700 until 1712, when he retired. He lived for a short period with Michael Perry
in 1694 and 1695, was apprenticed to Samuel Checkley for
six months in 1695, and finally served an apprenticeship
with Richard Wilkins beginning in 1697. Sewall opened
his own shop in 1699 or 1700 "near the Old Meeting House."
His name appears in the imprints of eleven known works,
four of which are by Cotton Mather (all published in
1701), and two of which deal with Sewall's father. In
1701 he possibly published Ebenezer Pemberton's <u>The
Souldier Defended & Directed</u>, a sermon preached on the
senior Sewall's election to captaincy in the Artillery
Company; the next year Sewall published Benjamin Colman's
<u>Faith Victorious</u> to commemorate the elder Sewall's retire-
ment from the captaincy.

References:

Littlefield, George E. <u>Early Boston Booksellers: 1642-
    1711</u>. Boston: Club of Odd Volumes, 1900; reprint
    edition, New York: Burt Franklin, 1969.

Sewall, Samuel. <u>The Diary of Samuel Sewall: 1674-1729</u>.
    Edited by M. Halsey Thomas. 2 vols. New York:
    Farrar, Straus & Giroux, 1973.

Joseph H. Seymour

Joseph H. Seymour (dates unknown) was an engraver. He published William Hayley's poem The Triumphs of Temper in 1794.

Francis Skinner

Francis Skinner (1709-1785), primarily a binder, also sold books at his shop in Fish Street. He spent most of his career in Newport, Rhode Island, but one known Boston imprint bears his name: William Walling's Wonderful Providence of God. Skinner sold that book in 1730.

References:

Spawn, William and Carol Spawn. "Francis Skinner, Bookbinder of Newport: An Eighteenth-Century Craftsman Identified by His Tools." Winterthur Portfolio, 2 (1965).

Thomas, Isaiah. The History of Printing in America. Worcester, Mass.: Isaiah Thomas, Jr., 1810; 2nd ed., revised, Albany, N.Y.: J. Munsell for the American Antiquarian Society, 1874; ed. Marcus A. McCorison, Barre, Mass.: Imprint Society, 1970.

John Smibert

John Smibert (d. 1751) was an artist who spent time in
Italy with Bishop Berkeley, with whom he came to America.
He arrived in Boston in 1729, and his greatest contribution to that city was as architect of Faneuil Hall. His
name appears in only one known imprint, Richard Gridley's
Plan of the City and Fortress of Louisburg. Smibert sold
that title at his shop "in Queen street" in 1746.

References:

Foster, William E. "Some Rhode Island Contributions to
the Intellectual Life of the Last Century." Proceedings of the American Antiquarian Society, 8
(1892).

Morgan, John H. "John Watson: Painter, Merchant, and
Capitalist of New Jersey, 1685-1768." Proceedings
of the American Antiquarian Society, 50 (1940).

Whitehill, Walter M. Boston: A Topographical History.
Cambridge: Belknap Press of Harvard University
Press, 1959.

459

William Spotswood

William Spotswood (c. 1753-1805), publisher and
bookseller, published over 120 titles in Boston,
one-fourth of which are plays. Primarily a
Philadelphia publisher from 1784 to 1805, he began publishing in Boston in 1793 at No. 55 Marlborough Street.
In 1798 he formed a brief partnership with Samuel
Etheridge before returning finally to Philadelphia in
1800.

Major Authors: Fanny Burney, Henry Fielding,
Hannah More, Joseph Priestley, Richard Brinsley Sheridan,
Isaiah Thomas.

Spotswood's specialty was drama. He published more
than twenty-five plays that range from Florian's Look
before You Leap to Sheridan's The Critic, both in 1795.
He also published Henry Fielding's The Fathers (1795)
and Hannah More's Search after Happiness (1796). This
number of plays reflects the growing secularization
of the age and the Bostonians' desire for dramatic entertainment after having been unable to see a play performed
for over four decades after 1750.

Spotswood published a variety of other books. He
published eleven children's books, including volumes by
Christopher Smart (1795), James Fordyce (1795), Anna
Barbauld (1795), Thomas Day (1796, 1798), and Mrs.
Pinchard (1798). He published moral tales by various
authors, and he was responsible for Isaiah Thomas almanacs from 1795 through 1800. He published books on travel
and places remote; Ann Radcliffe's Romance of the Forest
(1795); the first and only number of the Tablet (1795),
a newspaper; an edition of Hoyle's Games Approved (1796);
and the first Boston edition of Fanny Burney's Camilla
(1797).

460

William Spotswood

Some idea of Spotswood's relative prominence in the world of Boston publishing may be gained from the refusal by Jeremy Belknap of Spotswood's 1789 proposal for publishing The Foresters. Belknap chose the firm of Thomas and Andrews because of its extensive connections and its ability to push a sale. Spotswood clearly occupied a minor position in the publishing world of eighteenth-century Boston. His significance rests with the number of plays he published and the variety of his other titles.

Elizabeth Nelson Adams

Reference:

Silver, Rollo G. The American Printer: 1787-1825. Charlottesville, Va.: University Press of Virginia, 1967.

Robert Starke (or Starkey)

Robert Starke (or Starkey) (d. c. 1722) was active as a bookseller in Boston from 1717 to 1721. His name appears in eight known Boston imprints, five of which are titles by Cotton Mather. Starke conducted business "near the New North Meeting-House."

Reference:

Thomas, Isaiah. The History of Printing in America. Worcester, Mass.: Isaiah Thomas, Jr., 1810; 2nd ed., revised, Albany, N.Y.: J. Munsell for the American Antiquarian Society, 1874; ed. Marcus A. McCorison, Barre, Mass.: Imprint Society, 1970.

Robert Starkey (see Robert Starke)

Alexander Steele

Alexander Steele (c. 1744-1804), bookseller and binder, joined with others to publish the 1772 Massachusetts Calendar (1771).

462

Benjamin Sweetser

Benjamin Sweetser (1772-1837) established, with William
Burdick, the semiweekly Courier in July 1795 "opposite
the Court-House, Court-Street." After Burdick withdrew
in December 1795, Sweetser continued with the newspaper
at "No. 63 State-Street, directly opposite Messrs. Jones
Bass's Auction Room." That printing shop burned in March
1796, whereupon Sweetser bought the Federal Orrery,
changed its name to the Courier and General Advertiser,
and published it. He also published, between July and
October 1796, the Massachusetts Magazine. Sweetser's
name appears in the imprints of five known titles published in either 1795 or 1796.

References:

Brigham, Clarence S. History and Bibliography of Amer-
     ican Newspapers: 1690-1820. Vol. 1. Worcester,
     Mass.: American Antiquarian Society, 1947.

Mott, Frank Luther. A History of American Magazines:
     1741-1850. New York and London: Appleton, 1930;
     Cambridge: Harvard University Press, 1938;
     Cambridge: Belknap Press of Harvard University
     Press, 1957.

John Tappin

John Tappin (d. 1678) came with his parents to America from England in 1633. His name appears in one known imprint, John Allin's `The Spouse of Christ Coming out of Affliction. Samuel Green printed that title for Tappin in 1672.

Reference:

Littlefield, George E. Early Boston Booksellers: 1642-1711. Boston: Club of Odd Volumes, 1900; reprint edition, New York: Burt Franklin, 1969.

Isaiah Thomas

Isaiah Thomas (1749-1831), printer and bookseller, was the most important publisher in eighteenth-century America. During his most active period from 1780 to 1800 he established branches through partnership arrangements in more than a score of towns throughout New England, in New York, and in Baltimore. At the height of his prosperity in the 1790s he employed 150 people in one printing office, operating seven presses continuously. Thomas's various publishing ventures accounted for more than 900 books. He was the most prolific American publisher of Bibles, a leading producer of children's books, an early developer of music publishing, and a major printer of almanacs. His most important contribution to the growth of the publishing industry in the United

464

States was to pioneer the transition between the small, individual markets of the colonial book trade and the developing, national interests after the War of Independence. He was also a major influence in developing the character of American culture as distinct from its English origins. Thomas wrote The History of Printing in America, the leading work on the subject for more than a century, and he was the founder of the American Antiquarian Society.

Major Authors: Caleb Alexander, William Hill Brown, William Perry, Nicholas Pike, Mercy Otis Warren.

Thomas was born on 19 January 1749 into a New England family that had settled in Boston a century earlier. While his great-grandfather and grandfather were merchants, Isaiah's father, Moses, declined to follow in the tradition and tried his hand unsucessfully at being a tailor, sailor, soldier, storekeeper, schoolmaster, and farmer--the last in Hempstead, Long Island, where he met and married Fidelity Grant of Rhode Island. Moses died in 1752 and his widow was left with five children and little means to care for them. In 1756, when Isaiah, the youngest, was six years old, he was apprenticed to Zechariah Fowle, a Boston printer, who undertook to educate and train him in his own craft. Fowle, however, turned out to be unambitious, lazy, and ignorant, and Thomas was left to educate himself. Within two years, Thomas set the type for his first book, an edition of the New-England Primer (1757). During his apprenticeship he was helped by his master's partner, Samuel Draper, a good printer. By the time Thomas was twelve he could do most of the composition in the shop and help Fowle with the presswork. At thirteen he printed the New Book of Knowledge (1762) and included his own crude woodcuts. Thomas was virtually operating the shop when he was sixteen, and among the works that he was completely responsible for is Tom Thumb's Play-Book (1764), which he printed for Andrew Barclay, a bookseller. During his early years Thomas also received guidance from the printer Gamaliel Rogers.

Thomas harbored contempt for Fowle, and on 16 September 1765, following a serious quarrel, the young man broke his indenture and sailed for Halifax, Nova Scotia. He was not yet eighteen years of age. This was the start of a nearly continuous period of travel that extended over several years. On a number of occasions he had sought to journey to London where he might acquire the type of experience and skills in his craft not available elsewhere, but he never managed to make the trip abroad. In Halifax he worked for Anthony Henry, a printer with a reputation for indolence who published the Halifax Gazette. The management of the paper was left entirely to Thomas, but his activities in opposition to the Stamp Act led to the termination of his employment within six months. He returned to New England, worked briefly for Daniel Fowle, publisher of the New-Hampshire Gazette in Portsmouth, and moved over to the rival paper, the Portsmouth Mercury. His success on the latter paper was noted by Zechariah Fowle, who offered to take him back and forget the past. Thomas returned to his old job in Boston, but repeated quarrels again broke up the association and the young man resumed his travels. He made his way to Wilmington, North Carolina, and then to Charleston, South Carolina, where he settled down for two years as a journeyman for Robert Wells, publisher of the South Carolina and American General Gazette. During this time he met and married Mary Dill, a step he soon regretted when he learned of her free-wheeling past that included a bastard son.

In 1770, with extensive experience in newspaper publishing, Thomas returned to Boston with the idea of establishing his own publication. Once again he associated himself with Fowle, entered into a partnership on Salem Street, and embarked upon the publication of the Massachusetts Spy in spite of the fact that there were several other papers being published in the city. In October of that year, after moving the shop to Union Street, Thomas bought out his partner and was in business for himself. At first he intended to open his newspaper to the views of both loyalists and patriots, but he finally cast his lot with the cause of the latter.

466

His involvement in the politics of the ante-bellum years led to trouble with the English authorities, and he subsequently was forced to flee to Worcester, Massachusetts, where his business expanded only modestly. He won a contract to publish the annual broadsides listing the Harvard theses, he put out an edition of Ezekiel Cheever's Latin grammar, and he began the publication of almanacs. There were some adjustments in his personal life. His wife bore him a daughter, Mary Ann, and a son, Isaiah, Jr., and in 1777 he secured a divorce on grounds of infidelity. Two years later he married his cousin Mary, widow of Isaac Fowle. His business activities declined during the early years of the war, but as the Revolution began to draw to a close, Thomas entered the period of his career that would make him the leading publisher of his time.

In his rise to leadership in the publishing field, Thomas at first followed the course of other printer-bookseller-publishers. He established at least a small measure of security by publishing a successful periodical, turned to book publishing as the major portion of his business, and engaged in bookselling to move his stock faster by exchange arrangements with other bookseller-publishers. His genius, however, was as an entrepreneur who learned to adapt to the political, social, and economic changes of his time. His means of expansion during the earlier fragmented condition of the colonies and before the Federal unification afforded by the Constitution consisted largely of the establishment of branches through partnerships in cities and towns throughout New England and beyond. As the century began to draw to a close, Thomas developed the mass distribution techniques that were to gain momentum in the nineteenth century.

One of the earliest of his partnership branches was with Henry W. Tinges at Newburyport, but the most important was his association with Ebenezer T. Andrews, who joined in a three-way partnership with Thomas and John Sprague in Boston in 1788. Sprague left a year later, and soon the Boston firm of Thomas and Andrews

467

in Newbury Street became the largest and most important
in the network. The partnership lasted for more than
thirty years. Eventually, Andrews's business judgment
and entrepreneurial skill rivaled those of Thomas.

The full range of titles published by Thomas (most
in conjunction with Andrews after 1788) encompasses popular and serious material, including almanacs, children's
books, Bibles, textbooks, and even some erotica.

The famous Thomas almanacs were the most widely
circulated of the many almanacs published during that
period. After selling between 3,000 and 4,000 copies
annually during the 1780s, the 1797 edition, to cite
one profitable year, sold as many as 29,000 copies.
Thomas secured the calculations and other material
from Benjamin West, Dr. Samuel Stearns, and Daniel
George.

Thomas began publishing children's books by reprinting a number of John Newbery's chapbooks and other titles imported from England. Always taking into account
the particular needs of his markets, Thomas altered the
English texts to suit the American tastes by changing,
for example, references to royalty into American terms.
He began publishing his own series of children's books
with The Beauty and the Monster in 1785, and he introduced into America the use of stamped, illustrated paper
covers for children's books. All told, Thomas published
more than 100 children's books.

Even Thomas's Bible publishing ventures began with
books for children, including The Holy Bible Abridged
(1786) and A Curious Hieroglyphick Bible (1788). His
major Bible project was the simultaneous publication, in
the early 1790s, of two-volume folio and royal quarto
editions. His best known effort was the "standing Bible"
in which the type was kept standing for successive printings. The main advantage of such a technique was that
Thomas could print smaller, more predictable runs and
proceed rapidly with many subsequent printings. It en-
tailed a heavy investment in type but yielded large

savings in paper. For the project, Thomas ordered from London, in installments, the composed forms of type. The Bible took six years to complete. Published in 1797, it remained in print for many years.

Thomas's major achievements in mass distribution were in the field of textbook publishing. His earliest and most successful effort was with a speller. After trying vainly to buy the Massachusetts publication rights for Noah Webster's spelling book in 1783, he brought out his own New American Spelling Book two years later and was able to capitalize on Webster's success. Even more successful was a better spelling book by Professor William Perry of Edinburgh University that Thomas also published in 1785. It went through fourteen editions with total sales of 300,000 copies. He later published several editions of Perry's Royal Standard English Dictionary, beginning in 1788. It sold approximately 54,000 copies. In the process of distributing these popular books Thomas attempted to establish uniform pricing. That initiated a dispute that has engaged publishers and booksellers to the present day.

Although he was not the first to publish music books, Thomas published Silas Ballou's New Hymns on Various Subjects (1785) after securing music type from England. He also published belles-lettres, including the first American novel, William Hill Brown's The Power of Sympathy (1789), and Mercy Otis Warren's Poems, Dramatic and Miscellaneous (1790).

Standard European works that found prominent positions in the Thomas publication lists include Claude Millot's Elements of General History in five volumes (1789) and Blackstone's Commentaries in four volumes (1790). Although he made no other major attempt at publishing law titles, Thomas was the most important New England publisher of standard medical works. In 1793 he published editions of William Smellie's Set of Anatomical Tables and Charles White's Treatise on the Management of Pregnant and Lying-In Women. Of all the foreign medical

469

works published in Massachusetts at the time, Thomas accounted for more than half.

Thomas also published lighter material. Ballads and topical works such as books on shaking Quakers (1782) came off his presses, as did The Amours and Adventures of Two English Gentlemen in Italy (1795). He was often careful to bowdlerize the titles of some European works. One example is the original version of Dr. Faustus that had appeared in England as The History of the Damnable Life and the Deserved Death of Dr. John Faustus, D. D. Both the title and the text were changed for Thomas's American edition that was titled The Surprising Life and Death of Dr. John Faustus, D. D. (1795).

A favorite exercise in bibliographical speculation has been the question of whether Thomas was the publisher of the first American edition of John Cleland's Memoirs of a Woman of Pleasure, more popularly known as Fanny Hill. In the Thomas papers at the American Antiquarian Society is a letter from London bookseller Thomas Evans, dated 29 July 1786, concerning a shipment of books. The London dealer writes: "I hope I did not omit anything necessary to be mentioned, except one, which I fear I did, it was, I think, the Memoirs of a W. of P." Also among Thomas's effects are collections of newspaper volumes originally bound in marbled covers. When the marbling began to wear off, sheets were revealed that came from an edition of Cleland's erotic classic. Although the title page in the sheets bears a London imprint, the assumption is that Thomas published it without wishing to identify it with his own firm.

Recognizing the importance of the publisher's complete responsibility for producing books, Thomas made good use of his experiences with shortages and difficulties before and during the Revolution to develop a self-sufficient and profitable business. Not unlike more recent situations, newspapers during those years suffered critical shortages of paper, forcing them to reduce their size, to reduce their frequency of publication, or to suspend publication. Thomas had his own paper mill to supply a portion of his needs. He also introduced the use of wove paper that was developed by Baskerville in England in the 1750s. Also, Thomas had a bindery in the Worcester office.

As was customary in the book trade, Thomas maintained friendly relations with his colleagues and, on one occasion, he was able to round up and borrow some mathematical type that he needed for a publication. He also sought to organize the trade, and he was an advocate of regulating practices for the mutual benefit of publishers. He attended a major organizing meeting in Philadelphia in 1788 in which the aged Benjamin Franklin also participated. In spite of such attempts, however, the establishment of rules and regulations for the trade never proved successful.

Thomas's complete involvement in the world of books and publishing extended to his lifetime habit of preserving records of the trade. (He founded the American Antiquarian Society in 1812 and served as its president until his death.) He saved long runs of exchange papers and built up an extensive library. He made use of it, of course, in writing his monumental History of Printing in America, an ambitious project, but generously endowed with errors and gaps. It lists obscure biographical details on printers from earlier years whom he never met, but it offers virtually no personal information on Ebenezer Andrews, his partner for more than thirty years.

Thomas's skills as a printing craftsman never measured up to European standards, but they were far better than those of many of his colleagues in America. He was a shrewd businessman. That, combined with unlimited ambition in his earlier years and an alert grasp of the needs of the book-buying public throughout his career, made him preeminent among American publishers.

Jacob L. Chernofsky

471

References:

Shipton, Clifford K. Isaiah Thomas: Printer, Patriot
    and Philanthropist, 1749-1831. Rochester, N.Y.:
    Leo Hart, 1948.

Silver, Rollo G. The American Printer: 1787-1825.
    Charlottesville, Va.: University Press of
    Virginia, 1967.

Tebbel, John. A History of Book Publishing in the
    United States. Vol. 1. New York and London:
    Bowker, 1972.

Thomas, Isaiah. The History of Printing in America.
    Worcester, Mass.: Isaiah Thomas, Jr., 1810;
    2nd ed., revised, Albany, N.Y.: J. Munsell
    for the American Antiquarian Society, 1874;
    ed. Marcus A. McCorison, Barre, Mass.: Imprint
    Society, 1970.

Daniel Tillotson (or Tillotsen) (see Joseph Hawkins and
    Daniel Tillotson)

Shippie Townsend

Shippie Townsend (1722-1798) was an author of religious
titles who published two of his own works "at his house
in Cross-Street." He published A Practical Essay in
1783 and Repentence and Remission of Sins Considered
in 1784.

James Turner

James Turner (d. 1759), silversmith, engraver, and bookseller in Boston from 1744 to 1758, engraved, printed, and sold the last sixteen pages of John Barnard's New Version of the Psalms of David (1752).

Hezekiah Usher

Hezekiah Usher (1615-1676) was the first Massachusetts publisher and bookseller and the agent for the Society for the Propagation of the Gospel in New England (the New England Company). He sold the first edition of the Bay Psalm Book (1640); the first law book, The Book of the General Lawes and Libertyes (1648); and it was probably Usher who sent the Dunster and Lyon revision of the Bay Psalm Book to Cambridge, England, where it was printed for him in 1648. His first bookstore was located in Cambridge, but in 1642 he moved it to Boston.

Major Authors: Charles Chauncy, John Cotton, Samuel Danforth, Jonathan Mitchel, John Norton.

Usher was born in England and emigrated to Cambridge in approximately 1638, being admitted to the First Church as a freeman on 14 March 1639. He was married three times: to Frances, by whom he had six children and who died in 1652; Elizabeth, who died in 1670; and Mary, who outlived him. He operated his Cambridge bookstore for several years before moving to Boston in 1642. His name first appeared in an imprint in 1647 as the seller of Samuel Danforth's almanac. In

473

February of the same year he bought a lot near the market and built a house on it, the first floor given over to his store and the second providing living quarters for his family.

Despite the tremendous growth of the city during its first forty years, Boston was still too small to support a full time bookseller, and Usher consequently became a factotum for the small colony. He still sold books, published them on occasion, and acted as the agent for the New England Company, but he made his living as a merchant, exporting the colony's raw materials and importing manufactured goods and food that could not be grown there. Usher was prominent in civic affairs, holding a number of posts, and was a member of the Artillery Company. He abandoned the book business in 1669, his son John stepping in to take his place, and he devoted himself to the more lucrative business of exporting and importing. He died a comparatively wealthy man, leaving an estate valued at £15,358.

Usher either published or sold some of the most important titles printed in the early years of Massachusetts, including the Bay Psalm Book, John Cotton's Spiritual Milk for Boston Babes in Either England (1656), the first law book (1648), and, when the press was busy with the laws, it was probably he who sent the Dunster and Lyon revision of the Bay Psalm Book to England to be printed. The majority of Usher's ten known imprints, however, deal with the controversy surrounding the adoption of the Half-Way Covenant. By the 1660s the idealism and optimism that had spurred the establishment of the Massachusetts theocracy, an optimism that had been codified in the Cambridge Platform of 1649, was being severely tested by the lack of religious rigorousness in the colony's second generation. Two options were available to the leaders of Massachusetts: either to maintain the principles of the Platform of Church Discipline and risk the quick death of the Congregational churches through a lack of members, or to revise the Platform to allow the admission of people who could not otherwise meet the stringent requirements. At issue were the two basic questions of

474

whether to permit the children of noncommunicants to be baptized and whether to abandon the condition of church membership for citizenship. The decision of the 1662 Synod, which answered both questions in the affirmative, was published by Usher in 1662 as Propositions Concerning the Subject of Baptism and Consociation of Churches.

Despite the decision of the Synod, a strong minority opposition, led by Increase Mather and John Davenport, continued to argue against these changes in church polity. It appears that Usher agreed with the majority, for in 1669, when Davenport was made pastor of the First Church, Usher was a member of a group that seceded from the church and founded the Third Church (Old South). Although Usher disagreed with the dissenters, he took his responsibilities as a publisher seriously, and he published the first American edition of Charles Chauncy's Anti-Synodalia Americana, a rebuttal of the Synod's decision. His sense of fair play having been assuaged, his next three publications, John Allin's Animadversions upon the Anti-synodalia Americana (1664), Richard Mather and Jonathan Mitchel's Defence of the Answer (1664), and John Norton's Three Choice and Profitable Sermons (1664), with its "Copy of a Letter," all defend the Half-Way Covenant.

As the agent for the New England Company, Usher was instrumental in assisting John Eliot's missionary work among the Indians, chiefly by aiding in the printing of Eliot's Algonquian translations of catechisms, primers, sermons, and, most important, the first American Bible. He supplied the paper, the type, and the ink used by Cambridge printer Samuel Green in working off Eliot's translations. Usher assisted not only in America, but he also made frequent trips to England to buy supplies; on one such trip he bought a press, the second in the colony, and a large assortment of type valued at over £80. He also arranged the order for the specially cast font of type used in printing the Bible; and it was Usher who was responsible for shipping forty copies of the completed Bible to England, where they were circulated as proof that the missionary work among the Indians was

475

succeeding and insured the continued financial support of the New England Company.

Hezekiah Usher's importance as a publisher lies not in the number of his imprints but in their nature. By publishing titles in favor of the Half-Way Covenant, he unwittingly helped further the slow transformation of Massachusetts from a religious state to a secular one. Even more important, he acted as the midwife to the colony's printing industry. Without his assistance and without his financial support, for he often advanced the money for printing supplies out of his own pocket and waited as long as several years before being reimbursed by the New England Company, it is unlikely that printing would have been so quickly and so well established in Massachusetts. When Usher died, John Hull noted in his diary that he was "a pious and useful merchant."

James P. O'Donnell

References:

Littlefield, George E. Early Boston Booksellers: 1642-1711. Boston: Club of Odd Volumes, 1900; reprint edition, New York: Burt Franklin, 1969.

Littlefield, George E. The Early Massachusetts Press: 1638-1711. Boston: Club of Odd Volumes, 1907; reprint edition, New York: Burt Franklin, 1969.

Roden, Robert F. The Cambridge Press: 1638-1692. New York: Dodd, Mead, 1905; reprint edition, New York: Burt Franklin, 1970.

Winship, George P. The Cambridge Press: 1638-1692. Philadelphia: University of Pennsylvania Press. 1945.

Hezekiah Usher, Jr.

Hezekiah Usher, Jr. (1639-1697) was the son of the first American bookseller and brother to John Usher. His name appears in only two known imprints. He published a Psalter (1682?), and in 1692 he published Samuel Willard's Some Miscellany Observations on Our Present Debates Respecting Witchcrafts.

Reference:

Littlefield, George E. Early Boston Booksellers: 1642-1711. Boston: Club of Odd Volumes, 1900; reprint edition, New York: Burt Franklin, 1969.

John Usher

John Usher (1648-1726) was a wealthy bookseller who was established in business "near the Town-House" by his father, Hezekiah Usher, the first American bookseller, with whom he served an apprenticeship. John Usher's name appears in eighteen known imprints, with the most important one being Nathaniel Morton's New-England's Memoriall (1669), the first nonreligious work printed at the Cambridge Press. In 1772 he published The General Laws and Liberties of the Massachusetts Colony, "the first American book to be issued under an official privilege for exclusive sale." He was granted the right to print the laws for seven years; that was, in effect, the first American copyright. Usher became

477

active in governmental affairs after 1692, and only three
annual Tulley almanacs bear his name after that date.
Lawrence C. Wroth, writing in The Book in America, notes
that Usher "established the tradition of agressive vigor
in method coupled with dignity in the character of production that gave individuality to the Boston book trade
throughout the colonial period."

References:

Lehmann-Haupt, Hellmut. The Book in America. New York:
Bowker, 1939; revised and enlarged, New York:
Bowker, 1951.

Littlefield, George E. Early Boston Booksellers: 1642-
1711. Boston: Club of Odd Volumes, 1900; reprint
edition, New York: Burt Franklin, 1969.

Moore, John W. Moore's Historical, Biographical, and
Miscellaneous Gatherings. Concord, N.H.:
Republican Press, 1886; reprint edition, Detroit:
Gale Research, 1968.

Thomas, Isaiah. The History of Printing in America.
Worcester, Mass.: Isaiah Thomas, Jr., 1810;
2nd ed., revised, Albany, N.Y.: J. Munsell
for the American Antiquarian Society, 1874;
ed. Marcus A. McCorison, Barre, Mass.: Imprint
Society, 1970.

William Warden

William Warden (1761-1786) established, with his partner
Benjamin Russell, the Massachusetts Centinel: And the
Republican Journal in March 1784, a newspaper Russell
continued after Warden's death. In addition to the
Centinel, Warden and Russell printed Phillis Wheatley's
Liberty and Peace (1784), a Shippie Townsend sermon
(1784), and the anonymous Sans Souci. Alias Free and Easy
(1785).

References:

Brigham, Clarence S. History and Bibliography of Amer-
    ican Newspapers: 1690-1820. Vol. 1. Worcester,
    Mass.: American Antiquarian Society, 1947.

Buckingham, Joseph T. Specimens of Newspaper Literature.
    Vol. 2. Boston: Little and Brown, 1850.

Caleb Parry Wayne

Caleb Parry Wayne (1776-1849) established, in January 1798, the <u>Federal Gazette and Daily Advertiser</u>, the first daily newspaper in Boston (it became a semiweekly in March and ceased publication later that month). Wayne conducted business at "No. 17 Kilby Street, 3 doors from State-Street." Five other Boston imprints bear his name; all were published in 1798. Most of his career was spent in Philadelphia.

References:

Brigham, Clarence S. <u>History and Bibliography of American Newspapers: 1690-1820</u>. Vol. 2. Worcester, Mass.: American Antiquarian Society, 1947.

Buckingham, Joseph T. <u>Specimens of Newspaper Literature</u>. Vol. 2. Boston: Little and Brown, 1850.

Samuel Webb

Samuel Webb (1733-1792), who served an apprenticeship with Daniel Henchman, was a bookseller and binder in Boston from 1759 until his death. Eleven of the thirteen known volumes bearing his name as publisher appeared by 1766; two were published in 1774. Not one is significant. Webb conducted business "in Ann-Street" and, in 1774, "in Queen-Street."

Job Weeden and William Barrett

Job Weeden (c. 1756-1820) and William Barrett (c. 1765-1817) were partners in Boston in 1784 and 1785 at "south-side State-Street, and directly under Mr. Charles Shimmin's School." They published the Gentlemen and Lady's Town and Country Magazine between May and December 1784. Frank Luther Mott notes that therein "women were given special and explicit attention" for the first time in any American magazine. He also observes that "the typography was as bad as the syntax of the title." Weeden and Barrett published only two other known items, an edition of the Weatherwise almanac and Bryan Edwards's Thoughts on the Late Proceedings of Government, Respecting the Trade of the West-India Islands with the United States of America (1784), a volume printed in London. After the dissolution of the firm, Weeden continued as a printer in Boston until his death. In February 1785 Barrett established and published the American Journal; it continued into 1786. He was active as a publisher in Newburyport until 1797.

References:

Anon. "J. Weeden, Printer." Rhode Island Historical Society Collections, 12 (1919).

Brigham, Clarence S. History and Bibliography of American Newspapers: 1690-1820. Vol. 1. Worcester, Mass.: American Antiquarian Society, 1947.

Mott, Frank Luther. A History of American Magazines: 1741-1850. New York and London: Appleton, 1930; Cambridge: Harvard University Press, 1938; Cambridge: Belknap Press of Harvard University Press, 1957.

Ezra Waldo Weld

Ezra Waldo Weld (1765-1818) edited the Massachusetts Magazine with fellow printer William Greenough and the engraver Samuel Hill in 1794. In October of that year Weld began printing the Federal Orrery. He continued with that newspaper until June 1795 (accompanied by Greenough into April). Other than the magazine and the newspaper, Weld's name appears in fourteen known imprints. He collaborated with his partner Greenough on all of them, not one of which is significant. Weld and Greenough conducted business at "No. 42, Cornhill" or "No. 49, State-Street."

References:

Brigham, Clarence S. History and Bibliography of American Newspapers: 1690-1820. Vol. 1. Worcester, Mass.: American Antiquarian Society, 1947.

Mott, Frank Luther. A History of American Magazines: 1741-1850. New York and London: Appleton, 1930; Cambridge: Harvard University Press, 1938; Cambridge: Belknap Press of Harvard University Press, 1957.

David West

David West (1765-1810) began his publishing career in
1787. He shared many imprints with his brother, John,
and he formed partnerships with Oliver Greenleaf (1799-
1805) and Lemuel Blake (1809-1814). He published slowly
at first, but when he was responsible for forty titles in
1794, his career hit its peak. He specialized in no one
literary genre. He published religious works, textbooks,
plays, almanacs, travel books, government documents, and
novels, including Jeremy Belknap's The Foresters.

David Paul Ragan

John West

John West (1770-1827) began his career in 1793 upon the
advice of his brother, David. He spent his entire career
at No. 75 Cornhill. John published most of his works
with David; fewer than thirty titles bear his name alone.
His most active year was 1794, but by 1800 his name was
appearing in only ten imprints annually. Like his brother,
John published various materials. He published the second Boston directory, numerous almanacs, Psalters, clas-
sics, and novels.

David Paul Ragan

John Wharton

John Wharton (c. 1733-1768) and his partner Nicholas
Bowes succeeded Daniel Henchman in business and dealt
mainly in English books. They published ten known works
from 1761 to 1767, all of which are either practical or
religious.

Reference:

Thomas, Isaiah. The History of Printing in America.
    Worcester, Mass.: Isaiah Thomas, Jr., 1810;
    2nd ed., revised, Albany, N.Y.: J. Munsell
    for the American Antiquarian Society, 1874;
    ed. Marcus A. McCorison, Barre, Mass.: Imprint
    Society, 1970.

Joseph Wheeler

Joseph Wheeler (1640-1717) conducted business as a
seller of general merchandise "at the head of the
Dock." In 1697 he published two titles by Cotton
Mather, Great Examples of Judgment and Mercy (no copy
of which is known to exist) and The Thoughts of a Dying
Man. No other known book bears his name in an imprint.

Joseph Wheeler

Reference:

Littlefield, George E. Early Boston Booksellers:
     1642-1711. Boston: Club of Odd Volumes, 1900;
     reprint edition, New York: Burt Franklin, 1969.

White

White (given name and dates unknown) established, with
John Norman, the Boston Magazine in October 1783. They
were joined by Edmund Freeman in February 1784, but that
partnership lasted only through June of that year, at
which time White and Norman withdrew. White could have
been James White, although Lyon N. Richardson claims
that he was Joseph White. Possibly he was neither.

Reference:

Richardson, Lyon N. A History of Early American Maga-
     zines, 1741-1789. New York: Nelson, 1931;
     reprint edition, New York: Octagon, 1966.

James White

James White (c. 1755-1824), bookseller, printer, and publisher, began his career as a binder in 1776. He published books in partnership with Thomas Adams from 1778 to 1780 "in School-Street, next door to the Cromwell's Head Tavern." White published alone from 1781 to 1801, at which time he established a firm with Joseph Roby and James W. Burditt that lasted until 1808.

Major Authors: Jeremy Belknap, Caleb Bingham, Jonathan Edwards, James Fordyce, Lord Kames, Job Orton, John Palmer, Peter Thacher.

White entered the printing and publishing business in 1778 as a partner with Thomas Adams. They had no press or type, so they leased the office of Nathaniel Mills and John Hicks until 1780. White and Adams's major publication was the Evening Post, a newspaper that they began in October 1778. In March 1780 it became the Morning Chronicle; it ceased publication two months later. They published only four known items other than the paper: a 1778 broadside for the Continental Congress, John Lathrop's Consolation for Mourners (1779), a Nathaniel Low almanac (1779), and a 1780 publication for the Massachusetts Bay Colony.

After dissolving his partnership with Adams in 1780, White worked alone as a bookseller and printer from 1781 to 1801. He published sporadically through 1793, but he increased his activity in 1794 with energy that could not have been anticipated. The reason for the large number of volumes bearing his name from 1794 to 1800 is that most of them were joint publishing efforts. Most often he shared an imprint with Ebenezer Larkin, but he also shared projects with Samuel Hall, Isaiah Thomas, David West, John West, Benjamin Larkin,

and William Spotswood. Among his most important publications are Jonathan Edwards's Treatise Concerning Religious Affections (1794), the second edition of Jeremy
Belknap's The Foresters (1796), the first American edition of Lord Kames's influential Elements of Criticism
(1796), and three editions of Caleb Bingham's American
Preceptor (1796-1798). In 1799 White bought the Independent Chronicle from his former partner Thomas Adams.
His ownership lasted from 13 May 1799 until 15 May 1800.

James White was a printer and publisher of modest
accomplishments. His most significant publications are
probably the Evening Post and the 1796 edition of Lord
Kames's Elements of Criticism.

References:

Brigham, Clarence S. History and Bibliography of Amer-
      ican Newspapers: 1690-1820. Vol. 1. Worcester,
      Mass.: American Antiquarian Society, 1947.

Buckingham, Joseph T. Specimens of Newspaper Literature.
      Vol. 1. Boston: Little and Brown, 1850.

Joseph White

Joseph White (c. 1755-1836), printer, publisher, and bookseller, possibly began in business in 1782. From 1788 to 1793 he was in partnership with Charles Cambridge "near Charles-River Bridge," and together they produced more than half of White's publications. Without Cambridge the rate of White's titles decreased to an average of fewer than three a year. He was in business alone in Boston from 1793 until 1809, and in 1810 he relocated to Charlestown, Massachusetts, where he remained until 1826.

White's titles reflect the practical interests of his countrymen. Through 1800 he published six almanacs by Abraham Weatherwise, four by Benjamin West, and two by Samuel Bullard; seven editions of the New-England Primer; two children's books; and two song books. Of some interest is Robert Treat Paine's Adams and Liberty, a song that White published as a broadside in 1798. Most significant are his several editions of works by Daniel Defoe.

Timothy White

Timothy White (1724-1791), bookseller and binder, conducted business "a little above the Market." His name appears in only two known imprints. He published the New-England Primer Improved in 1766, and possibly the next year he published Joseph Alleine's Alarm to Unconverted Sinners.

Reference:

Thomas, Isaiah. The History of Printing in America. Worcester, Mass.: Isaiah Thomas, Jr., 1810; 2nd ed., revised, Albany, N.Y.: J. Munsell for the American Antiquarian Society, 1874; ed. Marcus A. McCorison, Barre, Mass.: Imprint Society, 1970.

Samuel Whiting

Samuel Whiting (dates unknown) published only one known title, the Memoirs of Capt Roger Clap (1774).

Stephen Whiting

Stephen Whiting (dates unknown), who conducted business "near the Mill Bridge," published Thomas Johnston's 1759 map of Quebec.

Richard Wilkins

Richard Wilkins (1623-1704) was a bookseller in Limerick, Ireland, before emigrating to America at age sixty for religious reasons. He opened a shop in Boston "near the Town-House." His name appears in four known imprints, and the authors he published were John Bailey (1689), Increase Mather (1693), Joshua Scottow (1696), and Samuel Sewall (1697). Samuel Gerrish served an apprenticeship with Wilkins, and when the master retired, Gerrish continued the business.

References:

Littlefield, George E. Early Boston Booksellers: 1642-1711. Boston: Club of Odd Volumes, 1900; reprint edition, New York: Burt Franklin, 1969.

Littlefield, George E. The Early Massachusetts Press: 1638-1711. Boston: Club of Odd Volumes, 1907; reprint edition, New York: Burt Franklin, 1969.

490

Sewall, Samuel. The Diary of Samuel Sewall: 1674-1729. Edited by M. Halsey Thomas. 2 vols. New York: Farrar, Straus & Giroux, 1973.

Thomas, Isaiah. The History of Printing in America. Worcester, Mass.: Isaiah Thomas, Jr., 1810; 2nd ed., revised, Albany, N.Y.: J. Munsell for the American Antiquarian Society, 1874; ed. Marcus A. McCorison, Barre, Mass.: Imprint Society, 1970.

John Mascoll Williams

John Mascoll Williams (1741-1827) published Samuel How's Simplicity of the Gospel Defended in 1772.

Nathaniel Willis (see Edward Eveleth Powars and Nathaniel Willis)

Joshua Winter

Joshua Winter (1723-1761) was a bookseller and binder at his shop "in Union-street near the Town Dock." His name appears in twenty-one known imprints from 1745 to 1761, none of which is significant. Winter had John Perkins as an apprentice, and Perkins succeeded him in business.

Reference:

Thomas, Isaiah. The History of Printing in America. Worcester, Mass.: Isaiah Thomas, Jr., 1810; 2nd ed., revised, Albany, N.Y.: J. Munsell for the American Antiquarian Society, 1874; ed. Marcus A. McCorison, Barre, Mass.: Imprint Society, 1970.

Abraham Wood

Abraham Wood (dates unknown) reportedly published Divine Songs Extracted from J. Hart's Hymns in 1792. No copy of that volume is known to exist.

James Woode

James Woode (dates unknown) joined with Joseph Browning and Obadiah Gill to publish Cotton Mather's The Way to Prosperity in 1690.

492

Alexander Young and
Thomas Minns

Alexander Young (1768-1834) and Thomas Minns (1773-1836)
were the publishers of the Massachusetts Mercury and were
official Massachusetts printers after 1796. They printed
over 100 titles through 1800. Young began his career as
partner to Joseph Belknap in 1791 at "No. 34, Newbury-
Street," although they moved later that year to the
"north side of the State-House, State-Street." Their
firm lasted only until 1792, at which time Young went
into business with Samuel Etheridge in Market Square.
They moved that same year "opposite the entrance of the
Branch-Bank, State-Street." In 1793 Young established
his own firm on the "north side of the State-House,
State-Street," at which site Minns joined him as a partner in 1794. They remained together until 1828.

Major Authors: Fisher Ames, Abiel Holmes, Joseph
McKeen, William D. Peck, Jonathan Strong, Peter Thacher,
Shippie Townsend.

Publisher Served: The Massachusetts General Court.

Young began in business with Joseph Belknap in
1791. They boasted of owning the first complete printing
press made in Boston. The eleven titles they printed are
varied; they include sermons, autobiographies, political
discourses, an history, an anthology of French quotations,
and a weekly newspaper, the American Apollo. The firm
was dissolved in May 1792.

Young next went into business with Samuel Etheridge.
Apparently this was not a satisfactory relationship, for
the association lasted little more than a year. They
printed only six titles, each in a different genre--a
textbook, a government document, a poem, a religious
discourse, a propaganda piece supporting the establishment

493

of a theater in Boston, and a triweekly (later semiweekly) newspaper, the Massachusetts Mercury. It was a telling period in Young's career in that he began work in two areas to which he would later devote much time, printing for the government and newspaper publishing.

After the firm of Young and Etheridge dissolved in August 1793, Young continued to publish the Mercury. During this time between partners he printed only one title independently, a sermon by Peter Thacher on the death of John Hancock. In April 1794 Young took Thomas Minns as a partner.

Some of Young's most important contributions were in the area of newspaper publishing. With Belknap he founded and published the American Apollo; with Etheridge he founded and published the Massachusetts Mercury. Minns, however, was apparently Young's equal. When Minns joined Young, the latter declared that he "thought proper to receive into connection in the publication of this paper, Mr. Thomas Minns, whose abilities and sedulous attention to the duties of his profession will probably conduce to render this work more extensively useful and interesting." Young and Minns proclaimed that they would "expose the machinations of the vindictive, and . . . support real merit, though laboring under the oppression of obloquy and misfortune. Fearless of consequences, the decent, the modest essays and animad-versions of the Theologian, the Moralist, and Politician, shall find a most ready insertion." Young and Minns re-mained editors of the Mercury into the 1820s.

The paper was mainly a semiweekly, although there is evidence that at one time they considered making it a daily. After securing the contract for government printing, the firm announced in the Mercury for 3 June 1796 that "having been honored with the appointment of Printers to the Commonwealth, they find it necessary to resign the idea of printing a daily paper."

During the latter half of the eighteenth century the government of Massachusetts had a number of official

494

printers, frequently more than one at a time. Although
it was a precarious post and although payment for work
rendered came slowly, the position of Printer to the
Commonwealth was prestigious and competition for the
contract was keen. It was the custom of the general
court to appoint the official printer at the beginning
of each session after all bids had been considered. For
political reasons the contract changed hands frequently.
Young and Minns petitioned for the position in 1794, but
it was awarded to Adams and Larkin. Throughout the session, the Senate unsuccessfully raised the question of
appointing a new committee to consider the printing contract. In 1796 it was decided that selection of the
printer should be by secret ballot, and petitions for
consideration were to be submitted by interested parties.
In the session of 1796 Young and Minns were successful in
their attempt and were named "Printers to the State."
The firm was able to retain the contract until 1800.

The primary function of the state printer was to
furnish a printing of the acts and laws of the general
court, but he also printed resolves, proclamations, reports, general orders, sermons, and miscellaneous papers.
Young and Minns printed all of these items.

In addition to their interest in newspapers and
their duties to the general court, Young and Minns were
interested in the theater. They printed broadsides for
the Boston Theatre, and they printed and sold, in 1792,
William Haliburton's Effects of the Stage on the Manners
of a People: And the Propriety of Encouraging a Virtuous
Theatre, a volume favoring the establishing of Boston
theater.

The firm printed, not surprisingly, about a dozen
sermons. Three are by Peter Thacher, the Congregational
clergyman who had ardently supported the American Revolution and later played an active part in Massachusetts
politics. Young and Minns also printed election sermons
that were customarily delivered to the general court on
election day. One of note is by Abiel Holmes, father of

495

Oliver Wendell Holmes, and another is by Joseph McKeen, first president of Bowdoin College.

The partnership of Young and Minns was lasting and prolific. It continued well into the nineteenth century, and it printed over 100 titles through 1800. They published the Massachusetts Mercury, but by far the greatest part of their work during this period was for the government. They were responsible for a wide variety of publications that reflect the interests of their times.

Jean Rhyne

References:

Brigham, Clarence S. History and Bibliography of American Newspapers: 1690-1820. Vol. 1. Worcester, Mass.: American Antiquarian Society, 1947.

Buckingham, Joseph T. Specimens of Newspaper Literature. Vol. 2. Boston: Little and Brown, 1850.

Meserve, Walter J. An Emerging Entertainment: The Drama of the American People to 1828. Bloomington and London: Indiana University Press, 1977.

Silver, Rollo G. "Government Printing in Massachusetts, 1751-1801." Studies in Bibliography, 16 (1963).

Silver, Rollo G. The American Printer: 1787-1825. Charlottesville, Va.: University Press of Virginia, 1967.

Name Index

Abercrombie, Robert, 119
Adam, Alexander, 35, 270
Adams, Abijah (brother to Thomas), 1
Adams, Abijah (father of Abijah and Thomas), 6
Adams, Amos, 2, 317, 322
Adams, Ann Lowder, 2
Adams, Hannah, 132, 172, 176
Adams, James Truslow, 165
Adams, John (father of Seth), 2
Adams, John (poet), 207-208
Adams, John (political leader), 125, 126, 129, 198, 226
Adams, John Quincy, 334, 336
Adams, Mary Lamson, 6
Adams, Samuel (political leader), 118, 125, 127, 134, 183, 339, 429
Adams, Samuel (publisher), 1
Adams, Sarah Swift, 2
Adams, Seth, 2-4, 312, 317-320, 328, 395
Adams, Thomas, 1, 5-10, 132, 227, 339-340, 390, 415, 486-487, 495
Adams, William, 21
Addison, Joseph, 76, 78, 139, 167, 334, 367

Agrippa, Cornelius (pseudonym), 184
Aitken, Robert, 24
Alden, John, 311, 317
Alden, John E., 365, 368
Alden, Priscilla, 311, 317
Alexander, Caleb, 270, 465
Alleine, Joseph, 46, 47, 311, 323, 489
Alleine, Richard, 394
Allen, Bezoune, 10, 63, 220, 221
Allen, Ethan, 78, 98, 173
Allen, James, 11, 137, 296, 426
Allen, John (author), 315
Allen, John (publisher), 10, 11-15, 66, 146, 203, 205, 213-218, 242, 277, 279, 281, 296, 394, 410
Allen, John Wincoll, 16
Allin, James, 422
Allin, John, 306, 464, 475
Alline, Henry, 137, 139
Allyn, John, 267, 271
Ames, Fisher, 493
Ames, Levi, 271
Ames, Nathaniel, 2, 100, 101, 103, 106, 108, 113, 114, 118, 123, 168, 215, 226, 311, 317-318, 343, 358-359, 395, 440-441, 447, 449
Ames, Nathaniel, Jr., 108, 441

497

Mitchelson, David, 161
Molière (Jean Baptiste
 Poquelin), 378
Monis, Judah, 228, 375
Montesquieu, Charles
 Louis de Secondat, 378
Moodey (or Moody), Samuel,
 239, 323
Moody, Eleazar, 270
Moody, Joshua, 59
Moody, Samuel (see Samuel
 Moodey)
Moore, John (author), 67
Moore, John (bookseller),
 346
Moore, Seth H., 375
Mordecai the Benjamite
 (pseudonym), 315
More, Hannah, 137, 139,
 334, 460
Moreau de Saint-Méry,
 Médéric-Louis-Elie, 378
Morgan, John, 74
Morse, Jedediah, 267, 271,
 376
Morton, Nathaniel, 230,
 307, 477
Morton, Sarah Wentworth,
 348, 351
Mott, Frank Luther, 250,
 277, 340, 418, 481
Murphy, Arthur, 156
Murray, James, 76, 78
Murray, Lindley, 351, 382
Musgrave, Philip, 194,
 323, 344, 376
Mycall, John, 24

Nancrede, Hannah Dixey,
 378
Nancrede, Joseph, 349,
 352, 377-385

Napoleon, 445
Negus, Edmund, 385
Newbery, John, 468
Newcastle, Duke of, 44
Newman, John, 132
Nichols, Francis, 385
Nichols, Jonathan, 386
Niles, Samuel, 102
Noble, Oliver, 370
Norman, John, 52, 71, 73,
 79, 197-198, 386-389,
 390, 485
Norman, William, 390
North, Frederick, Lord,
 225
Norton, John, 306, 473-475
Nourse, John, 5, 6, 7, 9,
 132, 227, 339, 390-391,
 415
Noyes, James, 93

Oakes, Urian, 230, 232
Oates, Titus, 278
Occom, Samson, 301
Odiorne, Thomas, 155
Odlin, John, 207
O'Keefe, John, 26, 39, 156
Oliver, Lieutenant Governor
 Andrew, 440
Orton, Job, 486
Osgood, David, 98, 436
Oswald, John C., 166
Otis, Harrison Gray, 443
 436
Otis, James, 123-124, 125,
 134
Oulton, Walley, 35, 379
Owen, John, 283

Pain, Philip, 232, 307
Pain, William, 388

Smith, Samuel Harrison, 336
Smith, William, 362
Southey, Robert, 348, 352, 382
Southwick, Solomon, 268
Sower, Christopher, 182
Spotswood, William, 155, 336-337, 349, 377, 380, 460-461, 487
Sprague, John, 18, 467
Sprague, Mary, 40
Stanhope, Philip (see Lord Chesterfield)
Starke (or Starkey), Robert, 11, 14, 84, 462
Starkey, Robert (see Robert Starke)
Stearns, Samuel, 108, 118, 123, 468
Steele, Alexander, 462
Steere, Richard, 82, 413
Sterne, Laurence, 159-161, 365, 367
Sternhold, Thomas, 318
Stiles, Ezra, 118, 121
Stillman, Samuel, 320, 348, 350
Stoddard, Solomon, 46, 47, 145, 213, 236, 241, 284, 286, 397, 409-410
Stone, Samuel, 205
Story, Joseph, 443
Stoughton, William, 306
Strong, Jonathan, 493
Strong, Nathaniel, 217
Sullivan, James, 6, 9, 139, 336, 340
Surr, T. S., 39, 379
Swan, Abraham, 176, 386, 388

Swan, Timothy, 386, 388
Swedenborg, Emanuel, 72
Sweetser, Benjamin, 62, 345, 463
Swienten, Gerard van, 98
Swift, John, 275, 440
Swift, Jonathan, 280
Symmes, Thomas, 200, 202, 220, 288
Symmes, William, 267, 271

Tappin, John, 464
Tate, Nahum, 312, 314, 318-319, 343, 449
Taylor, Edward, 208
Taylor, John, 420
Taylor, Samuel, 22
Taylor, Thomas, 62
Tebbel, John, 23, 59, 163-164, 168, 190, 293
Temple, Samuel, 270
Tennent, Gilbert, 100, 102, 282, 284, 287, 325
Thacher, Peter, 16, 203, 267, 271, 288, 341, 398, 486, 493-495
Thacher, Thomas, 178-180
Thayer, Nathaniel, 267, 271
Thomas, Fidelity Grant, 465
Thomas the Gageite (pseudonym), 315
Thomas, Isaiah, 11, 12, 18, 22, 26, 35, 42, 61, 66, 71, 78, 84, 107, 111, 113, 114, 129, 137, 139, 141, 151, 155, 165-166, 187-191, 193, 208, 210-211, 222, 240, 246, 248, 250, 260, 268, 289, 291, 295, 313, 332, 336-338, 348-349, 362, 370-371, 373, 379, 381, 383, 387,

Title Index

Title Index

Sacrificer, 202
Safety of Appearing at
    the Day of Judgment,
    236
Sailours Companion, 201
Saint's Jewel, 47, 207
Salem Gazette, 438
Sans Souci. Alias Free
    and Easy, 436, 479
Saturday Evening Herald,
    415
School of Good Manners,
    270
Scriptural Catechism, 65
Scripture History, 39
Search after Happiness,
    460
Seasonable Caveat against
    Believing Every
    Spirit: With Some
    Directions for Trying
    the Spirits, Whether
    They are of God, 288
Seasonable Thoughts on
    the State of Religion
    in New England, 152,
    153
Second Letter to a Friend,
    Giving a More Practical
    Narrative of the Defeat
    of the French Army at
    Lake-George, 121
Select Number of Plain
    Tunes Adapted to Con-
    gregational Worship,
    319
Self-Immolation, 39
Selling of Joseph, 13,
    217
Seneca's Morals, 35
Sentimental Journey
    through France and
    Italy, 367

Serious Call to the
    Quakers, Inviting Them
    to Return to Christian-
    ity, 243
Sermon against the Danger-
    ous and Sinful Practice
    of Inoculation, 302
Sermon Concerning Obedience
    and Resignation, 243
Sermon in Praise of
    Swearing, 58
Sermon Occasioned by the
    Execution of a Man
    Found Guilty of
    Murder, 115
Sermon on the Nature and
    Necessity of Conversion,
    121
Sermon Preached at Lexing-
    ton, on the 19th of
    April, 1781, 132
Sermon Preach'd at the
    Ordination of Mr. Samuel
    Whittelsey, Jun., 102
Sermon Preached before the
    House of Commons, on the
    31st of January 1688, 237
Sermon Preached in Trinity
    Church at the Funeral of
    Thomas Green, 108
Sermons on Sacramental
    Occasions, 189
Sermons to Young Women, 39
Several Poems, 180
Several Reasons Proving
    That Inoculation or
    Transplanting the Small
    Pox is a Lawful Practice,
    326
Several Sermons, 410
Short Account of the Solar
    System, 133

540

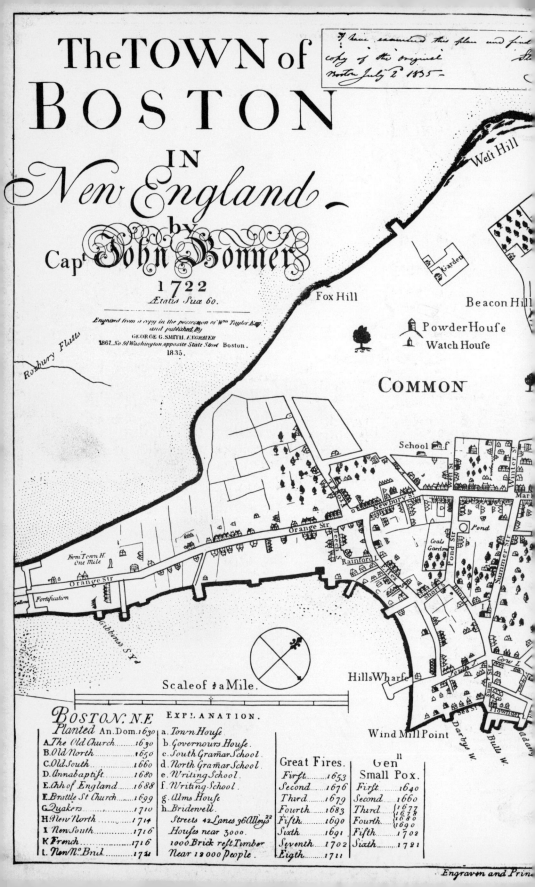

The TOWN of BOSTON

IN

New England

by

Cap.t John Bonner

1722

Ætatis Suæ 60.

Engraved from a copy in the possession of W.m Taylor Esq.
and published By
GEORGE G. SMITH, ENGRAVER
1867. No 91 Washington, opposite State Street Boston.
1835.

I have examined this plan and find [it] a copy of the original St..
Boston July 2 1835.

West Hill

Roxbury Flatts

Fox Hill

Beacon Hill

Garden

Powder House
Watch House

COMMON

School

Newbury St

Water St

Marl

Orange Str

From Town H.
One Mile

Orange Str

Fortification

Gallows

Gibbins Yd

Rainford L

Pond

Coals Garden

Pond Str

Sumner Str

Short S.t

Cow L.

Tenth

Hills Wharfe

Wind Mill Point

Darby W.

Bull W.

Scale of ⅛ a Mile

BOSTON. N.E
Planted An.Dom.1630

A. The Old Church	1630
B. Old North	1650
C. Old South	1660
D. Annabaptist	1680
E. Ch: of England	1688
F. Brattle St Church	1699
G. Quakers	1710
H. New North	1714
I. New South	1716
K. French	1716
L. New N.o Brick	1721

EXPLANATION.

a. Town House	
b. Governours House	
c. South Gramar School	
d. North Gramar School	
e. Writing School	
f. Writing School	
g. Alms House	
h. Bridewell	
Streets 42 Lanes 36 Alloys 22	
Houses near 3000.	
1000 Brick rest Timber	
Near 12000 People.	

Great Fires.

First	1653
Second	1676
Third	1679
Fourth	1683
Fifth	1690
Sixth	1691
Seventh	1702
Eigth	1711

Gen.ll Small Pox.

First	1640
Second	1660
Third	1677 1680
Fourth	1690
Fifth	1702
Sixth	1721

Engraven and Prin